The Challenge of Asylum to Legal Systems

The Challenge of Asylum to Legal Systems

Edited by

Prakash Shah

Cavendish
Publishing
Limited

London • Sydney • Portland, Oregon

First published in Great Britain 2005 by
Cavendish Publishing Limited, The Glass House,
Wharton Street, London WC1X 9PX, United Kingdom
Telephone: + 44 (0)20 7278 8000   Facsimile: + 44 (0)20 7278 8080
Email: info@cavendishpublishing.com
Website: www.cavendishpublishing.com

Published in the United States by Cavendish Publishing
c/o International Specialized Book Services,
5824 NE Hassalo Street, Portland,
Oregon 97213-3644, USA

Published in Australia by Cavendish Publishing (Australia) Pty Ltd
45 Beach Street, Coogee, NSW 2034, Australia
Telephone: + 61 (2)9664 0909   Facsimile: +61 (2)9664 5420

© Cavendish Publishing 2005

British Library Cataloguing in Publication Data

Shah, Prakash
The challenge of asylum to legal systems
1. Asylum, Right of – European Union countries
2. Refugees – Legal status, laws, etc – European Union countries
3. Refugees – Government policy – European Union countries
I Title
342.4'083

Library of Congress Cataloguing in Publication Data
Data available

ISBN-10: 1-85941-981-X
ISBN-13: 978-1-859-41981-6

1 3 5 7 9 10 8 6 4 2

Printed and bound in Great Britain

LIST OF CONTRIBUTORS

Sarah Craig is a Lecturer in Law at Stirling University. Before embarking on academic life, she worked as a solicitor for fourteen years, mostly in law centres. Her interest in immigration and asylum law arose while working at the Ethnic Minorities Law Centre in Glasgow, representing clients at immigration and asylum appeals at a time when pressure to curtail the appeals process was very strong. She is also a co-author of the recently published Scottish Executive Report *Human Rights in the Scottish Courts*, November 2004, and is currently investigating ways of analysing human rights arguments presented at the Immigration Appellate Authority.

Maria Fletcher has been a Lecturer in European Law at the University of Glasgow since 2002. Her primary field of research is EU Justice and Home Affairs (EU JHA) policy, with publications to date on EC immigration and asylum policies and EU criminal justice policy. She is a member of a small academic team on EU JHA policy which offers support and advice to the Scottish Executive. She lectures on EU law at undergraduate and postgraduate levels and has recently introduced a course on immigration and asylum law at the University of Glasgow.

Colin Harvey is Professor of Human Rights Law, Human Rights Centre, School of Law, Queen's University, Belfast, Northern Ireland. From 2000–04 he was Professor of Constitutional and Human Rights Law, School of Law, University of Leeds and co-convenor of the Human Rights Research Unit. He has previously taught at the University of Wales, Aberystwyth; the University of Michigan; and Adam Michiewicz University, Poznan, Poland. He was Refugee Co-ordinator for Amnesty International (Irish Section) 1998–2000 and a member of the Executive of the Committee on the Administration of Justice 1999–2000. He is on the Advisory Board of the British Institute of Human Rights, on the editorial board of *Human Rights Law Review* and *The Journal of Civil Liberties*, and the case editor for the *International Journal of Refugee Law*. He has published extensively in academic, and more popular, formats on issues of human rights law and politics. His major publications include *Seeking Asylum in the UK: Problems and Prospects*, 2000, Butterworths; *Human Rights in the Community: Rights as Agents for Change*, 2005, Hart; *Sanctuary in Ireland: Perspectives on Asylum Law and Policy*, 2004, Institute of Public Administration; *Human Rights, Equality and Democratic Renewal in Northern Ireland*, 2001, Hart (with Jo Shaw and John Morison); *Voices, Spaces and Processes in Constitutionalism*, 2000, Blackwell; and the *Special Issue on the Occasion of the 50th Anniversary of the European Convention on Human Rights*, 2000, Northern Ireland Legal Quarterly.

Steve Peers is a Professor of Law at the University of Essex. He is the author of *EU Justice and Home Affairs Law*, 1st edn, 2000, 2nd edn, 2005, Longman, and co-editor (with Angela Ward) of *The EU Charter of Rights*, 2004, Hart, and (with Nicola Rogers) of *EU Immigration and Asylum Law: Text and Commentary*, 2005, Martinus Nijhoff. He has written extensively on EU law issues, particularly EU immigration and asylum law, EU criminal and policing law, and human rights in EU law.

Dr Catherine Phuong is a Lecturer in Law at the University of Newcastle, UK. She has also been a visiting lecturer at the University of Lyon 2 (France) and a visiting research scholar at the University of Michigan (USA). She has taught at the International Summer School on Forced Migration, Refugee Studies Centre, Oxford. She has published several articles on international refugee law in journals, including the *International Journal of Refugee Law*, *Journal of Refugee Studies*, *Journal of Immigration, Asylum and Nationality Law* and the *International and Comparative Law Quarterly*. She has also just published a book entitled *The International Protection of Internally Displaced Persons*, 2005, CUP.

Keith Puttick is a Principal Lecturer in Law at Staffordshire University, and teaches employment law, public law and social welfare law and practice. He is a co-author of *Employment Rights*, 3rd edn, 2004, Pluto; and author of the Social Security and Community Care sections of Burton, Sir Michael (ed), *Civil Appeals* 2002, and revised edition 2005; *Welfare Benefits Law and Practice*, 9th edn, 2005; and *Child Support Law: Parents, the CSA and the Courts*, 2003, all published by EMIS Professional Publishing. His research interests and current work cover the areas of anthropology and law of welfare, work, and the family; public international law and EU law aspects of migration; and migrants' integration in host states' labour markets and communities.

Dr Valsamis Mitsilegas is Legal Assistant to the House of Lords European Union Committee. He formerly worked at the University of Leicester on an ESRC-funded project examining new challenges to security governance in the EU. He has published extensively in the areas of EU Justice and Home Affairs law and policy, transnational crime, money laundering and immigration and asylum. His major publications include *The European Union and Internal Security* (with Jorg Monar and Wyn Rees, 2003, Palgrave), book chapters and articles in various books and journals, which include the *European Law Review*, the *European Foreign Affairs Review* and the *Journal of Ethnic and Migration Studies*.

Roxana Rycroft is an interpreter and specialises in legal interpretation. She has therefore appeared as an interpreter in the immigration context, but also works in other contexts involving police, probation authorities and the courts in the UK. She holds an undergraduate degree in sociology from the University of Surrey at Roehampton and a Masters in Human Rights from the London School of Economics. Her areas of academic interest centre on legal provisions that relate to interpreting and the relationship between law, language and interpretation.

Dr Prakash Shah is a Lecturer at the Department of Law, Queen Mary, University of London where he convenes the London University LLM course on Comparative Immigration and Nationality Law, and teaches on the MSc in Migration. His publications include *Refugees, Race and the Legal Concept of Asylum in Britain*, 2000, Cavendish Publishing, and he has previously taught at the University of Kent at Canterbury and continues to teach at the School of Oriental and African Studies, London. He is Managing Editor of the *Journal of Immigration, Asylum and Nationality Law* and moderator for the Institute of Legal Executives immigration law examination. He is frequently consulted as an expert, particularly on issues of South Asian laws and cultures arising in the immigration context. Besides his interest in immigration, asylum and nationality law, he is also a specialist on ethnic minorities and law.

Dallal Stevens is a Lecturer in Law at the University of Warwick. Her research and teaching interests focus, generally, on migration and, in particular, on asylum and refugee law. She is the author of the recent book, *UK Asylum Law & Policy: Historical and Contemporary Perspectives*, 2004, Sweet & Maxwell, as well as numerous articles, book chapters and conference papers in this area. At Warwick, she has established a popular undergraduate module on refugee and asylum law and is involved in the supervision of doctoral candidates working on refugee-related issues. Dallal Stevens is an associate editor for *Immigration, Asylum and Nationality Law*, and is a trustee for the Immigration Advisory Service and the Electronic Immigration Network. She founded the migration law section of the Society of Legal Scholars.

Dr Robert Thomas is a Lecturer at the School of Law, University of Manchester. His principal research interests are in administrative law and immigration and asylum law. He has undertaken empirical research on entry clearance appeals by family visitors, and published scholarly papers on immigration appeals and the impact of judicial review on asylum policy. He has also acted as a specialist adviser to the House of Commons Constitutional Affairs Committee with regard to its inquiry into immigration and asylum appeals. He is currently undertaking a major empirical study of the operation of asylum appeals in the United Kingdom.

Ernst Willheim is a Visitor in the Law Program at the Research School of Social Sciences, Australian National University. Between 1967 and 1998 he worked for the Australian Attorney General's Department where he headed several policy and professional divisions, led Australian delegations to international conferences and appeared as counsel for the Australian Government in the High Court and other appellate courts. Since his retirement from government service he has undertaken research in several public law areas, including native title, racial discrimination, administrative law, judicial accountability, constitutional law, sovereign immunity and refugees. He has made submissions to parliamentary committees, critical of government legislation on human rights grounds, and assisted non-government organisations to make submissions to the UN's Human Rights Committee and Racial Discrimination Committee challenging Australia's compliance with international human rights obligations. He recently prepared a successful complaint, on behalf of an Aboriginal man, to the Committee on the Elimination of Racial Discrimination. He has published widely, particularly in the areas of constitutional law, administrative law, international law, environmental law, judicial accountability, Aboriginal issues and refugees.

Dan Wilsher, MA, LLM, is a non-practising solicitor and Lecturer in Law at City University, London. He was a member of the Law Society Immigration Law Panel. He practised in an immigration firm for a number of years before moving into academia. His current research interests are refugee/immigration law, competition law, EC law, corruption and good governance.

PREFACE

This book emerges from the series of papers delivered at the WG Hart legal workshop held from 30 June to 1 July 2004 at London's Institute of Advanced Legal Studies (IALS). The present writer had the privilege of co-convening the workshop with Prof Werner Menski of SOAS. It was the first time that the Hart series had featured immigration issues to any degree and it seemed an opportune time to raise the whole issue of *The Challenge of Migration to Legal Systems*, as the workshop came to be called. While this book has as its focus the issue of asylum for refugees, a parallel volume of the Hart workshop papers concerning other migration and diaspora related issues is also currently being finalised for publication.

Several events have combined to place migration issues near the top of the political and legal agenda in many countries, especially in so-called Euro-American countries. The European Union had just expanded in May 2004 to include 10 new Member States, and one of the critical issues of contention in the lead up to the increase in membership and in its aftermath was the freedom of movement that the new EU citizens would enjoy. The EU was itself engaged in reformulating its migration *acquis* with the clock having ticked past the point when a decision would have to be made as to whether to switch to qualified majority voting in the EU Council on immigration and asylum matters. Above all, and importantly for the present book, was the huge debate and ensuing legal changes that had followed the possibly long-term increase in the flow of asylum seekers in Europe, North America and Australia in the previous 20 or so years.

I would like to thank those without whose invaluable assistance the workshop proceedings and this subsequent publication could not have gone ahead. They include chiefly my Academic Co-Director, Prof Menski at SOAS, and the staff at the IALS who provided all the facilities, organised accommodation for participants, received papers, dealt with a huge number of administrative issues, and helped liaise with Cavendish Publishing. Among the staff at IALS, most thanks go to Belinda Crothers, whose modesty and graciousness are perhaps only equalled by her efficiency, as well as to Julian Harris and David Phillips. Thanks are also due to Ian Macdonald QC, who kindly agreed to give the opening address at the workshop, and to all the contributors represented in this present volume, who have all been wonderful to work with and have co-operated with my every awkward request. Finally, my appreciation must go to the staff at Cavendish, in particular, Sonny Leong, Jon Lloyd and Ewan Cooper who have worked to ensure that the publication of this collection goes ahead smoothly.

Prakash Shah, Queen Mary, University of London
March 2005

CONTENTS

INTRODUCTION

FROM LEGAL CENTRALISM TO OFFICIAL LAWLESSNESS?

Prakash Shah

The question of asylum for refugees has been one of the most intractable challenges to the legal systems of Western countries. In my view, which is largely conditioned by research and observation of developments in the UK, the questions and suggestions that were posed 20 years ago about how to deal with refugees and asylum seekers were quite different in some, sometimes subtle, ways to what is being suggested, argued about and actualised in policy today. In part, this change of emphasis can be explained by the ongoing efforts by Africans, Asians and Latin Americans (and those long-settled in Europe, such as Roma people) to seek refuge, work and a better life in the so-called developed West or in what, from another perspective, are white-dominated, Euro-American spaces.

Additionally, the states in these latter spaces have sought to deploy mechanisms over the last nearly two and half decades to bear down on such private attempts at self-determination. The change of emphasis that I am referring to is largely a function of the realisation that such efforts by the ordinary people of the collective 'South' are not coming under control by officially sponsored, legalistic methods. Thus what we see over those last two and half decades is a steady transformation from reliance on *legality* as a means of controlling access to asylum to a somewhat retaliatory resort to official non-legality or bare-faced brutality. Hence the title of the present chapter.

Traditional accounts of refugee law will normally refer to international obligations as contained in the 1951 Convention on the Status of Refugees and its 1967 Protocol; but how are we to explain the massive growth in refugee law that has taken place in Western countries only in the last two decades?[1] The 1951 Convention came about when a minimal number of refugees was seeking asylum in the West while the Iron Curtain later kept in check the number of refugees, who were in any case overshadowed by movements from the South, officially classed as labour migration. When the 1967 Protocol removed the dateline of 1 January 1951 the legal effect was to allow resort to the protection of the 1951 Convention to

---

1   For the UK, see, Harvey, C, *Seeking Asylum in the UK*, 2000, London: Butterworths; Shah, P, *Refugees, Race and the Legal Concept of Asylum in Britain*, 2000, London: Cavendish Publishing; Stevens, D, *UK Asylum Law and Policy: Historical and Contemporary Perspectives*, 2004, London: Sweet & Maxwell. For practitioner-focused perspectives, see Henderson, M, *Best Practice Guide to Asylum and Human Rights Appeals*, 2003, London: ILPA and Refugee Legal Group; Symes, M and Jorro, P, *Asylum Law and Practice*, 2003, London: LexisNexis; and Stedman, A and Hawkin, B, *A Practical Guide to Presenting Asylum and Human Rights Claims*, 2003, London: LexisNexis.

any refugee emerging after that date (as long as the geographical limitation to Europe was not maintained).

In retrospect this now seems like a huge, blank cheque written for the benefit of refugees then not even in being. Indeed, the possibility that large numbers of people from the South would come to Europe's doors was ruled out in the discussion leading to the 1951 Convention, and was strangely not factored in even in 1967. It seems, rather, that the predominant concern behind the 1967 Protocol was to allow the intervention by the United Nations High Commissioner for Refugees (UNHCR) in Africa and, later, in Asia and Latin America. In the first two continents Europe was losing control and American power was asserting itself – ironic when one considers the simultaneous movement towards political independence – while American hegemonic power in Latin America was also being established. Thus, simultaneous to the Cold War being fought by the James Bonds of Europe were the hot wars brought about by the large-scale militarisation of parts of Africa, Asia and Latin America. The UNHCR was embroiled in Cold War geo-politics in the South through massive 'aid' missions which, once we can see past the hubris generated by its definitional achievements, the OAU Convention on refugees was also aimed at underpinning.[2]

LEGAL CENTRALISM IN REFUGEE DETERMINATION PROCEDURES

It was only from the 1970s that perceptions of increases in the number of asylum seekers from the hot wars of the South began to cause concern in the Euro-American North. It was from this time that we can see the concern to institute procedures for the recognition of refugees in Western countries. This aim was encoded in the UNHCR Executive Committee's 1977 recommendation on refugee determination procedures. It is hardly conceivable that most Southern countries could initiate large-scale recognition procedures – the real addressees of this recommendation were Western countries that predicated their immigration control systems on 'strong-state' assumptions.

In Britain the recommendation was followed by advocacy, on the part of various parties, for legally predicated procedures for the recognition of refugees. Thus it was that the Immigration Rule changes in 1980 were made with the specific aim of distinguishing genuine refugees from those who were not genuine. Importantly, it was argued that unlike the admission in large numbers of refugee groups, the then current example being the Vietnamese 'boat people' from camps in Hong Kong, the Rule changes would allow legal mechanisms already embedded by the Immigration Act 1971 to determine refugeehood.[3] Similar initiatives were taken in several parts of the Euro-American world, notably in Germany and the United States.[4]

---

2   On the UNHCR, see Loescher, G, *The UNHCR and World Politics: A Perilous Path*, 2001, Oxford: OUP. The OAU is the Organization of African Unity.

3   See *op cit* Shah, fn 1, pp 114–35.

4   See Qureshi, S, 'Opening the floodgates? Eligibility for asylum in the USA and the UK', *Anglo-American Law Review*, 1988, pp 83–107, on parallels in the UK and USA; and Marshall, B, *The New Germany and Migration in Europe*, 2000, Manchester: Manchester UP, on Germany.

I am referring to this pattern of endowing official structures with the power to determine refugeehood as a species of 'legal centralism', after Griffiths who defines the term as the ideology that proclaims that 'law is and should be the law of the state, uniform for all persons, exclusive of all other law, and administered by a single set of state institutions'.[5] While we do not have the space here to develop this fully, it can be stated simply that asylum law in its legal centralist form has rested on the assumption that refugeehood is an individuated phenomenon that must be determined by official legal power only. This dismisses the role of, for example, migrant networks as the basis for alternative structures that indeed play a strong role in determining refugee flows. Such 'extra-legal' factors constantly invade the official legal sphere, which can increasingly be seen as more and more desperate to control their autonomy.

The ascent of legal power in the UK context was, however, a slow one and it was not until the Asylum and Immigration Appeals Act 1993 that a right of appeal was instituted for all rejected asylum seekers. This brought refugee law into its own in Britain. The interim period particularly from the 1980s had seen litigation brought by people claiming asylum, which was leading to large caseloads at the High Court in London. One major case in which the Government was embarrassed by charges that those returned to Sri Lanka had been tortured was nearly lost by the UK in Strasbourg. 'Nearly lost' because the quite inflated claims by UK Government lawyers about the extent to which judicial review entailed an examination of the merits of a particular case were believed by the European Court. That Court, having become a reluctant supervisory mechanism for a Europe increasingly unfriendly towards refugees from the South, probably also had its own motives for its conclusion in the *Vilvarajah* case that the UK had not violated the European Convention on Human Rights (ECHR).[6]

However, subsequent law-making was largely a result of the combination of large caseloads in the High Court, the perceived shaky position of judicial review as a proper remedy for rejected asylum seekers, and the huge build up of cases by a Home Office that was increasingly reluctant to issue refusals that would simply end up before the High Court. As indicated above, the ensuing 1993 Act allowed any rejected asylum seeker an appeal before an adjudicator, with possible further challenges. It is from this time that we see the rise of a *lex specialis* on refugee law in the UK, which parallels and feeds on similar developments elsewhere, especially in the Anglo-American, common law world.[7]

Adjudicators could now deal with the massive numbers of people who were being refused by the Home Office in the hope that this would be a cheaper alternative. This argument did not factor in the possibility that judicial review would continue to figure in the range of remedies available to the dissatisfied asylum seekers or their lawyers. More critically, the generation of legal power that

---

5   Griffiths, J, 'What is legal pluralism?', (1986) 24 Journal of Legal Pluralism and Unofficial Law 1, at p 3.

6   *Vilvarajah v UK* (1992) 14 EHRR 248.

7   Hathaway, JC, *The Law of Refugee Status*, 1991, Toronto and London: Butterworths, signals and anticipates these trends.

ensued was predicated on the tremendously arrogant claim that lawyers and official legal techniques could ascertain with some degree of certitude that a person who claimed to be a refuge was indeed one, and that anyone else must be bogus. Anyone who has read a Home Office refusal letter and witnessed an asylum hearing will immediately be struck by the strongly dismissive way in which the person, who ought to be most directly concerned with the refusal letter or subsequent legal proceedings, is dealt with. These are merely illustrations of the disempowering effects of legal procedures in the asylum field.

TO OFFICIAL LAWLESSNESS

From the above it might seem that the kind of legal strategies instituted to control asylum migration would result in the considerable oppression of asylum seekers; and they did. However, things have become much worse since then, as we are gradually moving away from a paradigm based on having at least a minimum set of legal guarantees for asylum seekers. Each further piece of legislation introduced – the Asylum and Immigration Act 1996, the Immigration and Asylum Act 1999, the Nationality, Immigration and Asylum Act 2002 and, most recently, the Asylum and Immigration (Treatment of Claimants, etc) Act 2004 – have led to asylum seekers being dealt with in a more and more arbitrary way. The number of Acts in the last decade or so, not to mention changes in practice and in the Immigration Rules, shows a typically gradualist, British way of moving along. The parallels in other European countries are quite striking however, either because continental ideas have eventually been adopted in Britain or because restrictive ideas have been exported across the Channel. This is no surprise as, since asylum came onto the European law-making agenda in the 1980s, much earlier than its formalisation in each subsequent European treaty, European officials have continued to exchange notes about worst practice. As several of the contributors to this book explain, the famed British Euro-scepticism only extends to rejecting proposals where legal guarantees might *enhance* the status of people claiming asylum or, more generally, of extra-European migrants. After examination of the EU's activities in the asylum field in recent years, several contributors to this book express scepticism whether there are any 'minimum standards' below which the treatment of asylum seekers is not allowed to fall, despite the Amsterdam Treaty's express proclamation that such standards should form the benchmark for the formulation of common laws.

These recent British, European and even Australian law-making agendas represent moves away from the legal centralist presuppositions of earlier days, and toward much more arbitrary and brutal ways of dealing with people claiming asylum. This may seem rather contradictory. After all, do we not have more law today, not less? We do indeed but, as Colin Harvey argues in this book, the quality of that law may be losing sight of some essential values that law ought to be informed by. I see here a deep scepticism about where this authoritarian law-making agenda is leading us, and a severe critique of value free positivism. The 2004 Act in the UK establishes new lows in this regard. It virtually instructs judicial officers to make findings against credibility, thus almost binding them to reject asylum appeals, if certain facts are deemed established. What indeed is the point of judicial oversight if such slot machine justice can mechanically produce the desired results?

What, it may be asked, about the new importance given to human rights values post-October 2000 in the UK? To answer this point I would draw on a speech given by the Indian writer, Arundhati Roy, when accepting the Sydney Peace Prize on 7 November 2004. She argues:

> Today, it is not merely justice itself, but the idea of justice that is under attack. The assault on vulnerable, fragile sections of society is at once so complete, so cruel and so clever – all encompassing and yet specifically targeted, blatantly brutal and yet unbelievably insidious – that its sheer audacity has eroded our definition of justice. It has forced us to lower our sights, and curtail our expectations. Even among the well-intentioned, the expansive, magnificent concept of justice is gradually being substituted with the reduced, far more fragile discourse of 'human rights'. If you think about it, this is an alarming shift of paradigm. The difference is that notions of equality, of parity have been pried loose and eased out of the equation. It's a process of attrition. Almost unconsciously, we begin to think of justice for the rich and human rights for the poor. Justice for the corporate world, human rights for its victims. Justice for Americans, human rights for Afghans and Iraqis. Justice for the Indian upper castes, human rights for Dalits and Adivasis (if that). Justice for white Australians, human rights for Aboriginals and immigrants (most times, not even that).

This evocative passage could be extended to the treatment of people who dare to claim asylum almost anywhere in the Euro-American world. They are relegated to receiving, if at all, treatment at the floor of human rights rather than being allowed to drink at the table like others. The fallacy of the human rights paradigm has therefore to be viewed very critically rather than as the be-all-and-end-all of justice for asylum seekers and refugees. A close examination of the immigration legislation, in particular the UK's 1999 Act, will make evident that there are ways that the executive can authorise the non-regard for human rights grounds so as to bind judicial authorities too. Such legally mandated blindness bears out Roy's point, above, that even human rights standards may not always be available to immigrants.

I have not yet mentioned the events of 11 September 2001, and deliberately so. This is partly because the shift to arbitrariness in asylum law and policy actually pre-dates them. However, if the catastrophic ethnic conflicts unleashed throughout the world by the end of the Cold War represented the collapse of the old international order, 11 September may mark the building of a new world order. Ernst Willheim's discussion in this book shows how Australian policy was already taking a turn for the arbitrary pre-11 September, although that date admittedly had the effect of notching up the level of restrictionism. Certainly, post-11 September we might be witnessing the self-fulfilment of the Huntingdonian vision of clashing civilisations. Developments since then in Europe, North America and Australia give much cause for concern as laws are following wider societal polarisation between the 'good' and 'bad' camps, crushing those on the wrong side of the fence, or those who do not wish to take sides.

The last decade of developments in Australia illustrates well the trend toward curtailment of judicial remedies. Since 1994, administrative decisions in refugee cases were only challengeable at the Australian High Court, but in September 2001 further legislation sought to oust the jurisdiction of even that Court. At least in Australia there remains some residual recourse to the courts under the system of constitutional review. The UK sought to copy the Australian model in defiance of the knowledge that there would not exist any remedy at all once a person had moved past the single-tier Asylum and Immigration Tribunal (AIT), as it will be known under the 2004 Act. This was a high point in attempts to resolve the issue of access to law for rejected asylum seekers who continued to bother the High Court/Administrative Court in significant numbers with claims for judicial review. Earlier moves to limit or remove appeal rights altogether had met with even more judicial reviews. Middle England, or that portion of it that cared enough, protested at the proposed removal of this constitutional safeguard, the contest having been transformed to one between the executive and the judges, and the Government had to back down on that measure.

Nonetheless, moves to limit public funding, that most critical subsidy for the costs of legal challenge, were already underway. Some law firms had taken the cue when the proposals were published in 2003 and decided that they could not conscientiously operate under the new regime. One can notice now that firms that remain in the market either work privately or, in those that continue to operate under the public funding regime, there is a worsening relationship with asylum seekers. Now law schools are also being urged to take on *pro bono* asylum work for indigent clients, based on the American model. As Sarah Craig and Maria Fletcher point out in this book, the 2004 Act rather insidiously vests the power to award legal costs, at the conclusion of proceedings, with the AIT or the 'appropriate court' of review. This means that there will be even less incentive to take cases through to appeal. Ultimately, it is the cutting back of funds, as the state gradually withdraws legal protection or simply removes the expectation that costs will be met, which determines the critical question of access to law. Middle England remains silent on this question and thus tolerates this official lawlessness – perhaps being kept busy (or distracted) with other issues such as the ban on fox-hunting.

How though do we explain the slide towards more draconian anti-law strategies to control or to 'deflect' (as Craig and Fletcher have it in this book) asylum migrants? There is surely some form of exploitation going on here where the state and its powerful agencies and sub-contractors can brutalise people and increasingly direct authoritarian measures, like systematic dispersal, detention or expulsion, against entire families with children. We could explain this in terms of a new type of political economy that continues to exploit such vulnerable people with the aim of diverting the use of resources to subsidise their activities on the pretext of securing borders. This can be placed within the wider picture of Euro-American societies increasingly living with the disconcerting consciousness that they are continuously transformed into extensions of the South through population movements and the formation of non-assimilating Afro-Asian-Latin diasporic communities in their midst. As discussed by some writers in our companion volume, *Migration, Diasporas and Legal Systems in Europe*, this introduces all sorts of questions that it seems we are hardly prepared to face.

OUTLINE OF CHAPTERS

The first six chapters in this book all deal in one way or another with the European context of law-making on asylum and linked issues. This reflects the importance the EU has acquired in recent years, having been endowed with constitutional power to make law in the asylum and migration area. Many of the developments in the UK and other EU states therefore now tend to follow the general agendas being thrashed out at EU level. A recent trip to Australia also revealed to me how closely EU developments are being watched there, and that the EU is very significant as an international actor in the refugee field, more generally influencing the rewriting of the international law on refugee protection in light of Euro-American interests.

Dallal Stevens directs our attention to the wider context of international population movements when discussing asylum migration. She provides an overview of developments so far on the Common European Asylum System (CEAS) and reflects on some of its critiques. She argues that Europe cannot proceed on the narrow policy-making basis that views asylum issues with a sort of tunnel vision. Instead, she sees that the discussions on asylum are actually intimately linked to, and have implications for, the way in which we theorise the legitimacy of state control of migration. She argues that the whole notion of unrestrained sovereignty as a basis for the control of migration needs to be revised. She highlights the challenge that migration and asylum migration in particular pose for the liberal democratic state as it tilts away from its liberal underpinnings and in the direction of nationalism. In addition, Stevens urges that asylum policy-making takes on board the question of the economics of migration and that it is in this context that a more rational approach needs to be developed.

Catherine Phuong is also mindful of the wider context of asylum migration and, like Stevens, takes head on the discussion about the management of refugee flows in light of recent proposals by the UK, the UNHCR and the European Commission, proposals which advocate the processing of asylum applications nearer to the countries of origin or in centralised EU reception centres. While anticipating that her suggestions may be viewed as 'controversial' by advocates of refugee protection, Phuong urges us to step back and read these proposals seriously, as they could form the basis of a more realistic policy for managing international refugee flows in light of states' concerns about regulating migration more generally. She expresses some caution, however, with regard to all the official proposals issued to date, arguing that they lack clarity in important respects and it is not always apparent how they might operate in practice.

Sarah Craig and Maria Fletcher show that the asylum procedures directive, a critical cornerstone of the CEAS, is likely in its current form to reduce legal protection standards for asylum seekers. Craig and Fletcher review the relevant provisions of the Directive and equivalent UK measures. In particular, they draw attention to safe country lists as a means of denying protection; the ways in which deemed behaviour by asylum seekers can lead to a reduction in guarantees; and the way in which remedies and appeal rights have been downgraded. We are seeing here a good example of the ways in which European states are using the mechanism of common law law-making to drive standards down and take steps toward a largely discretionary approach in the processing of asylum applications. We are also left with few illusions that in this area UK law seems to follow (or perhaps even lead) EU models, another sign that in the UK we are only selectively Euro-sceptical.

Steve Peers provides a critique of another of the building blocks of the CEAS – its legislation on family members and their treatment. This is a complex subject, not least because of the way in which the EU has approached law-making covering family members. There are several different documents, with some overlap, depending on whether one is a family member of an asylum applicant, of someone who already has protection (but then the question is what sort of protection), or whether one is subject to 'deflection', to use Craig and Fletcher's term, under the Dublin arrangements. Peers reviews the applicable instruments in light of human rights standards, and is severely critical of the confusing approach to law-making, arguing that while there is some protection, sometimes, for some people, there are also major gaps, incoherence, and a problem of generally low standards, leading to potential breaches of human rights.

A critique of the approaches to welfare provision for migrants, in particular under Directive 2003/9 on reception conditions, is provided by Keith Puttick. He prefaces his discussion by providing an overview about the way in which welfare provision for asylum seekers is increasingly controlled, with several vivid examples from the UK and elsewhere. Puttick argues that Directive 2003/9 still leaves a number of areas of the asylum support process unregulated by EU law, and that this gives considerable scope for Member States to continue to act independently and restrictively. He sees in this the risk that states will remain free to perpetuate certain objectionable policies, for example, their use of welfare restrictions as a means of discouraging the making of asylum applications, such as the withdrawal of welfare support as a 'removal' measure or the more general undermining of welfare universality principles. Crucially, Member States are also given a wide discretion whether to allow asylum seekers to work. Given the current ban on working in the UK, this seems like an illustration of what Stevens notes about the economically blind approach to asylum regulation. One could go further and speculate about the problems that persons living under such conditions are being driven to. Are we further nudging people into working illegally or will we hold against them the fact that they have at some point had recourse to public funds, perhaps using the fact to deny family reunion or to justify expulsion?

So far decision making in the EU Council has rested on unanimity voting. This procedure complicates decision making as restrictive Member State positions can determine the agenda for the whole Union. Valsamis Mitsilegas discusses how this has worked in the case of the asylum procedures and the reception conditions directives, particularly drawing on the evidence provided to the House of Lords Select Committee on the EU. He shows how particular restrictive Member State positions, especially those of the UK and Germany, have eventually been reflected in the texts of the directives. The UK (and Irish) position is obviously complicated as it enjoys an opt-in and an opt-out to common policies (while Denmark enjoys an opt-out). Mitsilegas shows that the UK's position on 'Schengen-building measures' is marked by its participation in the restrictive and enforcement measures but reluctance to participate in positive measures that might enhance the legal standing of migrants. The lack of clarity about when precisely the UK may opt in or opt out also means that it can sometimes bypass domestic scrutiny of proposed legislation. The UK (and Ireland) can also of course be refused participation in some areas, and it has experienced this very situation in connection with the European Border Guards Regulation, the other Member States thereby showing their frustration at the UK's piecemeal approach to participation. Finally, Mitsilegas also discusses the possible effects of changes in light of moves to 'communitarisation'.

Dan Wilsher then directs our focus to the international human rights law applicable when states detain migrants. This is an area of growing importance in migration law, as the frequency of detention, in particular of asylum seekers, seems to be on the rise. Wilsher mainly examines the legal decisions produced by the European Court of Human Rights and the UN Human Rights Committee, along with some domestic decisions of importance. Wilsher finds that the Human Rights Committee's case law under the International Covenant on Civil and Political Rights is sometimes in conflict with that under the ECHR. He prefers the former's balanced approach between the state's claim to detain people with the aim of controlling migration and a person's right to liberty, as compared to the European Court's more ambivalent position on individual liberty.

Colin Harvey stays with judicial decision making, mainly analysing leading British case law on refugees. In so doing he actually makes the wider point that there are certain values that underpin the legal order and that deserve to be analysed and remembered, particularly at times when those values are under threat of being relinquished by the spectre of threats to national security. These values, Harvey argues, should not just underpin judicial decision making, but ought to bind legal actors in other roles, too. In particular, however, he reminds us that in times when national security appears to be an argument overriding other claims to justice, judges must play an activist role in ensuring that the values embedded in the rule of law, which Harvey clearly views as a substantive concept linked to individual dignity, are adhered to.

The Immigration Appellate Authority is the main site of litigation of claims to refugeehood. Robert Thomas analyses the conflicts and tensions within this area of administrative law decision making. He identifies the inherent tension between the bureaucratic and legal models of decision making and, perhaps more critically, an inherent contradiction among the objectives of the system. More specifically, Thomas points out that the asylum sector of the legal process has been identified as an important cause of delay and therefore an impediment to the effective administration of removals. The conflicting pressures on the appellate authority have given rise to concerns about the quality of their decisions, thus confirming that such concerns are not confined to Home Office decision making, particularly in this high pressure, high-volume jurisdiction. Thomas does not find it surprising that both the adjudicators and the Tribunal have been criticised for the 'variable quality' of their decisions – he identifies a high rate of remittals from the Tribunal to adjudicators, while the Tribunal has itself not escaped criticism by the Court of Appeal. Thomas's unease about the pressure on adjudicators to produce determinations so quickly in relation to matters of such importance to individuals should be of considerable concern. This pressure also underpins the wider significance of his study, which shows us that the official legal process is itself constantly invaded by concerns that are extraneous to the determination of refugee status.

Through her experience as an interpreter and her observations of interpreting encounters, Roxana Rycroft provides a rare and devastating critique of the distortions in communication through which the asylum account emerges. In so doing she finds that the role of the interpreter as a conduit of information is at best a difficult one to fulfil, while it also hinders the communication process and may not even be conducive to the telling of the asylum seeker's story. Problems in the approach to asylum decision making are nowhere more clearly highlighted than in the dynamic interaction and the consequent writing up of the 'asylum encounter' in which major pitfalls of inter-linguistic and inter-cultural communication mean that the asylum seeker's story, upon which all subsequent processes and the fate of the asylum seeker hinge, turns out to be an inaccurate account of the experiences of the asylum seeker. Rycroft points out that the rigid linguistic and extra-linguistic demarcations involved in the giving and taking down of the asylum account make it such a selective and constrained one, and far from any real account of events that led to flight. Not only does the Home Office not consider the role of the interviewing officer as being to elicit relevant information that would assist the decision, she even finds that the Home Office employs adversarial tactics to set asylum seekers up to fail.

Ernst Willheim's account shows strikingly close parallels between Australian approaches to policy-making and those, discussed by other writers, of the UK and EU. We have already noted how the UK closely emulated the Australian ouster clause in the lead up to the passing of the 2004 Act. Australia appears to be leading the field in restrictive practices in many other ways. It is processing asylum applications extra-territorially, albeit at a very high financial cost, although this has not deterred some European leaders, including the British Prime Minister, Tony Blair, from actually considering this policy. Australia has been intercepting vessels on the high seas and deflecting them, something which joint EU patrols are also trying to achieve in the Mediterranean, with resulting higher death tolls as desperate sea-crossers undertake longer and more perilous journeys to avoid such patrols. Australia has systematic detention policies to detain those who arrive without authorisation and claim asylum, something that is becoming more and more routine in European countries as has the sustained propaganda campaign against asylum seekers, tirades against whom seem to be increasingly legitimised as electioneering tactics.

Charting the slide from legal centralism to brutality in asylum law I feel compelled to argue, as do all the writers in this volume, that a law-centred approach is certainly the preferable route to the protection of refugees. It is by no means the ideal, however, since official legal techniques also have their oppressive capacities in the field of asylum migration. Unfortunately, we now find ourselves in the position that even minimum legal guarantees are being chipped away quite fast, while existing legal processes get overloaded by an expulsion-oriented ethos that is less and less interested to learn about and take into account the subjective conditions of refugeehood. Regional and international protection systems have been ignored, emasculated or have simply been co-opted into the process of managing asylum migration at the behest of powerful states. As resources are transferred to the more authoritarian official and semi-official agencies we may sadly be witnessing the twilight of asylum law in the West.

CHAPTER 1

ASYLUM SEEKERS IN THE NEW EUROPE: TIME FOR A RETHINK?

Dallal Stevens

INTRODUCTION

Increasing numbers of asylum seekers to Europe over the last two decades have engendered a feeling of panic amongst EU Member States, which has resulted in a range of restrictive measures at both national and EU levels. Although the year 2003 witnessed a fall in asylum seekers to the EU,[1] a trend which appears to be continuing,[2] the legacy of rising numbers of asylum applications in the 1990s lends urgency to the quest for a firm solution to the asylum issue. It was only in May 2004 that the five-year plan on asylum, first conceived in Amsterdam, saw fruition in the partial realisation of the Common European Asylum System (CEAS). The adoption of the Dublin II Regulation,[3] and directives on reception conditions for asylum seekers,[4] on temporary protection in the event of mass influx of displaced persons,[5] on family reunification,[6] and on the definition of a refugee[7] provide the basis of a new 'harmonised' or 'communitarianised' asylum policy post-Tampere. Only the Procedures Directive remains outstanding, though the 'general approach' was agreed in the final hours before the deadline of 1 May 2004.[8]

---

1   A 22% decline in EU states, with the exclusion of Italy: UNHCR, *Asylum Levels and Trends: Europe and non-European Industrialized Countries, 2003*, 24 February 2004.
2   The 14 EU countries for which there was data (excludes Italy) registered a 15% fall in quarterly asylum applications. UNHCR, *Asylum Levels and Trends: Europe and non-European Industrialized Countries, First Quarter 2004*.
3   Council Regulation (EC) 343/2003 of 18 February 2003, establishing the criteria for determining the Member State responsible for examining an asylum application lodged in one of the Member States by a third country national.
4   Council Directive (2003/9/EC), on laying down minimum standards for the reception of asylum seekers.
5   Council Directive (2001/55/EC), on minimum standards for giving temporary protection in the event of a mass influx of displaced persons and on the measures promoting a balance of efforts between Member States in receiving such persons and bearing the consequences thereof.
6   Council Directive (2003/86/EC), on the right to family reunification.
7   Council Directive (Doc 8034/04, Asile 23), on the minimum standards for the qualification and status of third country nationals and stateless persons as refugees or as persons who otherwise need international protection and the content of the protection granted.
8   Council Directive (Doc 8771/04, Asile 33), on minimum standards on procedure in Member States for granting and withdrawing refugee status.

Tampere was not simply about advocating the introduction, in the short term, of minimum standards in the asylum and refugee fields; it also proposed that 'in the longer term, Community rules should lead to a common asylum procedure and a uniform status for those who are granted asylum valid throughout the Union'.[9] More generally, the European Council stressed 'the need for more efficient management of migration flows at all their stages'.[10] These longer-term goals were again articulated at Thessaloniki in June 2003, when the European Council 'reaffirmed the importance of establishing a more efficient asylum system within the EU to identify quickly all persons in need of protection, in the context of broader migration movements, and developing appropriate EU programmes'.[11] It is now impossible to approach the issue of asylum in Europe without consideration being given to the question of migration more generally.

This chapter offers some reflections on the future of asylum and refugee policy in the new Europe within the context of the wider debate on migration. It addresses three main aspects. First, it assesses briefly the ability of the CEAS to provide effective protection to asylum seekers and refugees. Secondly, it considers new approaches advanced by the EU Commission and United Nations High Commissioner for Refugees (UNHCR) to deal with the migration of asylum seekers. Thirdly, it argues that a whole range of underlying factors relating to asylum (and migration) in an increasingly globalised world are not adequately addressed by the EU or UNHCR initiatives, and that consequently EU asylum policy has entered a new phase of uncertainty.

THE CEAS

The background to the CEAS and the problems with the directives on procedures and refugee status and with the Dublin II Regulation have been addressed in some detail elsewhere.[12] For many, Tampere represented a milestone in its apparent commitment to 'an open and secure European Union, fully committed to the obligations of the Geneva Refugee Convention and other relevant human rights instruments',[13] and its reaffirmation of the 'absolute respect of the right to seek asylum' and the principle of non-*refoulement*.[14] Despite such assurances, the European Council on Refugees and Exiles (ECRE) published in June 2004 a rather damning report on the development of EU minimum standards for refugee protection from Tampere 1999 to Brussels 2004.[15] While acknowledging the

---

9   Presidency Conclusions, Tampere European Council, 15 and 16 October 1999, para 15.

10   *Ibid*, para 22.

11   Presidency Conclusions, Thessaloniki European Council, 19 and 20 June 2003, para 25.

12   See Stevens, D, *UK Asylum Law and Policy: Historical and Contemporary Perspectives*, 2004, London: Sweet & Maxwell; Boccardi, I, *Europe and Refugees – Towards an EU Asylum Policy*, 2002, The Hague: Kluwer Law International.

13   Presidency Conclusions, Tampere European Council, 15 and 16 October 1999, para 4.

14   *Ibid*, para 13.

15   ECRE, *Broken Promises – Forgotten Principles. An ECRE Evaluation of the Development of Minimum Standards for Refugee Protection, Tampere 1999 – Brussels 2004*, June 2004: available at www.ecre.org.

undoubted achievements of the past five years in the EU's asylum policy – the centrality of the 1951 Convention; the adoption of a refugee definition broadly reflecting international standards; the granting of a subsidiary form of protection in all Member States; the recognition of persecution by non-state actors and of gender-specific and child-specific forms of persecution; the provision of adequate reception conditions for asylum seekers – the report is still largely critical.[16] Much of the criticism is reserved for the yet unadopted Procedures Directive, which is described as 'gravely flawed'.[17] Of particular concern are the concepts of 'safe third country' and 'safe country of origin'. According to the proposed directive, a country may be considered safe for return of an asylum seeker despite not having ratified and implemented the 1951 Convention, not complying with other human rights obligations, and failing to have a prescribed asylum procedure in place.[18] In addition, ECRE objects to the introduction in the directive of a 'super safe third country' concept, according to which asylum seekers can be returned to a country without examination of their application so long as the country concerned has in fact ratified and observes the 1951 Convention and the ECHR, and has in place an asylum procedure prescribed by law.[19] The safe country of origin concept is also incorporated into the Directive. UK asylum lawyers have a long relationship with such a concept since its first appearance in UK law as the so-called 'white list' in the Asylum and Immigration Act 1996. Applications from listed countries are deemed to be unfounded and subject to accelerated procedures. While confirming the right to an effective remedy,[20] the directive also permits the use of non-suspensive appeals, thereby undermining the ability of asylum seekers to make use of such a right.

The Qualification Directive, too, attracts censure. The directive incorporates the internal protection alternative (IPA), widely practised by most states, but fails to provide any guidance to Member States on how to judge whether IPA is appropriate.[21] Furthermore, ECRE, while acknowledging the advances made in the directive through inclusion of subsidiary protection status, is concerned that the grounds giving rise to such status do not reflect the full spectrum of obligations under international human rights law;[22] nor do they guarantee those offered subsidiary protection equal rights to refugees.[23]

The Reception Directive implements a provision permitting Member States to 'refuse reception conditions in cases where an asylum seeker has failed to demonstrate that the asylum claim was made as soon as reasonably practicable after arrival'.[24] In the UK, this found form in the now notorious s 55 of the

---

16 *Ibid*, p 28.
17 *Ibid*.
18 *Ibid*, p 10; Art 27 (1), Doc 8771/04, Asile 33, 30 April 2004.
19 Article 35A, Doc 8771/04, Asile 33, 30 April 2004.
20 Article 38, Doc 8771/04, Asile 33, 30 April 2004.
21 ECRE, *Broken Promises – Forgotten Principles. An ECRE Evaluation of the Development of Minimum Standards for Refugee Protection, Tampere 1999 – Brussels 2004*, June 2004, p 13.
22 *Ibid*.
23 *Ibid*.
24 Article 16(2).

Nationality, Immigration and Asylum Act 2002. Such has been the strength of the campaign against s 55 that, finally, in late June 2004, the Government announced a climbdown, pending appeal to the House of Lords in the case of *Secretary of State for the Home Department v Limbuela, Tesema and Adam*.[25] As from Monday 28 June 2004, asylum seekers should not be refused state support unless it is clear that they have some alternative means of support.[26]

The objections rehearsed above are not new. James Hathaway, for example, in an article in the *European Journal of Migration and Law* in 2003, alerted readers to a range of problems with the proposed directives, many of which have not been addressed in the final agreed versions.[27] Even though he concluded by guardedly welcoming Europe's commitment to 'two courageous and principled steps – abolition of mandatory diversion to "temporary" protection, and the effective assimilation of refugees and other persons entitled to international protection against return', he cautioned against the exclusion of asylum seekers from refugee rights or any artificial restriction of the scope of refugee status and the content of protection standards.[28] More recently, a number of NGOs issued a strongly worded joint letter to Mr António Vitorino, Commissioner for Justice and Home Affairs, calling on the European Commission to withdraw its proposals for the Procedures Directive, many of which they deemed an 'abdication from international law'.[29] Steve Peers has questioned whether the proposed Procedures Directive constitutes 'an assault on human rights',[30] while the UNHCR has repeatedly argued against the extension of the safe third country concept in the directive and has warned that the EU seems, in its discussions, to be 'veering towards the "lowest common denominator"'.[31] After much deliberation, agreement was reached on 9 November 2004 by the EU Council on an amended Procedures Directive.[32]

Concerns about the actual contents of the directives aside, there is a pertinent issue for consideration relating to enlargement itself. Recent events, such as accession by the ten new Member States and agreement of the Constitution, raise further questions on the future of asylum policy within Europe. Clearly, in order to comply with the requirements of membership, the new states were obliged to adopt certain measures relating to asylum, measures that they have had no opportunity to influence. These states are arguably committed to the pre-CEAS model and, according to some commentators, may resist 'any attempts to develop

---

25 [2004] EWCA Civ 540.

26 Travis, A, 'Blunkett backs down on aid for asylum seekers' (2004) *The Guardian*, 26 June.

27 Hathaway, J, 'What's in a label?' (2003) 5(1) EJML 1–21.

28 *Ibid*, pp 20–21.

29 ECRE *et al*, Letter to Mr A Vitorino, Member of the European Commission, 'Re: Call for withdrawal of the Asylum Procedures Directive', 22 March 2004.

30 Peers, S, 'EU law on asylum procedures: an assault on human rights?' *Statewatch*, November 2003.

31 UNHCR, *Aide Memoire – Directive on Minimum Standards on Procedures for Granting and Withdrawing Refugee Status*, 18 November 2003.

32 Document No 14203/04 Asile 64, 9 November 2004.

the *acquis* in a more liberal direction', especially if required to introduce further changes to their domestic legislation.[33] According to this view, enlargement could impede a progressive – or human rights oriented – approach to a future EU asylum policy.

To conclude these preliminary remarks, despite the commitment of Tampere to the establishment of 'a Common European Asylum System, based on the full and inclusive application of the Geneva Convention',[34] there are clear question marks over whether the CEAS meets its international obligations, particularly in relation to the principle of non-*refoulement* and 'effective protection'. As the House of Lords EU Committee recognised, 'effective protection' is crucial in assessing proposals on removal of asylum applicants to third countries.[35] Although different bodies have expressed different views as to the conditions that must prevail for protection to be effective,[36] there is a general understanding that there must be a guarantee against *refoulement*. The House of Lords EU Committee, in an earlier report on minimum standards in asylum procedures, cautioned against the automatic application of guidelines in the Procedures Directive that would effectively replace individual consideration of cases and possibly lead to the inappropriate removal of asylum seekers to unsafe countries.[37]

ALTERNATIVE APPROACHES

The EU

Aside from concerns about the 'building blocks' of the CEAS, questions may also be asked as to whether the EU has met the broader migration objectives set by the Tampere Council. In March 2003, Tony Blair presented a 'concept paper', entitled a *New Vision for Refugees*, to European Council members on new approaches to asylum processing and protection.[38] Its main thrust was to improve the management of the asylum process globally by 'two complementary elements': 'measures to improve regional management of migration flows; and processing centres, on transit routes to Europe'. The latter proposal covered two contentious

---

33 Byrne, R *et al*, 'Understanding refugee law in an enlarged European Union' (2004) 15 European Journal of International Law 355.

34 Presidency Conclusions, Tampere European Council, 15 and 16 October 1999, para 13.

35 House of Lords EU Committee, 11th Report, Session 2003–04, *Handling EU Asylum Claims: New Approaches Examined*, HL Paper 74, paras 61–68.

36 See, for example, Commission Communication *Towards More Accessible, Equitable and Managed Asylum Systems*, COM (2003) 315 final, p 6; Lisbon Expert Roundtable, *Summary Conclusions on the Concept of 'Effective Protection' in the Context of Secondary Movements of Refugees and Asylum Seekers*, 9–10 December 2002, available at www.unhcr.ch.

37 House of Lords EU Committee, 11th Report, Session 2000–01, *Minimum Standards in Asylum Procedures*, HL Paper 59, 30 April 2004, paras 122–23.

38 For Tony Blair's letter of 10 March 2003 to the Greek Presidency and accompanying concept paper see www.statewatch.org/news/2003/apr/blair-simitis-asile.pdf; for a full copy of the proposal *New Vision for Refugees* see www.proasyl.de/texte/europe/union/2003/UK_NewVision.pdf (last visited 9.5.05).

suggestions: the so-called 'safe-havens' idea, according to which people could be moved from Europe to protected areas, and the establishment of 'transit processing centres' outside the EU to which asylum seekers could be sent to have their claims processed. While the paper did not receive from all Member States the support anticipated by the UK Government, it did prompt the Commission into action with the production of its own communication entitled *Towards More Accessible, Equitable and Managed Asylum Systems*.[39] In this document, the Commission drew attention once more to the objectives outlined at Tampere. Tampere had, it claimed, 'underlined the need for a comprehensive approach to migration and asylum, addressing political, human rights and development issues in countries and regions of origin and transit'.[40] It had also 'called for a greater coherence between the Union's internal and external policies, and stressed the need for more efficient management of migration flows at all their stages, in which the partnership with countries of origin and transit would be a key element for the success of such a policy'.[41] Recognising that there was 'a crisis in the asylum system', a 'growing malaise in public opinion' and rising abuse of asylum procedures, the Commission concluded that there was 'a real threat to the institution of asylum and more generally for Europe's humanitarian tradition'.[42] It proposed, therefore, that any new initiatives to help complement the stage-by-stage approach adopted at Tampere should be underpinned by 10 basic premises:

- full respect for international obligations;

- attention to the root causes of forced migration;

- provision of access to legal immigration channels;

- continuation of the fight against illegal immigration;

- full partnership with and between countries of origin, transit and first asylum and destination;

- improvement of the quality of decisions in the EU, consolidation of protection capacities in regions of origin, and treatment of protection requests as close as possible to needs;

- introduction of new approaches to complement the CEAS;

- discussions on new approaches to expedite negotiations on the first phase directives of the CEAS;

- adherence by new EU Member States, in their initiatives on asylum, to the UNHCR Agenda for Protection and Convention Plus; and

- respect for the EU's current financial perspective.[43]

---

39 COM (2003) 315 final.
40 *Ibid*, p 4.
41 *Ibid*.
42 COM (2003) 315 final, p 11. See, also, Commission Communication *On the Common Asylum Policy and the Agenda for Protection*, COM (2003) 152 final.
43 COM (2003) 315 final, p 12.

With these basic premises in mind, the Commission proposed that a new approach be based on three specific but complementary objectives: the orderly and managed arrival of persons in need of international protection in the EU from the region of origin; the sharing of burdens and responsibilities within the EU as well as with regions of origin enabling the EU to provide effective protection as soon and as close as possible to those in need of international protection; and the development of an integrated approach to efficient and enforceable asylum decision making and return procedures.[44] Meeting only a few weeks after the Commission published its principles and objectives, the Thessaloniki European Council seized the opportunity to invite the Commission:

> to explore all parameters in order to ensure more orderly and managed entry in the EU of persons in need of international protection, and to examine ways and means to enhance the protection capacity of regions of origin with a view to presenting to the Council, before June 2004, a comprehensive report suggesting measures to be taken, including legal implications.[45]

On 4 June 2004, the Commission finally published the results of its deliberations in a new communication: *Communication from the Commission to the Council and the European Parliament on the Managed Entry in the EU of Persons in Need of International Protection and the Enhancement of the Protection Capacity of the Regions of Origin: 'Improving Access to Durable Solutions'*.[46] With such a title, the document seemed to promise a more liberal and understanding approach to the quest for asylum. The opposite, however, is arguably true, for the Commission has now endorsed many of the UK Government's proposals in the criticised *New Vision for Refugees*.[47]

The 21-page communication addresses the two objectives set at Thessaloniki: exploration of all parameters in order to ensure more orderly and managed entry in to the EU of persons in need of international protection, and the examination of ways and means to enhance the protection capacity of regions of origin. In relation to the first, the Commission favours the establishment of a resettlement scheme, despite this being the least favoured of three proposals for durable solutions (voluntary repatriation, local integration, and resettlement) offered by the UNHCR.[48]

In 2003, the Migration Policy Institute, on behalf of the Commission, published a *Study on the Feasibility of Setting Up Resettlement Schemes in EU Member States or at EU level, Against the Background of the Common European Asylum System and the Goal of a Common Asylum Procedure*. The Commission, in calling for the study, made it clear that any resettlement scheme must be complementary to the process of

---

44 *Ibid*, p 13.
45 Presidency Conclusions, Thassaloniki European Council, 19 and 20 June 2003, para 26.
46 COM (2004) 410 final.
47 See, for example, Hayes, B, 'Killing me softly? "Improving access to durable solutions": doublespeak and the dismantling of refugee protection in the EU' *Statewatch*, July 2004.
48 See UNHCR, *Agenda for Protection*; UNHCR Executive Committee Conclusion No 95 (LIV) 2003, p i.

spontaneous asylum claims in EU Member States or at the borders. The study defines resettlement as 'the selection and transfer of refugees from a state in which they have sought protection to a third state which has agreed to admit them with permanent residence status'.[49] In endorsing resettlement, the Commission's stated objective is:

> to provide international protection and to offer a durable solution in the EU to those who genuinely need it and to facilitate their managed arrival in the EU, and to express solidarity with and share the burden of countries in the regions of origin faced with protracted refugee situations.[50]

According to the communication, 'the watchwords of such a scheme would be "flexibility" and "situation-specific"'.[51] This means that it would be adaptable 'to the differing characteristics of global refugee needs' and 'to the ability of Member States to resettle certain caseloads in given years'.[52] The EU anticipates the involvement of the UNHCR in the selection and referral of caseloads.[53]

While the Commission supported a resettlement scheme, it rejected the adoption of Protected Entry Procedures (PEPs) recommended by the Danish Centre for Human Rights in a second EU-commissioned study: *Study on the Feasibility of Processing Asylum Claims Outside the EU Against the Background of the Common European Asylum System and the Goal of a Common Asylum Procedure.*[54] According to the report, PEPs would allow a non-national to approach a potential host state outside his or her territory with a claim for asylum, or other form of international protection, and to be granted an entry permit in the case of a positive response to that claim, whether preliminary or final.[55] The authors of the study were convinced that PEPs could help address the problem of human smuggling and would also attract *bona fide* refugees. In the long term, they claimed, PEPs would also 'contribute to the establishment of a dialogue with would-be migrants at the earliest conceivable stage of the migration continuum'.[56] The study went on to propose that PEPs should be considered by the EU Member States as part of a comprehensive approach, complementary to existing territorial asylum systems. It concluded that such an approach would offer three different, but interlinked, contributions to extraterritorial refugee protection:

1   Assistance to regional first countries of asylum to handle larger quantities of protection seekers in full compliance with international norms.

---

49 *Study on the Feasibility of Setting Up Resettlement Schemes in EU Member States or at EU level, Against the Background of the Common European Asylum System and the Goal of a Common Asylum Procedure,* Executive Summary, p vi.
50 COM (2004) 410 final, para 27.
51 *Ibid,* para 25.
52 *Ibid.*
53 *Ibid,* para 23.
54 Noll, G, Fagerlund, J and Liebaut, F, Danish Centre for Human Rights, 2002, published May 2003.
55 *Study on the Feasibility of Processing Asylum Claims Outside the EU against the Background of the Common European Asylum System and the Goal of a Common Asylum Procedure,* Executive Summary, p 3.
56 *Ibid.*

2   PEPs offered by a single Member State for (a) individuals whose needs cannot be met by the first country of asylum due to qualitative limitations in its protection offer, and who possess specific links to that Member State, and (b) urgent cases.

3   A resettlement quota offered by EU Member States through a central agency, eg, UNHCR. The quota would be used to cater for protection needs which cannot be met either in the first country of asylum or through self-selecting extra-regional solutions. The quota would be exclusively protection-oriented, and thus free of utilitarian considerations benefiting Member States.

Despite the Danish Centre for Human Rights' very positive endorsement of PEPs, and the UNHCR's belief that such procedures could help order and assist the predictability of secondary refugee movements,[57] the Commission was less enthusiastic. There was not, it stated, 'the same level of common perspective and confidence among Member States as exists *vis à vis* resettlement'. Consequently, the Commission rejected establishing a PEP mechanism as a stand-alone policy proposal and opted for resettlement as its favoured solution. This despite a number of Member States having functioning PEPs in place.

Under the second objective set out in Conclusion 26 of the Thessaloniki European Council – 'to examine ways and means to enhance the protection capacity of regions of origin' – the Commission's 2004 communication goes on to set out a new policy framework. Referring to previous communications, the Commission calls for increased co-ordination between the EU's internal process and the external aspect of the governance of refugees.[58] The importance of sharing responsibility for managing refugees with third countries is underscored, as is the need for more effective co-operation to reinforce the protection capacities of countries receiving refugees.[59] The Commission accepts that new approaches to asylum need to focus more sharply on action to be taken outside the EU, within a framework of genuine burden and responsibility sharing.[60] This in order to improve the management of asylum-related flows within Europe and in the regions of origin. Finally, the communication clarifies that a number of programmes to establish or enhance asylum systems in third countries in line with UNHCR standards have been financed in the Balkans and Eastern Europe.[61]

The communication goes on to consider a global policy framework. Drawing on the UNHCR's own *Handbook on Strengthening Protection Capacities in Host Countries*,[62] the Commission argues that:

> the third country in the region of origin should be able to offer the possibility of eventual local integration to a refugee if one of the UNHCR-identified traditional

---

57   COM (2004) 410 final, para 35.
58   *Ibid*, para 38.
59   *Ibid*.
60   *Ibid*.
61   *Ibid*.
62   EC/GC/01/19, 4 September 2001.

other two durable solutions (resettlement or return to the country of origin) is not available, or while waiting for a durable solution.[63]

To do this, suggests the Commission, the EU should first look at how it guarantees protection to those in need – namely, the measures provided by Art 63 of the Amsterdam Treaty: minimum standards on qualification as a refugee, procedures, and reception conditions – and adopt them as the core of effective protection.[64] With this in mind, the document goes on to provide a 'benchmark' for effective protection:

(a) life and liberty are not threatened on account of race, religion, nationality, membership of a particular social group or political opinion;

(b) the principle of non-*refoulement* in accordance with the Geneva Convention is respected;

(c) the right to freedom from torture and cruel, inhuman or degrading treatment is respected, as well as the prohibition of removal to such treatment;

(d) the possibility exists to request refugee status and, where granted, to receive protection in accordance with the Geneva Convention; and

(e) the possibility exists to live a safe and dignified life taking into consideration the relevant socio-economic conditions prevailing in the host country.[65]

These standards are provided in the full understanding that many current refugee hosting countries fail to meet them, even where those countries are willing to offer protection. It is recognised that, before effective protection can be properly achieved in many third countries, the EU needs to provide financial and technical support to help build protection capacity.[66]

Finally, in order to address Thessaloniki's clear call for an integrated, comprehensive and balanced approach, the Commission would implement EU regional protection programmes. These would provide a 'tool box' of measures:

• action to enhance protection capacity;

• a registration scheme;

• an EU-wide resettlement scheme;

• assistance for improving the local infrastructure;

• assistance in regard to local integration of persons in need of international protection in the third country;

• co-operation of legal migration;

• action on migration management; and

• return to the country of nationality or a third country offering effective protection.[67]

---

63 *Ibid*, para 42.
64 *Ibid*, para 43.
65 *Ibid*, para 45.
66 *Ibid*, para 46.
67 *Ibid*, para 51.

Thus, in the new development phase of the CEAS, the Commission's recommendations revolve around two new initiatives: EU resettlement schemes and EU regional protection programmes. No new legislation is proposed and the Commission simply calls upon the Council and the European Parliament to endorse the communication. The main concern with all these proposals , for some critics, is that the EU is seeking to establish '"safe havens" in disguise', through regional protection, and is hoping to 'cherry-pick' refugees for resettlement in its territory.[68] The similarities with the UK's problematic *New Vision for Refugees* are obvious.

Despite the Commission's apparent endorsement of regionalisation of the asylum issue, recent events indicate that some Member States are reluctant to pursue variants of this policy. Plans announced by Germany and Italy to establish transit processing centres in Libya or Tunisia were rejected by France and Spain. The French Interior Minister, Dominique de Villepin, described the proposals as 'very destabilising' for the targeted countries, while the High Commissioner for Refugees, Ruud Lubbers, warned that plans by the EU to shift the asylum burden to developing countries would be 'doomed to failure' and would also 'seriously undermine the global refugee system to the detriment of everyone, including the EU itself'.[69] The Commission itself advanced a separate plan, with the endorsement of the Netherlands, whereby five UN refugee agency pilot projects would be funded in North Africa to upgrade existing processing facilities.[70] The estimated cost was 1 million euros, of which 80% would be paid by the EU and 20% by the Dutch. Though the UNHCR was to be closely involved, the aim was, once more, to ensure that asylum seekers remain in the region of origin rather than make their way to Europe.[71]

Though disagreement on certain aspects of EU asylum policy is very evident amongst Member States, the Presidency Conclusions of the Brussels European Council, held on 4 and 5 November 2004, confirm that asylum and migration are still issues of high priority. It has been agreed that the second phase of the CEAS will establish a common asylum procedure and a uniform status for those granted asylum or subsidiary protection.[72] The date for adoption has been set as the end of 2010. The Conclusions go on to discuss 'the external dimension of asylum and migration'. Partnerships with third countries,[73] with countries and regions of origin,[74] and with countries and regions of transit,[75] are endorsed within the

---

68 Hayes, B, 'Killing me softly? "Improving access to durable solutions": doublespeak and the dismantling of refugee protection in the EU' *Statewatch*, July 2004, pp 4–5.

69 'European Council agrees JHA programme for 2005–2010', *EurActiv*, 6 December 2004.

70 'EU divided over African asylum camps', *EurActiv*, 5 October 2004.

71 *Ibid.*

72 Presidency Conclusions, Brussels European Council, 4 and 5 November 2004, para 1.3.

73 *Ibid*, para 1.6.1: assisting third countries 'to improve their capacity for migration management and refugee protection, prevent and combat illegal immigration, inform on legal channels for migration, resolve refugee situations by providing better access to durable solutions, build border-control capacity, enhance document security and tackle the problem of return'.

74 *Ibid*, para 1.6.2.

75 *Ibid*, para 1.6.3.

proposals. The Commission is invited to develop EU regional protection programmes, in consultation and co-operation with the UNHCR. The Council also called for the establishment of an effective removal and repatriation policy, 'for persons to be returned in a humane manner and with full respect for their human rights and dignity'.[76] It is anticipated that discussions on minimum standards for return procedures and to support national removal efforts will be commenced in early 2005. Once more, what emerges from the Presidency Conclusions is that within the EU, asylum and migration are two sides of the same coin, and that one cannot be discussed without the other. This approach, which now seems entrenched within EU policy-making, will be of great concern to refugee-support groups and practitioners of asylum and refugee law, since, notwithstanding statements to the contrary, the human rights dimension of asylum is often lost in the migration debate.

The UNHCR

Recognising that there was gathering momentum for radical reform, the UNHCR also used the Blair concept paper as a launch pad for its own proposal in June 2003: the 'three-pronged approach'. This, too, focused on multilateral co-operation and equitable sharing of burdens and responsibilities. The three prongs were regional (improved access to solutions in the region of origin), domestic (improved national asylum system of the destination state) and EU (processing of 'manifestly unfounded' cases). The proposal provoked an intense debate, as well as some surprise that the UNHCR was prepared to impose quite a heavy burden on countries in the region of origin. However, the issue of concern for EU Member States was the 'EU prong', which envisaged an EU-based processing centre (within the EU) for cases composed primarily for economic migrants.

Following widespread discussions, the UNHCR produced in December 2003 an amended version of the 'EU prong'. The changes reflected the concern of the UNHCR about the draft Procedures Directive and about the potential impact of enlargement on the EU asylum regime. The revised proposal remained similar to the original in advocating reception and processing within the EU; settlement through burden-sharing arrangements for recognised refugees; burden-sharing in return operations; and a monitoring role for the UNHCR. It established a clear administrative structure: EU reception centres; an EU asylum agency (whose officers would take first instance decisions on asylum claims in EU reception centres); and an EU asylum review board (which would consider and decide appeals). The new proposal no longer recommended that EU-level processing be for 'asylum applicants originating from designated countries of origin who are primarily economic migrants resorting to the asylum channel'.[77] Instead, it suggests that EU reception centres could process the following: Dublin II transfers; cases from countries of origin whose asylum seekers are regularly

---

76 *Ibid*, para 1.6.4.
77 UNHCR Working Paper, *A Revised 'EU Prong' Proposal*, 22 December 2003, para 19.

rejected in high numbers in destination states; and/or cases from countries of origin that warrant pooling of resources to determine status because of their complexity.[78] The proposal also argued that it took account of problems likely to be faced by EU Member States, particularly those situated at external frontiers, as a result of implementation of Dublin II and Eurodac. Finally, it is claimed that 'the proposal provides a mechanism for a progressive shift from national to EU reception, processing and settlement/return arrangements'.[79] This is arguably the most radical aspect to the revised 'EU prong'. It should be noted that there are no details on judicial control or scrutiny of the agency or review board.[80]

It is clear from recent press statements issued by the UNHCR that it has grave concerns about the direction of EU policy. As Ruud Lubbers recently commented:

> The EU approach to asylum rests on a key premise: that all EU states have similar asylum systems of equally high quality. The harmonisation process, now entering its second five-year phase, is designed to bring national systems closer together. But there is a glaring omission: there is no system of burden-sharing. Instead, the tendency is to shift the burden to other EU states, or countries outside the EU that are ill-equipped to handle asylum claims.[81]

The UNHCR supports harmonisation of Member States' asylum laws and practices, and is in favour of greater financial and political investment in regions of origin, as well as the use of EU resettlement schemes. In so doing, however, it is treading a dangerous path, one that could easily lead to the very outcome which it seeks to avoid, the regionalisation of asylum policy beyond EU borders.

COMMENT

In April 2004, the House of Lords EU Committee reported on the new approaches to handling EU asylum claims advanced by the UK, the EC Commission and the UNHCR. While the Committee endorsed the Commission's view that any new approaches should be consistent with the ten premises outlined in the Commission's communication, there was little support for either the UK or UNHCR initiative. Summarised below are the Committee's principal objections:

- 'the new proposals do not provide the safeguards contained in national law';

- 'the UNHCR proposal, while envisaging the processing of applications within the EU, presupposes the existence of a common system of asylum rules across the Union. This is premature and, bearing in mind the difficulty states have found agreeing even minimum standards, unrealistic';

---

78   *Ibid*, para 7.
79   *Ibid*, para 19.
80   House of Lords EU Committee, 11th Report, Session 2003–04, *Handling EU asylum claims: new approaches examined*, HL Paper 74, para 77.
81   Lubbers, R, 'Make asylum fair, not fast' (2004) *The Guardian*, 3 November.

- the existence of a similar lacuna with regard to which country would assume responsibility for the asylum seekers. 'The lack of clarity on this issue leaves asylum seekers in a legal vacuum';

- 'the proposals have significant procedural and cost implications'; and

- 'the Government's proposals for regional protection areas are vague and unlikely to guarantee effective protection or durable solutions.'

The Committee took the view that 'rather than developing proposals for processing centres or regional protection areas, it would be preferable to devote resources to strengthening and accelerating asylum procedures in Member States and to ensuring high minimum standards at EU level.'[82]

Significantly, the Committee resisted the temptation to make any radical new proposal of its own with regard to EU asylum claims, preferring to revisit well-trodden territory. Its outlook could be accused of being too parochial. The Committee stressed that the quality of initial decision-making (in the UK) is the single most important component of an effective asylum system, urged the Minister to establish an independent body responsible for initial decision-making (similar to the Canadian model), supported the establishment of an independent documentation centre, managed on an EU or UNHCR basis, and considered prompt removal/departure of failed asylum seekers the best deterrent to unfounded applications.[83]

In none of these developments, including the House of Lords report, has consideration been given to the wider issue of migration in a global context. This is despite the call for 'a comprehensive approach, involving all stages of migration, with respect to the root causes of migration, entry and admission policies and integration and return policies'.[84] Current proposals continue to be purely reactive to the pressure felt by EU Member States because of the numbers of asylum applications, and therefore fail to provide any long-term holistic view. It is my contention that in order to arrive at an EU asylum policy capable of providing effective protection (in the wider sense) to refugees, and to address the concerns of EU Member States vis-à-vis uncontrolled migration, a much broader perspective must be taken. To date, the public debate on asylum within the EU has been too tightly circumscribed, though, privately, EU Ministers probably engage with the full range of issues at stake. Recent discussions on open borders, as well as the current challenges of migration in the 21st century, have given renewed salience to the migration debate, prompting the UK Government to adopt the term 'managed migration' to describe its new policy.[85] It is time the importance of

---

82 House of Lords EU Committee, 11th Report, Session 2003–04, *Handling EU Asylum Claims: New Approaches Examined*, HL Paper 74, paras 88, 97–101.

83 *Ibid*, paras 108–13, 116–18.

84 Presidency Conclusions, Brussels European Council, 4 and 5 November 2004, para 1.2.

85 See, for a useful summary of the main issues, Boswell, C and Crisp, J, *Poverty, International Migration and Asylum* 2004, UNU-WIDER, Policy Brief No 8; for the UK's view of managed migration see Blunkett, D, 'Managing migration in the 21st century', 12 November 2003, Speech to the Royal Institute of International Affairs.

certain factors on the future of EU asylum policy were more openly and fully articulated. Failure to do so is likely to result in further restrictions.

While this list is by no means intended to be exhaustive, some of the broader considerations in the current literature are as follows:

- theoretical perspectives;

- the issue of sovereignty;

- liberalism and democratisation;

- economic (and other) benefits;

- politics and policy; and

- human rights protection.

In the short space at my disposal here, I propose to outline briefly some aspects of the first four, since the last two have arguably been better rehearsed in the migration literature.

Theoretical perspectives

It is perhaps apposite to open here with a brief overview of some theoretical perspectives.[86] Three of the best known commentators on the ethics of migration are Rawls, Carens and Walzer. For many years, they have engaged with the debate on open borders. Though EU states are unlikely ever to subscribe to such a policy, the ethical arguments in favour of and opposed to more liberal migration can be illuminating and should not be dismissed out of hand. Carens's 1987 article in the *Review of Politics*, 'Aliens and citizens: the case for open borders', made an important contribution to the philosophical debate on migration.[87] In it he argued that the theories of Nozick, Rawls and utilitarianism all pointed towards acceptance of open borders.[88] Such a view of Rawls might have been a little premature. In *The Law of Peoples*, Rawls suggests that an important role of a people's government is to be 'the representative and effective agent of a people as they take responsibility for their territory and the size of their population as well as for maintaining its environmental integrity and its capacity to sustain them'.[89] He goes on to argue that a people (or their agent) should recognise that they cannot make up for their irresponsibility in caring for their land and conserving natural resources by engaging in war or by 'migrating into other peoples' territory

---

86   For a recent analysis of ethical considerations in the asylum context see Gibney, M, *The Ethics and Politics of Asylum*, 2004, Cambridge: CUP.

87   (1987) 49 Review of Politics 251–73.

88   For a discussion of Carens, see Meilander, P, 'Liberalism and open borders: the argument of Joseph Carens' (1999) 33 International Migration Review 1062–81.

89   Rawls, J, 'The law of peoples' (1993) 20 Critical Inquiry 47–48; repeated in Rawls, J, *The Law of Peoples*, 1999, Cambridge, Massachusetts: Harvard UP.

without their consent'.[90] At this point Rawls adds a footnote, as if as an afterthought: 'This remark implies that a people has at least a qualified right to limit immigration. I leave aside here what these qualifications might be.'[91] Rawls therefore sides with the case against open borders, albeit in fairly restricted terms, and does not engage in further analysis of the migration or asylum issues, leaving it to others to suggest the most appropriate regulatory framework.

More recently, Carens has moved away from positing open borders on ethical grounds to an acceptance that reality dictates that states believe they are entitled to control admission to their territories.[92] He argues that the moral responsibility of states for asylum seekers is greater than for refugees settled in camps.[93] This is on because of what might happen to an asylum seeker if returned to a country from which they are fleeing. In determining whether an asylum seeker is a refugee according to the 1951 Convention, Carens suggests that the Convention definition of a refugee should be revised to reflect a wider perspective, namely that: 'From a moral perspective, what should matter the most is the seriousness of the danger and the extent of the risk, not the source of the threat or the motivation behind it.'[94] Most asylum seekers, he believes, have mixed motivations for flight. He recognises, though, that any modification of the definition of a 'refugee' is likely to lead to restriction rather than expansion in the current climate.[95]

Walzer, by contrast, advocated the right to exclude some refugees on the basis of communitarian justice.[96] In *Spheres of Justice*, he poses the questions: 'Are citizens bound to take in strangers?'[97] 'Should victims of political or religious persecution be admitted?'[98] To some refugees, he suggests, we may have the same obligations as those owed to fellow nationals. In his view, asylum is granted for two reasons: because its denial requires the use of force against desperate people, and because the numbers likely to be involved are small and the people easily absorbed. This might have been the position in 1983 but, clearly, the same cannot be said today. EU Member States are fully prepared to remove individuals if deemed necessary; numbers of asylum seekers are no longer considered to be small; neither are asylum seekers and refugees necessarily easily integrated within the EU. Walzer was himself sceptical about open-ended admission, even of refugees. He concluded:

> The call 'Give me … your huddled masses yearning to breathe free' is generous and noble; actually to take in large numbers of refugees is often morally necessary; but the right to restrain the flow remains a feature of communal self-determination. The

---

90 *Ibid*, p 49.
91 *Ibid*.
92 Carens, J, 'Who should get in? The ethics of immigration admissions' (2003) 17(1) Ethics and International Affairs 95–110.
93 *Ibid*, p 101.
94 *Ibid*, p 103.
95 *Ibid*.
96 Walzer, M, *Spheres of Justice*, 1983, Oxford: Blackwell.
97 *Ibid*, p 45.
98 *Ibid*, p 49.

principle of mutual aid can only modify and not transform admission policies rooted in a particular community's understanding of itself.[99]

So where do these diverse theoretical considerations leave us? They point towards the conclusion that any construction – or reconstruction – of the EU's asylum policy should take account of much broader perspectives than currently articulated in EU deliberations and documentation. At the very least, they feed into a debate that ought to inform the EU's broader conception of its human rights obligations with regard to asylum.

Sovereignty

The question of sovereignty raises some challenging questions in the EU context. Sovereignty is regarded by many as 'the ultimate value in immigration matters' and usually relates to a state-centred notion of autonomy.[100] This is, of course, a myth, particularly in light of globalisation, since borders are now breached in numerous ways – by people, products and pollutants.[101] In relation to the EU, Kostakopoulou argues that 'the development of the Community legal order is a concrete manifestation of border-transcending communities on a transnational scale' but that the Community is not sovereign in the traditional sense as there is no single political centre in which power is vested.[102] European Member States have individually and collectively struggled to cope with asylum and immigration and the 'challenge to state autonomy and sovereignty' that they represent.[103] The combination of increasing migration and European integration can undoubtedly be seen to pose problems for national identity as well as the notion of sovereignty.[104] Have Member States transferred a part of their sovereignty to the EU in relation to the migration of EU nationals within the EU? Arguably, yes. The same cannot be said for the migration of non-EU nationals to the EU, although the creation of a CEAS and the implementation of some of the proposals in the new approaches could effect a quite radical diminution of sovereignty. Certainly, some of the ideas expressed by the UNHCR in its 'EU prong' anticipate the transfer of a degree of control over asylum to UNHCR officers. For this reason alone, the UNHCR's proposals are unlikely to meet with approval.[105] Some commentators regard the changes introduced by EU Member

---

99 *Ibid*, p 51.

100 Kostakopoulou, D, 'Is there an alternative to "Schengenland"?' (1998) XLVI Political Studies 891.

101 *Ibid*.

102 *Ibid*, pp 891–92.

103 Hollifield, J, *Immigrants, Markets, and States*, 1992, Cambridge, Massachusetts: Harvard UP, p 41.

104 Koslowski, R, *Migrants & Citizens*, 2000, New York: Cornell UP, p 14.

105 For an argument that the 1951 Convention has impinged little on sovereignty, see Dauvergne, C, 'Challenges to sovereignty: migration laws for the 21st century', UNHCR, *New Issues in Refugee Research*, Working Paper No 92, July 2003.

States to control migration – visas, carrier sanctions, tighter border controls, Eurodac, even the CEAS itself – as a reassertion of state sovereignty. This is a dubious assumption since state sovereignty can be seen to be altered by policy integration, irrespective of its purpose.[106] The process of enlargement also leads to transformation of the state sovereignty of applicant countries prior to accession as they seek to meet the EU conditions for entry.[107]

Liberalism and democratisation

It is now self-evident that the globalisation of markets has led to increased international migration. So too has the expansion of civil and social rights since 1945.[108] As a consequence, EU Member States find themselves in an untenable position. While their liberal values are extended to the new Member States as part of the 'club', rights of non-citizens continue to be downplayed. Hollifield, in his seminal work, *Immigrants, Markets and States*, argues that:

> [i]n liberal political systems the individual occupies a sacrosanct position, regardless of his or her contractual relationship with the state or society. Whether the motivation for migration is one part political and two parts economic or vice-versa should in principle make little difference to the way the individual is treated.[109]

Immigration, he suggests, 'continues to reflect a liberal paradox of rights versus markets'.[110] The same can be said of asylum. Indeed, the formulation of policy within the EU indicates a tendency to regard people as 'citizens first and humans second'.[111] Once this occurs, the danger is that nationalism, national interest and national security will take priority over universal ethics and human rights.[112] Asylum has certainly posed a challenge to liberal democratic states or to what Ruggie and Hollifield term 'embedded liberalism'.[113] The curb on access to asylum, the lowering of minimum standards, and the general limitation evident in European asylum policy of civil and political rights indicate an inexorable move away from liberal values.[114]

---

106 *Op cit*, Koslowski, fn 104, p 156.

107 *Ibid*, p 157.

108 *Op cit*, Hollifield, fn 103, p 41.

109 *Ibid*, p 231.

110 *Ibid*.

111 Walker, R and Mendlovitz, S, 'Interrogating state sovereignty' in Steiner, H and Alston, P, *International Human Rights in Context*, 1996, Oxford: Clarendon, p 153.

112 *Ibid*.

113 '[a]ny international order (or regime) contains within it the values or social purpose of the hegemonic state(s); hence the notion of an "embedded liberalism in the postwar economic order"', *op cit*, Hollifield, fn 103, p 27.

114 See, for a discussion of some of these issues, Boswell, C, 'Explaining European public policy responses to asylum and migration', Conference Paper at UNHCR-WIDER Conference on Poverty, International Migration and Asylum, Helsinki, 27–28 September 2002.

Economic benefits

In searching for solutions to the 'asylum problem', serious consideration has been given by the UK, EU and UNHCR to the role to be played by regions of origin. However, there is little in the EU proposals that indicate that the economics of migration have been taken into account. Much of the early work in this area was conducted on labour migration and refugees; little relates to the experiences of asylum seekers.[115] Recent research on worker remittances reveals their importance to the funding of developing countries; in fact, they appear to constitute the second largest source of external funding behind foreign direct investment for some developing countries.[116] Consequently, international migration (as defined by the share of a country's population living abroad) 'has a strong, statistically important impact on reducing poverty in the developing world'.[117] This has led some economists to conclude that borders should be opened and migration – whether labour or refugee – liberalised.[118]

EU Member States, despite their often stated commitment to improving the lot of the developing world, seldom address the issue of remittances in their formulation of asylum policy. Instead, work is seen as a 'pull factor' and, consequently, the right to work is withdrawn from asylum seekers in many EU states (until they receive refugee or other status). On the other hand, huge amounts are spent on reception, accommodation or detention centres and supporting asylum seekers with cash or vouchers. An additional financial factor for consideration is the contribution that can be made to an economy by refugees and asylum seekers. While a number of reports have studied the positive contribution to be made by refugees to the economy of host countries, more research needs to be undertaken on the role that can be played by asylum seekers. This is, of course, a problematic undertaking since many states now prohibit asylum seekers from working.

CONCLUSION

The CEAS, in providing the 'building blocks' of EU asylum policy, has been subject to criticism since the draft directives and regulation first appeared. While it would be facile to suggest that all aspects of the new regime are unacceptable, there are certainly major concerns with the Qualification Directive and, in particular, the draft Procedures Directive. Even the much heralded Dublin II Regulation, which was designed to solve the problems of the Dublin Convention,

115 Martin, S *et al*, 'Impact of asylum on receiving countries', March 2003, Discussion Paper No 2003/24, UNU-WIDER, p 6.

116 Ratha, D, 'Workers' remittances: an important and stable source of external development finance', in *Global Development Finance 2003*, 2003, World Bank.

117 Adams, R and Page, J, 'The impact of international migration and remittances on poverty', Conference Paper at DFID/World Bank Conference on Migrant Remittances, London, 9–10 October 2003, p 10.

118 See, for example, Harris, N, 'Migration without borders: the economic perspective' available at www.unesco.org/most/migration/paper_n_harris.pdf.

appears to suffer from the same flaws as its predecessor. Already there are reports emanating from the UK's Immigration and Nationality Department that EU states continue to refuse to take responsibility for asylum seekers who have reached the UK and whom the Home Office wishes to return under the provisions of the regulation.

Providing the foundations for a CEAS does not, of course, address the more complex questions surrounding the future of migration. Although 2003 and 2004 were important years in moving forward with thinking on longer-term solutions, in the judgment of the House of Lords and prominent NGOs, the proposals to date are substantially flawed. Though the EU might vaunt its achievements in the field of asylum law, it is still very far from the 'comprehensive approach to migration and asylum' that the Commission's 2003 communication recognised as essential and which the 2004 Brussels Presidency Conclusion reiterated.

This is not to suggest that a conflation of migration and asylum should be endorsed without question; therein lies another set of issues beyond the purview of this discussion. From the evidence that can be adduced at this point, however, it is likely that the EU's notion of 'comprehensiveness' will, in reality, be very limited. EU documentation continues to prove that the focus of the Commission and of Member States revolves around deterrence, exclusion and security, and human rights considerations are often subsumed into bland statements of principle. In arguing that EU policy elevates the causes and consequences of migration above the needs and human rights of asylum seekers, this chapter urges those engaging in the debate to explore more fully the myriad factors surrounding the issues of asylum and of migration more broadly. As has been repeatedly proven at national level, failure to do so will result in an EU asylum regime which meets the demands of states, but which has little to do with effective and durable protection.

CHAPTER 2

PROTECTING REFUGEES IN THE CONTEXT OF IMMIGRATION CONTROLS

Catherine Phuong

EU Member States are discussing new approaches to refugee protection. The results of the debate which is currently taking place will undoubtedly have an impact well beyond the EU and may signal an important shift in states' implementation of their international refugee protection duties under the 1951 Convention. The EU debate has been given renewed momentum by the UK proposal that suggested improved 'management of refugee flows' in regions of origin and the creation of transit processing centres outside the EU boundaries.[1] The proposal has produced strong reactions.[2] The United Nations High Commissioner for Refugees (UNHCR) announced its own proposal, which adopts some elements of the UK proposal: UNHCR's three-pronged proposal suggests that 'manifestly unfounded' cases should be processed in EU-based processing centres (EU prong), that refugees who have moved from a safe country of first asylum should be returned there (regional prong), and that remaining cases should be dealt with by the national asylum system of the destination state (domestic prong).[3] The European Commission had initially tried to distance itself from the UK and UNHCR proposals, and favoured the development of protected entry procedures and EU resettlement programmes.[4] More recently, it has shown greater interest in improving protection capacities in regions of origin.[5] There will undoubtedly be many more proposals to come as Member States are exploring new ways of managing refugee flows into the EU.[6]

---

1   See UK paper, *New International Approaches to Asylum Processing and Protection*, 10 March 2003. For a detailed analysis, see Noll, G, 'Visions of the exceptional: legal and theoretical issues raised by transit processing centers and protection zones' (2003) 5 European Journal of Migration and Law 303; and Loescher, G and Milner, J, 'The missing link: the need for comprehensive engagement in regions of refugee origin' (2003) 79 International Affairs 583.

2   See, for instance, Amnesty International, *UK/EU/UNHCR: Unlawful and Unworkable – Amnesty International's Views on Proposals for Extra-territorial Processing of Asylum Claims*, IOR 61/004/2003, 18 June 2003. See also House of Lords European Union Committee, *Eleventh Report of Session 2003–2004: Handling EU Asylum Claims: New Approaches Examined*, HL 74, 30 April 2004.

3   See UNHCR, *UNHCR's Three-pronged Proposal*, Working Paper, June 2003; and UNHCR, *A Revised 'EU Prong' Proposal*, Working Paper, 22 December 2003.

4   See *Towards More Accessible, Equitable and Managed Asylum Systems*, COM (2003) 315, 3 June 2003.

5   See *On the Managed Entry in the EU of Persons in Need of International Protection and the Enhancement of the Protection Capacity of the Regions of Origin – 'Improving Access to Durable Solutions'*, COM (2004) 410, 4 June 2004.

6   See, for instance Parker, G, 'Berlin in to push to set up EU camps in north Africa' (2004) *Financial Times*, 16 September.

The aim of this chapter is not to examine these proposals in detail. On the contrary, it tries to step back from them and provide its own analysis of the problems currently at hand. The chapter does not seek to propose some novel way of addressing the asylum crisis. There are already plenty of academic models that attempt to do so.[7] Its ambition is much more modest. Its aim is, first, to identify with more clarity the problems we should be trying to deal with. It is argued here that issues of refugee protection have to be addressed within the context of migration control strategies. These issues of refugee protection should not be seen solely in terms of state concerns. Indeed, the improved management of refugee movements is in the interests of both the host communities (in both industrialised countries and first asylum countries) and the refugees themselves. The chapter will then examine which avenues can be explored by states in order to reduce incentives for irregular migration, while at the same time preserving access to refugee protection, or even improving protection for the majority of the world's refugees. Finally, it will be argued that if such ideas are ever to lead to concrete proposals, EU Member States should carefully consider the legal parameters within which they will have to operate.

WHAT IS THE ASYLUM CRISIS?

There seems to be a consensus that the international refugee regime is in crisis.[8] Nonetheless, there are wide disagreements as to how to deal with that crisis. While most agree that the current situation is untenable, they disagree on what solutions should be adopted to address current problems. This failure to reach agreement on the remedies can be traced to a failure to agree, first, on the diagnosis of the problems. One therefore needs to identify with greater clarity the issues involved. When we talk about the asylum crisis, we usually refer to concerns about refugee protection. It is argued here that we should also address concerns about the management of refugee flows.

Current concerns about refugee protection are threefold. First, the concern is about refugees not having sufficient and adequate access to protection, whether it is in regions of origin or in industrialised countries. The growing efficiency of border management policies has made it increasingly difficult for some refugees to seek protection in the EU. Visa requirements and carrier sanctions are aimed at all would-be migrants without any distinction. Their 'unintended' impact is to prevent some refugees from entering the territories of EU Member States and therefore from activating those states' international obligations towards them.

Secondly, there is what I would call the problem of unfair 'distribution' of protection. Those refugees who are afforded protection in the EU are not

---

7   See, for instance, Hathaway, J and Neve, R, 'Making international refugee law relevant again: a proposal for collectivised and solution-oriented protection' (1997) 10 Harvard Human Rights Journal 117; and Schuck, P, 'Refugee burden-sharing: a modest proposal' (1997) 22 Yale Journal of International Law 243.

8   See Chimni, B, 'Reforming the international refugee regime: a dialogical model' (2001) 14 Journal of Refugee Studies 151.

necessarily those who are the most in need of it. Indeed, asylum seekers are often single men who have the social connections, the financial resources and physical resilience to undertake the long and expensive journey from their regions of origin. In the meantime, others, who may be more in need of protection outside their region of origin, remain in first asylum countries or displaced within their own country.

Thirdly, it appears that resources devoted to refugee protection are inequitably distributed among refugees. In 2003, out of the 9.7 million refugees who were of concern to UNHCR, more than 6 million were to be found in Africa or Asia.[9] The overwhelming majority of refugees is therefore hosted in developing countries with few resources. International agencies often have to assist these countries in coping with major refugee populations. UNHCR has an annual budget of US$1 billion and the number of persons of concern to the agency is 17 million.[10] In contrast, industrialised states spend around US$10 billion on processing the claims of less than one million asylum seekers who find their way into their territories.[11]

The first three problems, which have been identified so far, focus on refugee protection. Some people may refuse to identify any further problems. However, focusing on problems of access to protection only reveals one part of the overall picture, and attempts to address the issue of refugee protection in isolation from related migration issues are unlikely to succeed. There are linkages between asylum and migration.[12] Failure to acknowledge what is generally referred to as the asylum/migration nexus works to the detriment of any attempt to improve refugee protection.

Asylum is one form of migration. While states have the sovereign power to control entry into their territories, they have made a significant concession to their ability to exercise this power when it comes to a specific type of human rights victim who deserve international protection. States have thus accepted some limited international obligations with regard to refugees. The main obligation contained in the 1951 Refugee Convention is the duty not to return a refugee to any country where their life or safety would be at risk (prohibition of *refoulement* in Art 33). When a person entered the country and claimed asylum, the state has so far considered that it had to examine that claim in order to determine whether that person is a refugee. If the person is, the state is bound by its international obligations not to return the person to their country of origin. If the person is not a refugee, the state can exercise its sovereign power to let them stay on some humanitarian ground or to return them to their country of origin.

---

9   See UNHCR, *Refugee by Numbers (2004 edition)*, available at www.unhcr.ch.

10 *Ibid.*

11 See ECRE/USCR, *Responding to the Asylum and Access Challenge: An Agenda for Comprehensive Engagement in Protracted Refugee Situations*, 30 April 2003.

12 See Crisp, J and Dessalegne, D, 'Refugee protection and migration management: the challenge for UNHCR', UNHCR/EPAU, *New Issues in Refugee Research*, Working Paper No 64, August 2002. See, also, UNHCR Global Consultations on International Protection, *Refugee Protection and Migration Control: Perspectives from UNHCR and IOM*, EC/GC/01/11, 31 May 2001.

Since asylum migration is one form of migration for which states have accepted international obligations, migrants who do not need international protection have (understandably) sought to use this channel of migration. The development of rapid and inexpensive air transport, the spread of global communications and the enduring economic gap between developing and developed countries have prompted an increasing number of people to migrate to richer parts of the world and more stable democratic structures. In response to the growing pressures of irregular migration, EU Member States have imposed increasingly elaborate controls on entry into their territories. Some irregular migrants have thus turned to the asylum channel, which has remained open because states have committed themselves to keeping that door open. Refugee movements cannot be insulated from other forms of migration. One therefore needs to acknowledge the asylum/migration nexus and address the asylum issue within the broader context of migration control.

As a result, the problem of abuse of the asylum channel has to be considered. One, of course, cannot identify all asylum seekers as persons who do not need international protection, as the popular press does in some industrialised countries. Nevertheless, it must be conceded that a significant proportion of asylum seekers do not have any claim to protection. These are migrants who use the asylum channel for the reasons explained above. Their impact on national asylum systems is considerable. At the very least, they contribute to the spiralling costs involved in maintaining asylum systems. The human and financial resources committed to examining unfounded asylum applications could be put to a better use if invested in improving protection for refugees in first asylum countries.

There may be a danger that, in the face of the rising costs involved in national asylum systems and mounting public pressure, states may decide to renounce the international obligations that they have undertaken towards refugees. This is unlikely to happen in the short term since state parties have recently all reaffirmed their commitment to the 1951 Refugee Convention on the occasion of its 50th anniversary.[13] Nevertheless, the reported abuse of asylum procedures is leading some members of the public to lose confidence in the institution of asylum itself. One should not underestimate this trend that impacts on the level of states' commitments to refugees and integration outcomes. In the age of liberal democracies, voters have a significant impact on overall policy orientations.[14]

Regular economic migrants do not apply for asylum. Those economic migrants who do are irregular migrants. In most cases, they have only managed to enter the country with the assistance of smugglers. People smuggling has become a thriving industry with links to other types of transnational criminal activities. Irregular migration, which is sustained by smugglers, destabilises large parts of societies, in countries of departure, transit countries and countries of

---

13   See *Declaration of State Parties to the 1951 Convention or its 1967 Protocol Relating to the Status of Refugees*, HCR/MMSP/2001/9, 16 January 2002.

14   See Gibney, MJ, 'Liberal democratic states and responsibilities to refugees' (1999) 93(1) American Political Science Review 175.

destination. It exposes the migrants to great dangers to their physical safety. The only ones to benefit from irregular migration appear to be the smugglers and some refugees who would not have access to protection otherwise. Where access to protection is needed it should be provided through other, legal, means. One must note that such access may not always be needed: some refugees who use smugglers to come and seek protection in industrialised states are people who may have already found protection in a first asylum country, or could have sought and been provided with protection in a first asylum country. In other words, smuggling is closely linked to secondary movements of refugees.

The issue of secondary movements, which are also referred to as 'irregular movements', has recently become a focus of attention. It must be noted that the terms 'secondary' and 'irregular' should not be used interchangeably when referring to refugee movements; not all secondary movements are 'irregular' in the sense of refugees breaching immigration rules on entry. By the same token, all irregular movements of refugees are not necessarily secondary. The refugee movements that are problematic to states are those which are both secondary and irregular. Where the refugee has already found protection in one state, he should not be entitled to seek the protection of another. For instance, the 1951 Refugee Convention provides that its provisions do not apply to any person who has taken residence in a first asylum country (Art 1(E)). Moreover, UNHCR's Executive Committee has acknowledged that:

> Where refugees and asylum seekers move in an irregular manner from a country where they have already found protection, they may be returned to that country if
>
> (i) they are protected there against *refoulement* and
>
> (ii) they are permitted to remain there and to be treated in accordance with recognised basic human rights standards until a durable solution is found for them.[15]

Nevertheless, the Committee also cautioned:

> It is recognised that there may be exceptional cases in which a refugee or asylum seekers may justifiably claim that he has reason to fear persecution or that his physical safety or freedom are endangered in a country where he previously found protection. Such cases should be given favourable consideration by the authorities of the state where he requests asylum.[16]

It is worth noting that the 1951 Refugee Convention does not stipulate that a refugee has the choice of the country of asylum; but neither does it require a refugee to seek protection at the first opportunity. It does not require that a refugee travels directly from their country of origin to the state where they wish to claim refugee status (though the protection afforded by Art 31 lapses if they do not).[17]

---

15 See *EXCOM Conclusion No 58 (XL) on the Problem of Refugees and Asylum-seekers who move in an Irregular Manner from a Country in which they had Already Found Protection* (1989), para 25(f).

16 *Ibid*, para 25(g).

17 See Goodwin-Gill, G, 'Article 31 of the 1951 Convention relating to the status of refugees: non-penalization, detention and protection', in Feller, E *et al* (eds), *Refugee Protection in International Law: UNHCR's Global Consultations on International Protection*, 2003, Cambridge: CUP, p 194.

In any case, most refugees cannot travel directly to the EU and often transit through one or several countries *en route*. In some cases it may be fair to expect an asylum seeker to have requested asylum in the transit country if they 'already [have] connexion or close links' with that state.[18] A principle that refugees should remain where they have already found 'protection' appears to make sense. Considering that onward movements often take place with the assistance of smugglers, one can then understand why secondary movements may be a problem that should be addressed. At a minimum, if returns are envisaged to a third country, they should only take place where 'effective protection' is provided there. As will be examined below, the crucial issue would then be to determine what 'effective protection' means in the refugee law context.

It follows from this brief analysis that while there is no doubt that the international refugee regime is in crisis, considerable divergences can appear when attempting to identify the exact problems we should seek to address. We should not stop at identifying problems encountered by refugees alone, but also those problems encountered by states attempting both to manage migration and provide protection to refugees. This is not to say that state interests in migration control should take precedence over refugee rights, but that any serious discussion about the future of refugee protection should acknowledge that states, which remain the source of refugee protection by exercising their power to grant asylum, also have other interests at stake when they provide such protection.

REDUCING IRREGULAR MIGRATION, WHILE PRESERVING (OR EVEN IMPROVING) REFUGEE PROTECTION

If state interests are to be seriously taken into account, should measures aimed at improving refugee protection also aim to improve migration management? Proposals which seek exclusively to improve refugee protection are unlikely to be taken up by states. The challenge is to find some common ground that would allow us to improve refugee protection, while at the same time manage migration more efficiently. I will examine in turn the strategies that are commonly invoked to improve refugee protection on the one hand, and migration management on the other. I argue that there may be more common ground between these strategies than is generally believed.

Improving refugee protection in the context of immigration controls

Several measures that would improve refugee protection can be immediately implemented by states. Refugee determination procedures have been plagued by problems of delays, costs, poor quality of decisions, etc. There is still scope for

---

18 See *EXCOM Conclusion No 15 (XXX) on Refugees without an Asylum Country* (1979), para (h)(iv).

increasing the efficiency of these procedures. Resources should be 'front-loaded' in order to correctly identify as early as possible those who should be granted protection. Refugees would be recognised more rapidly and the incentives for irregular migration would be reduced, especially if removals of failed asylum seekers were enforced more systematically and rapidly.[19] Procedural efficiency may still constitute the most effective way to deter abuse of the asylum channel by irregular migrants with no claim for protection.

Protection capacities in first asylum countries can be strengthened with the assistance of UNHCR and industrialised states.[20] There are several reasons why it is in the interest of refugees that improved protection is provided as close as possible to the countries of origin. For one thing, refugees should not have to travel far to find safety. Secondly, repatriation is more likely to take place if refugees remain closer to their homes. Moreover, the UNHCR *Agenda for Protection* declared that burdens should be shared more equitably and that more efforts should thus be made to shoulder the burdens of first asylum countries.[21] Finally, strengthening protection capacities in regions of origin would also reduce incentives for onward migration, at least as far as those who move solely for protection reasons are concerned. Indeed, some refugees do not intend to seek asylum in industrialised countries when they leave their home. In many cases, it is the conditions in the first asylum country which prompt them to search for more durable solutions elsewhere.[22] The problem often lies in the fact that while first asylum countries usually maintain relatively open borders (partly because effective border controls are expensive) they often clearly oppose local integration.[23] In contrast, while industrialised countries have adopted strict immigration controls, most of them have so far allowed most recognised refugees to remain in the country on a permanent basis (with the notable exception of Australia).

Industrialised states are unlikely to relax their border controls, especially because security concerns have been added to popular demands for strict migration control. Nevertheless, the impact of such controls on refugees can be attenuated by the following measures. First, those refugees who cannot find durable solutions in first asylum countries could have improved access to protection through the more strategic use of resettlement programmes. Several countries such as the US, Canada and Australia already have well-established

19 See Gibney, M and Hansen, R, 'Deportation and the liberal state: the forcible return of asylum seekers and unlawful migrants in Canada, Germany and the United Kingdom', UNHCR/EPAU, *New Issues in Refugee Research*, Working Paper No 77, February 2003. See also Phuong, C, 'The removal of failed asylum-seekers', forthcoming in (2005) *Legal Studies*.

20 See UNHCR Global Consultations on International Protection, *Strengthening Protection Capacities in Host Countries*, EC/GC/01/19, 19 April 2002.

21 See UNHCR, *Agenda for Protection*, A/AC.98/965/Add.1, 26 June 2002 (3rd edn, October 2003), pp 56–65.

22 See, for instance, Chatelard, G, 'Iraqi forced migrants in Jordan: conditions, religious networks, and the smuggling process', WIDER Discussion Paper No 2003/34, April 2003.

23 For instance, Kenya categorically opposes the local integration of Somali refugees; see ECRE/USCR, *Responding to the Asylum and Access Challenge*, p 16.

schemes and EU Member States are considering setting up their own schemes.[24] So far, the established programmes benefit less than 1% of the world's refugees. The establishment and expansion of EU resettlement programmes may dissuade some refugees from trying to enter the EU through illegal means. Nevertheless, such a measure will only have a limited impact on secondary movements of refugees since any increase in the overall number of resettlement places will never match the number of refugees hoping to seek protection in industrialised countries. Moreover, those eligible for resettlement are, in theory, those who are most in need of protection, but not necessarily refugees who would have left the region of origin in the first place. Nonetheless, resettlement still constitutes an important symbolic gesture of willingness to share the burden of first asylum countries. It is argued here that there should be more strategic use of resettlement as an instrument of protection for those refugees who cannot find durable solutions in their first asylum country.[25]

Secondly, protected entry procedures could be set up, or enhanced where they already exist. This would allow refugees to apply for asylum from a first asylum country, or even from a country of origin, and be granted a visa allowing them to travel to the country of destination where the asylum application is processed. The EU is currently exploring the possibility of establishing a joint scheme.[26] The hope is that refugees will use this legal channel to enter the EU, rather than pay smugglers. The combination of resettlement programmes and protected entry procedures could greatly improve access to protection in the EU. However, EU Member States have not so far shown any great enthusiasm for the development of protected entry procedures.[27]

The above measures would deter those wanting to abuse asylum procedures, improve protection in first asylum countries, and establish legal channels for organised movements of refugees to industrialised countries. The measures could even produce these outcomes while still allowing for the maintenance of strict immigration controls. It remains to be seen whether protection capacities in regions of origin can be sufficiently improved, and whether expanded resettlement programmes and protected entry procedures could provide adequate access to protection. If they do, the numbers of asylum seekers travelling in an irregular manner to industrialised countries should diminish, and the costs of refugee determination procedures should follow the same downward trend. Resources could be diverted to development assistance in first asylum countries and even countries of origin. Those who are solely concerned with the welfare of

---

24 See Migration Policy Institute, *Study on the Feasibility of Setting Up Resettlement Schemes in EU Member States or at EU level against the Background of the Common European Asylum System and the Goal of a Common Asylum Procedure* (2003), http://europa.eu.int/comm/ justice_home/doc_centre/asylum/studies/docs/resettlement-study-full_2003_en.pdf.

25 UNHCR Global Consultations on International Protection, *Strengthening and Expanding Resettlement Today: Dilemmas, Changes and Opportunities*, EC/GC/02/7, 25 April 2002.

26 See Danish Centre for Human Rights, *Study on the Feasibility of Processing Asylum Claims outside the EU Against the background of the Common European Asylum System and the Goal of a Common Asylum Procedure* (2002), http://europa.eu.int/comm/justice_home/ doc_centre/asylum/common/asylumstudy_dchr_2002_en.pdf.

27 *Op cit*, fn 5, para 35.

refugees probably wish to leave it at that. However, it is highly unlikely that states would be willing to invest vast amounts of money in resettlement programmes and capacity building activities in first asylum countries unless the problem of irregular migration is addressed more directly.

Combating irregular migration while preserving refugee protection

Industrialised states all seek to combat irregular migration, while fulfilling their international obligations towards refugees. The focus of their attention is the smugglers and traffickers who facilitate irregular migration between developing countries and industrialised countries. As visa requirements do not distinguish between economic migrants and refugees, both use smugglers to enter industrialised countries. If states want to tackle the smuggling problem more aggressively they should also ensure that refugees no longer need to resort to smugglers to gain access to protection. Once such access is secured, states will be more justified in adopting more radical measures to combat smuggling.

States do try to co-operate with each other in order to dismantle trafficking and smuggling networks. However, focusing on the service providers is not sufficient and states also want to diminish the demand for the service. Smuggling responds to a demand for migration. There is no doubt that assistance should be provided in countries of origin and transit countries in order to reduce this demand for irregular migration.[28] Nevertheless, one should also recognise that these efforts are of limited value. Unless the economic gap between developing and developed states is dramatically reduced there will always be a demand for migration.

A supplementary strategy is to reduce the value of smuggling services. Irregular migrants who manage to enter industrialised countries currently have two choices. They can remain in the country illegally or present themselves to the authorities and claim asylum. While their claim is examined, states must proceed on the basis that the irregular migrants may be refugees and should therefore not be returned to their country of origin. So far, this has meant that they were allowed to stay in the destination country until their claim is decided. If they are declared to be refugees, they are granted refugee status and allowed to remain. If they have no claim for protection, they may be returned to their country of origin.

As far as those who do not need protection are concerned, they can be removed because states have no international obligations towards them. The problem raised by failed asylum seekers is that they generate unnecessary costs in national asylum systems in terms of processing their claims, providing support and enforcing their removal (where necessary). As mentioned earlier, improving the efficiency of asylum procedures and the enforcement of removals should deter these migrants from claiming asylum. Opening more legal channels of economic migration may divert some of these migrants away from the asylum channel.

---

28   *Op cit*, Loescher and Milner, fn 1.

There are enduring labour shortages in several sectors of the EU economy. Nevertheless, the types of migrants who currently burden asylum determination procedures may not match the categories of workers needed in European economies. One must concede that expanding legal channels of economic migration is a gamble, but EU Member States should consider this option more seriously. A targeted and incremental development of legal avenues for economic migration should be envisaged. Facilitating short-term migration movements of unskilled workers is in our EU economic interest and may divert some irregular migrants from the asylum channel and avoid the costs of processing unfounded claims.

Although these strategies have not been sufficiently explored yet, states have decided that economic migrants who lodge unfounded asylum applications may need further deterrence. Instead of being allowed to remain in the country while their claim is processed, these applicants may be transferred elsewhere in order to prevent absconding and to facilitate return to the country of origin. For this purpose, the UK has proposed that asylum seekers be immediately transferred to transit processing centres.[29] It is important to note that the UK document does not distinguish between refugees and others, but this is not anticipated to have a negative impact on refugees who would still ultimately be resettled in the EU. UNHCR made a similar proposition, with the difference that the 'EU reception centres' would be located within the EU.[30] Moreover, the centres envisaged by UNHCR would mainly process 'manifestly unfounded applications'.[31]

If the prospect of being transferred to transit processing centres is not sufficiently dissuasive for those who abuse the asylum channel, the UK envisages that the centres could also receive 'illegal migrants intercepted en route to the EU before they had lodged an asylum claim but where they had a *clear intention* of doing so' [emphasis added].[32] I do not see how a clear intention could be inferred other than by directly asking the intercepted migrants whether they wish to claim for asylum. I suspect that, once they are intercepted, most irregular migrants would lodge an asylum claim, even if they had no prior intention of doing so. In reality, interceptions would be undertaken to ensure that transit processing centres act as a deterrent not only for irregular migrants who abuse the asylum channel, but also for those who had no initial intention of doing so; that is, economic migrants who intended to remain illegally once in the EU.

States would argue that these proposals operate within the framework of international law since no asylum seeker would be returned home before establishing that they are not a refugee. In addition, the UK observes that '[t]here is no obligation under the 1951 Refugee Convention to process claims for asylum in the country of application'.[33] According to UNHCR, the Convention does not

---

29 *Op cit*, fn 1 (UK paper), pp 4–5.

30 *Op cit*, fn 3, pp 6–9.

31 Other categories of claims to be processed in the proposed EU reception centres were added in UNHCR, *A Revised 'EU Prong' Proposal*, p 2.

32 *Op cit*, fn 1 (UK paper), p 5.

33 *Op cit*, fn 1 (UK paper), p 6.

prevent a state from transferring responsibility for processing asylum claims in third countries.[34] Nevertheless, it is still argued here that transit processing centres should not be envisaged for a range of legal and practical reasons.[35] For instance, if transit processing centres are created, there will be high costs involved in the establishment and running of these centres. Transferring asylum seekers to and from these centres will also incur significant costs. If established outside the EU, the centres will require close co-operation with the state in which the centres are situated. Such a level of co-operation may not be so easy to secure.

Besides irregular migrants, who are essentially economic migrants, the other category of migrants smuggled into the EU is refugees. Most refugees flee to a first asylum country in the region of origin, and then travel in an irregular manner to industrialised countries, often via transit countries. It is precisely this type of migration, which is referred to as secondary movements, that states want to address in order to combat irregular migration. As explained earlier, there is nothing in the 1951 Refugee Convention that prevents a refugee from seeking asylum outside their region of origin. However, what states are clearly concerned about is the close relationship between secondary movements and smuggling, hence the recent search for 'incentives' to induce refugees not to appeal to smugglers to help them leave their first asylum country. As mentioned above, one obvious incentive to reduce secondary movements is to improve the level of refugee protection provided in first asylum countries. This would reduce the 'push' factor. Moreover, refugees can be directed to protected entry procedures and resettlement programmes, both of which will help to ensure that refugee movements are predictable.

Nevertheless, states may consider that the 'pull' factor, that is, permanent asylum in an industrialised state where average incomes are several times higher than in the first asylum country, is still too strong. The possibility that industrialised states are currently exploring is to return refugees to their first asylum country where they have already found or could have sought protection. States would not be breaching their international obligation under Art 33 of the 1951 Refugee Convention. Nevertheless, it will be argued later that states also have to take into account a range of legal constraints before any transfers to regions of origin are envisaged.

Combating irregular migration and improving refugee protection?

While industrialised states are unlikely to invest significant amounts of human and financial resources in resettlement programmes and capacity building in regions of origin without being able to combat smuggling more aggressively, it is also to be expected that first asylum countries will never accept transfers of

---

34   See House of Lords European Union Committee, *Eleventh Report of Session 2003–2004*, para 82.

35   *Op cit*, Noll, fn 1.

refugees without gaining any benefit for themselves. It is argued here that, contrary to the general perception, proposals to combat smuggling can contribute to improve the protection afforded to the majority of the world's refugees. This could be achieved where first asylum countries can 'exploit' industrialised states' desperate desire to address the problem of irregular migration.

First asylum countries could be placed in the strong bargaining position where they would only accept transfers of refugees *if* industrialised states commit themselves to resettlement and assistance to strengthen protection capacities in regions of origin. In this context, transfers of refugees to first asylum countries could no longer be perceived as mere burden shifting or as the result of unilateral exclusionary policies. Industrialised states would not be seen as seeking to exclude refugees if they commit to take on a substantial number of refugees (not just a few hundred) through resettlement programmes. These would be refugees who cannot not find durable solutions to their plight in the first asylum country, that is, those who are most deserving of protection, but who could never have acquired the resources to be smuggled into an industrialised country. Special assistance would be provided to these refugees to facilitate their integration in the host society. The general public would probably be much more sympathetic and welcoming toward these refugees and therefore less reluctant to commit national resources to refugee protection.

As for the refugees who remain in the first asylum country, they would also benefit from industrialised states' new engagement in regions of origin. The savings made on in-country processing would be invested in capacity building in first asylum countries in the region/s of origin that accept transfers of refugees. The outcome may well be that industrialised states will still be spending up to US$10 billion a year on refugees, but this sum would be mainly spent on refugee protection itself or protection-related activities (aid, peacekeeping, etc), rather than processing asylum seekers, up to half of whom are not refugees.

Transfers of refugees to regions of origin without any substantive accompanying measures are clearly unacceptable. Transfers which are coupled with strong commitments to improve refugee protection in regions of origin raise interesting possibilities that need to be explored more fully. Once one overcomes the initial aversion to transfers and envisages the issue of refugee protection in a global context, one realises that transfers could constitute the key to improved protection (through resettlement) for the greater number of refugees in regions of origin and the highest level of protection for those who need it. Those concerned with the welfare of refugees should see an unexpected opportunity here. In this 'ideal scenario' there would no longer be any demand for smuggling services because of the lack of incentives to migrate in an irregular manner to industrialised countries.

To recap, those who have no need for protection are processed upon arrival and returned to their country of origin. Those who do need protection, but had already found it (or could have found it) in a first asylum country, are returned to their region of origin. In each case, no migrant would achieve their intended migration outcome. Irregular migrants may react by choosing to remain illegally once in the country. To counter such possibility, some states may suggest that the solution would be not to let irregular migrants enter the country in the first place, but to intercept them and transfer them immediately to transit processing centres. Faced with such a prospect, there would no longer be any incentive to migrate in an irregular manner. Those who wish to migrate to industrialised countries should use expanded resettlement programmes or protected entry procedures if they are refugees, or legal channels of family or labour migration if they are not.

One could even argue that both states and refugees would benefit from such a situation. All the problems identified in the first part of this chapter would be solved. Obviously, states would finally manage to reduce smuggling. Refugees would only move in an orderly manner. The number of asylum seekers to be processed would diminish. In accordance with the principle of burden sharing, the savings made on processing, which could amount to several *billion* US dollars, could be spent more usefully on expanding resettlement programmes, improving protection in first asylum countries, assisting refugees to come and increasing development aid more generally. Refugees who wish to seek protection in industrialised states may not all be granted this possibility, but the situation of the greater number of refugees remaining in regions of origin could improve dramatically. Moreover, those granted asylum in industrialised states through resettlement would be those most deserving of protection, not those who manage to make the journey because of good connections and financial means. Finally, this ideal scenario would take place within the framework of the 1951 Refugee Convention since no refugee would at any point be returned to a country where they had a fear of persecution.

At this stage of the analysis, while one cannot help feeling uncomfortable with the scenario envisaged above, some may concede that they would have fewer objections to transfers/returns of refugees to regions of origin *provided that* protection is available there, that resettlement programmes are set up and that savings made on in-country processing are reinvested in improving protection in regions of origin. If one tries to think about refugee protection not only in the EU context, but in the more global context, transfers of refugees to regions of origin may afford an opportunity to provide protection in the EU to those who really need it, as well as better protection to the vast majority of refugees remaining in first asylum countries. Those concerned with the welfare of *all* refugees should consider this opportunity carefully. Of course the crucial concept which needs to be examined now is that of protection in the region of origin. The mistake which must not be made here is to exclude all returns to regions of origin on the sole basis that the refugees will never enjoy the same living standards in regions of origins as in the EU. In other words, one should draw a distinction between protection from persecution and protection from poverty.

DEFINING PROTECTION IN THE CONTEXT OF SECONDARY MOVEMENTS

If refugees can be returned to a first asylum country where 'effective protection' is available, there is a concern that this notion will be interpreted restrictively. More generally, the proposals may lead states to interpret their obligations under the 1951 Refugee Convention in a minimalist fashion. Two main questions need to be considered. First, there is no doubt that current proposals are based entirely on the premise that protection can be provided to refugees in regions of origin. It is absolutely astounding that neither the UK nor UNHCR have provided any detail about their understanding of the concept of 'effective protection'.[36] One should note that the word 'effective' is redundant to the extent that protection must always be effective. Protection that is not effective is simply not protection. The second and related question that should be addressed is to what extent states can be held responsible for failures to provide protection in the first asylum country.

The most fundamental obligation contained in the 1951 Refugee Convention is the prohibition of *refoulement*. It follows that where transfers to a third country are envisaged, one must first establish that the refugee will not be persecuted there. One has to concede that it is unlikely that a person has a well-founded fear of persecution both in the country of origin and a third state. Nevertheless, states should always envisage this possibility in order to avoid a breach of their fundamental obligation under Art 33. There has never been any doubt that Art 33 also prohibits indirect *refoulement*. States cannot transfer a refugee to a state which, in turn, would return the refugee to a place where they have a well-founded fear of persecution; nor can states begin a chain deportation.

One could suggest that the receiving state should always be a party to the 1951 Refugee Convention. However, this is not a necessary, nor a sufficient, condition. What should be scrutinised is the actual practice of the receiving state. Nonetheless, where the receiving state is a party to the 1951 Refugee Convention, UNHCR can exercise its supervising role under Art 35 of the Convention. Similar arguments can be made with regard to the other human rights instruments which are mentioned below: while accession to these treaties is preferable, it is the actual practice of states that should be examined.

It is by no means sufficient that states do not return a refugee to another state where their life or freedom would be threatened on one of the Convention grounds. UNHCR's Executive Committee adopted Conclusion No 58 stating that refugees could be returned to a first asylum country provided that they be 'permitted to remain [in the third country] and to be treated in accordance with recognised basic human rights standards until a durable solution is found for them'. In order to identify these basic human rights standards one can refer to what is commonly known as the International Bill of Rights, which is composed of the Universal Declaration of Human Rights and the two international covenants.[37] The notion of *basic* human rights standards implies that these

36 UNHCR had merely commissioned a paper and convened a roundtable on the topic. See Legomsky, SH, 'Secondary refugee movements and the return of asylum-seekers to third countries: the meaning of effective protection' (2003) 15 International Journal of Refugee Law 567; and *Summary Conclusions on the Concept of 'Effective Protection' in the Context of Secondary Movements of Refugees and Asylum-seekers*, Lisbon Expert Roundtable, 9 and 10 December 2002.

37 *Universal Declaration of Human Rights*, GA Res 217 A (III), 10 December 1948, hereinafter *Universal Declaration*; *International Covenant on Civil and Political Rights*, 16 December 1966, 999 *UNTS* 171, hereinafter *ICCPR*; and *International Covenant on Economic, Social and Cultural Rights*, 16 December 1966, 993 *UNTS* 3, hereinafter *ICESCR*.

standards should be applied in all circumstances and that there should never be any derogation from them. States who are parties to the above treaties should not be able to evade their obligations not to breach non-derogable rights by simply transferring the person to another jurisdiction. The list of non-derogable rights contained in the International Bill of Rights is fairly limited. The Universal Declaration is not a legally binding treaty. The ICESCR does not contain any provision dealing with derogations. Article 4(2) of the ICCPR lists the provisions that are non-derogable, which include Arts 6 (right to life), 7 (torture and cruel, inhuman or degrading treatment), 8(1) and (2) (slavery and servitude) and 18 (freedom of thought, conscience and religion). However, one can also distinguish the notion of basic human rights from the concept of non-derogable rights, which are not necessarily the most fundamental human rights.

The concept of protection should clearly include, at a minimum, protection of basic economic and social rights. The ICESCR imposes on states, who are parties to it, a number of core obligations 'to ensure the satisfaction of, at the very least, minimum essential levels of each of the rights is incumbent upon every State party'.[38] Protection should therefore include access to essential foodstuffs, essential primary health care, basic shelter and housing, and basic primary education. Nevertheless, developing countries may choose to what extent such access is granted to non-nationals (Art 2(3)). Such limitation is partly offset by the fact that the 1951 Refugee Convention provides a stronger basis protecting some of the refugee's economic rights.[39]

If a state, which is party to the ICCPR and/or the ICESCR, returns a person to a territory where their basic human rights are breached, it may be in violation of that state's obligations under the Covenants. The Human Rights Committee has unequivocally stated that:

> if a State party extradites a person within its jurisdiction [in such circumstances], and if, as a result, there is a real risk that his or her rights under the Covenant will be violated in another jurisdiction, the State party itself may be in violation of the Covenant.[40]

This argument was made with regard to Art 7, but could apply to other Articles of the Covenants. All EU Member States are also parties to the Convention against Torture.[41] Article 3 of that Convention explicitly states that no one should be returned to a state 'where there are substantial grounds for believing that he would be in danger of being subjected to torture'.

The ECHR also imposes legal constraints on removals to third countries. The most relevant provision is undoubtedly Art 3. In the landmark case of *Soering*, the European Court of Human Rights established that no one should be extradited to

---

38 See *The Nature of State Parties' Obligations (Art 2, Para 1) – General Comment No 3*, 14 December 1990, E/1991/23.

39 See Hathaway, JC, 'The international refugee rights regime' (2000) 8(2) Collected Courses of the Academy of European Law 135.

40 See *Ng v Canada*, CCPR/C/49/D/469/1991, 7 January 1994, para 14.2.

41 *Convention against Torture and Other Cruel, Inhuman or Degrading Treatment or Punishment*, 10 December 1984, 23 *ILM* 1027 and 24 *ILM* 535.

a state where they would face a real risk of serious ill-treatment by that state.[42] Article 3 also applies where the risk of ill-treatment emanates from non-state agents and where state authorities are unable to afford protection.[43] Nevertheless, the Court has also stated that 'given the fundamental importance of Article 3 in the Convention system, the Court must reserve to itself sufficient flexibility to address the application of that article in other contexts which might arise.'[44] Accordingly, it has established that, in very exceptional circumstances, Art 3 may also be engaged where a person is returned to a situation, rather than specific acts, exposing them to serious ill-treatment.[45]

There is some uncertainty as to what constitutes inhuman and degrading treatment for the purposes of Art 3. Nonetheless, the Court has recently given some guidance as to the types of treatment which may fall within the definition of ill-treatment prohibited by the Convention. The Court has stated that:

> [a]s regards the types of 'treatment' which fall within the scope of Article 3 of the Convention, the Court's case-law refers to 'ill-treatment' that attains a minimum level of severity and involves *actual bodily injury* or *intense physical or mental suffering*. Where treatment humiliates or debases an individual, showing a lack of respect for, or diminishing, his or her human dignity, or arouses feelings of fear, anguish or inferiority capable of breaking an individual's moral and physical resistance, it may be characterised as degrading and also fall within the prohibition of Article 3.[46] [Emphasis added]

The threshold set by Art 3 is high. Nonetheless, it is worth noting that the Court has not foreclosed any further development of its jurisprudence on Art 3 in the context of removals.

Other Articles of the Convention should be considered when examining the legality of transfers of refugees to third countries. The Court has explicitly considered that Art 8 could be engaged in removal cases. In the early cases, Art 8 was successfully invoked only where the removal decision would impact on the enjoyment of family life of those already established within the territory of a state party to the Convention. Indeed, the Court focused on whether the refusal to permit entry or the expulsion of the spouse, child or parent of a settled person amounted to an 'interference' with that person's right to respect for family life.[47] For such an interference to exist, the applicant has to demonstrate that they cannot follow their spouse and establish their family life elsewhere.[48] In the context of transfers of refugees to a third country, states must thus ensure that the refugee does not have close family ties with a person who is settled in their territory and, if the refugee does, that the family can relocate in the third country. More recently,

---

42 See *Soering v United Kingdom et al* (1989) 11 EHRR 439.
43 See *HLR v France* (1998) 27 EHRR 29.
44 See *D v United Kingdom* (1997) 24 EHRR 423, para 49.
45 *Ibid*.
46 See *Pretty v United Kingdom* (2002) 35 EHRR 1, para 52.
47 See *Abdulaziz, Cabales and Balkandi v United Kingdom* (1985) 7 EHRR 471.
48 See Rogers, N, 'Immigration and the European Convention on Human Rights: are new principles emerging?' (2003) 1 European Human Rights Law Review 53.

the Court has shifted its attention to the rights of private life of the person to be removed. In *Bensaid*, it declared that a decision to remove a person to a situation in which they would face treatment that does not reach the severity of Art 3 'may nonetheless breach Article 8 in its private life aspect where there are sufficiently adverse effects on physical and moral integrity'.[49] It is worth noting that Art 8 was broadly interpreted to include elements such as gender identification, name, sexual orientation, sexual life, mental health and so on.[50] This case should be seen as an important development since there is no longer a requirement to establish close family ties with a person who is settled in the territory of a contracting state. So far, the Court has not found that a removal decision constituted a violation of Art 8 on the sole ground that the person will face a severe interference with their private life, but states should be aware that it is clearly open to suggestion that some removal decisions may breach this provision.

Article 6 (right to fair trial) has mainly been invoked in extradition cases. Although the Court has stated that an extradition decision could breach Art 6 where there is a risk of a 'flagrant denial of a fair trial' in the requesting country,[51] it has so far refused to examine any issue arising under Art 6 in extradition cases.[52] Transfers of refugees to a third country would rarely be challenged under Art 6, unless the refugees would face trial in the third country and there is evidence that they will be denied a fair trial. Article 9 (freedom of thought, conscience and religion) has never been successfully invoked to challenge a removal decision.[53]

There is no doubt that state parties to the European Court of Human Rights (ECHR) should always consider the foreseeable consequences of their acts of removal. It is now widely accepted that where there is a real risk that the person facing the possibility of removal will face ill-treatment amounting to torture or inhuman or degrading treatment within the meaning of Art 3, the state deciding their removal is in breach of its Convention obligations. However, other articles of the Convention can also be engaged when envisaging transfers of refugees to third countries, even in situations where the refugees would face treatment falling short of Art 3 ill-treatment. Transfers of refugees to a third country may amount to a breach of Art 8. Future developments on Arts 6 and 9 should also be scrutinised. Decisions to transfer a refugee to a third state would be in contravention of the Convention where the refugee faces a serious risk of a gross violation of any of their Convention rights. The severity of the violation should not be assessed solely with reference to Art 3, as evidenced by the Court's recent decision in *Bensaid*.

A separate but related question that needs to be examined is to what extent the sending state can be held responsible for subsequent breaches of the refugee's rights in the third state. There should be a clear distinction between those acts which were foreseeable consequences of the transfer and those which were not.

---

49 See *Bensaid v United Kingdom* (2001) 33 EHRR 10, para 46.

50 *Ibid*, para 47.

51 See *Soering v United Kingdom*, para 113. See, also, *MAR v United Kingdom* (1996) 23 EHRR CD 120.

52 See *Mamatkulov and Abdurasulovic v Turkey* (2003) 14 BHRC 149.

53 See *R v Special Adjudicator ex p Ullah* [2004] UKHL 26.

Where the receiving state fails to provide protection to the refugee (by breaching any of the rights identified above) and such failure was foreseeable at the time of transfer, the sending state is not responsible for the failure itself, but for carrying out the transfer in contravention of its international obligations.

A mere possibility that the refugee's right(s) will be breached in the receiving state is not sufficient. It has to be a 'serious risk' or a 'real risk'. The responsibility of the sending state will not be engaged where the risk is merely 'speculative' or 'based on largely hypothetical factors'.[54] The central issue is whether the breach was foreseeable in the light of the circumstances known or which ought to have been known to the sending state at the time of the transfer. Nevertheless, events subsequent to the transfer may still be useful to assess the sending state's responsibility.[55] Where the receiving state violates the refugee's rights, but such event was not foreseeable at the time of transfer, it is unlikely that the sending state could be held in any way responsible for the violation. Nevertheless, there is a remote possibility that if the sending state sets up its own 'facilities' (for example, regional protected areas) to protect the transferred refugees in the receiving state, it exercises extra-territorial jurisdiction over these facilities and could be held responsible for certain human rights violations taking place there. The European Court of Human Rights has recognised that a state exercises extra-territorial jurisdiction 'when the ... state, through effective control of the relevant territory and its inhabitants abroad as a consequence of military occupation or through the consent, invitation or acquiescence of the Government of that territory, exercises all or some of the public powers normally to be exercised by that Government'.[56]

There are a range of legal constraints which EU Member States should take into account when envisaging transfers of refugees to first asylum countries or any other third state. The challenge is to ensure that refugees are not returned to a country where protection is not available, while at the same time creating opportunities for some transfers to take place to carefully selected countries. It must be remembered that smuggling will only be eliminated, resettlement programmes expanded and increased assistance to refugees in first asylum countries provided, on the condition that some transfers of refugees take place.

CONCLUSION

There is no doubt that a number of the ideas examined in this chapter will be perceived as highly controversial by some people. Any proposal, or even suggestion, that the current international refugee protection regime should be reformed is almost invariably met with suspicion by those concerned with the

---

54 See *Bensaid v United Kingdom*, paras 39 and 48.
55 See *Cruz Varas and Others v Sweden* (1992) 14 EHRR 1, para 76.
56 See *Bankovic and Others v Belgium and 16 Other Contracting States* (2001) 11 BHRC 435. See also *Loizidou v Turkey* (1997) 23 EHRR 513.

welfare of refugees.[57] However, there should be an honest recognition that states cannot continue to provide refugee protection in the way they have done in the last fifty years and that the general public's support for the institution of asylum is waning. Fresh thinking about how to provide refugee protection in the 21st century, in the context of migration control strategies, is urgently needed.

This chapter does not endorse the UK or UNHCR proposals. Nonetheless, it argues that some of the ideas contained in these proposals should be carefully scrutinised, rather than completely discarded. The proposals were not articulated in a manner that allows us to understand how they would work to the benefit of both states and refugees worldwide. This chapter has tried to distance itself from the proposals and go back to identifying the problems we should be trying to solve. It argued that the asylum/migration nexus should be taken more seriously for the simple reason that states that provide protection to refugees also have other concerns, such as migration control, to address. This chapter went on to examine what strategies can be explored in order to reduce incentives for irregular migration, while at the same time preserving, or even improving, protection for a broader number of refugees. A central feature of these strategies is the transfers of refugees to first asylum countries where protection is available. It is therefore crucial to come to a clear understanding of what protection means in this context. Consequently, the final part of the chapter attempted to define the concept of protection, with reference to international human rights and refugee law.

UNHCR could play a crucial role in assisting states to implement their obligations both to refugees and their own citizens. In the context of the Convention Plus initiative, the agency is contributing to the discussion on irregular secondary movements of refugees and asylum seekers.[58] However, such discussion remains unfocused.[59] It needs to be based on a more thorough analysis of the issues involved: why refugees move in an irregular manner from their first asylum country; how measures designed to control irregular secondary movements can be implemented in a protection-sensitive manner; what protection should be available to refugees in the first asylum country; how protection can be provided with the assistance of industrialised states; how these various issues can and should interlink; and so on.

We are still a long way from implementing any of the proposals suggested in this chapter and a number of questions remain. For one thing, where do we start? On the one hand, transfers of refugees to first asylum countries can only be envisaged where protection is available. On the other hand, protection may only be available where EU Member States make a firm commitment to investing massive financial and human resources in first asylum countries, which will only happen when resources can be diverted from Member States's overburdened

---

57 *Op cit*, Hathaway and Neve, fn 7, p 151.

58 See *Convention Plus Issues Paper Submitted by UNHCR on Addressing Irregular Secondary Movements of Refugees and Asylum-Seekers*, FORUM/CG/SM/03, 11 March 2004.

59 See, for instance, *Informal Record – Constitutive Meeting of the Core Group on Irregular Secondary Movements of Refugees and Asylum-Seekers, Geneva, 11 March 2004*, FORUM/CG/SM/02, 23 March 2004.

asylum systems, that is, when transfers take place. States could start by implementing measures to improve access to protection in regions of origin and industrialised countries, while gradually and carefully considering accompanying measures to tackle smuggling in a protection-sensitive manner. Previous experience, such as the Comprehensive Plan of Action for Indo-Chinese refugees, has shown that the success of such strategies is often dependent on close co-operation amongst a small group of states focusing their efforts on a specific caseload of refugees. States may want to proceed cautiously and first identify which caseload of refugees could benefit from a comprehensive arrangement. The Commission is now working on an EU regional protection programme that may be implemented within the next few years.[60] It remains to be seen what this programme will actually involve and how it will be implemented.

The chapter has identified a number of challenges involved in the implementation of the new strategies to provide refugee protection and one must also remember that these are not magic formulas for solving the current crisis.[61] Nevertheless, provided that states proceed carefully, it may be worth taking these risks in the interests of the refugees themselves.

---

60   *Op cit*, European Commission, fn 5, para 57.
61   See Crisp, J, *Refugee Protection in Regions of Origin: Potential and Challenges*, 1 December 2003, available at www.migrationinformation.org/Feature/print.cfm?ID=182.

CHAPTER 3

DEFLECTING REFUGEES: A CRITIQUE OF THE EC ASYLUM PROCEDURES DIRECTIVE

Sarah Craig and Maria Fletcher

This chapter takes the theme of asylum procedures and reveals how access to a full, fair and effective asylum determination process in the UK is likely to be eroded further, thanks to recently agreed legislation at European Community level. The EC Procedures Directive,[1] if adopted in its current form, fails to secure an acceptable minimum standard of procedural protection and rights for persons fleeing persecution and represents an obstacle in the way of the Community's long-term aim of achieving a harmonised asylum procedure. The Procedures Directive also provides a clear example of how legal systems and procedures can be manipulated in order to distort and undermine refugee protection. Therefore, in this context the question is not so much how migration poses a challenge to legal systems, but rather the extent to which legal systems are challenging migration.

The premise of this chapter is that a right to claim asylum pursuant to the 1951 UN Convention Relating to the Status of Refugees (Refugee Convention) necessarily includes a right to a process of individual determination. Moreover, this requires that the decision maker must allow the applicant to remain in the host state for the duration of their claim. Requisite procedural guarantees must be in place to ensure that any hearing is fair, but additionally and crucially, *access* to such procedures and guarantees must be secured. Yet, despite these obligations recent trends amongst policy makers at the national and Community level limit, partially or completely, access to a full asylum determination process. The result is that persons seeking international protection may be deflected away from having a determination of their claim with the full range of procedural safeguards and rights or they may be deflected from access to an asylum procedure altogether. The adoption of these 'deflection' techniques or mechanisms limits access to those *procedural* guarantees necessary in order to secure a fair hearing and, as such, necessarily undermines the very *substance* of refugee protection.

This chapter will be split into four sections. First, in order to understand the current disappointing situation as regards the Community procedures legislation, the background to common rules on asylum procedures in the European

---

1 The original Commission proposal for a Council Directive on minimum standards and procedures in Member States for granting and withdrawing refugee status was COM (2000) 578 final. This chapter is based on the amended draft version found at Council Doc 8771/04, Asile 33, 30 April 2004. At the time of going to press the latest version is Council Doc 14203/04, Asile 64, 9 November 2004. This version postpones the adoption of a minimum common list of safe countries of origin until after the adoption of the Directive. We refer to this in the text where appropriate.

Community is outlined. Secondly, we discuss some difficulties inherent in asylum decision-making with particular reference to UK practice, and evaluate the Procedures Directive in this respect. The main focus of the chapter is the third section, which identifies and critiques some of the deflection mechanisms used in the Procedures Directive. The deflection methods discussed are: the application of various safe country concepts, the imposition of procedural rules relating to the applicant's behaviour and, finally, the failure to guarantee in-country rights to appeal. In relation to each of these mechanisms, the minimum rules laid down in the Procedures Directive will be examined with reference to standards, obligations and guarantees laid down in international refugee law, human rights law and European Community law. The fourth and final section will consider some of the general legal implications of the Procedures Directive and, looking to the future, various legal options available to mitigate its negative content and impact will be examined.

THE EC PROCEDURES LEGISLATION IN CONTEXT

Procedural norms: relevant sources

Our basic premise is that the right to claim asylum, as enshrined in the 1951 Refugee Convention and its 1967 Protocol, necessarily requires that procedures for determining refugee status are both *fair* and *accessible*. If procedures are not fair and accessible the very notion of refugee protection is undermined. Effective procedures form part of the right to claim asylum and therefore their formulation and implementation deserve intense consideration and constant scrutiny. A framework of standards and how to interpret them can be deduced from a variety of legal sources at the international and European levels.[2]

All Member States are signatories of the Refugee Convention and its 1967 Protocol, and Art 63(1) EC Treaty provides that the EC must act in accordance with them. The Refugee Convention establishes the definition of a refugee[3] and enshrines such *jus cogens* norms as non-discrimination in relation to race, religion and country of origin[4] and non-*refoulement*.[5] For the purpose of interpreting the extent of procedural standards inherent in the Refugee Convention, the UNHCR

---

2   Reference is made here only to those key sources and principles against which the deflection techniques discussed in this chapter may be appraised. For a comprehensive discussion of all of the binding standards relevant to the appraisal of the Procedures Directive see Costello, C, *Analysis and Critique of Council Directive on Minimum Standards and Procedures in Member States for Granting and Withdrawing Refugee Status*, 30 April 2004, ILPA, Chapter 1, available at www.ilpa.org.uk/submissions/AsylumProcedures Directive.htm.

3   Article 1A.

4   Article 3.

5   Articles 32 and 33 impose a duty upon signatory states not to expel or return 'a refugee in any manner whatsoever to the frontiers of territories where his [or her] life or freedom would be threatened' on Convention grounds (race, religion, nationality, membership of a particular social group or political opinion).

Handbook[6] and the Conclusions of the Executive Committee of the Convention ('EXCOM Conclusions') are relevant and influential, although not legally binding. As an undisputed minimum, the Refugee Convention definition of refugee and the principle of non-*refoulement* imply that asylum claims are assessed on an individual and personal basis. The UNHCR Handbook also lays down some basic requirements for asylum determinations, including the need to inform the applicant of the procedure to be followed and the requirement that in the event of non-recognition of status at first instance, an applicant should be given a reasonable time to appeal that decision.[7] The Refugee Convention does not have an international dispute resolution mechanism capable of providing adjudication on the extent of its scope and application in the event of individual complaints. This function has, to date, been carried out by the relevant authorities (such as immigration officials, tribunals and courts) in the signatory states, but with the exercise of EC competence in the asylum field (which is required to respect the Refugee Convention) it is likely that the European Court of Justice will be called upon to fulfil this role in the future as far as EU Member States are concerned.[8]

All Member States are signatories to the European Convention on Human Rights and Fundamental Freedoms (ECHR) and are subject to the jurisdiction of the European Court of Human Rights. In relation to asylum procedure the ECHR is initially disappointing as a source of law. Article 6, the right to a fair hearing, only applies to the determination of 'civil rights and obligations' and criminal trials. Immigration and asylum decisions are regarded as administrative in nature and, therefore, somewhat controversially, the obligations pursuant to Art 6 have been held not to extend to asylum determinations.[9] However, UK courts have found that Art 6 norms can apply to immigration cases,[10] and the European Court of Human Rights has held that Art 3, combined with Art 13, requires that a fair determination process be made available where torture has been alleged.[11]

EU law enshrines binding general principles of law that may inform the content, interpretation and implementation of asylum procedures legislation. Most obviously, the respect for fundamental human rights is enshrined as a general principle of Community law and a founding principle of the EU.[12] Human rights standards, as drawn from the ECHR and constitutional traditions common to Member States, bind the EU institutions and the Member States when they are implementing Community law and are therefore binding on the EU's legislature. Additionally, the Charter of Fundamental Rights of the European Union,[13] 2000,

---

6   *Handbook on Procedures and Criteria for Determining Refugee Status under the 1951 Convention and the 1967 Protocol relating to the Status of Refugees*, HCR/IP/4/Eng/REV.1, re-edited, Geneva, January 1992.

7   Paragraph 192.

8   See Guild, E, 'Seeking asylum: Storm clouds between international commitments and EU legislative measures' (2004) 29(2) ELR 198, p 205.

9   *Maaouia v France* (2001) 33 EHRR 42.

10   *Asifa Saleem v SSHD* [2000] 4 All ER 814.

11   *Jabari v Turkey* [2001] INLR 136; *TI v UK*, [2000] INLR 211; *Hatami v Sweden*, 56/1998/962/1177, 9 October 1988; and *Hilal v UK* (2001) 33 EHRR 2.

12   Article 6 EU.

13   OJ [2000] C364/01.

lists the full range of rights recognised by the EU. This Charter is not currently legally binding, although it has been referred to in the preambles of recent EC legislation, in numerous Opinions of several Advocates General[14] and in several Court of First Instance judgments.[15] The Charter enshrines a right to asylum (Art 18), protection in the event of removal, expulsion or extradition (Art 19) and a right to an effective remedy and to a fair trial (Art 47), which, unlike the similar ECHR provision, is not limited to civil rights and should therefore extend to immigration decisions.

Other relevant instruments include the 1984 UN Convention against Torture, the Universal Declaration of Human Rights (Art 14(1)), the International Covenant on Civil and Political Rights 1966 (Art 14(1)), and the UN Convention on the Rights of the Child 1989.

It is clear, therefore, that international refugee law, ECHR case law and EU law create standards and principles that are binding upon Member States and the EU. Where appropriate, this framework of standards in relation to asylum procedures should be reflected in emerging legislation at the Community level. It would seem, however, that despite numerous references to upholding principles of international refugee law and human rights law in the European treaties,[16] in European Council Conclusions, and even in the Procedures Directive itself, certain provisions of the Directive present a very real possibility of breach of such norms.

The development of common procedural standards at the EC level: a mixed history

Despite the existence of binding norms, the history of the development of an approach, at the European level, to asylum procedures reveals a staggering lack of conformity in practice. Following a report submitted by the EC immigration ministers to the Maastricht Summit in December 1991 three Resolutions dealing with asylum procedures were approved in December 1992. These so-called 'London Resolutions' dealt with 'manifestly unfounded applications for asylum',[17] and 'safe' countries.[18] Therefore, the predominant approach from the outset was to approximate mechanisms for limiting access to national adjudication procedures. In any case, these early efforts to approximate procedures failed. The soft-law nature of resolutions meant that implementation was ad hoc and compliance rates were poor.

---

14 For example, Tizzano AG in Case C-173/99, *BECTU*, 8 Feb 2001; Jacobs AG in Case C-270/99P, *Z v Parliament*, 22 March 2001; and Case C-50/00P, *Unión de Pequeños Agricultores v Council*, 21 March 2002; Stix-Hackl AG in Case C-60/00, *Carpenter*, 13 September 2001.
15 For example, Case T-177/01, *Jégo-Quéré et Cie SA v Commission*, judgment of 3 May 2002.
16 Article 63(1) EC and Art 6 EU.
17 SN 4822/1/92 WGI 1282 of 2 December 1992.
18 SN4823/92 WGI 1283 of 19 November 1992.

A degree of procedural approximation was regarded as the most feasible and effective first step to longer-term substantive harmonisation, which itself was regarded as necessary in order to legitimise the approach to burden sharing of asylum applications already established in the Dublin Convention.[19] The Dublin system, rightly or wrongly, was based on the assumption that an asylum application lodged anywhere in the Community would have an identical outcome and, therefore, its legitimacy vis à vis other international obligations rested on the assumption of the equivalence of Member States' asylum adjudication systems.[20] On this basis, procedural approximation should clearly have pre-dated any attempt to organise the distribution of asylum applications between the Member States.

The Treaty of Amsterdam, in force from 1 May 1999, finally brought a significant amount of immigration and asylum policy within the competence of the European Community. Article 63 EC conferred competence on the Community to introduce, by 1 May 2004, a number of measures on asylum. The following measures had been formally adopted by that date:

- Decision 2000/596/EC on the European Refugee Fund;[21]

- Regulation 2725/2000, establishing a common EU database for the fingerprints of asylum seekers and persons found irregularly crossing the border (Eurodac Regulation);[22]

- Directive 2001/55, establishing a common temporary protection system for persons fleeing conflict in the event of a mass influx (Temporary Protection Directive);[23]

- Directive 2003/9, establishing minimum standards on the reception of asylum seekers in Member States (Reception Conditions Directive);[24]

- Regulation 343/2003, on the allocation of responsibility for determining asylum applications among the Member States (Dublin II Regulation);[25] and

- Directive 2004/83, on minimum standards for the qualification and status of third country nationals or stateless persons as refugees (Qualifications Directive).[26]

---

19 The 1990 Dublin Convention on State Responsibility for Asylum Applications [1997] OJ C254/1 has since been replaced and amended by a Community legal act, namely the 'Dublin II' Regulation 343/2003, [2003] OJ L50/1.
20 Boccardi, I, *European and Refugees: Towards an EU Asylum Policy*, 2002, The Hague: Kluwer Law International, p 101.
21 [2000] OJ L252/12.
22 [2000] OJ L316/1. Also Reg 407/2002, [2002] OJ L62/1.
23 [2001] OJ L212/12.
24 [2003] OJ L31/18.
25 [2003] OJ L50/1.
26 [2004] OJ L304/12.

The Procedures Directive, which forms the focus of this paper, was not formally adopted by 1 May 2004. In terms of protection of asylum seekers it is particularly disappointing that this piece of legislation is the last to be agreed because until such time as the procedures are fully standardised in the EU, many of the mechanisms, protections and rights guaranteed in the other 'building block' legislation will be undermined.

Upon adoption, the Procedures Directive will form the final legislative 'building block' of the first phase in achieving a Common European Asylum System (CEAS),[27] a goal set by the EU Member States at the Tampere European Council meeting in October 1999. The Tampere Conclusions outlined the programme for implementing the new powers conferred upon the Community by the Treaty of Amsterdam. In what may be described as the high-point of European immigration and asylum policy, the Conclusions state that:

> the aim is an open and secure European Union, fully committed to the obligations of Geneva Refugee Convention and other relevant human rights instruments, and able to respond to humanitarian needs on the basis of solidarity.

It reaffirmed the importance that the EU and the Member States attach to absolute respect for the right to seek asylum, and it agreed to work towards the creation of a CEAS, based on the full and inclusive application of the Refugee Convention, thus ensuring that nobody is sent back to persecution and respecting the principle of non-*refoulement*.

There is no doubt that the protection objectives of the Tampere mandate remain an important benchmark in the development of the CEAS, but more recent European Councils have added other objectives, changing the tone somewhat. The emphasis at the Seville European Council in June 2002 shifted towards ensuring 'swift and effective' protection for refugees, while making sure abuse of the system is prevented and failed applicants are returned to their country of origin more quickly. The European Council at Thessaloniki in June 2003, *inter alia*, invited the Council to examine 'the possibilities to further reinforce the asylum procedures in order to make them more efficient with a view to accelerating as much as possible, the processing of non-international protection-related applications'.

Reading between the lines, the recent emphasis is on identifying those individuals deemed unworthy of having their claim assessed with the full raft of procedural rights and guarantees, fast-tracking them in a variety of ways through the national systems or removing them from the systems altogether. The Member States appear to be less concerned about adopting common, strong and fair procedural safeguards and guarantees for those individuals seeking to invoke their rights to international protection in the EU and more concerned about limiting access to fair procedures.

---

27 The second phase of the CEAS will see the creation of a single asylum procedure applicable throughout the EU. The Commission launched discussion on the form and nature of the second phase in its Communication *A More Efficient Common European Asylum System: The single Procedure as the Next Step*, COM (2004) 503, 15 July 2004.

The mood amongst the Member States reflects broader public concerns, often whipped up by the right-wing press, about the 'abuse' or misuse of the asylum system and the numbers of individuals seeking asylum.[28] This exclusionary mood has spilled over from the Member States into the emerging legislation at both national and EC levels. Nowhere is this more obvious than in relation to the Procedures Directive.

Political agreement on the Procedures Directive: refugee protection undermined?

On 29 April 2004 the Justice and Home Affairs Council in Luxembourg reached political agreement on the 'general approach'[29] of the Procedures Directive. It was anticipated that formal adoption would follow shortly thereafter. However, the long and tortuous negotiation process continued and the latest political agreement was reached on 9 November 2004. This remains subject to reconsultation with the European Parliament. Final adoption is now expected by mid 2005.

The failure to formally adopt this Directive prior to the 1 May 2004 deadline means that the ten new Member States are to be included in the decision-making process. Although the fifteen 'old' Member States may hope that the 'new' Member States will respect the consensus that has been achieved, legally there is nothing preventing one or more of the new States from taking issue with the Procedures Directive in its current formulation and blocking the unanimous vote that is required. However, given the new Member States's geographical positions in the enlarged EU, their relative inexperience in relation to the legal processing of asylum claims and their pre-accession duty to introduce measures to comply with EC asylum policy to date, they are unlikely to object to the illiberal nature of the Directive.[30]

The response to this politically agreed version of the Procedures Directive has been mixed. In a press release, dated 30 April 2004, welcoming the Council's agreement on the CEAS, the Commission was (surprisingly) warm in its praise of the Directive saying that it will 'ensure that throughout the EU, all procedures at first instance are subject to the same minimum standards, while maintaining consistency with international obligations in this field'. A rather different tone was adopted by UNHCR in its press release of the same day:

> Taking a very good European Commission draft as its starting point, the long process of inter-state negotiations has resulted in an Asylum Procedures Directive which contains no binding commitment to satisfactory procedural standards, allowing scope for states to adopt or continue worst practices in determining

---

28 Although, as Richard Rawlings pointed out in the Hart Workshop, 2004 discussions, no evidence has been submitted to support the claims of abuse of the system.

29 Brussels, 30 April 8771/04, Inter-institutional File: 2000/0238 (CNS).

30 For more on the formation and impact of asylum law on the enlarged EU see Byrne, R, Noll, G and Vedsted-Hansen, J, 'Understanding refugee law in an enlarged European Union' (2004) 15 European Journal of International Law 355.

asylum claims. UNHCR is disappointed that EU states have failed to live up to the commitments they made at the beginning of the harmonization process in Tampere in 1999.[31]

Despite the words of praise from the Commission, there is no doubt that the Directive agreed is an exceptionally watered down version of the Commission Proposal.[32] The text of the Procedures Directive as it stands is incredibly disappointing. It is complex, often vague, and lacks coherence. Moreover, the content of the Directive, in terms of procedural guarantees and access to those guarantees, is problematic from a legal perspective, raising as it does, questions of compatibility with established norms of international refugee law, human rights law and EC law.[33]

The minimum standards enshrined in the Directive indeed provide example after example of national worst practice reflecting the lowest common denominator approach to procedural protection. Worse still, the Directive is littered with possibilities to enable Member States to derogate from these lowest, and sometimes already qualified, procedural guarantees, rendering them at best elusive and at worst illusory. The non-governmental organisation the European Council on Refugees and Exiles (ECRE) comments that the Directive contains 'a catalogue of discretionary clauses and represents a piece of legislation with a negligible level of approximation on issues of fundamental importance for the guarantee of fairness in the determination of asylum claims across Europe'.[34] The high levels of discretion conferred upon Member States by the Procedures Directive serve to undermine some of the crucial harmonisation achievements of the other building block asylum legislation. For instance, the broadly welcome consensus upon the definition of a Convention 'refugee' secured in the Qualifications Directive may be nullified in practice given the possibilities in the Procedures Directive for Member States to deflect people away from a fair determination process. Put simply, a common standard of protection cannot be achieved for applicants as long as they have different chances of accessing that protection in different Member States. At a more general level, the high level of

---

31 UNHCR Press Release, 'UNHCR regrets missed opportunity to adopt high EU asylum standards', 30 April 2004.

32 COM (2000) 578, 20 September 2000; OJ [2001] C 62 E/231 and amended proposal COM (2002) 326, 18 June 2002; OJ [2002] C 291 E/143.

33 Amnesty International has commented that:

   [t]he directive on asylum procedures, approved in April 2004, is a striking example of the influence of national agendas on the harmonisation process. After years of arduous negotiations, this directive has become a mere catalogue of national practice, allowing member states to retain national legislation which includes significant departures from accepted international refugee and human rights law.

   (Amnesty International, *The European Union – Now More Free, Secure and Just? Amnesty International's Human Rights Assessment of the Tampere Agenda*, Brussels, 2 June 2004.)

34 European Council on Refugees and Exiles (ECRE), 'Broken promises – forgotten principles. An evaluation of the development of EU minimum standards for refugee protection, Tampere 1999 – Brussels 2004' June 2004, 27, www.ecre.org/positions/Tampere_June_04.shtml.

discretion contained in the Directive serves to undermine the harmonising national laws that lie at the heart of the long-term goal of a CEAS.[35]

PROBLEMS IN ASYLUM DECISION-MAKING – THE UK EXPERIENCE AND THE PROCEDURES DIRECTIVE

Chapter II of the Procedures Directive sets out the minimum standards of decision-making. In this section we show, with illustrations from the UK asylum process, how, even with the benefit of the full guarantees contained in Chapter II, there are difficulties inherent in the asylum decision-making process, particularly for women and those who give inconsistent accounts. It will become clear that the procedural guarantees in Chapter II are both insufficient and excessively qualified. Most applicants could be deflected away from the full decision-making process, often by methods and in circumstances that are questionable in terms of standards enshrined in human rights and refugee law.

Screening and deflection

When an application for asylum is made in the UK, basic screening details in relation to identity, nationality, journey and basis of claim are recorded. The information gained is used to decide how the claim is dealt with, deflection being one possibility at that stage. For example, where screening reveals that the claim was made late, or that the applicant travelled through a safe country *en route* to the UK, then the applicant may not get access to the full decision-making process. Vulnerable applicants, such as women and separated children, run the greatest risk of not having their claims considered fully. The 1991 UN Guidelines on the Treatment of Gender Related Claims for Refugee Status, recognise this (at para 57):

> Sometimes, women who arrive as part of a family unit are not interviewed or are cursorily interviewed about their experiences, even when it is possible that they, rather than their husband, have been the targets of persecution. Their male relatives may not raise the relevant issues because they are unaware of the details or ashamed to report them.

While Art 5(2) of the Directive provides that all adults should have the right to make a separate application for asylum, in practice the Directive has not improved the situation for women. Article 5(3) says that dependent adults can have applications submitted on their behalf provided they consent, and their consent will be sought no later than at the interview stage. As only the main applicant is interviewed, it is not clear how adult dependents who wish to claim individually will be separately identified. Unless interviewed separately in private, women who do not wish to disclose their abuse to their husbands may

---

35 The limitation of secondary movements of asylum seekers influenced solely by the diversity of applicable rules is one of the main purposes of the CEAS.

not reveal details at the interview stage and will not benefit from the right to make a separate application.

Late claims

Under UK rules the decision maker *can* regard an asylum application as being less credible on the ground that it was made late;[36] and under new provisions,[37] a decision maker *'shall'* regard an applicant's credibility as damaged when the application is made after receiving an immigration decision, or after the applicant been arrested, unless the claim relies solely on matters which arose after receiving the decision, or it was not possible to apply before being arrested.

While the Procedures Directive[38] says that an application cannot be refused or excluded from examination solely on the ground that it is not made as soon as possible, it does allow accelerated decision making to be used for late applications where no reasonable cause for that delay exists,[39] thus sanctioning an approach which is sceptical of all 'late' applications.

In 2001, two thirds of all asylum seekers in the UK made their claim 'in country'.[40] While an asylum application made late simply to frustrate removal will justifiably attract scepticism, lateness alone is not a reliable indicator of credibility, and the European Court of Human Rights has said that the application of strict time limits to asylum applicants is inappropriate.[41] This was also recognised by a 1996 UK Social Security Advisory Committee report, which said:

> There are many valid reasons why people do not make their claim immediately on arrival. Lack of knowledge of procedures, arriving in a confused and frightened state, language difficulties or fear of officialdom may all be insuperable barriers to making any kind of approach to the authorities at port of entry.[42]

Interview

The full decision-making process in the UK involves Home Office officials making decisions based on a substantive interview, usually conducted through an interpreter. The interview usually supplements submissions made on a statement of evidence form, which contains questions directed at establishing whether the applicant meets the criteria for refugee status. While the provisions about

---

36 HC 395, para 341(i).
37 Section 8 of the Asylum and Immigration (Treatment of Claimants, etc) Act 2004.
38 Article 7(1).
39 Article 23(4)(I).
40 Asylum Statistics UK 2001, Home Office Research Development and Statistics Directorate, 31 July 2002, www.homeoffice.gov.uk/rds/immigration1.html.
41 *Jabari v Turkey* [2001] INLR 136.
42 Quoted in *R v Secretary of State for Social Security ex p B and JCWI* [1997] 1 WLR 275.

interview confidentiality and absence of family members in Arts 10 and 11 of the Procedures Directive are welcome, the right to a personal interview is restricted to the main asylum applicant so, as noted above, women's claims, in particular, may be overlooked. Article 10 also describes a wide range of situations where an interview need not take place at all. These include where a 'meeting' has already taken place, where it is not 'reasonably practicable' to hold an interview (for example, because the applicant is unfit to be interviewed), where the information given indicates that the application is unfounded, where the applicant comes from a safe country of origin or has travelled through a safe third country, or where the application is being made to frustrate or delay removal.[43] The Directive also allows decisions to be made without an interview if applicants fail to turn up for an interview appointment without a reasonable excuse, fail to respond to requests for information or fail to comply with duties to report to the authorities.[44] In some cases the authorities can also treat these applications as abandoned.[45] The provisions in Art 12 of the Directive about records of interviews are also disappointing. The record does not need to be a complete transcript and need only record the essential information,[46] although the requirement that the record be made available to the applicant and that the applicant be given the chance to indicate their agreement or otherwise is helpful.[47]

Inconsistencies in the asylum account

In order to reflect the difficulties that asylum seekers face in proving their claims, the standard of proof applied to asylum claims is said to be lower than the normal civil standard of proof. However, if the claim is not credible, it will fail, and inconsistencies between accounts are often given as a reason for disbelieving a claim. In the UK, the interview is supposed to supplement the statement of evidence form by getting more information about the claim; but in practice the credibility of the asylum applicant is damaged if the details at interview are not consistent with those on the statement of evidence form. The Directive once more endorses the UK's approach to inconsistencies in accounts by stating that applicants who have made 'inconsistent, contradictory, unlikely or insufficient representations'[48] can be refused the opportunity of being interviewed, or otherwise have their applications 'accelerated'.

This approach to inconsistencies in accounts is at odds with the 1992 UNHCR Handbook on Procedures and Criteria for Determining Refugee Status which says (at para 199) that applicants should be given the benefit of the doubt and acknowledges that inconsistencies are not the same as lies:

---

43 Article 10(2).
44 Article 20 and Art 33.
45 Article 20.
46 Article 12(1).
47 Article 12(3).
48 Article 23(4)(g).

> While an initial interview should normally suffice to bring an applicant's story to light, it may be necessary for the examiner to clarify any apparent inconsistencies and to resolve any contradictions in a further interview, and to find an explanation for any misrepresentation or concealment of material facts.

An approach which regards inconsistencies as lies is also at odds with the approach taken in human rights cases involving torture. In *Hatami v Sweden*,[49] the Commission found a violation of Art 3 where a claim had been refused on the ground of inconsistencies in the account given. The Commission criticised the interviewing process used and stated 'complete accuracy was seldom to be expected of victims of torture'.

Legal assistance[50]

The Procedures Directive provides that applicants can request legal assistance at any stage,[51] and the UK authorities cannot refuse it, but they are not required to provide it free of charge until the appeal stage,[52] and at the application stage the asylum seeker can be required to pay for it. This is illogical, since a valid initial decision requires the full participation of the applicant in the decision-making process, and legal representation enables that participation to occur.

The Directive confers a large amount of discretion on the Member States, in their national legislation, to limit free legal assistance further. For instance, even at the appeal stage, free legal assistance could be limited to the first tier of appeal only, and does not have to be provided for second tier appeals and judicial reviews. Moreover, it may be granted only for appeals that are likely to succeed, the only safeguard being that provision of free legal assistance should not be arbitrarily restricted.[53] Assistance may be provided only through designated providers, and can be made available subject to certain upper financial limits.[54]

The current UK system,[55] which allows for legal assistance to be provided throughout the process from application and interview through initial decision and appeal to judicial review, looks set to be the next target for levelling down as a result of this Directive. This has been foreshadowed in new legislation which sets strict time limits for applications for statutory review of decisions of the new Asylum and Immigration Tribunal, and (in England, Wales and Northern Ireland, but not Scotland) leaves the decision whether to grant legal assistance to the courts.[56]

---

49 56/1998/962/1177, 9 October 1988.
50 Since April 2000, this has been called 'Public Funding' in England, Wales and Northern Ireland. The term 'Legal Aid' applies in Scotland.
51 Article 13(1).
52 Article 13(3).
53 Article 13(3)(d).
54 Article 13(3)(c) and 13(5).
55 Administered in England and Wales by the Community Legal Service Fund, and in Scotland by the Scottish Legal Aid Board, under separate provisions.
56 Section 26 of the Asylum and Immigration (Treatment of Claimants etc) Act 2004, inserting new s 103D in the Nationality Immigration and Asylum Act 2002.

Interpreters and translators

Interpreters and translators play an important role in the asylum process. Most cases involve the use of an interpreter and the translation of documents. As described above, the claim could fail because of inconsistencies in the asylum account, and these can easily arise from inaccurate translation or faulty interpretation. In the UK at present, interpretation costs associated with legal representation can usually be met out of public funds, and the relevant decision maker (whether it be the Home Office or the Immigration Appellate Authority) will routinely provide an interpreter if the applicant's first language is not English.[57]

The Procedures Directive does not require interpretation services to be made available across the board. There is no automatic right to an interpreter where the applicant's first language is not English (even for a personal interview with the authorities).[58] Rather the State must deem an interpreter 'necessary' where 'appropriate communication cannot be ensured without such circumstances',[59] and where interpretation services are provided they must be paid for out of public funds. This is another area where 'levelling down' may occur. Also, the standard of 'appropriate communication' may be interpreted differently by each Member State authority, thus creating an uneven playing field. The Directive's failure to ensure the availability of interpretation and translation services will impede effective and open communication with the asylum applicant, will increase the chances of reaching wrong decisions, and will be likely to increase the number of time-consuming appeals.

METHODS OF DEFLECTION

Having outlined the procedural guarantees that should, in principle, attach to an examination of an asylum application, and some of the problems that can arise in the asylum application process, we will now look in more detail at some methods adopted to deflect access to full examination procedures and, as a corollary, those procedural guarantees.

The basic rule laid down in the Directive is that 'Member states shall process applications for asylum in an examination procedure in accordance with the basic principles and guarantees of Chapter II'.[60] Moreover, Member States must ensure that the procedure is concluded as speedily as possible, without prejudice to an 'adequate and complete examination', and shall inform the applicant of any delay or provide an expected time frame for a decision when no decision can be taken within six months.[61]

---

57 See the chapter in this book by Roxana Rycroft who discusses the dynamics of interpreting.
58 Article 11.
59 Article 9(1)(a).
60 Article 23(1).
61 Article 23(2).

The Directive, however, also constructs a complex system of procedural routes and requirements that will effectively prevent full access to the Chapter II guarantees for the majority of applicants. At the simplest level, the Directive can be said to create three procedures: *regular, accelerated,* and *specific.* It also refers to three types of application: *inadmissible, unfounded* and *manifestly unfounded.* The Directive is constructed so as to concentrate solely on listing extensive circumstances pursuant to which access to Chapter II guarantees may be limited or access to a procedure may be denied altogether.

Access to a *regular* procedure with the raft of Chapter II minimum guarantees is residual in that such a procedure only applies when *accelerated* and *specific* procedures do not. Procedures may be *accelerated* (or prioritised) in a very large number of circumstances,[62] most of which concern the specific behaviour of the applicant in submitting their application, and therefore have no bearing on the substance of the claim. This list is non-exhaustive and the open-ended discretion of the Member States in respect of accelerated procedure is limited only by the requirement that they must remain 'in accordance with the basic principles and guarantees of Chapter II'. Given the inadequate nature of the Chapter II guarantees in the first place, this requirement does little to alleviate concerns and, in any case, it is questionable whether full compliance is possible or likely in practice. Expedited procedure is bound to cut corners in the decision-making process or else there would be no material distinction between a regular and accelerated procedure. It is hard to accept the suggestion that an accelerated procedure is the same as a regular procedure in terms of procedural guarantees, and different only in length. Something would surely have to give.[63] Indeed it becomes clear, when one reads on in the Directive, that the vast majority of circumstances that give rise to *accelerated* procedure may also lead to applications being deemed *unfounded* or *manifestly unfounded.*[64] It is for Member States to determine what these guarantees would entail. Additionally, some grounds for *accelerated* procedure, including where a non-Member State is considered as a first country of asylum or as a safe third country for the applicant, may also result in the application being deemed *inadmissible.*[65] Given that this means that there is no obligation on the Member State to consider the merits of the case at all, there is clearly a departure from Chapter II procedural guarantees in the *accelerated* procedure.

Finally, *specific* procedure may be applied to subsequent applications for asylum, to border applications and to 'safe third country' applications.[66] The nature and content of the *specific* procedure is left to the Member States, but it is made clear that the procedure may derogate from the basic principles and guarantees in Chapter II.

---

62 Reading Arts 23(3) and 23(4) together.
63 There is no indication of a distinction in time frames between regular and accelerated procedures in the Directive.
64 Article 29(2). Note that the category of 'manifestly unfounded' may be used 'if it is so defined in the national legislation'.
65 Article 25(2)(a)–(g) includes a total of seven circumstances that may lead to an application being deemed inadmissible.
66 See Art 24, in conjunction with Arts 33–35.

The possibilities for deflection from 'an adequate and complete examination' permeate the Directive and, indeed, the whole examination process such that a so-called *regular* procedure is likely to be the exception rather than the norm. Beneath the three simple categories of procedure lies a multitude of complexities, not least that the nature and substance of the procedure applied in relation to any applicant may change at various points in the application process. Three examples of deflection methods are discussed here.

Deflection technique 1: 'Safe' countries

The first deflection method concerns applications that may be legitimately processed elsewhere. According to this method, applicants can[67] be removed to another 'safe' state to have their application considered there. EC law enshrines four different categories of safe countries; 'Dublin EU safe', 'safe third country', 'supersafe third country' and 'safe country of origin'. The 'Dublin EU safe' category is established in the Dublin II Regulation[68] while the latter three categories are enshrined in the Procedures Directive. Serious concerns about the compatibility of safe country principles with refugee law and, in particular, the principle of non-*refoulement* and Art 3 of the ECHR[69] have been raised. In addition the application of safe country principles may perpetuate the problem of 'refugees in orbit'.

1 'Safe third country'

This principle is laid down in Art 27 of the Procedures Directive. In general terms, safe third countries are deemed to be stable and free from political oppression, so that the authorities of the EU Member State in which the application is lodged may legitimately remove the applicant to the applicable safe third country. The principle is based on the contention that 'the claimant may be safely sent somewhere other than their country of origin or where they fear persecution'.[70] This means that, in effect, the application of the safe third country concept is a

---

67   To date, operational difficulties have meant that the use of safe country mechanisms has been limited. It remains to be seen whether efforts will be made to improve co-operation in the future in the light of the EU endorsement of safe country principles.

68   Council Regulation 343/2003, establishing the criteria and mechanisms for determining the Member State responsible for examining an application for asylum lodged in one of the Member States by a third country national, 18 February 2003, OJ [2003] L 50/1. This Regulation, known as 'Dublin II', replaced the Dublin Convention agreed in 1990 but not in force until 1997. Except where other provisions apply (relating, for instance, to family connection and the issuance of a visa), the general principle is that the state responsible for determining an asylum claim is the first Member State at which the asylum seeker arrives.

69   The Court of Human Rights has made it clear, in *TI v UK* [2000] INLR, that the application of safe country procedures does not affect the responsibility of the removing state to ensure that the applicant is not exposed to treatment contrary to Art 3 ECHR.

70   Clayton, G, *Textbook on Immigration and Asylum Law*, 2004, Oxford: OUP, p 400.

means by which Member States can shift the burden of processing asylum applications to outside of the EU. Where it is believed that an applicant should have applied elsewhere pursuant to this principle, the Directive stipulates that the application may be regarded as either unfounded or inadmissible and therefore subject to *accelerated* or *specific* procedures.[71] This principle constitutes a powerful method of deflecting applicants away from the asylum determination process in Member States and, as such, constitutes one of the most worrying developments in the Directive.

The criteria for the determination of countries as safe must be adequately construed and robustly enforced to ensure that individuals will not be removed to places where they are at risk of persecution, torture or inhuman or degrading treatment. According to international law, the primary responsibility for international protection remains with the state where the asylum claim is lodged. Accordingly, any transfer to a third country may only be envisaged where a third country is safe for the individual applicant, where that country agrees to admit the applicant to a fair determination procedure and where there is a meaningful link between the applicant and that third country.

The criteria established in the Directive fail to comply with these standards. According to Art 27(1), Member States may only apply the safe country concept where the competent national authorities are satisfied that the following conditions prevail in a third country:

(a) life and liberty are not threatened on account of race, religion, nationality, membership of a particular social group or political opinion; and

(b) the principle of non-*refoulement* is respected; and

(c) the prohibition on removal in breach of the right to freedom from torture and cruel and inhuman or degrading treatment as laid down in international law is respected; and

(d) the possibility exists for the applicant to request refugee status and, if found to be a refugee, to receive protection in accordance with the Geneva Convention.

Article 27(3)(b) obliges Member States to provide the applicant with a document informing the authorities of the third country that the application has not been examined in substance, and Art 27(4) obliges Member States to admit an applicant to a procedure when an applicant is refused entry into the territory of the safe third country. Neither of these safeguards amount to guaranteed access to a fair determination procedure in the third state.

Member States are permitted to draw up their own lists of safe third countries provided that the general criteria for designation are met.[72] The possibility of ensuring a level playing field is thereby undermined at the first hurdle of

---

71 Article 29(2) and Art 25(2)(c) respectively.
72 Member States are required to inform the Commission periodically of their lists of safe third countries.

designation. In terms of rules relating to the *application* of the safe third country concept, weak minimum standards combined with excessive state discretion once again undermine a common approach and effective protection. The Directive provides that rules on application of the principle must be laid down in national legislation and that, as a minimum, they should include rules requiring a link between the person seeking asylum and the third country to which it is proposed that the asylum seeker will be returned. It is left to the Member States to decide on the extent of the connection as long as it would be 'reasonable' for that person to go to that country. Therefore, there appears to be nothing preventing Member States from adopting a broad interpretation of this provision and even including mere transit through a country as a link sufficient to justify returning an applicant to that country. Additionally, Member States must have rules on methodology for the application of this principle to a particular country or applicant, 'including case by case consideration of the safety of the country for a particular applicant *and/or* national designation of countries considered to be generally safe' (emphasis added). Finally, rules must be introduced, 'in accordance with international law, allowing an individual examination of whether the third country is safe for a particular applicant which, as a minimum, shall permit the applicant to challenge the application of the safe third country concept on the grounds that he/she would be subjected to torture, cruel, inhuman or degrading treatment or punishment'.[73] Should this minimum approach be followed, there would be no clear obligation to consider the application of the principle to each individual applicant prior to a decision of inadmissibility; there would merely be a right for an applicant to challenge such a decision.

In relation to appeal procedures, the Directive provides that applicants must have the right to 'an effective remedy' where a decision of inadmissibility is taken pursuant to the safe third country principle,[74] but requires Member States to provide rules (in accordance with their international obligations) for the grounds of challenge to such a decision.[75] The question of whether the appeal has suspensive effect is left up to the Member States.[76] So, even if an individual has been subjected to appalling treatment, if the country is deemed by a Member State to be generally safe, then the application could be refused without individual consideration of the applicant's circumstances. In this case, individual consideration will only take place when the applicant challenges the refusal of protection, and that challenge may have to be taken after removal and from the country in which the treatment took place. Application of the safe third country principle, in that it denies an in-country right of appeal, risks breaching the principle of non-*refoulement* and undermines the very nature of an asylum claim by requiring that it be proven that the particular applicant is at risk from persecution. Moreover, non-suspensive appeals are not regarded as an effective remedy in international law, as we shall see later in more detail.

---

73   Article 27(2)(c).
74   Article 38(1)(a)(i).
75   Article 38(3)(c).
76   Article 38(3)(a).

2 Supersafe third countries

The category of safe third countries provides for at least the possibility of a rebuttal in individual circumstances. The Directive also provides for a category of so-called 'supersafe' third countries for which there may be 'no, or no full, examination of the asylum application and of the safety of the applicant in his/her individual circumstances ...'.[77] The concept of sending applicants to supersafe countries could apply where the competent authorities establish that an applicant is seeking to enter or has entered illegally into its territory from a designated supersafe country. Such a concept 'denigrates protection issues to matters of mere border control, effectively allowing illegal entry to determine asylum claims, in contravention of Article 31 of the Refugee Convention'.[78] An applicant would not have their individual application examined in substance and they would most likely be immediately removed from the territory of the Member State. The only procedural safeguards applicable to the applicant would be that they must be informed that a decision is being based solely upon this specific principle, and they must be provided with a document informing the authorities of the third country, in the language of that country, that the application has not been examined in substance. As with the safe third country principle there is no requirement that such communications are in a language that the applicant understands or that the Member State obtains assurances that the third country will process the applicant's claim.[79] The risks of chain *refoulement* and refugees in orbit are all too obvious.

A third country would be considered super-safe where four conditions are met:[80]

(a) where the country in question has ratified and observes the Geneva Convention without any geographical limitations; and

(b) where that country has in place asylum procedures prescribed by law; and

(c) where that country has ratified and observes the ECHR, including the standards relating to effective remedies; and

(d) where that country has been so designated by the Council in accordance with the procedure laid down in the Directive at Art 35A(3).

These determination criteria are stricter than those laid down for determining a safe third country in that they demand a higher level of legal commitment, on the part of the third country, to asylum law and relevant instruments of international law. The main difference is that 'safe' third countries must apply the protections set out in the two Conventions (Refugee Convention and ECHR) and must have a system for dealing with those seeking protection, whereas to be 'supersafe' the

---

77 Section VI, Art 35A.
78 *Op cit*, Costello, fn 2, p 51.
79 Where the third country does not admit the asylum applicant however, Art 35A(6) requires that the Member State provide access to a procedure.
80 Article 35A(2)(a)–(d).

country must have *formally ratified* the Conventions and have an asylum procedure *prescribed by law*. Moreover, by requiring formal ratification of the ECHR, the concept of supersafe third countries is necessarily limited in geographical scope.

The condition that the Council must designate a third country as supersafe for the purposes of this provision,[81] was no doubt intended to restrict the use of this concept and to ensure a common list of countries for Member States. However, even this limiting provision is qualified, rendering it effectively empty in the short term. Until such time as the Council has adopted a common list, current Member State designated safe countries can be used in place of the common list provided the other three criteria mentioned above are met.[82] There would, therefore, be an uneven application of this controversial principle until the Council adopts its common list, with consequent increased chances of *refoulement*. It is notable that although Member States cannot designate countries as supersafe (once the Council has done so), they are *required* to lay down in national law 'modalities for implementing' the principle.[83] This is particularly worrying because at present the principle of supersafe countries is only adopted by a few Member States. The Directive will effectively force Member States to introduce this principle into their national systems. In relation to the content of implementing methods, the Directive is silent and therefore does not require that there be a meaningful link between the applicant and the third country or that the applicant may challenge the application of the concept in their individual case. The Member States are given a free hand limited only by the requirement that the methods must be in accordance with the principle of non-*refoulement* under the Refugee Convention, including provisions for exceptions from the application of this article for humanitarian or political reasons or for reasons of public international law. Scepticism remains:

> Despite the fact that Member States are required to take the principle of non-refoulement into account in devising the rules to implement this provision, it is unacceptable that Member States are allowed to outright deny access to an asylum procedure to all asylum seekers arriving from such countries and strip them of any rights to rebut that presumption of safety.[84]

As if to emphasise the exceptional nature of this procedure, the Directive provides not only that specific procedures may be introduced that derogate from the basic Chapter II guarantees,[85] but also that a completely separate body may be established in order to deal with such cases.[86] Isolating such cases so obviously from the normal institutional and procedural framework of asylum adjudication

---

81 Acting by qualified majority on a proposal from the Commission and after consultation of the European Parliament: Art 35A(3).
82 Article 35A(7).
83 Article 35A(4).
84 *Op cit*, ECRE, fn 34, p 11.
85 Article 24(2).
86 Article 3A(3).

accentuates the underlying desire to remove applicants immediately to supersafe countries without any regard whatsoever for their individual safety and thereby exacerbates the possibility for *refoulement*.

3 Safe countries of origin

The safe country of origin concept is detailed in Arts 30, 30A and 30B of the Directive. As with the other categories of safe countries in the Directive, safe countries of origin must be non-EU states that are deemed to be generally stable and free from political oppression. However, unlike the safe and supersafe third country concepts, the safe country of origin concept refers to the country of habitual residence or nationality of the asylum applicant and enables Member States to deflect applications away from the full determination procedure where the applicants are nationals or habitual residents of a generally safe country.[87] The possibility to rebut the presumption of safety requires the applicant to submit 'serious grounds for considering the country not to be a safe country of origin in his/her particular circumstances in terms of his/her qualification as a refugee'.[88] In the context of an accelerated procedure this may prove difficult and on that basis it is questionable whether the Directive provides sufficient consideration of whether a country is safe for the particular applicant in line with international law. Moreover, this concept, distinguishing as it does on grounds of country of origin, discriminates on grounds of nationality, which may be in breach of international norms.

A minimum common list of third countries that shall be regarded by Member States as safe countries of origin will be adopted by the Council following the adoption of the Procedures Directive.[89] It had long been intended to include a minimum common list of safe countries of origin in the Directive itself. However, despite lengthy negotiations, Member States could not unanimously agree upon a common list. In order to prevent further delay of the adoption of the Directive as a whole, it was agreed in November 2004 that the decision to adopt a common list should be severed from the main negotiations and postponed until after the adoption of the Directive. It was also agreed that the common list would be adopted by the Council acting by qualified majority on a proposal from the Commission and after consultation of the European Parliament. Using a similar procedure, it will also be possible to amend the common list by adding or removing third countries.

There is little doubt that the use of the qualified majority voting procedure will ease the adoption of a minimum common list of safe countries of origin. It is likely however, to mask discrepancies rather than address them. Moreover, it may be argued that the use of this decision-making procedure is legally incorrect since it

---

87 These applications can be treated as unfounded and subjected to accelerated procedures. See Article 30B(2).
88 Article 30B(1).
89 See Art 30, Council Doc 14203/04, Asile 64, 9 November 2004.

does not correspond to the procedure envisaged by Art 67(5) of the EC for such measures (codecision).[90] A further problem is raised by the mandatory nature of the application of the safe country of origin principle. It effectively obliges those Member States who do not currently recognise this principle to dilute their standards of protection for asylum applicants in order to comply with the Directive. This arguably goes beyond the permissible legal competence to introduce Community 'minimum standards' in relation to asylum procedures.

In addition to the common list, Member States are permitted to maintain or draw up their own lists of safe countries of origin, using the criteria set out in Annex II of the Directive. The designation criteria laid down in Annex II stipulate that the country must be shown to be one that is 'generally and consistently' free from persecution, torture or inhuman or degrading treatment or punishment, and the threat of indiscriminate violence in situations of armed conflict.[91] Moreover, Member States can retain legislation in force at the time of the adoption of the Directive, which allows for the designation of countries as safe countries of origin, or part of a country as safe, or a country or part of a country as safe for a specified group of persons in that country, simply where Member States are 'satisfied that persons in the third country concerned are generally[92] neither subject to persecution,[93] torture, inhuman or degrading treatment or punishment'.[94]

There is no doubt that in making an assessment of whether a country may be regarded as safe for these purposes, considerations other than those listed above may creep in, for instance where Member States have particular historical ties and special individual relations with an individual third state. The Directive, by enabling Member States to have their own lists, in addition to the common list, perpetuates the uneven playing field that exists for those seeking asylum in the EU. It also fails to impose strict, efficient and regular review requirements which

---

90 Article 67(5) states that the codecision procedure shall apply to the adoption of measures provided for in Art 63(1) provided that the Council has previously adopted Community legislation defining the 'common rules and basic principles' governing these issues by way of unanimity. It would be reasonable to assume that the Procedures Directive defines the 'common rules and basic principles' governing procedures for granting or withdrawing refugee status and therefore any further implementing measures should be adopted pursuant to the codecision procedures.

91 This assessment is to be made on the basis of: the legal situation; the application of the law within a democratic system; the general political circumstances within a country, by taking particular account of the observance of the ECHR, the International Covenant on Civil and Political Rights, 1996 (ICCPR) and the Convention against Torture; respect of the Refugee Convention principle of non-*refoulement*; and provision for a system of effective remedies against violations of these rights and freedoms. In making an assessment based upon these criteria, Member States are to draw on data provided by a range of sources, including the UNHCR and the Council of Europe, and Member States must keep the Commission informed of their national lists. The Commission, in making proposals for the common EU list 'where necessary', must also draw upon a range of available data.

92 A preambular recital will contain the only safeguard in this respect, such that 'where an applicant shows that there are serious reasons to consider the country not to be safe in his/her particular circumstances, the designation of the country as safe can no longer be considered relevant for him/her'.

93 According to the definition established in Art 9 of the Qualifications Directive.

94 See Art 30A(2) and (3).

are vital given the speed at which the political circumstances in a country can deteriorate.

Deflection technique 2: Applicant's behaviour

A further deflection technique adopted in the Procedures Directive is that of making the nature of the examination procedure and the guarantees pursuant thereto, dependant upon the fulfilment of specific 'obligations or requirements' by the individual applicant. From the moment a prospective applicant enters a Member State with the intention of submitting an application for asylum to the moment of a final decision on the claim, there are a multitude of procedural requirements in place to be met by the applicant. At one level this is sensible to ensure effective decision making and as a means of preventing abuse of the asylum system. At another level, however, it may undermine the refugee protection system altogether if procedural impropriety leads too easily to a discrediting of the applicant's substantive case. The Procedures Directive fails to strike a balance between fair procedural requirements and guarantees by making the latter heavily dependent on the former and by conferring a wide discretion on Member States to require procedural co-operation and penalise non-compliance.

Article 9A of the Directive, entitled 'Obligations of the applicants for asylum', stipulates that Member States may impose certain co-operation obligations upon applicants in order to ensure smooth processing of the application. A non-exhaustive list of suggested obligations is laid down in Art 9A of the Directive and the consequences of non-co-operation include fast tracking or deemed withdrawal of the application as laid down elsewhere in the Directive.[95] The Directive confers a wide discretion on Member States to establish duties of procedural compliance, and the exercise of that discretion may result in similar procedural impropriety being treated with varying levels of severity in different Member States.[96]

1 Supply of personal documentation

An accelerated procedure may be used when:

> the applicant has not produced information to establish with a reasonable degree of certainty his/her identity or nationality, or, it is likely that, in bad faith, he/she has destroyed or disposed of an identity or travel document that would have helped establish his/her identity or nationality.[97]

In addition, one of the suggested procedural obligations on the asylum applicants in Art 9A relates to personal documentation. States are authorised to demand that

---

95 Articles 20 and 33.

96 For example, in the UK, a non-compliance refusal can require the applicant to put their case for the first time at the appeal stage.

97 Article 23(4)(f) and Art 29(2).

applicants produce documents in their possession that are relevant to the application, including their passports.[98] Obviously, where an applicant has no relevant identification papers, for whatever reason, they have nothing to produce. The failure to produce documents, even where the applicant does not have any documents to produce, will be deemed as failing to co-operate with the authorities and, in practice, is likely to have a detrimental impact on any consideration of their application.

2 Arriving without documents and genuineness of the claim

Penalties for asylum seekers who arrive without documents have ostensibly been introduced to deal with the problem of people trafficking, where agents give their clients forged papers and compel them to destroy those documents before they reach immigration control. However, these penalties punish the victim, not the trafficker. They also leave the asylum seeker in a no-win situation because possession of a passport has been taken to indicate an absence of persecution, as the UN Handbook says (para 47):

> A typical test for the well-foundedness of fear will arise when an applicant is in possession of a valid national passport. It has sometimes been claimed that possession of a passport signifies that the issuing authorities do not intend to persecute the holder, for otherwise they would not have issued a passport to him.

The Procedures Directive therefore leaves the asylum seeker in a double bind. It permits Member States to use lack of papers as a reason to deflect people from the full decision-making process. It also leaves those applicants who do have papers open to the allegation that they must have nothing to fear because they were able to travel on their own passport.

Deflection technique 3: Effective remedy?

The third deflection technique comes during the appeals stage of the examination process and relates to the limitation on an applicant's right to appeal in-country. Applicants may be effectively deflected from having access to their full appeal rights, which is in breach of international law norms that state that asylum procedures must include the right to an appeal and an appeal is only effective if it is suspensive.[99] In practice a non-suspensive appeal is likely to have a detrimental impact on the final determination of any claim.

The right to remain in-country during the appeal stage of the procedure is not guaranteed by the Directive. Put in other terms, the Directive does not guarantee the suspensive effect of appeals and applicants may therefore be deported while their appeal is pending. This policy decision is reflected in two articles of the Directive. First, according to Art 6, applicants are allowed to remain in the

---

98   Article 9A2(b).
99   *Op cit*, fn 11.

Member States only until a decision has been made by the determining authority at first instance.[100] Secondly, Art 38, on 'appeal procedures', introduces the concept of an 'effective remedy' and lists the decisions against which the Member State shall ensure that applicants have the right to such a remedy before a court or tribunal.[101] It is clear, however, that the concept of 'effective remedy' is left to the discretion of the Member States and, therefore, it is they who decide whether the remedy includes a suspensive right to appeal against a negative decision.[102] This leads to the ironic possibility that applicants may be returned to the unsafe country from which they fled or another state that might send them there, pending a decision on their appeal, rendering a successful appeal virtually useless. The chances of an applicant being able to secure effective legal representation and put forward a strong case *in absentia* from abroad are drastically reduced.

As a limited safeguard, Art 38(3) stipulates that national rules relating to non-suspensive appeals must be made in accordance with international obligations, and rules must be laid down on 'the possibility of legal remedy or protective measures where the appeal does not have suspensive effect'. Presumably, the legal remedy envisaged would be an injunction or interdict preventing removal, both of which require speedy and efficient legal advice. It is unclear at this stage whether this safeguard is sufficient to ensure that Member States comply with international law requirements for effective remedies. The Directive fails to provide for suspensive appeals and leaves it up the Member States to decide how to formulate the rules which comply with international obligations rather than setting out the norms that should apply.

LEGAL RESPONSES AND CONCLUSIONS

Just as the Member States (notably the UK) succeeded in reducing the levels of support offered to asylum applicants in the EC Reception Conditions Directive, so too the Member States have battled to ensure that access to a full and fair examination procedure is curtailed as far as possible in the Procedures Directive. The concept of asylum no longer appears to be viewed as an international law obligation *per se* with protectionist and human rights roots, but rather as a social menace and something to be dealt with swiftly, severely and with scepticism, except in the most extreme and blatant circumstances of need.

---

100 Subject to limited derogations.

101 Article 38(1). Article 38 also requires Member States to provide time limits and other necessary rules for the applicant to exercise their right to an effective remedy, and permits Member States to lay down time limits for the court or tribunal to examine the decision of the determining authority. See paras 2 and 4 respectively.

102 It is notable that the provision in the original Commission draft of the Reception Conditions Directive stating that material reception conditions must be ensured to applicants and their families during their admissibility, accelerated and other procedures and during appeals does not appear in the final version of the Directive.

The main legal consequences of adopting the Directive in its current form are threefold. In terms of compatibility with relevant existing legal frameworks, it would appear that the Directive leaves itself wide open to criticism and potential legal challenge. Member States seem to have used the creation of a common European asylum policy as an opportunity to further reduce legal protection in their own asylum regimes and to ignore, limit and reinterpret their obligations created pursuant to international norms.

A further potential legal consequence of the Directive is the lowering of protection standards in some Member States. The Directive does not contain a 'stand-still' clause to prevent those Member States with stronger protections from lowering them to the level stipulated in the Directive. Moreover, Member States may feel under political pressure to reduce standards so as not to be regarded as a 'soft touch' or as a more attractive option for asylum seekers. It remains to be seen whether Member States will decide to succumb to the concerns about asylum shopping or decide to retain and introduce higher standards of protection in conformity with the Tampere commitments they signed up to.

Finally, the adoption of the Directive will have the effect of undermining what limited progress has been made in the other EC asylum legislative building blocks. The failure of the Directive to enshrine uniform procedures and standards of protection throughout the Member States necessarily impacts upon the attainment of reception conditions and undermines the application of a common definition of who is a refugee. It would appear, from both an individual and collective perspective, that the Procedures Directive is the weakest link in the Community's asylum legislative package. Numerous legal responses, each of which could mitigate the negative impact of this piece of legislation, are considered below.

First, the formal adoption of the Procedures Directive requires a unanimous vote in Council. The postponement of this formal adoption until after 1 May 2004 leaves the door open to any of the new Member States to exercise their veto and thus block the adoption of the Directive as it stands. This would send the legislators back to the drawing board, an unenviable prospect indeed, but one that may secure a better outcome in the long term.

Secondly, if adopted in its current form, legal challenge may come by way of Art 230 EC, which provides a mechanism for the *direct* challenge of Community measures, including directives, before the European Court of Justice (ECJ). Given the stringent standing requirements for direct challenges from individuals it is more likely that only a privileged applicant – a Member State, the European Parliament, the Council or the Commission – would bring a challenge to the Procedures Directive before the European Court of Justice. Of these privileged applicants, it is most likely that the European Parliament would bring any action for judicial review given the role played by the others in the decision-making process.[103] The grounds for challenge under Art 230 EC are threefold: 'lack of

---

103 The argument for relaxing the rules on standing to enable individual or group action is particularly strong in this field given the potential impact that the legislation has on the lives of asylum applicants.

competence, infringement of an essential procedural requirement or infringement of this Treaty or of any rule of law relating to its application.' Annulment of the Directive by the European Court of Justice is arguable on all of these grounds.

In relation to competence, it seems that certain provisions of the Directive exceed the competences conferred by the EC Treaty. The example of the mandatory application of the supersafe third countries principle was cited earlier to demonstrate how the Directive does more than establish 'minimum standards'.

The case for annulment is also arguable on grounds of procedural impropriety. It can be argued that the provisions in the Directive establishing a mechanism for the adoption of common lists of safe countries of origin (Art 30) and supersafe third countries (Art 35) are procedurally flawed in that they require a qualified majority vote in Council and mere consultation of the Parliament in breach of Art 67(5) of the EC Treaty. Assuming the adoption of the Procedures Directive represents the final piece of building block legislation 'defining common rules and basic principles' in relation to asylum, the adoption of safe lists of countries must be deemed to 'implement' such common rules and therefore should be adopted by co-decision. On the basis that these improper procedures 'taint' the whole Directive with illegality, and assuming that the Directive is read as establishing a whole system, rather than a range of discrete measures, it is submitted that there are sound legal grounds for annulment of the Directive in its entirety.[104]

The ECJ's power to annul a measure because it infringes any rule of law relating to the application of the Treaty enables it to strike down legislation that is not in accord with the general principles of Community law (most notably fundamental rights and the right to an effective remedy) and other relevant norms enshrined in international instruments that are binding on the EU.

Legal challenge to the Directive may also come to the ECJ from national courts. The preliminary reference procedure enables national courts to send questions on the interpretation or validity of Community law (including Directives) to the ECJ.[105] However, in relation to asylum and all other Title IV EC issues, jurisdictional limits apply such that only the national court of final instance can refer questions to the ECJ.[106] Peers argues that this should not preclude lower national courts from being able to issue interim measures under limited conditions, to assist individuals affected by the potentially invalid legislation.[107] The preliminary reference procedure has yet to be successfully invoked in relation to a Title IV EC issue.[108]

---

104 *Op cit*, Costello, fn 2, Chapter 3; and for a discussion of the legal possibilities for challenging EC asylum law generally, see Peers, S, 'Challenging the validity of EC immigration and asylum law' (2003) 17(1) Immigration, Asylum and Nationality Law 25.

105 See Art 234 EC.

106 Article 68 EC.

107 Peers, S, 'Who's judging the watchmen? The judicial system of the "Area of Freedom, Security and Justice"' (1998) 18 YEL 337, 354–56.

108 Case C-51/03 *Georgescu*, 31 March 2004, was the first Title IV EC preliminary reference to reach the European Court of Justice, but was deemed inadmissible as it was not referred by a court of final instance as required by Art 68 EC.

The Directive is intended to introduce common 'minimum standards' only, thereby enabling Member States to introduce or maintain more favourable standards on procedures for granting and withdrawing refugee status.[109] Non-governmental organisations must maintain constructive dialogues with national governments and increase pressure on Member States to retain, introduce and apply higher protection standards in their national legislation.

The European Commission must make effective use of the legal enforcement mechanism at its disposal to ensure correct implementation and compliance. Article 226 EC enables the Commission to bring a Member State before the European Court of Justice where the Commission considers that a Member State is in breach of its obligations under Community law.

The formal adoption of the Procedures Directive will mark the end of the first phase of the CEAS and a period of 'bedding in' and compliance monitoring has been anticipated. ECRE comments that:

> it is of crucial importance that the processes of transposition and monitoring be prioritised, in order to ensure that an adequate assessment of impact of this set of minimum standards on refugees in Europe informs any further harmonisation.[110]

However, the Commission, even prior to the formal adoption of the Procedures Directive, has published a communication outlining its preparatory plans for a further legislative proposal in this field.[111] This communication demonstrates the Commission's recognition of potential protection gaps created by the building block legislation and the Commission's desire to close those gaps by proposing consensus-based legislation.[112] However, it is only by fulfilling its role as both initiator of legislation and enforcer of Community law that the Commission can play a credible role in the development of the CEAS. Resources must be made available for policy enforcement, as well as policy development.

Assuming adoption of the Directive as it stands, high expectations will undoubtedly be placed upon the judiciary at national and European level to interpret the Directive and any implementing measures in accordance with human rights and refugee law. At the national level, the judiciary has earned itself a reputation for being rather liberal in its interpretation and application of asylum law.[113] To date, the judiciary have, for the most part, resisted bowing to executive

---

109 Although only 'insofar as those standards are compatible with this Directive', Art 4.

110 *Op cit*, ECRE, fn 34, p 6.

111 *A More Efficient European Asylum System*, COM (2004) 503, 15 July 2004.

112 The Commission proposes an innovative method of pre-legislative consensus building amongst the Member States in the Communication, no doubt in a bid to avoid the extensive unpicking of its legislative proposals as happened in the first phase of the CEAS. It is worth noting that future asylum legislation will be adopted pursuant to the Art 251 EC co-decision procedure.

113 See, for instance, *R v Immigration Appeal Tribunal ex p Shah (United Nations High Commissioner for Refugees intervening)* [1999] 2 AC 629; *Bugdaycay v Secretary of State for the Home Department* [1987] AC 524; *R v Secretary of State for the Home Department ex p Adan* [2001] INLR 44, HL; and *R (Anufrijeva) v Secretary of State for the Home Department* [2004] 1 AC 604. See Colin Harvey's chapter in this collection for further detailed evidence of the UK judges' willingness to try to combine fairness to the individual with effective management of the asylum process.

policy preferences in the field of asylum;[114] indeed they have even been willing to rule against certain restrictive measures contained in recent UK legislation in this field. Despite this welcome judicial activism in recent times, in practice only limited reliance can be placed upon the judiciary given that it can only interpret the restrictive legislation and implementation measures in force, and then, only when a case is brought before it. At the least, we must hope that the senior judiciary continue to interpret asylum legislation in the light of broader protection and rights norms and take seriously the potential for higher levels of protection than those found in the Procedures Directive.

There will undoubtedly be similarly high expectations of the ECJ to provide a clear and robust interpretation of the Directive, consistent with international law obligations and general principles of Community law. However, placing too much reliance upon the ECJ would be unwise for a number of reasons. First, the ECJ can only exercise its jurisdiction where it is properly seized to do so. Unless and until privileged applicants challenge the Directive pursuant to Art 230 EC, or the Commission initiates infringement proceedings pursuant to Art 226, or national courts of final instance refer questions on the interpretation or validity of the Directive, the ECJ remains powerless. These jurisdictional requirements and hurdles highlight a wider principled objection to the judicial interpretation of fundamental rights-sensitive legislation in that the judicial approach would inevitably develop on a piecemeal and ad hoc basis over an extended period of time. Secondly, even when the ECJ is successfully seized judicial expansiveness is by no means guaranteed. To date, the ECJ has resisted making reference to the EU Charter of Fundamental Rights in its judgments, despite reliance upon it in several Court of First Instance judgments and in the Opinions of certain Advocates General. Enshrining, as it does, a clear right to asylum and protection in the event of removal, expulsion or extradition combined with a right to an effective remedy and a fair trial that goes beyond the scope of the similar ECHR right, the ECJ should make use of the Charter as an interpretative tool when called to rule upon the Procedures Directive.

The recent Treaty establishing a Constitution for Europe[115] provides for the incorporation of the European Union Charter of Fundamental Rights into the full legal framework of the EU. The legal transformation of the EU Rights Charter will only happen following ratification of the constitutional Treaty by all of the Member States, a process that may be, at best, protracted or, at worst, result in failure. Assuming the EU Rights Charter were to bind the EU institutions and the Member States when implementing EU law what, if any, added value would the Charter provide in respect of asylum procedures? The ECHR and the EU Rights Charter are intended to be compatible, so where EU Charter rights are similar to ECHR rights, the former are to be afforded the meaning and scope of the latter.

---

114 On the other hand, there appears to be a worrying deference to executive decision making where issues of national security permeate asylum cases. For an indepth discussion of this interface between judicial scrutiny and executive policy, see the chapter by Colin Harvey.

115 OJ [2004] C310. The process of formal ratification is underway.

However, the Charter also adds that EU law shall not be prevented from providing more extensive protection (Art 52(3)); so it may be possible for the Charter to confer more rights than the ECHR. For instance, the right to an effective remedy and a fair trial (Art 47) enshrined in the EU Charter is not limited to civil rights and obligations and therefore would include any rights arising from the immigration and asylum provisions under Title IV of the EC Treaty. Of potential significance is the interpretation of the 'right to asylum' laid down in Art 18 of the EU Rights Charter, as compared with the more widely understood refugee law norm of a 'right to claim asylum', which is a right to have a claim determined. What is clear, however, is that the ECJ would be required to interpret the EU Rights Charter as a legally binding piece of EU law.

Upon ratification of the Treaty establishing a Constitution for Europe, the EU will seek accession to the European Convention on Human Rights. EU accession would give the European Court of Human Rights a clear jurisdiction over any matter of Convention rights that involved EU institutions and thus the European Court of Human Rights would become the court of final jurisdiction in relation to most EU human rights issues. Although rules on the exact working relationship between these two Courts are, as yet, unclear, it would seem that an additional body scrutinising and interpreting human rights standards can only strengthen the EU's commitment to and compliance with human rights.

Of the above possible legal responses, some are clearly more imminent, feasible and effective than others. However, each of them offers a means by which the legal system could be used to challenge or bolster (in terms of human rights protection) the Procedures Directive. Many of the low standards of protection and deflection practices enshrined in the Directive were previously enshrined, or have been recently replicated, in the UK context, making the prospect of higher standards unlikely, at least in the short term. The Directive's failure to afford sufficient minimum standards of procedural protection to asylum seekers is disappointing at many levels. It not only undermines both the credibility of the EU as a legal organisation 'founded on principles of liberty, democracy, respect for human rights and the rule of law,' but also undermines the concept of refugee protection more broadly.

CHAPTER 4

EC LAW ON FAMILY MEMBERS OF PERSONS SEEKING OR RECEIVING INTERNATIONAL PROTECTION

Steve Peers

The treatment of family members of persons seeking or receiving international protection is an important practical issue for all individuals who have to flee their country of origin due to persecution, civil war, or risks of serious breaches of their basic human rights. Their family members, if left behind in the country of origin or a country of transit, might not be safe. Even if they are, the family has been split up, causing emotional and practical difficulties for all its members. How soon can they be reunited, and what conditions will they face? Will there be adequate income, accommodation and health care for the family, and how will the children adjust to a different school system, probably in a different language?

When developing a 'Common European Asylum System' (CEAS) as agreed by the Tampere European Council (summit meeting) of 1999, the EU had the chance to address these issues coherently and fairly. The EU has since adopted or agreed much legislation on various aspects of asylum and immigration law. How well has it met this challenge? Unfortunately, as we shall see, while EC law on this subject has managed to ensure a minimum level of protection for certain categories of family members as regards certain rights, this legislation contains major gaps, is in many respects incoherent, and in some areas sets standards so low that it does not ensure fair treatment of family members, and may even violate the minimum standards set by international human rights law.

INTERNATIONAL LAW AND HUMAN RIGHTS LAW FRAMEWORK

The admission of family members of refugees is not an express right under the 1951 Geneva Convention on the status of refugees, but is referred to in the Final Act of the Conference that drew up the Convention, and has been supported in many conclusions of the UNHCR Executive Committee. In the absence of precise obligations set out in international treaties, there is a wide, state practice of admitting the family members of refugees and those in need of temporary protection, as well as great divergence in approaches to this issue. Moreover, many states prefer not to admit the family members of persons seeking international protection or those with a recognised need for subsidiary protection.[1]

---

1   For an overview of the international obligations relating to family reunion for persons seeking protection or recognised as having protection needs, and the national application of those obligations, see Jastram, K and Newland, K, 'Family unity and refugee protection', in Feller E, Turk, V and Nicholson, F (eds), *Refugee Protection in International Law: UNHCR's Global Consultations on International Protection*, 2003, Cambridge: CUP, p 555.

Within Europe, some greater degree of clarification of obligations in this area might be expected pursuant to the European Convention on Human Rights (ECHR), and particularly the case law of the European Court of Human Rights (ECtHR). Article 8(1) of the ECHR obliges states to respect the right to private and family life, subject to limitations set out in Art 8(2), while Art 3 of the ECHR provides that no one may be subjected to torture or other inhuman or degrading treatment, without any limitation or derogation.

The case law of the ECtHR indicates that while Art 8 of the ECHR is relevant to family reunion issues, it usually has a very different impact depending on whether the issue is the initial admission of family members or the expulsion of family members after their initial entry. In the case of initial admissions, the ECtHR is loath to find that there has even been an interference with the right to respect for family life, on the grounds that the ECHR does not protect the right of married couples to choose the country of their residence, and that there is usually no bar (in the view of the Court) to the ability of married couples and their children to taking up joint residence in another country.[2] This approach is particularly clear in the judgments of *Abdulaziz and Others v UK*, *Gul v Switzerland* and *Ahmut v Netherlands*.[3] However, in one case, *Sen v Netherlands*,[4] the Court has found that refusal to admit constituted a breach of Art 8, where in the circumstances the family had several children split between the home and host state and it would have been too great a burden to remove the children in the host state where they were already settled.

In the case of expulsions, the protection for individuals is much stronger, with the Court ruling that removal of family members is, in principle, always an infringement of Art 8(1) of the ECHR, which has to be justified by Art 8(2) of the ECHR. Article 8(2) permits interference with Art 8(1) rights on several grounds, including public safety, economic interests and national security, where the interference is necessary in a democratic society. The extensive case law of the ECtHR on this issue indicates that states are obliged to balance the interest of the family member who may be removed against the interests of the state, taking into account, on the one hand, the extent of the links which the expellee has formed with the host state and the difficulty that the expellee would face maintaining family life following expulsion to another state, and on the other hand, the gravity of the public interests that might be furthered by removal, considering, in particular, the seriousness and pattern of any crimes committed by the person concerned.[5] Recently, there has been a particular focus in the case law on whether

---

2   For an analysis of the case law as it applies to family reunion of persons seeking or receiving protection, see Lambert, H, 'The European Court of Human Rights and the right of refugees and other persons in need of protection to family reunion' (1999) 11 IJRL 427; and Anderfuhren-Wayne, C, 'Family unity in immigration and refugee matters: United States and European approaches' (1996) 8 IJRL 347, pp 354–69.

3   *Abdulaziz and Others* v *UK* (Series A, No 94); *Ahmut v Netherlands* (Reports 1996-VI); *Gul v Switzerland* (Reports 1996-I).

4   *Sen v Netherlands*, judgment of 21 December 2001, not reported.

5   From an extensive literature, see, for instance, van Dijk, P, 'Protection of "integrated" aliens against expulsion under the European Convention on Human Rights' in Guild, E and Minderhoud, P (eds), *Security of Residence and Expulsion: Protection of Aliens in Europe*, 2001, The Hague: Kluwer, p 23.

the expellee's family members can hope to resume family life in practice with the expellee in the expellee's home state; this question is obviously most relevant where the family member has the nationality of the host state.[6]

Also, the ECtHR has indicated that states must guarantee a core of procedural rights, inherent in Art 8, in expulsion cases.[7] This ruling is important because Art 6 of the ECHR, which guarantees the right to a fair hearing to determine criminal charges or civil rights, does not apply to immigration disputes.[8]

To what extent do these rules apply to persons seeking or receiving international protection? The ECtHR has had only limited opportunities to rule on this issue. Two judgments are relevant.[9] First, in the important case of *Gul* v *Switzerland*,[10] Mr Gul had made an unsuccessful application for asylum in Switzerland, but had been granted a humanitarian residence permit in light of the length of time he had lived in Switzerland and the illness of his wife (who had joined him there). He then applied for his two children who remained in Turkey to join their parents (a third child had been born in Switzerland). The European Commission on Human Rights, which at the time had a role screening complaints brought within the Convention system, held the complaint as regards his oldest child inadmissible, but ruled in his favour as regards the second child. However, the ECtHR rejected Mr Gul's arguments as regards his second child, stressing that his application for asylum had been unsuccessful, that he had caused the initial separation from his second child, that his subsequent visits to Turkey showed that it was safe for him to return and that he could transfer most of the benefits he was receiving in Switzerland to Turkey. Although his wife was ill, it had not been proven that she could not receive care in Turkey, and she had been well enough to visit Turkey with her husband. The second child had grown up in Turkey and was familiar with the cultural and linguistic environment there. Furthermore, the Gul family did not have permanent residence status in Switzerland, but only a humanitarian residence permit. It should also be observed that the Gul family had not made an Art 3 complaint before the Court.

In the other judgment, *Nsona* v *Netherlands*, the two applicants, both Zairean nationals, had claimed to be related (as aunt and niece). The aunt had applied for refugee status in the Netherlands, and been given a humanitarian residence permit. She later tried to enter Dutch territory with the other applicant, at that point claiming the latter as her daughter. The Dutch authorities had refused entry and returned the child to Zaire. The ECtHR ruled there was no breach of Art 3 as regards the refusal to allow the child to enter (as the state is entitled to refuse entry to persons as long as that does not breach the Convention), the state's treatment of her during expulsion or the care arranged for after her return to Zaire; it had not

---

6 Case law starting with *Boultif v Switzerland*, judgment of 2 June 2001 (Reports 2001.IX).
7 *Al-Nashif v Bulgaria*, judgment of 10 June 2002, not reported.
8 See *Maaouia v France* (Reports 2000-X).
9 *Op cit*, fn 3, *Gul v Switzerland*; and *Nsona v Netherlands* (Reports 1996-V).
10 *Op cit*, fn 3.

been alleged that she faced a 'classic' Art 3 risk from state or non-state agents in Zaire upon her return. An Art 8 claim was rejected, on the grounds that the Dutch Government was entitled to disbelieve the applicants' claims in light of the aunt's initial deceit.

These judgments have been followed in a number of admissibility decisions of the Court or Commission. The *Kusungana v Switzerland* decision concerned the Art 8 complaint of an Angolan teenager whose father had made an unsuccessful asylum request in Switzerland some years earlier, but who had been allowed to stay following his marriage to an Angolan woman with a renewable Swiss residence permit.[11] The child's mother in Angola had died, and he subsequently sought to join his father's family in Switzerland. However, the Commission rejected his Art 8 complaint, reasoning that the child had extensive links in Angola and that the father had made no real connection with the child before the latter's arrival in Switzerland. There was no consideration of whether the father (or step-mother) would face any Art 3 risk if they returned to Angola, or indeed whether they would face any difficulties returning to Angola at all,[12] as the Commission appeared to presume that the father could not expect to enjoy any family life with his son in any location under the circumstances.

In *Bouhadef v Switzerland*,[13] the Court was unconvinced by the Art 3 claim made by the applicant (a rejected asylum seeker) and his family. It then ruled inadmissible an Art 8 claim, on the grounds that the family's links were entirely with Algeria.

In *PK v Switzerland*,[14] a Sri Lankan asylum seeker had withdrawn his asylum claim after receiving a residence permit, and then married a Sri Lankan woman with her own residence permit. However, he later lost his job, and the Swiss authorities sought to expel the entire family (by then also including two young children). The Commission ruled that the applicant's Art 8 claim was inadmissible, on the grounds that the state had an economic justification for removing him and that his family would face no difficulty following him, as his wife was also Sri Lankan and the children were an adaptable age. No Art 3 claim was raised.

In *OHS and GR v Finland*,[15] the Commission ruled inadmissible an Art 8 claim by two Iraqi Kurds. One of them had entered Finland earlier, requested asylum, and received a temporary residence permit. It is not clear what happened to her asylum claim. She briefly returned to (Kurdish) Iraq to marry the other applicant, and then argued that the Finnish authorities' refusal to admit him breached Art 8 (and other Convention Articles). The Commission reasoned that there was no breach of Art 3, in particular because the level of suffering occasioned by immigration decisions did not normally reach the threshold of treatment

---

11   Decision of 6 April 1998, not reported.
12   They had a young child who had been born in Switzerland.
13   Decision of 12 November 2002, not reported.
14   Decision of 17 April 1997, not reported.
15   Decision of 21 May 1997, not reported.

prescribed by Art 3 and because immigration decisions connected with family life normally fell to be addressed by Art 8. However, it appears also that the Commission did not believe that either applicant faced an Art 3 risk in the 'classic' sense if they were to develop their family life in Iraq. The Art 8 claim was then ruled inadmissible in light of the failure to succeed on Art 3 grounds, also taking into account that the wife's initial argument for admission into Finland was based on her unmarried status.

In *Aboikonie and Read v the Netherlands*,[16] the Commission ruled a complaint by a Surinamese national (a rejected asylum seeker) and his (naturalised) Dutch wife inadmissible.[17] First of all, it rejected the Art 3 claim, considering that there was not sufficient evidence of a real risk of Art 3 treatment if the husband were returned to Surinam. Then the Commission rejected the husband's Art 8 claim, in light of various criminal convictions by the Dutch courts, considering that the wife and the two older children were of Surinamese origin anyway and that the two younger children were adaptable.

In *KK v Switzerland*, following a previous rejection of an asylum request by a Sri Lankan woman, she made a fresh request for asylum after marrying a Sri Lankan man resident in Switzerland, also an asylum seeker. This fresh request was rejected as inadmissible by the Swiss authorities, but her husband's application was still pending; also, she was expecting his child. The Commission rejected her Art 8 claim as inadmissible on the grounds that her asylum claim had been definitively dismissed before the point when she established family life in Switzerland, therefore she had no reason to imagine that she could develop family life in Switzerland. No Art 3 claim was raised, and the status of her husband as an asylum seeker was not considered at all by the Commission.

In *Salazar v Sweden*,[18] the Commission ruled an Art 8 complaint inadmissible following its dismissal of the Art 3 argument made by a Peruvian family who faced expulsion from Sweden back to Peru.[19] Since there was no real risk (in the Commission's view) of treatment in breach of Art 3 in the receiving state, it followed that there was no bar to resuming family life there.

In *Solomon v Netherlands*,[20] the asylum application of the Nigerian applicant (with a Dutch partner and daughter) had already been rejected in domestic proceedings, and no Art 3 claim was raised before the Court, so the Art 8 argument was rejected on the usual grounds that there was no bar to establishing family life in the state of origin.

Finally, in the *Afonso and Atonio* decision,[21] the husband and father of the two applicants had entered the Netherlands several years earlier, and had applied for

---

16 Decision of 12 January 1998, not reported.
17 The couple also had four children residing in the Netherlands, all also (naturalised) Dutch citizens.
18 Decision of 7 March 1996, not reported.
19 In fact, the father had already been expelled and the other family members were in hiding in Sweden.
20 Decision of 5 September 2000, not reported.
21 Decision of 8 July 2003, not reported.

asylum there. He was eventually granted a residence permit as part of a 'tolerance' policy of non-enforcement of expulsions in light of the situation in the country of origin (Angola). The two applicants, his wife and daughter, eventually sought to join him in the Netherlands, which they were able to enter on the basis of a Schengen visa issued by Portugal. Due to these circumstances, the wife's asylum claim in the Netherlands was rejected as inadmissible, on the grounds that Portugal was responsible for considering the claim, pursuant to the Dublin Convention.[22] The ECtHR ruled the Art 8 claim of both applicants as inadmissible, taking into account the safety of the country of origin in light of more recent political developments; it also dismissed the Art 3 claim of the applicants as inadmissible on the same grounds, apparently assuming that the application of the Dublin Convention would have no impact on the Art 3 argument.[23] The lack of documented substantiation of the marriage between the husband and the wife was also a factor taken into account by the Court; and even though the husband and father had since obtained Dutch nationality, his Angolan background meant that it would not be difficult for him to resume his family life in his country of origin.

It can be seen that in neither judgment and in none of the admissibility decisions was any of the family members a recognised Geneva Convention refugee. In several cases, one of the relevant family members had a form of humanitarian residence permit, although it seems likely that at least some of these cases would not have qualified for subsidiary protection status under the EC's new Directive.[24] Nevertheless, in each of those cases wherever an Art 3 risk was in fact alleged, the Court or Commission assessed whether an Art 3 risk would in fact prevent the take up of family life in the country of origin. In one case (*KK*), the family member was an asylum seeker, but the Commission simply failed to comment on the status of the family member at all in that case, and no Art 3 issues had been raised. In several cases, none of the family had any form of residence connection in the host country, and in the absence of success in claiming Art 3 grounds, the Art 8 claims were therefore bound to fail. None of the cases referred to above took the Court's judgment in *Boultif* into account, perhaps because all of the family members in these judgments were either foreigners or naturalised citizens of the host state and were therefore outside the scope of the *Boultif* judgment.

It is unfortunate that the case law has not yet given any clear indication of the family reunion rights of individuals seeking or needing protection. However, it is submitted that logically the only interpretation of the Convention consistent with

---

22 The decision does not make clear what happened (if anything) to the Portuguese consideration of the asylum claim, although it appears that the first applicant was not (at least initially) removed to Portugal pursuant to the Dublin Convention.

23 This is consistent with the well-known *TI v UK* decision (Reports of Judgments and Decisions 2000-III) holding that the application of the Dublin Convention cannot preclude consideration of whether there is an Art 3 ECHR risk (including a 'chain' Art 3 risk) in another EU Member State (although the Court did not refer to this earlier decision).

24 See the section on 'Substantive EC law' below.

its wording and the case law is that the family members of any person who can show a real risk of Art 3 treatment in the country of origin must be admitted to the host state and allowed to reside there, whether or not they accompany the person under risk upon their initial entry to the host state, or join them in the host state later. Only this interpretation would respect the non-derogability of Art 3, which means that it is simply unjustifiable to demand that to expect the person with an Art 3 risk enjoy family life in the country where they face that risk. It is irrelevant what status (refugee, subsidiary protection, temporary protection) the person with the Art 3 risk has, as there is nothing in Arts 3 or 8 ECHR to suggest any distinction between such groups in this regard. In fact, Art 14 ECHR (non-discrimination as regards any rights granted by the Convention) should preclude any distinction between such groups.

There could be several highly limited exceptions, though. First, if the family members have a different nationality from the person facing the Art 3 risk, then an ECHR signatory state could argue that family life could be established in the country of origin of the family members. For example, if an Iraqi national residing in an ECHR signatory state has an American spouse, in principle it would not violate Art 8 to decide that family life should be enjoyed in the US (assuming that the latter state is willing to admit the Iraqi spouse). Secondly, if one or more of the family members (including the person facing the Art 3 risk) has very strong links to another country, other than the country of origin, the host state, or the state of nationality of any of the family members, and that state is willing to accept the entire family, then family life could be enjoyed in that state. So, adapting the prior example, if the American spouse has permanent residence status in Canada, there is no Art 8 breach if an ECHR signatory insists that family life should be enjoyed in Canada instead. Finally, if any of the family members (including the person facing the Art 3 risk) have committed acts that are sufficiently objectionable as to justify a state's interference with the right to family life in accordance with Art 8(2) of the ECHR, then the family members could be denied entry or expelled; even the person facing the Art 3 risk could be expelled. The combination of Arts 3 and 8 should produce a *stronger* right to family life, in light of the absolute character of Art 3; but not an *absolute* right to family life, in light of the permitted limitations upon Art 8.

However, these exceptions must logically be subject to certain conditions. First of all, it should be recalled that there is nothing in the Convention to prevent each family member of a person with an Art 3 risk from showing that they also face an individual Art 3 risk in any other country (including a 'chain' Art 3 risk). In that case, the family member's position must also be assessed in light of Art 3, not Art 8. Next, obviously no expulsion to any other country could take place if there was an Art 3 risk (including a 'chain' Art 3 risk) to any of the family in that country. In particular, an expulsion of any of the family to the country of origin could not be justified under any circumstances. Such an expulsion would impermissibly give priority to the limitations permitted by Art 8(2) over the non-derogability of Art 3, as the person facing the Art 3 risk could not possibly resume family life without submitting themselves to an Art 3 risk. Finally, it should be recalled that for refugees, Art 32 of the Geneva Convention precludes their expulsion to any other state (regardless of whether the expulsion to that state would violate the non-*refoulement* rule), except on specified public order grounds. So, taking that rule together with Arts 3 and 8 of the ECHR, the family members of a refugee cannot be expelled unless the refugee can also be expelled pursuant to the Geneva Convention. Even in that case, the family members might have a separate claim to stay, on grounds of the need to protect their private life in the host state.[25] In any case, where the family members of the person facing an Art 3 risk have the nationality of the host state, then the *Boultif* judgment applies to give them extra protection against expulsion.

What about family members of asylum seekers, or other persons seeking international protection? It is arguable that Member States must allow them to enter and reside pursuant to Art 8 as long as the claim for international protection has not been finally rejected, subject to the same limitations outlined above. Otherwise the asylum seeker would have to choose between not enjoying family life at all, and the possible application of an Art 3 risk if he returned to the country of origin. It should be recalled that Art 3 imposes a number of implied procedural obligations on states.[26]

EUROPEAN COMMUNITY LAW FRAMEWORK

Following the entry into force of the Treaty of Amsterdam on 1 May 1999, the EC has power to adopt measures concerning the key areas of asylum law: asylum responsibility, reception conditions, definition of a refugee, asylum procedures, subsidiary protection, temporary protection and 'burden-sharing'.[27] Furthermore, the EC has also had powers as from the same date to adopt immigration law measures, which may also be relevant to persons seeking or receiving protection, because relevant immigration law issues not within the scope of the EC's asylum law powers also arise for such persons.[28] The planned EU Constitution would expand the EU's powers over both immigration and asylum, but is not discussed further in this chapter as its entry into force is still uncertain.[29]

Since the asylum provisions of the EC Treaty do not confer any explicit competence in relation to family members of persons seeking or receiving international protection, the treatment of such family members is either an ancillary issue in proposed or adopted EC asylum legislation, or addressed in EC immigration legislation. In particular, the EC institutions had by 30 July 2004 adopted or agreed in principle asylum legislation on the issues of: the

---

25 See *Slivenko v Latvia*, judgment of 9 October 2003 (Reports 2003-X).
26 See, for example, *Jabari v Turkey* (Reports of Judgments and Decisions 2000-VIII).
27 Article 63(1) and (2) EC.
28 Article 63(3) and (4) EC.
29 For the Constitution, as agreed by the 'Giscard Convention' in July 2003, see OJ 2003 C 169. For the Constitution, as agreed in June 2004 at the end of the subsequent intergovernmental conference and signed on 29 October 2004, see Council doc CIG 87/04, 8 August 2004.

responsibility for asylum seekers (Reg 343/2003),[30] the replacing of the 1990 Dublin Convention;[31] the reception conditions for asylum seekers (Directive 2003/9);[32] the definition of refugee and subsidiary protection status (Directive 2004/83), including the content of such status;[33] the asylum procedures (agreed in April 2004);[34] and the temporary protection (Directive 2001/55).[35] All of these measures included some provisions relevant to family members of persons seeking or receiving protection.

As regards immigration law, family reunion with refugees is covered by the main EC Directive on family reunion (Directive 2003/86),[36] but sponsors with subsidiary or temporary protection, or who are seeking any type of status, are excluded from the scope of that Directive,[37] even though persons with subsidiary protection had been included within the initial proposal.[38] However, persons with refugee or subsidiary or temporary protection status, or persons seeking any such status, are excluded from other proposed or adopted EC immigration legislation, most particularly Directive 2003/109 on the status of long-term resident, third-country nationals,[39] which had originally included refugees (and pursuant to a separate proposal, persons with subsidiary protection) within its scope.[40] Further relevant proposals in the field of immigration law are likely to be forthcoming; in

---

30 OJ 2003 L 50/1. Member States were obliged to apply the Regulation by 1 September 2003. An implementing Regulation was adopted by the Commission (Reg 1560/2003, OJ 2003 L 222/3, in force 7 September 2003).

31 OJ 1997 C 254. The Convention still governs the issue of asylum responsibility as between Denmark and the other Member States (except for those Member States joining the EU in 2004).

32 OJ 2003 L 31/18. Member States must apply the Directive by February 2005.

33 OJ 2004 L 304/12.

34 The text agreed in principle by the Justice and Home Affairs Council on 29 April 2004 is in Council doc 8771/04, 30 April 2004. This text will undergo some technical editing before its formal adoption by the Council, including changes in the numbering of its Articles; all references in this chapter are to the version before editing in doc 8771/04. Member States will have two years to apply the Directive after its adoption and publication. Adoption is likely to take place by summer 2005.

35 OJ 2001 L 212/12. Member States were obliged to implement the Directive by 31 December 2002, except Ireland, which opted in to the Directive subsequently and had to apply it by 31 December 2003 (Commission Decision 2003/690, OJ 2003 L 251/23).

36 Articles 9–12 of the Directive (OJ 2003 L 251/12). Member States must apply the Directive by 3 October 2005.

37 Article 3(2) of the Directive (ibid).

38 See the section on 'Substantive EC law' below.

39 Article 3(2)(b), (c) and (d) of the Directive (OJ 2004 L 16/44). For other proposals, see the exclusions in the agreed text of the Directive on admission of students, pupils, volunteers and trainees (Art 3(2)(a) of Council doc 8013/04, 31 March 2004), in the proposed Directive on admission for employment or self-employment (Art 3(3)(b) of COM (2001) 386, 11 July 2001) and the proposed Directive on admission of researchers (Art 3(3)(a) in COM (2004) 178, 16 March 2004).

40 See Article 3 of the proposal for a Directive (COM (2001) 127, 13 March 2001) and Art 22 of the initial proposal for a directive on refugee and subsidiary protection status (COM (2001) 510, 12 September 2001).

particular, the Commission has committed itself to propose a measure extending Directive 2003/109 to refugees and persons with subsidiary protection.[41]

Refugees and other persons seeking or receiving international protection, and their family members, are also arguably covered to some extent by the EC's association agreements with non-EU countries, which often confer some rights concerning immigration or at least the status of migrants and their family members after admission.[42] Refugees and their family members are certainly covered by the EC free movement law rules on co-ordination of social security, and such rules have been extended (with some limitations) to all other third-country nationals and their family members; but the rules only apply to those third-country nationals who have moved between Member States.[43]

It should be recalled that the UK, Ireland and Denmark have an 'opt-out' from EC immigration and asylum law. The UK has chosen to opt in to every asylum measure and Ireland has chosen to opt in to almost all of them, but both of these Member States opted out of the family reunion Directive,[44] and Denmark is only covered by the Dublin Convention. Also, the Dublin rules apply to Norway and Iceland,[45] and soon Switzerland.[46]

Finally, it should be recalled that human rights form part of the general principles of EC law that the Court of Justice protects.[47] Such rights are derived from the national constitutional orders of the Member States and the international treaties on which they have collaborated. The ECHR has a special place as a source of these principles,[48] and the judgments of the ECtHR are taken into account regularly by the EU's Court of Justice.[49] In particular, the latter Court has frequently recognised that the EC legal order gives protection to the right to

---

41 See the statement in the minutes of the Council meeting adopting the Directive, welcoming the Commission's commitment to table the proposal 'within one year, and possibly by the end of 2003, to taking into account' a study on the transfer of protection status (see Statement 220/03 in the summary of Council acts in Nov 2003, Council doc 16382/03, 7 Jan 2004). The Commission later announced that it would not make this proposal in 2004 (COM (2004) 534, 30 July 2004, Annex II).

42 See the Opinion and judgment in Joined Cases C-95/99 to 98/99 *Khalil and Others* and C-180/99 *Addou* [2001] ECR I-7413, where the point was relevant but was not referred to the Court of Justice by the national court; and comments in the case note on this judgment by Peers, S (2002) 39 CMLRev 1395.

43 See *Khalil* and *Addou* (*ibid*) and Reg 859/2003 (OJ 2003 L 124/1).

44 Ireland has not opted in to the reception conditions Directive and opted into the temporary protection Directive only after its adoption (see fn 34, above). Both the UK and Ireland opted in to Reg 859/2003 on third-country nationals' social security (*ibid*).

45 See treaty with the EC (OJ 2001 L 93/38), in force since 1 April 2001 (OJ 2001 L 112/16).

46 A treaty to this effect, between the EC and Switzerland, was agreed in principle in May 2004, and signed in October 2004. For the text see COM (2004) 593, 14 September 2004.

47 The long-standing case law of the Court of Justice on this point has been entrenched by Art 6(2) of the Treaty on European Union (TEU).

48 Case 222/84 *Johnston* [1986] ECR 1651.

49 See Peers, S, 'The European Court of Justice and the European Court of Human Rights: comparative approaches' in Orucu, E (ed), *Judicial Comparativism in Human Rights Cases*, 2003, UKNCCL, pp 107–29.

family life, and has referred to some relevant ECtHR case law on the issue.[50] The EU Court has also referred to Art 3 of the ECHR in passing,[51] but has not yet had occasion to rule on whether this right (or, for that matter, the right to seek and enjoy asylum or any other asylum-related right) forms part of the general principles of EC law, or on the relevance of ECtHR judgments on Art 3 of the ECHR. While a number of relevant rights are protected in the EU's Charter of Rights, the Charter will not be discussed further in this chapter as it is not yet legally binding, pending ratification of the EU's draft Constitution.[52]

SUBSTANTIVE EC LAW

The framework for analysis of family reunion legislation in this chapter is fourfold.[53] First, how is the sponsor defined? Secondly, how are 'family members' defined? Thirdly, what are the conditions of entry for family members? Finally, what is the family member's status after entry?

Definition of sponsor

The main distinction between sponsors is between those sponsors who are seeking protection and those sponsors who have a recognised need for it. Within each of these groups, distinctions can be further drawn between those who seek or have received recognised protection as refugees under the Geneva Convention on the status of refugees, or subsidiary protection, or temporary protection. As we shall see, there are also further distinction as regards family members, between those who accompany the sponsor at the time of initial entry, those who seek reunion with the sponsor later and those whose relationship is only formed after entry.

It should also be noted that the agreed Directive on asylum procedures would, in addition, have an impact on family members as regards the asylum procedure.[54] Member States will be obliged to permit every adult having legal capacity to make an application on their own behalf.[55] However, Member States

---

50   See Case 249/86 *Commission v Germany* [1989] ECR 1263; Case C-60/00 *Carpenter* [2002] ECR I-6279; Case C-459/99 *MRAX* [2002] ECR I-6591; Case C-413/99 *Baumbast and R* [2002] ECR I-7091; Case C-257/00 *Givane* [2003] ECR I-345; Case C-109/01 *Akrich* [2003] ECR I-9607; and Joined Cases C-482/01 and C-493/01 *Oliveri* and *Orfanopolous*, judgment of 29 April 2004, not yet reported.

51   See Case C-112/00 *Schmidberger* [2003] ECR I-5659.

52   See fn 29, above. The draft Constitution would also require the EU to accede to the ECHR, which could also be relevant to asylum and family reunion issues.

53   This framework is taken from the companion piece to this chapter, which assesses EC family reunion rules applying to all persons *other* than those seeking or receiving international protection: see Peers, S, 'Family reunion and Community law' in Walker, N (ed), *Towards an Area of Freedom, Security and Justice*, 2004, Oxford: OUP.

54   See fn 34, above.

55   Article 5(2), asylum procedures Directive, see fn 34, above.

may opt that applications may be made on behalf of the applicant's dependants; in that case, it must be ensured that dependent adults consent to this collective application, failing which consent they must be permitted to apply in their own name.[56] Member States may also determine in national law the cases in which minors can make applications on their own behalf.[57] Where a collective application is made, Member States may issue a single decision covering all dependants,[58] holding a personal interview for each dependant is only an option for Member States,[59] and Member States may treat a subsequent separate application by a dependant as inadmissible if there are no facts relating to the dependant's situation which justify consideration of the separate application.[60] Personal interviews will normally take place without family members, unless the Member State's authorities consider it necessary to have the family members present for an 'appropriate examination'.[61]

(a) Sponsors seeking protection

EC legislation addresses the family members of asylum seekers in Directive 2003/9 on reception conditions for asylum seekers.[62] There is no proposed or adopted EC legislation regarding the family members of persons seeking subsidiary or temporary protection, but Member States are free to apply Directive 2003/9 to persons seeking subsidiary protection if they wish.[63] Also, the old and new rules on responsibility for asylum seekers (the previous Dublin Convention on responsibility for asylum applications and the 'Dublin II' Regulation which replaced it from 1 September 2003) had or have an impact upon the family members of asylum seekers and (indirectly) upon those seeking other forms of international protection.[64] Although the responsibility rules (including the special provisions allowing for states to 'opt out' of the normal rules, which are sometimes applied to ensure family reunion) are not formally family reunion rules, responsibility for asylum seekers entails accepting their entry onto the territory, and so where responsibility is premised on a family link, the result is to ensure family reunion; but conversely where other criteria for responsibility are

---

56 Article 5(3) of the asylum procedures Directive, see fn 34, above. There is no definition of 'dependants'.

57 Article 5(4)(a) of the asylum procedures Directive, see fn 34, above. There is no definition of 'minors' in general, although there is a common definition of 'unaccompanied minor' (Art 2(h) of the Directive).

58 Article 8(3) of the asylum procedures Directive, see fn 34, above.

59 Article 10(1) of the asylum procedures Directive, see fn 34, above. Member States may also determine in national law the cases in which they will give minors a personal interview.

60 Article 25(2)(g) of the asylum procedures Directive, see fn 34, above.

61 Article 11(1) of the asylum procedures Directive, see fn 34, above. There is no definition of 'family members'.

62 See fn 32, above.

63 See Art 3(4) of Directive 2003/9 (ibid).

64 See fns 30 and 31, above.

given precedence over family links, then family reunion will be prejudiced.[65] The Dublin rules do not apply to persons seeking subsidiary protection.

As regards asylum procedures, Member States which apply a 'single procedure' for both Geneva Convention refugee applications and subsidiary protection applications (as defined in Directive 2004/83) will be obliged to apply the asylum procedures Directive to all such cases.[66] Member States may also apply the asylum procedures Directive to all claims for international protection.[67]

(b) Sponsors with protection

As for family members of persons with recognised protection, the general family reunion Directive covers family reunion with refugees, defined as 'any third-country national or stateless person enjoying refugee status in accordance within the meaning of the Geneva Convention'.[68] Sponsors must have a residence permit for a period of over one year and a reasonable prospect of obtaining permanent residence; this criterion may be more difficult for refugees to fulfil, given that the EC legislation on long-term residents does not (yet) apply to them.[69]

The initial proposal for the general family reunion Directive had covered family reunion with persons with subsidiary protection,[70] but this category of sponsors was removed in the 2000 version of the proposal,[71] and not restored in a revised text in 2002,[72] or in the text of this Directive as agreed in February 2003 and adopted in September 2003.[73] So no adopted or proposed EC measure covers family reunion with persons with subsidiary protection; the Commission has reneged on its 2000 promise to propose legislation to cover such persons at an early date.[74]

---

65 See the discussion of case law and practice in: Hurwitz, A, 'The 1990 Dublin Convention: a comprehensive assessment' 11 IJRL 646, at pp 653–56 and 661–63; Loper, F, 'The Dublin Convention on Asylum: interpretation and application problems' in Marinho, C (ed), *The Dublin Convention on Asylum: Its Essence, Implementation and Prospects*, 2000, Maastricht: EIPA, pp 26–27; 'Practical cases' in *ibid*, pp 33–34, 49–51 and 63–64; Vermeulen, B, 'The application of Article 3(4) of the Dublin Convention on Asylum in Dutch case law' in *ibid*, p 53; and Klug, A, 'The Humanitarian Clause of the Dublin Convention and Family Protection' in *ibid*, p 69.
66 Article 3(3) of the procedures Directive (fn 34, above).
67 Article 3(4) of the procedures Directive (fn 34, above).
68 Article 2(b), Directive 2003/86 (fn 36, above).
69 They will of course be able to make an argument based on their access to permanent residence status as provided for in national law, or (if they are Turkish) the EC's association agreement (on this issue, see the section on 'Substantive EC law').
70 COM (1999) 638, 1 Dec 1999.
71 COM (2000) 624, 10 Oct 2000.
72 COM (2002) 225, 3 May 2002.
73 See fn 36, above.
74 See the explanatory memorandum and the preamble to the 2000 version of the proposal (see fn 71, above).

As for accompanying family members, the 2004 Directive on the definition of 'refugee' and subsidiary protection and the content of status covers them. Family members of refugees or persons with subsidiary protection are only covered by this Directive if they are 'present in the same State in relation to the application for international protection'.[75]

Finally, the temporary protection Directive adopted in 2001 contains family reunion rules for persons covered by a Community temporary protection regime as defined by that Directive. On the other hand, that Directive does not govern the status of persons (or their family members) within national temporary protection schemes.[76] The application of the Directive in practice is dependent on a Council decision to apply the Directive to establish the Community regime for a particular mass influx or threatened mass influx of persons. However, no such decision had been taken by the end of May 2005.

Definition of family members

The definition of family has been contested in the various Council measures under discussion or adopted. With each proposal, the Commission has suggested a broad concept of 'family', including the extended family. However, the Council has usually agreed only to cover the nuclear family within EC measures. For asylum seekers, Directive 2003/9 defines family as spouses or unmarried partners in a stable relationship, if 'the legislation and practice of the Member State concerned treats unmarried couples in a way comparable to married couples in its law relating to aliens', and unmarried dependent minor children of the couple or the asylum applicant regardless of whether born in wedlock or adopted as defined by national law.[77] The family must already have existed in the country of origin (ruling out application of the Directive to family formation) and the family 'must be present in the same Member States in relation to the application for asylum'. Member States can also apply the Directive to 'close relatives' dependent on the asylum seeker, or for humanitarian reasons.[78]

Subsequently, the Council followed this template in Reg 343/2003 on responsibility for asylum applications. The definition of 'family members' here is identical to that in Directive 2003/9, except that the family members need merely be 'present in the territory of the Member States' and family members also comprise the 'father, mother or guardian when the applicant is a refugee and unmarried'.[79] However, the requirement of prior family formation in the country of origin does not apply to the allocation rule conferring responsibility on a

---

75 Article 2(h) of the Directive, see fn 33, above.
76 Directive 2001/55, see fn 35, above. Member States had to apply the Directive by 31 December 2002.
77 Article 2(d) of Directive, see fn 32, above.
78 Article 4 of Directive, see fn 32, above.
79 Article 2(i) of Reg 343/2003, see fn 30, above.

Member State where a family member of an applicant has recognised Convention refugee status in another Member State. Presumably this distinction was inserted into the Regulation so that this allocation rule remained consistent with the previous equivalent rule in the Dublin Convention.

Similarly, during discussion of the proposal on the definition and content of refugee and subsidiary protection status, the Council agreed that family members were only covered 'insofar as the family already existed in the country of origin'. The list of family members is identical to that in Directive 2003/9, with the necessary difference that a child of the couple or of the *beneficiary* of international protection is covered, rather than the child of the couple or the asylum *applicant*.[80]

For family reunion with refugees, covered by the general family reunion directive, the definition of 'family members' is the same as that applying to other third-country national sponsors governed by the Directive, with certain exceptions. The general rules provide that Member States must authorise entry of family members, defined as spouses or minor children (including adopted children) of the couple, or minor children (again including adopted children) of one of the couple (that is, stepchildren) where the parent has custody and the child is dependent. Member States may admit children subject to a joint custody decision if the non-custodial parent has given their consent.[81] As for unmarried partners, Member States have an option to admit them under the Directive if they are in a 'duly attested stable long-term relationship' or a 'registered partnership', along with the unmarried minor children or dependent adult children (as defined in the Directive) of such partners.[82] There is no requirement of comparability with the rules applicable to married couples. Member States may also admit the dependent parents or grandparents of the sponsor or spouse, or the dependent unmarried adult children of the sponsor or spouse.[83] Special rules preclude admission of more than one spouse in cases of polygamy, and give Member States the option as to whether to admit children of such further spouses; permit Member States to set a minimum age for the sponsor or spouse (maximum 21 years of age) before the spouse can enter; and permit Member States to retain laws setting out special requirements where the children of the sponsors are over the age of 15.[84] It should be noted that several of the restrictive provisions in the Directive are the subject of a pending annulment action by the European Parliament, for alleged breach of human rights.[85]

The first special rule for refugees is that one condition applying to other sponsors does not apply to them: Member States cannot apply an optional restriction (an integration requirement) applicable to children over the age of 12, where the sponsor is a refugee.[86] Also, Member States have an option to admit

---

80 Article 2(h) of the Directive, see fn 33, above.
81 Article 4(1), Directive 2003/86, see fn 36, above.
82 Article 4(3), Directive 2003/86, see fn 36, above.
83 Article 4(2), see fn 36, above.
84 Article 4(3) to (5), see fn 36, above.
85 Case C-540/03, *European Parliament v Council*, pending.
86 Article 10(1), see fn 36, above, referring to the third sub-para of Art 4(1).

even further family members than those mentioned in that Directive, if those family members are dependent on the refugee.[87] Conversely, there is one restriction that only applies where the sponsor is a refugee. Usually, the Directive applies expressly regardless of whether the family relationship predated the sponsor's entry,[88] but as regards refugees, Member States have an option to restrict the application of the special refugee Chapter in the Directive to cases of family *reunion* only, leaving cases of family *formation* (where the refugee marries after entry into the Member State's territory) outside the scope of the Directive.[89] Since this is a power to limit application of the special *Chapter* to such persons, not to exclude them from the scope of the Directive entirely, then such persons must still be covered by the rest of the Directive. There is also a special rule in favour of unaccompanied minors who are refugees, where Member States are obliged to admit direct ascending relatives (such as parents or grandparents) without applying the strict conditions that usually apply to such entry. Member States also have an option to admit the guardians of unaccompanied minors.[90] The special rules applicable to refugees are without prejudice to 'any rules granting refugee status to family members';[91] as we have seen, the asylum procedures Directive will bring some limited harmonisation to that area.

However, the Council proved willing to take a slightly broader approach in the temporary protection Directive. Here 'family members' are defined, along with the standard definition of spouses, partners and children as found in other asylum measures, as including other close relatives who were part of the family unit at the time of the relevant events and who were wholly or mainly dependent on the sponsor at the time.[92] There is a requirement in all cases that the family relationship already existed in the country of origin and the family was separated due to the events which gave rise to the temporary protection claim.

Conditions of entry

For asylum seekers, there is no express right to family reunion in the reception conditions directive, so the question of conditions for such reunion is irrelevant, unless it could be argued (rather ambitiously) that a right of entry is a corollary of the 'family unity' provision in the Directive. However, the Regulation on responsibility for asylum seekers contains a relevant general provision and two relevant new rules for responsibility as compared to the Dublin Convention. The general provision provides that a Member State is responsible for a minor (as defined in the Regulation) accompanying a parent or guardian, whether or not the minor is considered to be an asylum seeker. The same provision applies to

---

87 Article 10(2), see fn 36, above.
88 Article 2(d), see fn 36, above.
89 Article 9(2), see fn 36, above.
90 Article 10(3), see fn 36, above. For the definition of 'unaccompanied minor', see Art 2(f).
91 Article 9(3), see fn 36, above.
92 Article 15(1) of Directive, see fn 35, above.

children born after the asylum seeker has arrived within the EU.[93] As for the new criteria, the first of these allocates responsibility to the Member State where an unaccompanied minor has a family member who is legally present;[94] and the second (now third in the order of criteria, following the previous criterion allocating responsibility to a Member State where the applicant has a family member who is a recognised Convention refugee) allocates responsibility to the Member State where an applicant's family member has applied for refugee status, if that application has not yet been the subject of a first decision regarding the substance.[95] There is no definition of 'legally present' in the first of these new grounds for responsibility, so it may be arguable whether reunion with an asylum seeker is covered by this ground. The importance of this distinction is that the condition, in the latter new ground, that the asylum application be pending would not apply to unaccompanied minors if asylum seekers are deemed to be 'legally present'. Also, the criterion for responsibility for 'unaccompanied minors' is apt to mean reunion with family members granted subsidiary protection status or even applying for that status, depending on the national and (eventually) EC law on this issue.[96]

For recognised refugees, the Directive on refugee definition and content does not contain an express right to family reunion. So unless the Dublin rules are relevant, any rights to entry must be found under the Directive on family reunion. The general conditions for family reunion under this Directive apply, with certain exceptions for refugee sponsors. Refugees need not necessarily show documentary evidence of the relationship; they are exempt from the possible resources, sickness insurance and accommodation requirements that Member States may impose; and they are exempt from the waiting period which Member States may insist upon before authorising reunification.[97] However, the references to the conditions of public policy *et al* apply equally to family reunion for refugees, with no express reference to the obvious difficulties that refugees would have living with their family members in the country of origin. Moreover, Member States may impose the resources, sickness insurance and accommodation requirements where reunion would be possible in a third country with which the sponsor or family member has special links,[98] or where an application for reunion

---

93 Article 4(3) of Reg, see fn 30, above.

94 Article 6 of Reg, see fn 30, above. 'Unaccompanied minor' is defined in Art 2(h).

95 Article 8 of Reg, see fn 30, above.

96 For those with recognised subsidiary protection status, the right to a residence permit provided for in the Directive on the definition and content of refugee and subsidiary protection status surely means that such persons will have to be considered 'legally present' for the purposes of Reg 343/2003, unless Member States apply the apparent derogation applicable to such family members (see Arts 23(2) and 24(2) of the Directive, see fn 33 above, discussed further, below).

97 See Arts 11 and 12. However, the exemption from the resources, sickness insurance and accommodation requirements only extends to reunion with the spouse and children as defined in Art 4(1), not to reunion with any other family members.

98 This proviso is logically connected to the principle of 'safe third country' as applied to asylum law, although here a 'third country' presumably means any state outside the EU, rather than (in EC asylum law) any state other than an EU Member State or the country of origin. Also, the 'safe third country' principle permits an asylum application to be rejected on the grounds that the asylum application 'should' have been made elsewhere, but here the rule applies when refugee status has already been recognised.

is submitted more than three months after the sponsor's refugee status is 'granted' (*sic*). They can also impose integration requirements on the sponsor or family members after entry, although it is not clear what will happen if those requirements are then 'failed'.[99]

As for the EC temporary protection rules, Member States have to reunite 'core' family members (whether they are scattered throughout the Member States or have not yet entered any Member State), but have an option whether to admit the non-core family, 'taking account on a case-by-case basis the extreme hardship they would face' in the absence of reunification.[100] However, Member States appear to have discretion as to where the reunion takes place.[101]

Status after entry

If Member States permit family members to join asylum seekers, or are obliged to do so by virtue of the rules on asylum responsibility, or find that family members have entered with the asylum seeker, there is still, as discussed above, an option under the agreed asylum procedures Directive to deny asylum seeker status to the family members, subject however to the family member's consent (if the family member is an adult). Directive 2003/9 leaves it up to each Member State to determine whether an asylum seeker's family is covered by the asylum application, and therefore by the Directive,[102] although following adoption of the procedures Directive, a coherent interpretation of the two Directives would surely mean that Member States must apply the reception Directive to any family member of an asylum seeker who files a separate application pursuant to the procedures Directive.[103] Where family members are covered by the Directive, Member States are obliged to take 'appropriate measures to maintain as far as possible family unity' in their territory, if Member States provide asylum seekers with housing.[104] The detailed provisions on housing require Member States to ensure 'protection of [the] family life' of asylum seekers and 'if appropriate' to lodge minor children of asylum seekers or asylum-seeking minors with a parent or adult family member responsible for them.[105] Vulnerable minors must have access to special social services.[106] Education of minor children of asylum seekers must be provided on 'similar' conditions to host state nationals, as long as an expulsion measure is not enforced, but this education can be provided in accommodation centres and there are provisions for delayed entry into the education system or the provision of alternate education.[107]

---

99 Article 7(2) of Directive 2003/86, see fn 36 above.
100 Article 15(2) and (3) of Directive 2001/55, see fn 35, above.
101 Article 15(5) of Directive 2001/55, see fn 35, above.
102 Article 3(1) of Directive 2003/9, see fn 32, above.
103 Article 3(1) of Directive 2003/9, see fn 32, above.
104 Article 8 of Directive 2003/9, see fn 32, above.
105 Article 14(2)(a) and (3) of Directive 2003/9, see fn 32, above.
106 Article 18(2) of Directive 2003/9, see fn 32, above.
107 Article 10 of Directive 2003/9, see fn 32, above.

For the family members of recognised refugees joining their family members later, the normal status rules in the family reunion directive apply.[108] These provide for access to education, employment, self-employment and vocational training on the same conditions as the sponsor (now implicitly entailing a reference to the adopted Directive on the content of refugee status, which regulates refugees' access to employment), but with a possible waiting period (maximum one year) for access to employment or self-employment and possible restrictions for non-core family members. Core family members also have the right to an autonomous residence permit (separate from the sponsor's permit) after five years, or earlier in certain circumstances. There are no special rules in the Directive on the content of refugee status to take account of family members who entered as asylum seekers, but were permitted to stay on family reunion grounds without consideration of the claim by the authorities. However, it is obviously arguable that where family members do not qualify for autonomous status, they can still revive or launch a fresh claim for protection in the event that they would otherwise face removal from the country. This is supported by the express text of the family reunion Directive, which is expressly without prejudice to any rules on the refugee (and presumably the subsidiary protection) status of family members.[109]

For family members accompanying recognised refugees or persons with subsidiary protection status, the Commission had proposed that they obtain the same status as the sponsor.[110] The Council rejected this suggestion, providing instead for a complex compromise. Article 23 of the Directive first of all requires family unity to be maintained. Next, it requires Member States to extend all the benefits in Arts 24 to 34 to family members 'in accordance with national procedures' and if compatible with the personal legal status of the family member. This comprises rights to a residence permit, travel documents, access to employment, access to education,[111] social welfare, health care, accommodation, free movement, integration and repatriation, along with special rules for unaccompanied minors. It does not include a right to refugee or subsidiary protection status as such, and in particular it does not comprise a right to non-*refoulement*; and there are no alternative rules protecting against expulsion of family members in the absence of a non-*refoulement* rule. For that matter, there are no rules in the Directive protecting against expulsion (as distinct from non-*refoulement*) of refugees.[112]

Moreover, there are some key restrictions on these rights. It may be argued what the references to national procedures or compatibility with personal legal

---

108 Articles 14 and 15 of Directive 2003/86, see fn 36, above.

109 Article 9(3).

110 Article 6 of proposed Directive on definition and content of status, see fn 40, above.

111 In this case it is not entirely clear whether minor children of refugees would have the same rights as their adult parents to education in Art 27, or the broader rights which the Directive confers on minor *refugees*.

112 The distinction between Arts 32 and 33 of the Geneva Convention is discussed further in the section on the international and human rights framework above.

status mean; the Directive also provides that Member States can 'define the conditions applicable' to family members of subsidiary protection beneficiaries, as long as they are guaranteed an adequate standard of living.[113] The family members can also be excluded from these rights if they are covered by the exclusion clauses applicable to the beneficiaries of international protection;[114] it is not clear whether this clause applies in all cases or just those cases where the family members apply for protection in their own name. It would certainly be objectionable to apply an exclusion clause to a person who has not even applied for refugee or subsidiary protection status, and who therefore has not been able to invoke procedural rights to argue against the application of the exclusion clause. Benefits can also be withdrawn for reasons of national security or public order.[115]

Finally, the temporary protection Directive does not expressly address the question of whether family members have any claim to temporary protection, or the rights granted to beneficiaries of that protection, in their own right.[116] Nor is there any alternative form of status provided for family members of beneficiaries.

ASSESSMENT

The first aspect of the EC rules on family reunion in this area that strikes the reader is the possible areas of confused overlap between various relevant rules. First of all, it is not clear whether persons seeking international protection or with a recognised international protection status, or their family members, can also still rely on rights which they may be granted according to association agreements between the EC, its Member States and non-EU states, in addition to the rules in the recent EC legislation. Some national courts have assumed that refugees (at least) cannot rely on the association agreements, but this interpretation is highly questionable.

Another area of possible overlap is between the family reunion Directive and the Dublin II rules (although not in the UK and Ireland, where only the Dublin II rules apply). This overlap derives from the rule in the Dublin Convention (now in the 'Dublin II' rules) that the family member of a refugee, as defined in those rules, *must* be admitted to the refugee's host state without any conditions applying, if the family member applies for refugee status. Under the family reunion Directive there is a more direct right of family reunion for family members of recognised refugees; but there are divergences in the two rules between the definition of sponsors, the definition of family members, the conditions of entry and the status after entry (where, at best, the reception conditions Directive would apply to asylum-seeking family members, at the option of the Member State responsible for the application). Various complications could result, in particular if an asylum

---

113 Article 23(2).
114 Article 23(3).
115 Article 23(4).
116 See Arts 8–14 of Directive 2001/55.

seeker is a minor and the move to join their parent extinguishes their right to apply for asylum pursuant to the options granted to Member States by the procedures Directive.[117]

Next, the relationship between the Dublin II rules and the temporary protection Directive is unclear, particularly as regards family members. Neither the original Dublin Convention nor its replacement Regulation made any reference to beneficiaries of temporary protection or their family members, leaving a risk that the family would be separated as a result of the application of the Dublin rules. The temporary protection Directive does specify that the Dublin Convention rules apply within the context of that Directive, and that, in particular, the state responsible for considering an asylum application of a beneficiary of temporary protection is the state that has accepted a transfer of that person onto its territory. [118] In fact, such a rule does not appear in the Dublin Convention (or the replacement) Regulation, so it is really a second rule in addition to the Dublin rules. Also, this second rule appears to have a different personal scope to the first rule: since it applies only to 'beneficiaries' of temporary protection, arguably it does not apply to their family members. Furthermore, there appears to be a third rule regarding family members, for the Directive specifies that the place of their reunion is left to Member States' discretion.[119]

It can be argued that a coherent interpretation of the rules means that where a family member of a beneficiary of temporary protection applies for asylum, then the general reference to the Dublin rules in the Directive applies (and arguably also the 'special' Dublin rules, if family members can be considered beneficiaries), instead of the rule relating to family members; the latter rule would only apply to family members who do *not* apply for asylum. This could cause complications where, pursuant to the procedures Directive, Member States do not permit minor children to apply for asylum. Moreover, it could be argued that in the absence of a general rule in the Dublin II Regulation ensuring that all references to the Dublin Convention should now be taken as references to the Regulation, then the Dublin Convention, rather than the Regulation, would still govern responsibility for asylum claims made by persons covered by the temporary protection Directive.[120] This would be important in practice, since many persons covered by temporary protection will be asylum seekers whose claims are put on hold, who therefore would be entitled to be joined by their (asylum-seeking) family members under the Dublin II Regulation, but not under the Dublin Convention.[121] So far, the issue

---

117 This complication could also result under the Dublin II rules if the child asylum seeker is moved to join an asylum-seeking parent.

118 Article 18 of the Directive, see fn 35, above.

119 Article 15(5).

120 Article 24(3) of the Dublin II Reg (see fn 30, above) states that the references to the Dublin Convention in the Eurodac Regulation should now be taken as references to this Reg. Arguably this has an *a contrario* effect. However, Art 24(1) of the Dublin II Regulation, which states that the Regulation replaces the Convention, arguably has the effect of amending all other cross-references to the Convention.

121 See Art 17 of the Directive and Art 8 of the Regulation. However, Art 19 of the Directive permits Member States to ban persons from holding temporary protection and asylum-seeker status concurrently. If Member States take up this option, it will deter asylum applications.

of the relationship between the Dublin rules and the temporary protection Directive has not been relevant in practice, as the Directive has not been invoked. For family members of temporary protection beneficiaries, that is just as well.

The second striking defect of the EC rules on this subject is the incoherent approach as between categories, in particular between the family reunion Directive and the refugee definition and content directive. While the two Directives do not overlap, they are each addressed to a category of family members of refugees and so one would expect a considerable degree of consistency since there is no convincing reason to treat the two categories differently. However, the two categories are governed by different definitions of 'family member', as well as by quite different rules on the status of family members. The family reunion Directive contains far fewer rules on status than the 2004 Directive, but does at least contain rules restricting expulsion of family members of refugees, which the later Directive lacks. Also, the family reunion Directive contains procedural rights, whereas the later Directive contains none.[122]

The third and greatest disappointment with the Community's foray into regulating the area of family members of persons seeking or in receipt of international protection is its failure to set sufficiently high standards. This is particularly obvious as regards subsidiary protection, where there is no EC law right of family reunion at all and a very limited and unclear status for the accompanying family members. There is no EC law provision providing for reception conditions for the family members of persons seeking subsidiary protection (and indeed no EC law provision providing for reception conditions for the persons seeking such protection). Without a procedures directive applying to subsidiary protection, there is nothing in EC law to regulate the position of family members who might make a separate claim for subsidiary protection.[123] The Dublin rules do not provide for unity of the family of persons with subsidiary protection, never mind unity of the family of persons applying for subsidiary protection on the same basis as asylum seekers' families. Given that the ECHR, as interpreted above, entails a core right of family reunion for persons with subsidiary protection, it is unfortunate that such a right is not secured by Community legislation.

As for the family members of persons with temporary protection, while there is a right to family reunion with core family members, the EC rules set too low a standard in two areas: the apparent rule that family members will be reunited in a Member State decided upon at Member States' discretion, and the absence of any provisions on status of the family members. Since many persons enjoying temporary protection have an underlying claim to recognition as a refugee, any forced movement to another state would breach the provisions of Art 32 of the

---

122 Perhaps such rights were omitted because the procedural rights relating to one of the main objects of the Directive, the definition of 'refugee', are set out in a separate directive. But the procedures Directive does not contain rules relating to disputes over the status of family members (or concerning disputes over recognised refugees' status, for that matter, apart from the grant or withdrawal of that status).

123 However, as already noted, there is a right under the ECHR for family members to make a separate Art 3 ECHR claim; but such a claim, if successful, will not necessarily confer subsidiary protection status.

Geneva Convention, which precludes expulsion of refugees except in limited circumstances. Furthermore, whichever of the many possible interpretations of the relationship between the temporary protection Directive and the Dublin rules is applied, there is a risk of splitting up family members.

The low standards are also obvious as regards the family members of asylum seekers, where there is no right of family reunion and Member States have discretion as to whether to apply the low standards in the reception Directive to family members.

As regards the family members of persons with refugee status, there is at least a right of family reunion in the family reunion Directive and a set of standards applicable to family members who accompany the asylum seeker. However, there is no protection against expulsion or *refoulement* for accompanying family members set out in EC law, even though there is a strong argument that the ECHR and Geneva Convention rules, taken together, require such protection to be provided.[124] There are also some very broad provisions in the 2004 Directive that could be interpreted to give discretion to Member States to limit the rights of accompanying family members. As for family reunion with refugees, there is protection against expulsion, but few other provisions on their status. Although the conditions for family reunion are more favourable than the general rules, they are still questionable in light of the analysis of the impact of the ECHR set out above.[125] It is doubtful whether the option to impose the stringent normal conditions in the Directive to applications for family formation (as distinct from reunion) and the option to insist upon an application within three months after 'granting' refugee status or else the income, sickness insurance and accommodation requirements will be applied, are compatible with human rights law. There is also a risk that the option to insist on the application of the income, sickness insurance and accommodation requirements in cases of links with a third country could be incompatible with human rights law in specific cases.

CONCLUSIONS

The EC rules on the reunion with, and the status of, the family members of persons seeking or receiving international protection set disappointingly low standards in several respects, and have a lack of internal coherence, both where the legislation overlaps and where two nearly identical categories of family members are treated quite differently. This is a classic example of the absence of 'joined-up' policy-making within the EU, and certain provisions in the legislation apparently fall below even the minimum standards set by the ECHR as regards family reunion with persons seeking or receiving international protection. It can only be hoped that as the EC moves toward the second stage of establishing a CEAS, due attention will be paid to remedying these significant defects.

---

124 See the analysis above.
125 *Ibid.*

CHAPTER 5

TOWARDS A JUST EUROPEAN WELFARE SYSTEM FOR MIGRANTS?

Keith Puttick

The addition of Title IV to the Treaty Establishing the European Community (TEC), providing for the progressive establishment of 'an area of freedom, security and justice', has been seen as problematic – partly because of the obvious tensions between freedom of movement, immigration, and 'security'.[1] Despite this, Title IV is an important landmark. As well as facilitating incorporation of the Schengen *acquis* into the Treaty on European Union, and the further development of free movement principles, it authorises a wide range of measures on asylum and immigration, including the regulation of third country nationals' ability to enter, work, and reside in the EU, and for safeguarding their rights and welfare in the process. By authorising minimum standards for the reception of asylum seekers, Art 63 also gave the Community the opportunity for a solution to one of its most serious and intractable problems: the need for a uniform, EU-wide system of support for asylum claimants.

In seeking to improve third country nationals' rights through a new Council Directive on entry and residence for the purpose of employment in the EU (first published in 2001: COM (2001) 386 Final) – an objective which will also address states' problems resulting from demographic changes in the population, declining birth rates, and labour shortages (Art 6 of the Preamble) – reaching agreement was never going to be easy. The project has also proven technically difficult given the complexity of current restrictions on non-EU citizens accessing work and social protection systems, or simply residing in EU states. This can be seen in the labyrinthine restrictions faced by 'guest workers' from Turkey, or Maghreb countries like Morocco, and under the EU's Euro-Mediterranean association agreements with countries providing such labour. At present there is only limited scope for movement and residence by such workers in parts of the EU in which they are not actually working.[2] So it has been no great surprise that progressing the scheme, particularly on the contentious issue of aligning employment and social security conditions more closely with those of EU citizens, has been

---

1   Church, C and Phinnemore, D, *The European Treaties: From Rome to Maastricht, Amsterdam, Nice and Beyond*, 2000, London: Penguin, pp 258–63.

2   *Nour Eddline El-Yassini v Secretary of State for the Home Department* [1999] ECR I-1209 EU: Case C-416/96; and van der Mei, AP, *Free Movement of Persons within the European Community: Cross-Border Access to Public Benefits*, 2003, Oxford: Hart, pp 167–77.

difficult.[3] When acceptable arrangements are, in time, agreed (possibly by the end of 2005, at least in respect of the 'principles' on which legislation will be based), the Directive will give important new opportunities and rights for workers from third countries and their family members, and promote key common policies. It should also address the complex integration objectives involved.

Three countries – Denmark, Ireland and the UK – maintain Title IV 'opt-ins' and 'opt-outs'. This is symptomatic of the lack of consensus that persists over Title IV objectives. Whilst these states can accept any specific measures they support – as seen with the UK's support of Directive 2003/9[4] – the opt-outs, and the numerous protocols and declarations used by states to qualify their support of measures, are indicative of the divisions that still persist about *how* Title IV objectives should be progressed.[5] In a number of cases the concerns highlight some fundamental disagreements, for example over states' commitment to implementing social and economic 'cohesion' objectives, and aligning employment, in-work support, and welfare rights with those of their own nationals. In this chapter I consider these points further in the context of the state's welfare role in supporting (and regulating) migration and asylum; and then offer a critique of aspects of national measures and EU legislation like EC Directive 2003/9.

MEMBER STATES' SUPPORT FOR 'NEW ARRIVALS'

The idea that income benefits, healthcare, and social services support should extend to new arrivals from outside their territory – and do so as a legal *right* – is

---

3   Restrictions on social rights have been among the changes made to the Draft Directive, so that these will be 'incremental', linked to 'length of stay', and 'less exhaustive' than measures like Directive 2003/109 on third country nationals who are long-term EU residents; Explanatory Memorandum to the Draft, p 14. Directive 2003/109 was accepted, but as the recital indicates only on the basis that 'integration' rights are qualified; and applicants must have adequate resources, including sickness insurance, 'to avoid becoming a burden for the Member State'. However, the Charter of Fundamental Rights of the European Union very explicitly states that 'Nationals of third countries authorised to work in Member States are entitled to working conditions equivalent to those of citizens of the Union'; see Part II, Title I, Art II-75, para 3, OJ 2004 C310/45, Vol 47 (16 December 2004). A contentious area is whether this should encompass in-work 'welfare', such tax credits, which are essential in supporting low-paid work, but which are not seen by all states as necessary to support segmented markets and low-paid workers as they are in economies like the US and UK; see Alstott, A, 'The earned income tax credit and the limitations of tax-based welfare reform' (1995) 108 Harvard Law Review 533, pp 534–44; and Puttick, K, '2020: A welfare odyssey – a commentary on "Principles into Practice" and the reform programme' (1999) 28 Industrial Law Journal 190, pp 191–94.

4   See Preamble, para 19, of that Directive; and Directive 2003/86, Preamble, para 17. Arguably, such 'cherry-picking' fundamentally weakens the effectiveness of the EU's programme, and undermines the objective of creating a 'common policy'.

5   A 'soft-law' approach to harmonising asylum laws, based on lowest common denominators, eg in dealing with asylum applications, is arguably a by-product of this, and has been problematic, as anticipated several years ago in Guild, E, 'The impetus to harmonise: asylum policy in the European Union' in Nicholson, F and Twomey, P *et al* (eds), *Refugee Rights and Realities: Evolving International Concepts and Regimes*, 1999, Cambridge: CUP, pp 334–35.

still unwelcome, even threatening, for some European states and their citizens. This can be seen each time the wrath of the media and popular antipathy falls on new arrivals perceived as 'economic migrants', 'benefits tourists', or 'health tourists'. The destabilising effects of this are most apparent in relation to the asylum seeking process when new arrivals are seen as abusing immigration, asylum, and welfare systems.[6]

In the process of operating immigration controls and status 'gateways' as a condition of state support for non-EU nationals after entry, and despite the EU's developing agenda, Europe is still for the most part a place where Member States are able to make their own rules, and pursue their own social and economic objectives within a 'bounded world' in which members of the political community avoid, if they possibly can, 'sharing with anyone else'.[7] In the case of asylum, the issues are more complex. In addition to national restrictions, cornerstone features of the support system are also rooted in public international law, notably the Refugee Convention 1951. However, the 1951 regime, whilst requiring states to provide support to *refugees* in various ways – including access to wage-earning employment, housing, public relief, social security, and so forth – failed to make explicit provision for *applicants* for such status during the reception phase. As a result, states have been free to develop (and restrict) their own national arrangements, so that their legal systems vary significantly in the levels of support they offer. In turn, countries like the UK with their (relatively) more generous welfare arrangements have been reducing migrants' access to welfare support, partly in order to reduce the perceived 'pull' factor seen as attracting migrants to their territory. The problem has only just started to be addressed at EU level through measures like Directive 2003/9, designed to lay down minimum reception standards.[8]

In operating support systems, governments are clearly influenced by a range of policy concerns including macro-economic 'efficiency' and social justice considerations. Popular hostility towards migrants is clearly another factor, and

---

6   States are increasingly restrictive in prescribing approved methods of claiming asylum, usually requiring claims to be made at the port of arrival. In-country applications may be possible, as in the UK's case; for example, permitting an application for variation of leave to enter and remain; Symes, M and Jorro, J, *Asylum Law and Practice*, 2003, London: LexisNexis Butterworths, pp 414–16. To deter in-country applications, systems increasingly provide for reduced support, or *no* welfare support (as with the UK's s 55 of the Nationality, Immigration and Asylum Act 2002). On such differentiation in Australia's reception support arrangements, see Odhiambo-Abuya, E, 'Asylum law: temporary and permanent protection programs in Australia – solutions or created problems?' (2004) 18(2) Immigration, Asylum and Nationality Law 115, p 136.

7   Walzer, M, *Spheres of Justice: A Defence of Pluralism and Equality*, 1983, Oxford and New York: Martin Robertson/Basic Books, p 31. This has become progressively more difficult in the face of global pressures, labour shortages, and the transfer of welfare costs from employers to the state.

8   Controversy surrounds even the existence of such a 'pull' factor, and yet it is a potent factor informing welfare policy, featuring strongly in the dispute between the UK and France over the Sangatte Refugee Centre; see Phuong, C, 'Closing Sangatte: the legal implications of the asylum dispute between France and the UK' (2003) 17(3) Immigration, Asylum and Nationality Law 157, pp 157–60.

history plainly shows just *how* potent this has been in shaping states' regimes.[9] The reasons for such hostility, and states' readiness to respond to it, are complex; but any anthropology of 'welfare' – that is, the pooling of risk and resources by the organised community (latterly the state) – is about priorities, and states generally give a higher priority to meeting the needs of 'their own' ahead of the claims of newcomers and 'outsiders'.[10] Reciprocity is also a decisive aspect. In the modern context, support is often only provided as a form of 'balanced', or conditional reciprocity.[11] Without the newcomer offering something in *return* for the support given by the host community there *is* no perceptible 'reciprocity'. Such ideas can be seen in action, and transposed to a modern setting, particularly in the context of expectations that migrants should be seen to be giving something *back* to their host communities. In the face of media predictions of a flood of new arrivals from Eastern Europe Accession States after 1 May 2004, the UK Government put measures in place to ensure that welfare support would *only* be available to those who 'come here to assist in meeting our skills shortages', and to 'work hard'.[12]

---

9   On 'efficiency' aspects of welfare interventions, see Barr, N, *The Economics of the Welfare State*, 2004, Oxford: OUP, pp 64–88. Cohen, S, *Immigration Controls, the Family and the Welfare State*, 2001, London: Jessica Kingsley Publishers, pp 181–203, tracks the history of popular hostility to migrants in the UK, and the relationship between immigration control and welfare support, starting with the Aliens Act 1905, the withdrawal of support for aliens in the 1920s, and later defining points.

10 'Modern denizens' has also been used to describe this group. When borders are crossed, and they arrive in their new destination, their status transforms to the rather more pejorative 'migrant', with civil, political, and social rights coming under attack after entry; Read, M and Simpson, A, *Against a Rising Tide: Racism, Europe and 1992*, 1991, London: Spokesman, p 30.

11 Sahlins, M, *Stone Age Economics*, 2004, London: Routledge, pp 191–204. Much of modern welfare is still founded on such principles, and this in turn has led to ECHR jurisprudence characterising contributory benefits, and paid-for services, as a form of 'property' for the purposes of Art 1 of Protocol 1 rather than as just distributions out of tax-funded 'schemes of social solidarity'; Lewis, J and Bowers, J, 'Article 1 of Protocol 1, ECHR – the peaceful enjoyment of property?' (2000) 7(6) Welfare Benefits: Law and Practice 17, pp 18–20; and Bowers QC, J and Lewis, J, *Employment Law and Human Rights*, 2002, London: Sweet & Maxwell, pp 17–18. Yet non-contributory, unreciprocated welfare distributions, such as social housing to the homeless, income support, etc, are essential for the purposes of maintaining social cohesion – especially for groups who are unable to work (or are prevented by state interventions from doing so), and who thus *cannot* 'reciprocate'. This is now part of what has been called the welfare 'mosaic' (see Barr, N, *ibid*, pp 6–9) and it is a form of 'welfare' that is particularly important for groups like new migrants. One of the reasons why New York is one of the few US states to protect, under its constitution, rights to unreciprocated welfare support is due to its location as a first port of call for European migrants – many of whom have had, and still have, significant welfare needs. On the operation of such systems, see Hershkoff, H and Loffredo, S, *The Rights of the Poor*, 1997, Carbondale and Edwardsville: SIUP/American Civil Liberties Union, p 3.

12 Prime Minister's Official Spokesman, 9 February 2004. These points were then implemented by the Accession (Immigration and Worker Registration) Regulations 2004, SI 2004/1219, and the Social Security (Habitual Residence) Amendment Regulations 2004, SI 2004/1232, ensuring that all such entrants first obtain a job, register, and complete a year's employment *before* being able to receive benefits, tax credits, social housing, etc. The restrictions have since been seen as counterproductive, as they impede efforts by employers, and government agencies (including those of the Department of Work and Pensions (DWP) and the Department of Trade and Industry (DTI)), to attract new skilled staff from Accession States into low wage sectors in high cost areas such London and the South East; and where transitional support is essential, for example in meeting housing costs. In *R(H) v Secretary of State for Work and Pensions* [2004] 3 CMLR 11 a judicial review of the regulations, invoking Art 7(2) of EC Regulation 1612/68, was partially successful on the basis that once employment is obtained discrimination in employment and welfare benefits matters is *not* permitted.

Similar considerations continue to inform the regime put in place by the Asylum and Immigration (Treatment of Claimants, etc) Act 2004, for example, using 'integration' loans instead of benefits and social services for refugees (s11); or by making the provision of accommodation for failed asylum seekers conditional on participation in unpaid 'community activities'.[13]

In the bigger picture, EU reception regimes can still leave migrants caught between two *very* hard places, that is, the denial of access to employment (or safe employment) *and* essential state welfare. This marks migrants out as having some of the worst living conditions of any social group in the community, and often significantly worse than other claimants living on mainstream state benefits.[14] Despite this, public concerns about migrants' threats to jobs, culture, and welfare systems continue to be an important factor in determining new immigration, welfare, and labour laws. In their responses to such pressure, governments may themselves be part of the problem.[15] Indeed, it was government action that precipitated the UK's continuing round of welfare restrictions on asylum seekers and those subject to immigration control. After housing and mainstream benefits were withheld from 'in-country' asylum seekers under the Asylum and Immigration Act 1996 (extending restrictions already in place for those in breach of immigration controls), Sue Willman recalls how advice bureaux and law centres like her own were 'overwhelmed by desperate clients who had no food and who in some cases were sleeping in the streets'.[16]

This prompted the courts to intervene in *R v Hammersmith and Fulham London Borough Council ex p M* (1998) 30 HLR 10, and decide that those 'in need of care and attention' continued to be eligible for help from local authorities under the s 21(1)(a) of the National Assistance Act 1948 (NAA). After local authorities then found themselves administering housing and subsistence-level support for thousands of people who had nowhere else to turn, the Government went into

---

13 Section 4(6)–(9) of the Immigration and Asylum Act 1999, inserted by s 10(1) of the 2004 Act. More recently, see the changes in the Immigration and Asylum Bill 2005.

14 Flaherty, J, Veit-Wilson, J and Dornan, P, *Poverty: The Facts*, 2004, London: Child Poverty Action Group, pp 199–201; and Palmer, G, Rahman, M and Kenway, P, *Monitoring Poverty and Social Exclusion*, 2003, York: New Policy Institute/Joseph Rowntree Foundation. Measurement of poverty and social exclusion among migrants may often engage indicators besides low income (Palmer *et al* at 2), including dependency on benefits (at 4, 5); unemployment (at 17); not in education, training or work (at 19); suicide (at 21); mental health (at 32); non-participation in civic organisations (at 40); and housing in temporary accommodation (at 49). The overall effect of this is to massively diminish social rights of the kind envisaged in Marshall, TH, *Citizenship and Social Class*, 1950, Cambridge: CUP, and Marshall, TH, 'Citizenship', in Marshall, TH and Bottomore, T (eds), *Citizenship and Social Class*, 1997, London: Pluto. Such principles are evident in Tampere objectives (discussed below) and are informing Title IV objectives seeking to approximate living standards of third country nationals to those of EU citizens.

15 A strand of 'moral panic' theory focuses on governments' role in mobilising popular antagonisms; Hall, S *et al* (eds), *Policing the Crisis*, 1977, London: Holmes and Meir/Macmillan, pp 16–18.

16 Willman, S, 'Who is responsible for supporting asylum-seekers?' (2001) 8(5) Welfare Benefits: Law and Practice 22, pp 22–23. These events undoubtedly marked the start of the present statutory framework; see Willman, S, Knafler, S and Pierce, S, *Support for Asylum-Seekers*, 2004, London: Legal Action Group, pp 48–55; and Clements, L, *Community Care and the Law*, 2004, London: Legal Action Group Publications, pp 147–51.

overdrive to warn about the country's welfare services being 'overwhelmed', and unable to cope. This continued to be a centrepiece in the case for *further* rounds of restrictions after 1999; and has been a key element, since 1999, in justifying the progressive removal of the last vestiges of mainstream benefits and community care assistance from asylum seekers and those subject to immigration control.[17]

After the mechanism in s 55(1) of the Nationality, Immigration and Asylum Act 2002 (NIA) was created, whereby support may be withheld from asylum seekers who do not make their claims as soon as reasonably practicable after arrival in the UK, the support regime entered a new crisis period. This has been punctuated by periodic human rights-led, court interventions to mitigate the worst effects of what, at times, has become a truly oppressive system. An intriguing insight into the scale of the crisis was provided when a Court of Appeal judge, Sir Stephen Sedley, spoke out at the Legal Action Group annual conference in London in 2003. He said that it had only been the combined 'triple effect' of, first, the Human Rights Act 1998, secondly, s 55 (10) of the Nationality, Immigration and Asylum Act 2002 (which enables support to be given, notwithstanding s 55(1), to avoid a breach of human rights), and, thirdly, the courts' power to make emergency interim orders (requiring support to be given), that was saving many asylum seekers and their dependants from 'starving in the streets'. More recently, the Court of Appeal in the *Limbuela* case utilised Art 3 of the ECHR and what must be seen as a judicially-created 'right to support' – based on principles laid down in *Pretty v United Kingdom* [2002] 35 EHRR 1 – to ensure asylum seekers receive essential welfare support when other sources of assistance are unavailable.[18] If a definitive history of the period between 1996 and 1999 ever comes to be written it is very likely that government warnings about a crisis in the support system will be seen to have become something of a self-fulfilling prophesy.

GLOBAL MIGRATIONS, LABOUR MARKETS AND 'WELFARE'

Despite the increased use of welfare restrictions to deter unwelcome forms of migration and asylum, and to facilitate removals[19] – a process also evident at

---

17   See *Fairer, Faster and Firmer: A Modern Approach to Immigration and Asylum* (White Paper Cm 4018, July 1998), and *Secure Borders, Safe Haven – Integration with Diversity in Modern Britain* (White Paper, Cm 5387, 2002); and the explanations that preceded s 14(2) of the Homelessness Act 2002 (introducing exclusions of asylum seekers, and those subject to immigration control, from housing allocations). Residual community care support is still available to meet exceptional needs that go beyond financial destitution, or when NASS support is not provided notwithstanding the 'destitution' requirements added in s 21(1A) by s 116 of the 1999 Act; see, for example, *R (Mani) v Lambeth Croydon London Borough Council* [2003] EWCA Civ 836; (2003) 6 CCLR 376, pp 384–87: and cases discussed by Puttick, K, 'Social security and community care' in Sir M Burton *et al* (eds), *Civil Appeals*, 2005, Welwyn Garden City: EMIS, Vol II, at Q800–04 and Q1001–1101.

18   *Secretary of State for the Home Department v Limbuela* [2004] QB 1440; [2004] 3 WLR 561; and see Puttick, K, 'Asylum support and *Limbuela*: an end (finally) to s 55?' (2004) 18(3) Immigration, Asylum and Nationality Law 186, pp 191–94.

19   Sections 9 and 10 of the Asylum and Immigration (Treatment of Claimants, etc) Act 2004. It is not clear, though, how this is necessarily a 'better approach' given the ensuing problems of destitution, the likelihood of claimants going 'underground', and the cost to local authorities when children are taken into care at public expense, as considered by the HC Home Affairs Committee Fifth Report (2003–04) (at para 40).

present in jurisdictions like the Netherlands (directed even at long-standing residents as well as unwelcome new arrivals) – most European states, like the UK, cannot disregard entirely the welfare needs of migrants entering their territories. In practice the distinction between regular and irregular (or 'atypical') migration also breaks down in the face of the significant and complex needs that new arrivals may have at the reception stage, as well as later in time. Apart from reception arrangements, governmental welfare systems are, in any case, essential in sustaining managed, regular migration, and in order to make a reality of EU freedom of movement principles. A number of factors are at play; but a key one is that third country nationals – whether they are working lawfully or not – often find themselves employed in segmented labour markets where there are poor working conditions and fewer occupational benefits to meet in-work welfare or more general needs. High turnover in such markets often dictates a need for significant levels of income replacement and state welfare assistance between periods of work. Away from employment-related needs, government schemes also play a vital integration role – especially through public sector housing, health and education systems.

In the newer Eastern European EU states, where welfare systems in the post-Communist era are still developing, a number of factors have prompted radical overhauls of state support, especially in response to the needs for a more mobile workforce, and the growth in temporary employment and residence.[20] Elsewhere in Europe, other considerations inform migrants' state support arrangements. In countries like Spain, where there is a heavy dependence on seasonal workers from the Maghreb countries, state support systems plays a vital role in facilitating employment, especially given the absence of occupational benefits in low-wage sectors like agricultural and food processing. Even in those parts of Europe where access to the labour market *is* readily available for new arrivals, and employment law interventions mean that a job (with adequate wages, occupational benefits, etc) *is* capable of becoming the main source of 'welfare' for the migrant (and any family dependants) – something which Third Way principles dictate is essential to obviate dependency on state assistance[21] – welfare needs can still remain high.

In practice, migrants can experience serious problems in accessing support. There are many reasons for this. In the first place, the host country may simply not

---

20 Andor, L, *Hungary on the Road to the European Union: Transition in Blue*, 2004, New York: Praeger; and Dziewiecka-Bokun, L, 'Poverty and the poor in Central and Eastern Europe', in Gordon, D and Townsend, P (eds), *Breadline Europe: The Measurement of Poverty*, 2000, Bristol: Policy Press.

21 Welfare claimants are urged to 'be independent' of the state, and are promised that legislation will 'make work pay', notably through tax credits and minimum wage interventions; see the *New Welfare Contract* in *New Ambitions for Our Country: A New Contract for Welfare* (March 1998, Cm 3805). UK Third Way approaches, though, are viewed critically elsewhere in Europe; see, for example, Esping-Andersen, G (with Gallie, G, Hemerijck, A and Myles, J), *Why We Need a New Welfare State*, 2002, Oxford: OUP, p 5. However, immigrants and asylum claimants are generally kept out of the ambit of Third Way measures and are often unable to work in order to be independent, and the UK's policy of excluding them from the labour market has been held not to be unlawful or irrational; *R v Secretary of State for the Home Department ex p Jammeh* [1999] Imm AR 1, CA.

provide much in the way of support. France, for example, is not traditionally noted for the quality of its support services for new third country arrivals, whether they are barred from taking up employment or not – which was probably one of the factors informing decisions by new arrivals, including residents at the Sangatte refugee camp, to try to progress on to the UK.[22] Other factors go beyond substantive welfare and support rights. I have in mind the problems of discrimination claimants can experience in securing substantive employment rights, access to income support systems like tax credits, and in the adjudication of sickness benefits, maternity-related rights, and so forth, which depend on employer co-operation.[23] In some cases state welfare provision is simply not geared up to meeting the support needs of ethnic minorities. This is something touched on in discourses on hybridisation and harmonisation of laws. It also raises doubts about states' *willingness* to adjust to pluralising pressures of the kinds described by Werner Menski and Mathias Rohe.[24] In the UK *some* progress is evident on this deficit in state welfare provision, for example in measures to meet the needs of polygamous households. An example is the State Pension Credit Act 2002, and 'polygamy payments' which supplement guarantee credits for additional wives.

For those who are excluded from employment, it is often the case that the combined effects of exclusion from mainstream employment, *and* inability to access state welfare – barriers linked in each case to immigration status – are contributing factors that prompt migrants to undertake highly exploitative, and sometimes dangerous, jobs in the most unregulated areas of Europe's labour markets.[25]

A further negative by-product of labour restrictions, linked to immigration and asylum status, is the difficulty of enforcing employment contracts and welfare rights that are dependent on lawful employment and 'employee' status. The inadequacy of government measures in the aftermath of tragedies, like the deaths of the young Chinese cockle-pickers in Morecambe Bay, produced outpourings of national rage, some of it directed against the government, and demands for 'action'. The newspapers sported headlines like 'Slavery 2004 – How Migrants are Lured to Britain to Work for 10p a Day and Fed on Dog Food' (*London Evening Standard*, front page, 13 February 2004); and 'MP Pleaded for Action on Cockling

---

22 *Op cit*, Phuong, fn 8.

23 *Service Delivery to Customers from Ethnic Minorities*, 1997, Benefits Agency; Mason, D, *Race and Ethnicity in Modern Britain*, 2000, Oxford: OUP; and Wayne, N, *Race Inequality in the Benefits System*, 2003, London: Disability Alliance. The Race Relations (Amendment) Act 2000 bars out discrimination in public decision making (including immigration-related welfare adjudication), but there are limits to how much such legislation can achieve, as considered at a joint conference on the subject, *Delivering Race Equality and Good Race Relations* (Commission for Racial Equality and Refugee Council, 24 November 2003).

24 In the volume accompanying the present one (Shah, P and Menski, W (eds), *Migration, Diasporas and Legal Systems in Europe*, forthcoming, London: Cavendish Publishing).

25 *Op cit*, Mason, fn 23, p 30; and Puttick, K 'Atypical and migrant workers' in Painter, R and Puttick, K, *Employment Rights*, 2004, London: Pluto, Chapter 22. *Op cit*, Symes and Jorro, fn 6, pp 444–45; and *op cit*, Willman, Knafler and Pierce, fn 16, p 37 *et seq*, discuss the current restrictive procedures regulating access to the UK labour market.

Danger' (*The Times*, 12 February 2004). Apart from a highly ineffectual licensing measure, the Gangmasters (Licensing) Act 2004, directed at gangmasters who supply labour and employers who use the gangmaster system to recruit (mainly in sectors such as agriculture and catering), little has been done to deal with the inherently weak position such workers are in at the private law level vis à vis their employers. Nor has action been taken to strengthen the role of regulatory agencies when they become aware of breaches of protective legislation. To do so would, no doubt, draw government agencies closer to the problems of the poor working conditions faced by illegal workers, and to some extent make those agencies complicit. Even when such workers have enforceable rights, for example not to be required to work hours in excess of working time limits, and agencies such as the DTI have duties to intervene, the obstacles to the practical realisation of those rights are enormous.[26]

Yet despite these problems that inhibit state welfare take-up, it is generally *only* the state that has sufficient resources to deal with the scale and complexity of welfare needs and support for employment. Modern state welfare systems have now adapted to most of the range of problems produced by the migration process. Although they have not been well-equipped to handle large-scale migrations, recent events, including the mass displacement of sizeable communities in former Yugoslavia, show how European states have *had* to adapt to such scenarios. This fact is now acknowledged by the enactment of Directive 2001/55 which requires states to provide support for such groups, and meet minimum standards of 'temporary protection'. Exceptionally, and in the absence of such state support, communities may be resolute and strong enough – and sufficiently well resourced – to meet their own welfare needs. This was a feature of the support given by the Kenyan Asian community to new arrivals from Kenya in the weeks that followed publication of the Commonwealth Immigrants Bill 1968.[27] Quite apart from legal considerations, in the modern context it is not good politics for governments *not* to render assistance – particularly when humanitarian needs dictate that they should, and the plight of newcomers attracts sympathy and media attention. This was amply illustrated when the Australian Government was subjected to a barrage of worldwide criticism when in 2003 it refused to yield to requests to permit refugees sanctuary: and permit their ship, the *MV Tampa*, to enter an Australian port – even after urgent calls for humanitarian support and safe haven.[28]

---

26 *Ibid*, Painter and Puttick, pp 503–05. On bars to welfare support linked to employment and residence status, see Puttick, K, *Welfare Benefits Law and Practice*, 2005 (9th edn), Welwyn: EMIS Publishing, Chapters 2 and 9.

27 That community 'rose to the challenge' of what became known as 'the Exodus', and organised the assistance required; Shah, R, 'A wrong righted: full status for Britain's 'other' citizens' (2003) 17(1) Immigration, Asylum and Nationality Law, p 5.

28 Willheim, E, '*MV Tampa*: the Australian response' (2003) 15(2) Immigration, Asylum and Nationality Law, p 159; and see, also, Shah, P, 'Australian immigration and asylum Law: an outsider's perspective' (2004) 18(1) Immigration, Asylum and Nationality Law 49 on the factors precipitating Australians' concerns about arrivals on their northern shores.

The truth of the matter is that most national frameworks maintain tight control over their welfare schemes and access to their labour markets. In doing so, they are able to utilise a range of status measures, even as a means of preventing their own nationals accessing state support – as can be seen in the use of the 'habitual residence' rule.[29] To that extent, for some claimants citizenship and nationality may be becoming less significant in terms of access to social rights than their ability to assist host states in meeting their labour needs – particularly during periods of skills shortages. This is one reason why current initiatives to extend entry rights to third country nationals have become such a priority. However, the perceived need among states to preserve *some* semblance of differentiation, particularly in the politically sensitive areas of employment and social rights, is another factor prompting states to preserve control over their welfare systems. In combination with the ability to bar out employment, such control also provides a potent means of *removing* those no longer welcome.

Given that this is something which Member States are unlikely to be willing to change, and because the EU is currently unable to insist on what Tamara Hervey has called 'top-down' regulation of national security schemes or 'replacement with a European-level social security regime', the best that can be expected for the time being is 'voluntary convergence' of EU support systems. This does not add up to much of a European policy, let alone substantive rights[30]; and even the less ambitious objective of agreeing 'transnational citizenship rights' and 'common principles' in this area is proving elusive.[31]

POST-TAMPERE: A CHANGING POSITION?

Disputes like Sangatte, and altercations between Germany and Italy after Kurdish refugees landed on the Italian coast, crossed Italy, entered Bavaria, and made asylum and welfare claims in Germany, clearly acted as a catalyst to develop common policies. In the latter case, Gunther Beckstein, Bavaria's Interior Minister was reported by the *Financial Times* on 8 January 1998 as saying (at p 2) that: 'More than half of all people who come to Europe want to live in Germany because the law is more liberal and welfare payments are higher than in other countries.' The flows of refugees into EU countries in the aftermath of the break-up of Yugoslavia and from war zones like Afghanistan also prompted action, and led the special meeting of the European Council in Tampere in October 1999 to lay down principles for working towards a Common European Asylum System (CEAS).

---

29 This can prevent UK citizens obtaining welfare support until habitual residence is established after an 'appreciable period of residence'; *Gingi v Secretary of State for Work and Pensions* [2002] 1 CMLR 20, CA, applying *Nessa v Chief Adjudication Officer* [1999] 1 WLR 1937, HL: and holding that there was no 'rule' on free movement established by the ECJ in *Swaddling v Adjudication Officer* (C90/97) [1999] All ER (EC) 217 which prevents the UK imposing such requirements.

30 Hervey, T, *European Social Law and Policy*, 1998, London: Longman, pp 82–83.

31 Baubock, R, *From Aliens to Citizens: Redefining the Status of Immigrants in Europe*, 1994, Aldershot: Avebury. On new welfare models, giving EU-wide rights on a more qualified basis, see *op cit*, Esping-Andersen, fn 21, pp 1–25.

The focus was not just on giving meaning and legal effect to the principle of non-*refoulement*. Acceptable conditions of support, primarily to enable refugees to remain in the country in which they arrive, were also seen as an urgent priority.

The Tampere 'conclusions', and later initiatives at the Laeken, Seville, and Lisbon European Councils, also sought to translate some of the more aspirational aspects of the Charter of Fundamental Rights of the European Union (2004), and non-discrimination principles in public international law, into positive obligations on Member States – an objective made clear in the Preamble to Directive 2003/9, para 6; but how far have measures like Directive 2003/9 succeeded in *delivering* on such objectives? The Directive offers important insights into the way EU common policy objectives in Art 63 are being implemented, and so a more detailed consideration of the scheme is merited.

DIRECTIVE 2003/9: COMMENTARY ON SPECIFIC REQUIREMENTS

The purpose of the Directive was to lay down minimum standards for the reception of third country nationals and stateless persons who make an application for asylum at states' borders or in their territories as asylum seekers. Family members, treated as such according to national law rather than under the Directive, are also within the scope of the measure (Arts 1–3). In order to maintain subsidiarity principles in Art 5 of the Treaty, considerable discretion has been left to Member states on implementation, and the Directive expressly preserves Member States' ability to introduce *more* favourable provisions (Art 4). This could, in time, prove problematic as all the indicators, to date, suggest that rather than such diversity in provisions what is needed is uniform provision consistently applied in all EU states. In the period leading up to the implementation date 6 February 2005 it became clear that some states, including the UK and the Netherlands, were intent on introducing some significant 'conditioning' on take-up of reception support. This appears to be permitted, albeit implicitly. In the UK's case, despite setbacks in the *Limbuela* case, the Government has consistently said that it intends to 'stand by' the policy objectives underpinning the s 55 of the NIA so that support can be withheld from applicants who do not make asylum claims as soon as reasonably practicable after their arrival.[32]

Given the way that immigration and asylum controls are inextricably linked to welfare support, *some* of the Directive's measures are particularly helpful. For example, documentation provisions in Art 6 mean that within three days of an application being lodged with the competent authority, certification of 'asylum seeker status', and confirmation of permission to stay in the receiving state's territory, pending applications being examined, must be given. This is likely to be important in the UK's context given the delays claimants can experience in

---

32   Statement on s 55 of the Nationality, Immigration and Asylum Act 2002: Court of Appeal Judgment 21 May 2004 (Home Office, Stat 017/2004).

receiving the documentation needed to facilitate support, as highlighted in the *Mersin* and *Arbab* cases.[33]

Conditions that require that recipients of support must remain on the territory of the host state are linked to reception requirements. This was one of the outcomes sought by the UK and other countries experiencing the problem of arrivals by migrants passing through other EU states' territories, for example in the Bavaria-Italy dispute. It is only when there are 'serious humanitarian reasons' that require an asylum applicant's presence in another state that the host state is authorised to provide travel documents to facilitate such travel (Art 6(5)). Freedom of movement is closely regulated in accordance with Tampere principles, and this includes restrictions by which claimants can be confined within the territory of the host state, and within 'an area assigned to them by that State' as long as the assigned area does not 'affect the unalienable sphere of private life', and permits 'sufficient scope for guaranteeing access to all benefits' under the Directive. Article 7 contains important powers which enable Member States to decide on residence, notably for reasons of public interest, public order, or the 'swift processing and effective monitoring' of an application'. For 'legal reasons', or reasons of public order, an applicant can be confined to a particular place (Art 7(3)); and provision of material conditions may be made conditional on complying with residence conditions. The Directive does not bar out detention, though, even for families. Although an appeal opportunity is given by Art 21 to contest a detention decision, the Directive does not regulate the detention process according to any specific *standards*; and this is likely, in most EU jurisdictions, to leave intact the discretionary powers of individual immigration officers.[34] Another area in which the Directive seems deficient, relates to families and the obligations on states to ensure that provision, including adequate accommodation, is provided for applicants and dependent family members.

Although states are obliged (by Art 8) to maintain 'as far as possible' family unity, and it is stated that the 'best interests of the child is to be the primary consideration', there is a surprising lack of specificity when it comes to detailed requirements for *realising* these important objectives. In the UK context, especially in areas where there may be shortages of adequate and suitable housing stock

---

33 *R v Secretary of State for the Home Department ex p Mersin* [2000] INLR 511, where it was noted that the Home Office is 'habitually guilty of unreasonable and unlawful delays in the dispatch of status letters'; and see *R (Ali Mohamed Al Haj Arbab) v Secretary of State for the Home Department* [2002] EWHC 1249; [2002] Imm AR 536. If such delays result in benefits or other welfare support being withheld, damages for breach of duty of care can be awarded; *R (Kanidagli) v Secretary of State for the Home Department* [2004] EWHC 1585.

34 On UK powers of detention in Sched 2, para 16, and Sched 3, para 2 of the Immigration Act 1971; and s 62 of the Nationality, Immigration and Asylum Act 2002, see, generally, *op cit*, Symes and Jorro, fn 6, pp 18–35); and on the controversies involved, see Cole, E, 'The detention of asylum-seeking families in the UK' (2003) 17(2) Immigration, Asylum and Nationality Law 94. On the inadequacy of effective appeal and review routes as an EU-wide concern, and detention as a disproportionate administrative measure, see Boeles, P, Brouwer, E, Woltjer, A and Alfenaar, K, *Border Control and Movement of Persons: Towards Effective Legal Remedies for Individuals in Europe*, 2003, Utrecht: Standing Committee of Experts in International Immigration, Refugee and Criminal Law, pp 12–14.

(particularly in London and the South East), it is likely to continue to be difficult in practice to achieve practical implementation of the family unity principle. For that reason it becomes necessary to see what the permitted fallback positions can be; for example, when there are delays in being able to meet special needs housing requirements during the reception stage. In practice, even when local authority social services have assessed families as having special needs for support under s 17 of the Children Act 1989, or when special needs legislation like the National Assistance Act 1948 is engaged for adult claimants, courts are often reluctant to make mandatory orders that have the effect of displacing local authorities' day-to-day management of the allocation of housing, particularly when this means asylum seekers and others are seen to 'jump' waiting lists and accorded higher priority than others. However, there are important exceptions and precedents like the *Batantu* case in which a mandatory order *was* granted.[35]

A further problem, in this context, is that the scheme appears to do very little to regulate accommodation and support rights after applications for asylum status have *failed*; or when the person is not in the asylum claims system at the point their needs fall to be assessed. When asylum seekers' applications fail, the extent to which states are obliged to maintain support will, it seems, remain primarily a matter for the state's own immigration, welfare and asylum systems under the Directive. This is a seriously problematic area in the UK, and the Directive's failure to regulate the process more effectively is very unfortunate. For the foreseeable future, national law and priorities will continue to prevail. The courts, for their part, have been increasingly careful not to interfere unduly in Home Office powers; and this can make litigation particularly difficult. Even the priorities of children and the family appear, at times, to rank lower in the pecking order than Home Office powers of removal.[36]

Despite the emphasis on family unity principles, the Directive has plainly not done much to slow down government plans to ratchet up restrictions in the support regime to withdraw support from failed asylum seekers and their family

---

35 *R (Batantu)* v *Islington LBC* [2001] 33 HLR 76; (2001) 4 CCLR 445, where the claimant, a refugee from the Congo, with exceptional leave to remain in the UK, had severe mental health problems, and lived with his wife and four children in high rise accommodation; and where the family was assessed as in urgent need of re-housing; and see *R (Wahid)* v *London Borough of Tower Hamlets* (2001) 4 CCLR 455; [2001] EWHC Admin 641, discussed in 'Community care services, mental health, and re-housing rights – the limits of judicial review' (2001) 8(6) Welfare Benefits: Law and Practice 14.

36 There is currently no automatic eligibility for support – either from NASS, the benefits system, or a local authority, particularly for those not co-operating with removal directions (given the restrictions in Sched 3 of the NIA). Support is largely discretionary, although the regime gives a strong steer in identifying the circumstances in which support should *not* be withdrawn without other arrangements being put in place; see, for example, s 18(1)(e), (2) of the NIA, which treats a failed asylum seeker as *still* an 'asylum seeker' for the purposes of support, even after a claim has been determined, if the claimant's household includes a dependent child under 18. Section 17 of the Children Act 1989 assessments for children in needy migrant households must have regard to Art 8 ECHR requirements, and take account of the child's needs, and links with UK-based family members; *R (M) v Islington LBC* [2003] 2 FLR 903, pp 918–20; reversed [2004] 2 FLR 867, pp 883–85, 892, CA; and see Coker, J, Finch, N and Stanley, A, *Putting Children First*, 2002, London: Legal Action Group Publications, pp 42–76.

members. This much is clear from the Asylum and Immigration (Treatment of Claimants, etc) Act 2004. The Government sees this as entirely consistent with the spirit and letter of the Directive, which is why that Act was able to add para 7A (as a new, fifth class of claimant: 'failed asylum seeker with family') to those rendered ineligible for support under Sched 3, para 1 to the NIA 2002. What is more, s 9(3) of the 2004 Act barred out appeals against the withdrawal of such assistance. The Directive's failure to do more to regulate removal powers is very surprising, particularly given the serious concerns there must be about any further extension of states' use of powers to withdraw essential day-to-day welfare support to effect removals. In debates on the 2004 Act, there were doubts expressed about *how* such powers would be exercised in practice, and whether they could be fairly used without running the risk of infringing Art 8 ECHR rights. The Home Affairs Committee was assured that immigration officers would receive 'guidance' to ensure assistance would not be withdrawn until after interviews, and decisions would be based on 'clear evidence' that the criteria for withdrawal were met. Nevertheless, such guidance is expected to be mainly non-statutory and 'non-binding'.[37]

Access to employment

In what is one of the most important elements in the legislation, Member States' authorities are again given wide discretion; in this case to determine the period, starting with the date an application for asylum is lodged, during which applicants will not have access to the labour market (Art 11). It is only after a decision is *not* taken within a year, and if the delay cannot be attributed to the applicant, that the state must then decide the conditions for granting the applicant access to employment (Art 11(2)).[38]

This has been interpreted to confer a 'right to work' from that point, but this interpretation must be doubted – especially as conditioning processes remain largely unregulated. The best that can be said is that once conditions are set and work is permitted, access cannot be withdrawn – at least until a negative decision on the asylum claim (and appeal) is notified. During appeals, access to employment may not be withdrawn, at least where an appeal against a 'negative decision' has 'suspensive effect' (and, of course, it may not).

---

37   HC Home Affairs Committee, First Report of Session 2003–04, para 62; and see the Fifth Report, paras 42 and 43. Among other things, there were concerns about whether the removal of support would be a proportionate response as a means of facilitating removal, and providing 'incentives' to leave.

38   The UK position, despite being characterised as 'discretionary', is already seen as largely compliant. The Immigration Minister, Beverly Hughes, in July 2002 indicated that the UK practice (after February 2005) would be to permit employment if a determination is not made within a year; see the note 'Asylum seekers working concession' in 18(1) Immigration, Asylum and Nationality Law 54. The courts are reluctant to interfere in employment restrictions; see the *Jammeh* case (fn 21, above).

Welfare support and housing

Member States are required by the Directive to ensure 'material reception conditions' are in place to assist applicants from the point when they make their application in accordance with national procedures and to 'ensure a standard of living adequate for the health of applicants and capable of ensuring their subsistence' (Art 13). Means-testing is permitted, something which in the UK is already a feature of the National Asylum Support Service (NASS) support arrangements in Part VI of the Immigration and Asylum Act 1999, the Asylum Support Regulations 2000, SI 2000/704, and in measures in the NIA (primarily within the definitions of 'destitution'). What the Directive does not do, however, is regulate the support claims, adjudication, and appeals process with any great specificity – something which is bound to be problematic in some EU jurisdictions.[39] Although the UK's housing provision and other forms of social security provision have been characterised as 'largely discretionary', public law principles, assisted by ECHR requirements, apply to decisions refusing or withdrawing it. If appeal rights are not available (and in the UK they are very tightly restricted) and support is *withdrawn* unlawfully the decision can be quashed in judicial review proceedings.[40] Test case litigation, which has highlighted some of the more negative aspects of the UK's support regime, including the 'dispersal' policy, has generally been unsuccessful – even when the circumstances indicate that ECHR rights are clearly in issue after applicants are placed in poor quality, unsuitable accommodation.[41]

In one particularly important area of the scheme, the Directive requires states to meet the requirements of those with special needs (Arts 13(2) and 17). The general principle in Art 17(1) is that states must take into account 'the specific situation' of vulnerable people, such as minors, unaccompanied disabled people, the elderly, pregnant women, single parents with minor children and people who have been subjected to torture, rape or other forms of serious psychological, physical or sexual violence. In the UK context, including those cases where NASS

---

39 Article 21 leaves the process of contesting decisions to 'procedures laid down in national law'; so it does nothing to improve the highly restrictive asylum support appeals regime in ss 103 and 104 and Sched 10 of the NIA. With Community Care, which delivers most of the assistance required by the more vulnerable asylum applicants, and dependants with special needs, the absence of appeal rights in most aspects of the system means that disputing decisions is largely relegated to judicial review or administrative complaints; see *op cit*, Puttick, fn 17, pp Q800–04; and *op cit*, Clements, fn 16, pp 531–42.

40 See *R (Hamid Ali Husain) v Asylum Support Adjudicator and Secretary of State for the Home Department* [2002] ACD 10; [2001] EWHC Admin 852, (2001) *The Times* 15 November. Despite the way enabling powers in s 95(1) and Pt VI of the 1999 Act are couched in discretionary and permissive terms, some commentators do regard the scheme as, in practice, providing 'entitlements'; see, for example Billings, P and Edwards, R, 'Safeguarding asylum seekers' dignity: clarifying the interface between Convention rights and asylum law' (2004) 11(2) Journal of Social Security Law 83, p 84.

41 In one case a family was dispersed to a notoriously dangerous and racist housing estate: but whilst confirming that Art 3 of the ECHR could be engaged, the court declined to intervene after concluding that the level of state protection required had to be commensurate with the degree of 'risk' in each case; *R (Mehmet Gezer) v Secretary of State for the Home Department* [2003] EWHC 860; [2003] HLR 64.

does not deliver support, this requirement does not, in fact, add anything to the qualitative aspects of the assessment and delivery process. Special needs over and above those delivered through NASS will generally trigger a right to a Community Care assessment; and unless the procedures adopted for carrying out and then implementing the results of assessment satisfy Public Law Standards it is likely that review rights will be triggered. The point has been illustrated by cases like *Batantu*[42] when the Administrative Court made a mandatory order requiring suitable accommodation to be provided after delays in re-housing.

CONCLUSIONS

The new reception standards in Directive 2003/9, and the other measures taken under Art 63, such as the family reunification procedures in Directive 2003/86, Directive 2001/55 on temporary protection for displaced persons, and Directive 2004/84 on minimum standards for determining the status of third country nationals and refugees (which also clarify the extent of rights to social protection and 'welfare' such groups should be afforded), are important steps in establishing an EU-wide support system for new arrivals. However, in key areas Directive 2003/9 has not delivered what was needed.[43] In particular, there are significant aspects of the asylum support process that remain unregulated, leaving considerable scope for Member States to act independently. In some cases this has plainly left the door open to national measures. Some of these, I suggest, are inherently objectionable – particularly in their use of welfare restrictions as a means of introducing disincentives for those who may well be genuine asylum seekers seeking to make *bona fide* asylum applications; institutionalising the withdrawal of welfare support from needy people as a 'removal' measure; and otherwise undermining welfare universality principles. In the last respect, there is surely a moral deficit created when legal rights to essential welfare support are differentiated according to nationality and migration status, rather than on the basis of need. To date, EU legislation, and the emerging blueprint for new initiatives in respect of third country nationals entering the EU, fall well short of the 'active and dynamic welfare state' and 'sustainable social justice' ideas mooted at Tampere, and which informed Lisbon European Council's conclusions in March 2000.[44]

These shortcomings are already proving to be problematic in some EU states. In the face of global pressures, and continuing migration into the Community, the need for improved social protection systems, consistently applied across the EU,

---

42 *Op cit*, fn 35.

43 On implementation in the UK, see the Asylum Seekers (Reception Conditions) Regulations 2005, SI 2005 No 7; Part 11B of the Immigration Rules (HC 395); and the Asylum Support Regulations 2000, SI 2000 No 704, as amended.

44 Esping-Andersen, G, *Why We Need a New Welfare State*, developing earlier themes in Esping-Andersen, G, *The Three Worlds of Welfare Capitalism*, 1999, Cambridge: Polity; on the EU's future role in developing new welfare initiatives, see the observations of Frank Vandenbroucke, Minister for Social Affairs and Pensions, Belgian Federal Government, in his Foreword, at x–xxiv.

is not simply going to go away. One predictable corollary of having inadequate welfare support arrangements *and* a bar on access to safe, well-rewarded employment, is the risk that a sizeable proportion of all new arrivals will continue to work in the informal economy, and be exploited in some of the worst, most unregulated, and dangerous sectors of Europe's labour market. Concerted measures to avoid this are well within the EU's area of legislative competence and should, arguably, be treated as 'cornerstone' Title IV and Employment and Social Policy objectives. As with other aspects of the 'common policy', though, action is well overdue.

CHAPTER 6

A 'COMMON' EU IMMIGRATION AND ASYLUM POLICY: NATIONAL AND INSTITUTIONAL CONSTRAINTS

Valsamis Mitsilegas[1]

The Amsterdam Treaty raised high expectations for the development of a common policy on immigration and asylum in the European Union. The 'communitarisation' of immigration and asylum policy, large parts of which became post-Amsterdam first pillar matters (in Title IV of the EC Treaty), was central in creating such expectations. The Community was granted competence to adopt a series of measures in areas ranging from asylum (including minimum standards on reception conditions, procedures and the definition of a refugee) to immigration (including visas, conditions of entry and residence in the EU of third country nationals and illegal immigration and residence) and border controls.[2]

Further impetus to such communautarisation was given by the Treaty provision that rules on external border controls, the movement of third country nationals, and asylum should be adopted within five years after the entry into force of the Amsterdam Treaty.[3] The European Council in Tampere raised the stakes further by calling on Member States to work towards the establishment of a common asylum system (para 13) and emphasising the need for approximation of national laws on the conditions for admission and residence of third country nationals (para 20) and the legal status of third country nationals (para 21). The Tampere Conclusions also called for tough measures against illegal immigration, especially trafficking in human beings, and measures ensuring the rights of victims of trafficking (para 23).

The five years since the entry into force of the Amsterdam Treaty have now passed (the Treaty entered into force on 1 May 1999). It is thus an opportune and appropriate moment to embark on a stocktaking exercise and examine how far the goals set out in Amsterdam and Tampere have been achieved and its expectations met. Notwithstanding Treaty 'communitarisation', intergovernmental elements in decision making on immigration and asylum, such as unanimity in the Council, a limited role of the European Parliament (consultation) and the possibility of a number of Member States (the UK, Ireland and Denmark) not to participate in EU policies, remained. Much has been written on the limitations that these more intergovernmental elements might impose on the development of EU common

---

1 Legal Assistant, Select Committee on the European Union, House of Lords. The views expressed here are personal and do not reflect the views of any Member, Officer or member of staff of the House or of the House of Lords corporately.
2 Articles 61–63 of the Treaty establishing the European Community (TEC).
3 Article 61a TEC.

standards on immigration and asylum, but not much on the impact these provisions have had in practice.

It is the issue of the actual impact of these provisions that this chapter will examine by focusing on how Member States used the more 'intergovernmental' Treaty provisions in negotiations in order to achieve their individually desired outcomes and what impact this has had thus far on the development of a common EU policy on immigration and asylum, and the nature of this policy. The analysis will be based primarily on the stance of the UK Government, as it unfolded during the parliamentary scrutiny of EU draft legislation by the House of Lords Select Committee on the European Union. On the basis of the lessons learned thus far, an attempt will be made to assess the viability of a common EU asylum and immigration policy in the light of the provisions of the draft Constitutional Treaty.

UNANIMITY

General

Unanimity has generally been viewed as a factor hindering meaningful harmonisation. It has been noted that unanimity in the Council tends to lead to agreements where the most reluctant actor determines the pace and the level of achievement.[4] This leads to the Commission anticipating the position of the most reluctant government when tabling proposals, thus perpetuating harmonisation by the lowest common denominator.[5]

In the case of many immigration and asylum legislative proposals post-Amsterdam, even the above predictions would prove to be over-optimistic. There is even an instance of proposed legislation, the draft Directive on the conditions of entry and residence of third-country nationals for the purpose of paid employment or self-employed economic activities,[6] in effect being defeated in the Council by some Member States questioning the existence of EC competence in the field. A number of other proposals have been eventually agreed, with many of their agreed provisions falling far short of the initial Commission proposal, both in the level of harmonisation and in the degree of protection granted to asylum seekers and migrants. It is no coincidence that this lowering of standards was particularly prominent in 'protective' measures, granting third country nationals positive rights, and not in enforcement/restrictive measures, which Member States appeared much readier to agree.

---

4   Egstroem, O and Joensson, Ch, 'Negotiation in the European Union: bargaining or problem-solving?' (2000) 7 Journal of European Public Policy 684, p 690.
5   Lavenex, S, 'The Europeanization of refugee policies: normative challenges and institutional legacies' (2001) 39 Journal of Common Market Studies 851, p 865.
6   COM (2001) 386 final, 11 July 2001.

The asylum procedures Directive

The draft Directive on asylum procedures has proven the most controversial and difficult to agree measure from the Commission 'asylum package' proposals (the others being proposals on reception conditions, the definition of a refugee and the Dublin II Regulation). The procedures Directive was the first to be tabled by the Commission in 2000 (and re-tabled in 2001) and the last to be 'agreed' by Member States. In an effort to reach the Treaty deadline of 30 April 2004, which had obtained greater political significance in view of enlargement (which meant that it would be easier for common standards to be unanimously agreed prior to the entry of ten more Member States in the EU), Member States reached a 'general approach' to the proposal at the Justice and Home Affairs Council of 19 November 2004. The draft has gone back to the European Parliament, which must be re-consulted since the text has been changed fundamentally since its last reading.

A detailed analysis of the Directive negotiations and their outcome falls outside the scope of this chapter.[7] Member States had to grapple with some difficult and sensitive issues, such as the concept of safe country of origin and safe third country, what constitutes 'effective protection', the issue of free legal advice and appeals in asylum procedures. Many Member States played the unanimity card in an effort, if not to transpose their own domestic system in the Directive, at least not to have to alter their existing domestic system at all after the Directive had been adopted. At the same time, some Member States attempted to achieve a result that would be consistent with proposed domestic legislation negotiated in parallel with the EU measure. Only a week before the April Justice and Home Affairs (JHA) Council, a Home Office Minister told Sub-committee E of the House of Lords EU Committee that there were a number of 'red lines' in the negotiations, which the UK Government would not cross.[8] Reporting on the JHA Council at the House of Commons, the same Minister said:

> I made clear that the UK would not accept anything which would prevent us from pursuing the approach in the Asylum and Immigration (Treatment of Claims, etc) Bill whereby an applicant who has transited a safe third country before coming to the UK may only challenge his removal on ECHR grounds.[9]

In the light of such attitudes, and taking into account the different procedures in Member States, reaching some sort of agreement on the issues appears to be quite an achievement. However, in the case of the procedures Directive this has led to both a dilution of common standards and a lowering of protective standards for asylum seekers. A good example of this is the provision on appeals. The rule in the Commission's initial proposal was that appeals must have suspensive effect and, subject to three derogations, the applicant may remain in the territory or at the border of the Member State concerned while awaiting the outcome of the

---

7   For a detailed analysis, see Craig and Fletcher, Chapter 3 this book.
8   *Further evidence by Caroline Flint MP on Asylum Procedures*, House of Lords EU Committee, 18th Report of Session 2003-04, QQ3–7.
9   *Hansard*, HC Deb Col 1424W, 24 May 2004.

appeal.[10] Four years later, Member States have reached a general approach on a provision which states that:

> Member States shall, where appropriate, provide for rules in accordance with their international obligations dealing with the question of whether the remedy pursuant to paragraph 1 [on the right to an effective remedy] shall have the effect of allowing applicants to remain in the Member State concerned pending its outcome.[11]

Member States must act 'where appropriate' and consider 'whether to allow applicants to remain'; not only has the explicit rule of the suspensive effect of appeals been removed from the text, but the text does not contain any sort of meaningful common standard on the right of the asylum seeker to remain in the territory of Member States pending an appeal.

A radical transformation from the Commission's initial proposal is also evident in the provisions on accelerated procedures. The five relatively short Articles in the Commission's proposal have been replaced by a series of lengthy provisions aiming to cover all possible circumstances when an application can be considered inadmissible or manifestly unfounded. The direction of the debate and content of the provisions raised concerns with NGOs and led to the intervention of UNHCR, which spoke against the adoption of these standards and put forward its own proposals on a centralised system of asylum procedures in the EU.[12] The definition of the safe third country concept has been central to the debate; Member States have come up with a number of criteria and safeguards in Art 27(1) and (2)[13] – including nationally determined rules requiring a 'connection' between the asylum seeker and the third country concerned, based on whether it would be reasonable for that person to go to that country.[14] This is, however, a general criterion for the crucial concept of effective protection and its content is left to Member States to determine.[15] There had been an attempt to establish more concrete criteria but this has been abandoned in view of the lack of agreement between Member States.[16]

Further concerns were raised by the inclusion in the Directive of the concept of 'super-safe' third countries – Member States may provide that no examination of the asylum application and of the safety of the applicant takes place where it has

---

10   Article 33(1) of COM (2000) 578 final.
11   Article 38(3)(a) of Doc 871/04, 30 April 2004.
12   These proposals were examined in detail in the House of Lords EU Committee Report entitled *Handling EU Asylum Claims: New Approaches Examined*, 11th Report, session 2003–04, HL Paper 74.
13   For a detailed analysis, see the chapter by Craig and Fletcher.
14   Article 27(2)(a). These criteria have been severely criticised by the European Council for Refugees and Exiles, which noted that the criteria 'fail to ensure that a person is only sent to a country which has ratified and implemented the 1951 Refugee Convention, adheres to other human rights standards and has an asylum procedure in place prescribed by law'. ECRE, *Broken Promises – Forgotten Principles*, 2004, p10 (available at www.ecre.org).
15   On different views on what constitutes effective protection, see House of Lords EU Committee, *Handling EU Asylum Claims*.
16   *Further evidence by Caroline Flint*, Q44 (see fn 8 above).

been established that the applicant is seeking to enter illegally or has entered illegally in the Member State from a safe third country.[17] The criteria for determining safety are minimal and less extensive than the criteria for the safe third country in Art 27.[18] The European Council on Refugees and Exiles (ECRE) notes that this means that Member States are allowed to outright deny access to an asylum procedure and to strip the asylum applicant of any rights to rebut the presumption of safety – the risks of *refoulement* are clear and Member States are not obliged to obtain assurances that the third country will process the asylum claim.[19] According to the UK Government, the provision was inserted, after German insistence, to address provisions in German domestic law whereby an asylum seeker may be refused entry to German territory at the border.[20] The UK Government also noted that this is not an issue for the UK as the provisions are aimed at countries with a land border.[21] However, this is not evident from the text of the Directive itself, and, even if this is the case, the implications of this provision for the rights of asylum seekers after enlargement, when the EU's neighbouring countries not bound by the Community *acquis* may be considered safe under it, may be considerable. This is yet another case where national standards have been introduced in an EU measure, and which may lower protection standards considerably.

The reception conditions Directive

Another asylum measure, the content of which was shaped by Member States playing the unanimity card, is Directive 2003/9/EC which lays down minimum standards for the reception of asylum seekers.[22] Member States were very close to agreeing a text by the summer of 2002. According to the Explanatory Memorandum (EM) accompanying one of the Directive drafts in May 2002, deposited for scrutiny at the House of Lords EU Committee and the European Scrutiny Committee at the House of Commons, Member States had reached a general approach at the JHA Council on 25 and 26 April 2002 and political agreement in the Council was scheduled for the JHA Council on 13–14 June 2002.[23] It was noted in the EM that there were no outstanding points of concern for the UK Government on the wording of the draft Directive.[24]

However, things changed dramatically in the next months following pressure from the UK and Germany. In the UK, negotiations on the Directive were going on

---

17 Article 35A(1))

18 Article 35A(2) refers to the ratification and observance of the provisions of the Geneva Convention without any geographical limitations, having in place an asylum procedure prescribed by law, ratification of the ECHR and observance of its provisions and designation by the Council.

19 *Op cit*, ECRE, fn 14, p 11.

20 *Further evidence by Caroline Flint*, Q54 (see fn 8 above).

21 *Ibid*, Q57.

22 OJ L31, 6 February 2003, p 18.

23 EM of 17 May 2002, para 19.

24 *Ibid*, para 16.

in parallel with discussion in Westminster about the Nationality, Immigration and Asylum Act 2002. One of the most controversial elements of this Act, s 55, allows for the exclusion of benefits from asylum seekers who had not applied for asylum upon arrival in the UK. This was confirmed by David Blunkett (who was then the Secretary of State for the Home Office), who wrote to the House of Commons in October 2002 saying that the Presidency agreed that the Council should work with a view to incorporating an addition to the Directive, proposed by the UK, to allow a Member State to refuse support in cases where the applicant does not submit their claim as soon as reasonably possible.[25]

Notwithstanding reactions by some Member States,[26] the Council accepted verbatim the UK proposal (which was adopted in exactly the same terms as domestic law).[27] Article 16(2) of the Directive states that Member States may refuse reception facilities in cases where an asylum seeker has failed to demonstrate that the asylum claim was made as soon as reasonably practicable after arrival in that Member State. This provision did not exist either in the original Commission proposal,[28] or in any of the Council drafts before autumn 2002, including the draft which was scheduled for political agreement in June 2002. It is yet another example of Member States using unanimity to export standards which they are aiming to impose domestically – and at the same time challenging the human rights of asylum seekers.[29] It must be noted that s 55 has been the subject of critical comments by English courts and members of the judiciary in so far as it may breach Art 3 of the ECHR – this led to an announcement by the Home Secretary in December 2003 that those asylum seekers who can give a credible explanation within three days of their arrival of how they arrived in the UK will be considered to have made their claim as soon as reasonably practicable.[30]

The German objection centred on the right of asylum seekers to have access to domestic labour markets. The initial Commission proposal stated that Member States must not forbid asylum applicants, and their accompanying family members, access to the labour market for more than six months from the lodging

---

25 *Hansard*, HC Deb Col 631W, 28 October 2002.

26 See Guild, E, 'Seeking asylum: storm clouds between international commitments and EU legislative instruments' (2004) 29 European Law Review 198, p 216, according to whom the Member State reacting was Sweden. Reporting on the November 2002 JHA Council, Lord Filkin for the UK Government wrote that 'with the exception of one Member State, Ministers agreed to amend Article 16 in line with the UK proposal'. *Hansard*, HC Deb Col WA94, 17 December 2002.

27 For a comparison, see Council doc 14658/02.

28 For an analysis of the background and content of the proposal, see Rogers, N, 'Minimum standards for reception' (2002) 4 European Journal of Migration and Law 215. See also the House of Lords EU Committee Report on *Minimum Standards of Reception Conditions for Asylum Seekers*, 8th Report, session 2001–02.

29 The UK (and German) position on the reception conditions Directive was criticised by Sarah Ludford MEP. See her letter in *The Guardian*, 30 December 2002.

30 See Stevens, D, 'The Nationality, Immigration and Asylum Act 2002: secure borders, safe haven?' (2004) 67 Modern Law Review 616, pp 620–22. For discussion on further developments see Keith Puttick's chapter in this volume.

of an asylum application.[31] According to David Blunkett in October 2002, 'one Member State maintained the view that the provision on access to labour markets should be deleted'.[32] This Member State was presumably Germany, which proposed an amendment to Art 11(2) that would, if the amendment was agreed, state that if a decision at first instance has not been taken within one year from the presentation of an asylum application, 'Member States shall decide under which conditions access to the labour market for the applicant can be granted'.[33]

The final version included a text similar, but not identical to, the German proposal. Article 11(2) states that if no decision is taken within a year, 'Member States shall decide the conditions for granting access to the labour market'. This provision is far from granting an unambiguous right of access to labour markets to an asylum seeker. It is narrower than the original Commission proposal, which granted access after six months (not a year) and included accompanying family members (not only the asylum seeker) in its scope. It has been reported that there are already different interpretations among Member States, with Germany arguing that it is up to Member States to decide, while the Danish Presidency (under which the proposal was agreed) took the view that access would be granted after one year.[34] This makes Art 11(2) a prime candidate for interpretation by the Court of Justice in Luxembourg. However, in a matter so crucial to the reception and integration of asylum seekers in Member States, the ambiguity of the provision and the lowering of the protection standards for asylum seekers and their families is regrettable.

Finally, one cannot help but note the outcome of negotiations on access of asylum seekers to vocational training. The Commission proposal included a similar clause to the one on access to labour markets and stated that Member States could not forbid access to vocational training for the asylum seeker and their accompanying family members for more than six months after the lodging of the asylum application.[35] The final version merely states that Member States 'may allow asylum seekers access to vocational training irrespective of whether they have access to the labour market'.[36] The provision appears to be purely discretionary and its value in developing minimum or common standards is questionable.

OPT-IN/OPT-OUT

General

An example of flexibility in EU law post-Amsterdam is provided by the arrangements between Member States that wanted to push ahead with the

---

31   Article 13(1).
32   *Hansard*, HC Deb Col 631W, 28 October 2002.
33   Council doc 14658/02, 22 November 2002.
34   *European Report*, No 2732, 30 November 2002, P IV-10.
35   Article 14(1).
36   Article 12.

communitarisation of immigration and asylum policies and the integration of the Schengen *acquis* in the Treaties and Member States, such as Denmark, Ireland and the UK, which were not willing to follow this pace.[37] In the form of an EU Treaty, these countries were given the option not to participate in proposals introduced under Title IV of the Treaty establishing the European Community (TEC) or to participate in proposals building upon the Schengen *acquis*. For the UK, the special position on border controls has been justified on the basis of the island geography of the country and the fact that the bulk of arrivals into the UK take place in ports and airports – this made systematic immigration checks the most convenient means of immigration control. For cultural and historical reasons, these external controls had allowed the UK to avoid the use of identity checks and identity documentation internally.[38]

The UK 'borders' Protocol maintains the right of the UK to verify the right to enter the UK of other EU nationals and to determine whether or not to grant other persons permission to enter the UK.[39] However, the modalities for UK participation differ on the basis of whether EC proposals are Title IV proposals or Schengen-building measures. The 'Title IV' Protocol allows the UK to opt into a proposal within three months after it has been presented to the Council, or to take part in it after its adoption.[40] The decision is thus purely for the UK to make. According to the Schengen Protocol, on the other hand, if the UK wants to take part in a Schengen-building measure, this has to be approved unanimously by the Schengen members. There is a real prospect, therefore, that an application for the UK participation may be rejected. Shortly after the adoption of the Amsterdam Treaty, it had been noted that the determination of whether a measure is Schengen-building or not is crucial.[41] This is essentially a political decision, and it has been predicted that it may cause tensions between the UK and Schengen states.[42]

In 1999, Jack Straw, the then UK Home Secretary, made a statement on the UK's policy on participation in Title IV measures. He noted that the UK Government's starting point was the Protocol on Frontier Controls, but that the

---

37 On these separate arrangements in general see Hailbronner, K, *Immigration and Asylum Law and Policy of the European Union*, 2000, The Hague: Kluwer Law International, pp 103–06; and Peers, S, *Justice and Home Affairs Law*, 2000, Harlow, London, New York: Longman, pp 53–60.

38 Evidence by Mr John Warne, then Director of the Organised and International Crime Directorate, Home Office, to the House of Lords EU Committee (Sub-committee F), *Schengen and the United Kingdom's Border Controls*, 7th Report, session 1998–99, Q23. For a critique of these arguments see Wiener, A, *Forging Flexibility – The British 'No' to Schengen*, ARENA Working Paper, Oslo, available at www.arena.uio.no.

39 Article 1.

40 Articles 3(1) and 4.

41 See the evidence of Mr Fortesque, then in the JHA Task Force in the Secretariat-General of the Commission, to the House of Lords EU Committee (Sub-committee F), *Schengen and the United Kingdom's Border Controls*, 7th Report, session 1998–99, para 32.

42 Monar, J, *Flexibility and Closer Cooperation in an Emerging European Migration Policy: Opportunities and Risks*, CESPI Working Paper, Rome, p 22, available at www.cespi.it.

UK was keen to engage in co-operation in all areas of present and future JHA co-operation that does not conflict with the UK frontiers control. The UK was interested, *inter alia*, in taking part in police and criminal law co-operation deriving from the Schengen provisions (including the Schengen Information System) and in developing co-operation on asylum. On immigration, Mr Straw noted:

> Our intention to maintain our frontier controls has implications for our participation in the direct operation of external frontier controls. For similar reasons, enhanced visa co-operation raises difficulty for us. But, within this constraint, we shall seek discussions with European Union colleagues to maximise the scope for mutual operational co-operation in combating illegal immigration, without prejudice to the maintenance of our national immigration controls. We shall also look to participation in immigration policy where it does not conflict with our frontiers-based system of control.[43]

The way in which this policy statement was applied by the UK Government in subsequent negotiations is examined below.[44]

UK 'opt-ins'

In line with Mr Straw's statement, and as seen above, the UK has opted into the negotiation and adoption of measures on asylum. On immigration, participation focused primarily on enforcement measures, such as the Regulation establishing Eurodac, the Directive on mutual recognition of expulsion decisions, Directives on carriers' liability and their obligation to communicate passenger data, and a Directive on the facilitation of the entry and residence of third country nationals in the EU.[45] The logic of British participation in some of the immigration control measures has been questioned, given that these are 'essentially commitments as among states between which border controls have been abolished'[46] – indeed, the facilitation and carriers' liability Directives are both Schengen-building measures. However, what this demonstrates is the UK policy of having two (instead of one) layers of stringent border and immigration controls (one at EU and one at national level) and the willingness of the UK to negotiate in order to shape the outcome of enforcement proposals.

A prime example of this policy is the stance of the UK regarding the draft Directive imposing obligations upon air carriers to transmit passenger data to

---

43 *Hansard*, HC Deb Col 381, 12 March 1999.
44 It is interesting to note the interpretation of the UK's position given by the Department of Constitutional Affairs. In a letter, dated 28 June 2004, to Lord Grenfell, the Chairman of the House of Lords EU Committee, on a Title IV proposal for a Regulation creating a European order for payment procedure (civil law), Lord Filkin stated that: 'each proposal is considered on a case-by-case basis but, unless a proposal affects the UK's border controls, the general policy is to opt-in unless there are strong reasons for not doing so.'
45 For a reasonably up-to-date list of the immigration opt-ins, see the Written Answer of the Immigration Minister, Mr Browne, *Hansard*, HC Deb Cols 204–205W, 29 June 2004.
46 Ryan, B, 'The United Kingdom' in Higgins, I and Hailbronner, K (eds), *Migration and Asylum Law and Policy in the European Union*, 2004, Cambridge: CUP, p 453.

border control authorities. This was a Title IV initiative by the Spanish Government and political agreement was reached at the April 2004 JHA Council, meeting the Amsterdam deadline.[47] The draft Directive was heavily criticised as being ineffective, imposing disproportionate duties on carriers and providing no remedies for aggrieved individuals.[48] Notwithstanding these reactions, and even though the UK Government accepted that, in many respects, the proposal was ineffective and, in any case, it would not change the UK's domestic arrangements, the UK decided to opt-in to the measure.[49] The UK Government framed the measure as a counter-terrorism measure and played the unanimity card in an attempt to water down the stringent data protection safeguards included in earlier drafts. Aided by the political impetus created after the Madrid bombings, the UK succeeded in lowering the standards in this context. Facing opposition from the House of Lords EU Committee, the UK Government decided to override the parliamentary scrutiny reserve and agree the measure in April regardless.[50]

UK 'opt-outs'

The UK Government's reluctance to participate in more positive measures was criticised by the House of Lords EU Committee in its Report, *A Common EU Policy on Illegal Immigration*.[51] In its response, the UK Government rejected the criticism as inappropriate and reiterated Mr Straw's statement.[52] However, UK Government practice thus far does justify the Committee's criticisms, as UK participation in positive measures has been minimal.[53] The following examples demonstrate the UK's reluctance to opt into any proposal that would give rights to third country nationals.

(a) Directive on short-term residence permits for victims of human trafficking

According to this Directive, Member States can give victims of human trafficking or smuggling, who co-operate with the police and provide information on trafficking, a short-term residence permit. Victims will be given a short reflection period determined by national law to think about whether they will co-operate

---

47 Council Directive 2004/84/EC of 29 April 2004 on the obligation of carriers to communicate passenger data, OJ L261, 6 August 2004, p 24.
48 See House of Lords EU Committee, *Fighting Illegal Immigration: Should Carriers Carry the Burden?* 5th Report, session 2003–04 and the evidence from the industry and NGOs.
49 *Ibid.* See, in particular, the letter of 9 October 2003 from Caroline Flint to Lord Grenfell.
50 Letter from Caroline Flint to Lord Grenfell of 11 May 2004 HL, EU Committee, Correspondence with Ministers 25th Report, session 2003–04 HL Paper 140, pp 118–19.
51 37th Report, session 2001–02, HL Paper 187.
52 Letter of 28 January 2003 from Lord Filkin to Baroness Harris of Richmond HL, EU Committee, Government responses for session 2001–02, 48th Report, session 2002–03, HL Paper 195, p 74.
53 For an overview, see Ryan, *op cit*, fn 46.

with the authorities. If they agree to co-operate, the national authorities will decide whether or not to issue the victim with a short-term residence permit. The final version of the Directive is much vaguer than the Commission's initial proposal, which called for a thirty-day reflection period and a six-month residence permit.

The UK Government decided not to opt-in. The reason was not, as one might expect, the possible granting of six-month residence permits, but the thirty-day reflection period proposed by the Commission combined with the perceived wide scope of the proposal. In a letter to the Chairman of the House of Lords EU Committee, Lord Filkin, then Home Office Minister, noted:

> ... although it is difficult to estimate the number of people who might eventually qualify for a short-term permit under the terms of the proposed Directive, it seems equally clear that the impact of allowing the majority of illegal entrants an automatic 30-day reflection period would far outweigh the likely effect of granting 6 months leave to remain to those who are subsequently found to qualify for the proposed permit. The fact that the reflection period does not create any entitlement to residence under the proposed Directive does not affect this position. The fact that the Immigration Service would be unable to take any action against the illegal entrant for 30 days is disruption enough.[54]

It is clear that the overwhelming factor that influenced the decision on whether to participate was the perceived potential of abuse of border controls by victims of trafficking. This 'logic of abuse' eclipsed any consideration of the need to protect vulnerable victims. This is also evident in a written answer by Lord Filkin in the House of Lords, in which he wrote that: 'any blanket grant is open to abuse and may create a perverse incentive for traffickers to exploit more victims by suggesting that they will be granted automatic reflection delays if they are trafficked.'[55] It is hard to see how this is a realistic scenario – would traffickers encourage victims to take part in schemes to denounce them, would they urge victims to present themselves to the authorities? It is very disappointing that this 'logic of abuse'[56] has prevented participation in a measure that does not even give unconditional protection to victims of trafficking, but provides some rights only at the discretion of the police and on condition that the victim becomes an informer. Non-participation does not sit very comfortably with the commitment of the UK to protect victims of trafficking in the UN Human Trafficking Protocol that accompanies the 2000 UN Transnational Organised Crime Convention.

---

54 Letter of 12 July 2002 HL, EU Committee, Correspondence with Ministers, 49th Report, 2002–03, HL Paper 196, p 221.

55 WA 149, HL *Hansard*, 27 June 2002.

56 This logic was also reflected in the UK Government's stance on the Directive on free movement of EU citizens in relation to family members: OJ L 158, 30 April 2004, p 77. The UK was against a number of the Commission proposals on the rights of family members (who in general are in a 'less unlawful' situation than illegal immigrants). In opposing a measure which would enhance the rights of EU citizens, and give rights to vulnerable third country nationals who have been married to EU citizens, the Home Office evoked the abuse of marriages of third country nationals to European Economic Area (EEA) citizens (letter of 29 November 2001 from Angela Eagle to Lord Brabazon of Tara) and stated that 'while we have no definite statistics, our experience shows that abuse of EC law by third country nationals is a growing problem' (letter of 17 December 2002 from Lord Filkin to Lord Grenfell).

(b) Directive on the admission of third country nationals for scientific research

This is a proposal that would introduce new procedures under which it would be for the host institution of a researcher in a Member State, and not immigration authorities, to make checks on the researcher. Any immigration checks would be confined to establishing the identity of the researcher and that the researcher does not present a threat to public order, security or health. The proposal aims to foster mobility and enhance the competitiveness of EU research institutions in the world. It differs from other legal immigration measures in encouraging mobility of a particular category of (highly skilled) entrant.[57] In this context, there may be a crossover or overlap between Home Office responsibilities and the responsibilities of departments, such as the Department of Education and Skills and the Office of Science and Technology.[58]

The UK Government decided to 'opt-out' of the proposal.[59] It has noted that, like the Directive on the admission of third country nationals for study purposes, the issues in the Directive:

> ... go to the heart of the UK's ability to set out our own policy in relation to the admission of third country nationals. Whilst the Directives offer a restrictive form of mobility, it remains in conflict with the UK's ability to make decisions on applications on the bases of the Immigration Rules.[60]

The extent to which other departments outside the Home Office have been consulted on the matter is unclear,[61] although the choice to opt-out may conflict with other policies that may be endorsed by other Government departments.

(c) Directive on the status of legally resident third country nationals

The Directive determines the terms of conferring and withdrawing long-term residence status by EU Member States to legally resident third country nationals

---

57 See letter of 13 May 2004 from Lord Grenfell, Chair of the HL EU Committee, to Caroline Flint.

58 *Ibid.*

59 Letter of 26 October 2004 from Caroline Flint to Lord Grenfell.

60 *Ibid*, para 22. See also EM on the Communication from the Commission on the First Annual Report on Migration and Integration, 8 September 2004, para 14 for similar sentiments.

61 The response of 22 June 2004 from Caroline Flint to Lord Grenfell states that: 'The [Education] Minister, Charles Clarke, has had sight of the Home Secretary's recommendation to opting-in to this measure and will be responding by 22 June, we are not aware as to his views. We have not, to date, consulted with the OST. As a matter of interest, Home Office officials are also currently in consultation with officials from the Department for Work and Pensions...'

and establishes the rights that this status entails.[62] The UK Government decided not to participate in the proposal and justified the 'opt-out' as follows:

> The proposed Directive would give long-term residents from one Member State the effective right to enter a second Member State and apply for residence there, provided they met certain conditions. We believe that, whilst the proposed Directive contains many provisions which are entirely consistent with our policy on participation in EU immigration measures, giving third-country nationals an enforceable right to enter the UK, without any checks or safeguards, is not.[63]

Underlying this stance is again a fear of abuse of immigration controls. There is also a level of confusion – and certainly a lack of clarity – on what constitutes border control. Under the borders Protocol, the UK maintained the right to determine whether or not to grant permission to third country nationals to enter the UK; but this control appears to be related to the crossing of external borders, and not to the conditions of admission of third country nationals to the territory of a Member State. So the emphasis of the UK Government upon the sanctity of national border controls in its decision to opt out of measures related to the admission of third country nationals to enter and reside in the UK seems somewhat misplaced. Indeed, it may be argued that some illegal immigration measures (such as the Directive obliging carriers to transmit passenger data prior to departure and the carriers' liability directive) – to which the UK has opted in – are much more linked to border controls than measures regulating the admission of third country nationals in Member States.

Measures where UK participation was rejected by other Member States – the example of the European Border Guard

The prospect of EU enlargement led Member States and the Commission, in the early 2000s, to start considering ways to enhance the management of the EU's external borders. Calls were made for a more co-ordinated management of the EU external borders, with the Commission (but not the Council) using the term 'European Corps of Border Guards'. An external border practitioners common unit was created within the Council, centres of excellence were created and various joint operations started to be organised at external borders. The UK took part in a number of these operations and led one of them (on maritime borders); the UK also hosted a centre of excellence in Dover.[64]

Notwithstanding the UK's frontier opt-out, the British Government was very keen to participate in joint border controls. The UK saw great value in operational

---

62 Directive 2003/109, (2004) OJ L16/44. For an analysis see Peers, S, 'Implementing equality? The Directive on long-term resident third-country nationals' (2004) European Law Review 437.

63 Letter of 7 August 2001 from Lord Rooker to Lord Brabazon of Tara, appendix 4 in House of Lords EU Committee, *The Legal Status of Long-term Resident Third-country Nationals*, 5th Report, session 2001–02.

64 For a detailed analysis of all these developments see HL EU Committee, *Proposals for a European Border Guard*, 29th Report, session 2002–03.

co-operation in border controls, and believed it could offer expertise. It was no surprise therefore that, when the Commission put forward a proposal for a regulation establishing an EU Agency for the Management of the EU External Border, the UK officially notified the Presidency of its wish to participate in the Regulation.[65]

However, the Schengen Member States did not accept the UK's request. The Regulation was framed as a 'Schengen-building' measure and the UK (and Ireland) were excluded.[66] The UK will be invited to sit at meetings of the Agency's Management Board, but will have no vote. The Management Board will examine requests by the UK and Ireland for participation in the activities of the agency. Such participation is a very limited role (with practically no say in decision making) and understandably the exclusion from the Regulation caused disappointment to the UK Government. In a letter from Flint to the House of Lords EU Committee, it was noted that:

> As negotiations progressed, it became clear that despite recognition from other Member States that UK participation is desirable on an operational level, and that there is some political impetus for reaching an imaginative solution, they were unwilling to show sufficient legal flexibility to accommodate us.[67]

Member States could indeed have shown sufficient flexibility. One way would be for the measure to be considered a Title IV measure dealing with border management. Another way would be to treat the Regulation as a Schengen-building measure, but to recognise that the control of EU external borders extends beyond the Schengen area, especially if one takes into account the control of maritime borders, a topic about which the UK has participated at length. As Baroness Scotland noted in the House of Lords debate on the European Border Guard Report, the UK has participated in around three-quarters of recent operational activities of the EU external borders.[68]

However, other Member States were not minded to show flexibility. This is a direct consequence of the UK's piecemeal approach to EU immigration policy. It confirms that the 'pick and choose Europe' that the UK advocates as its approach to EU immigration matters is counterproductive, and the UK leverage in important negotiations limited.[69] The European Border Agency is the cornerstone of future EU policy and operations on border controls and illegal immigration – and the Schengen Member States will not show the political will to include countries that do not participate wholeheartedly.

---

65 EM, 7 February 2004.
66 Doc 9018/04, 30 April 2004, Recital 25.
67 Letter of 24 March 2004 from Caroline Flint to Lord Grenfell, HL EU Committee, Correspondence with Ministers, 25th Report, session 2003–04, HL Paper 140, pp 120–21.
68 *Hansard*, HC Deb Vol 656, Col 366, 8 January 2004.
69 Speaking on EU immigration policy in the House of Commons debate Tony Blair, the UK Prime Minister, justifying the UK 'opt-out' from these measures, said: 'The simple position is that we are entitled to decide whether we opt in to any of these measures. That is the pick and choose Europe, if you like'. *Hansard*, HC Deb Col 58, 8 November 2004, 1.

Many would argue that the UK participation in measures destined to regulate an area without internal frontiers is illogical. The outcome of the negotiations on the European Border Agency, and the Visa Information System,[70] where the UK was similarly excluded, confirm the view that the selective opt-in position for the UK and Ireland does not detract from the fact that the new area of freedom, security and justice has been constructed on the assumption that both countries will normally not participate in migration policy applying to that area.[71] It remains to be seen if the UK will manage to reverse the political stance of Schengen Member States to exclude it from EU immigration policy via a legal route, by its challenge, in the Court of Justice in Luxembourg, of the legality of its exclusion from the Border Agency Regulation I.[72]

THE CONSTITUTIONAL TREATY

A major development in the Constitutional Treaty[73] is the true communitarisation of immigration and asylum policies. Law-making in these areas will take place under the 'legislative' procedure – with qualified majority voting and co-decision – which will give the European Parliament, traditionally more integrationist than the Council in these areas and more protective of the immigrant and the asylum seeker, a much greater influence and say.[74]

---

70 Although the UK Government does not participate in the EU common visa list, it applied to take part in the Decision establishing a Visa Information System: OJ L 213, 15 June 2004, p 5. The lack of consistency in the approach is evident – the measure was labelled Schengen-building and UK participation was excluded. According to the UK Government, the EU 'should not place legalistic hurdles in the way of sensible co-operation between those in Schengen and those outside it': Letter of 10 May 2004 from Caroline Flint to Lord Grenfell, HL EU Committee, Correspondence with Ministers (see fn 67), p 136.

71 *Op cit*, Monar, fn 42, p 11.

72 See letter of 27 October 2004 from Caroline Flint to Lord Grenfell. The Minister notes that:

    [w]e are making the challenge because we consider that the UK has been wrongly prevented from participating in adoption of the Border Agency Regulation and it is important to establish the correct legal position, both in relation to this Regulation and future Schengen Building Measures.

73 Doc CIG 87/1/04 REV 1, 13 October 2004.

74 Article 67(5) of the TEC as amended in Nice states that asylum proposals (still on minimum standards) will be adopted by co-decision provided that the Council has previously adopted Community legislation defining the common rules and basic principles governing these issues. It is not clear whether agreement in all four proposals of the asylum package is required for Art 67(5) to be triggered and the next stage to begin. At this stage, the Council is nearly there, with three out of four measures of the asylum package being agreed and the Procedures Directive being at the stage of a 'general' approach' (even though the subsequent JHA Council of 19 July spoke of political agreement). Can Member States embark on negotiations for a further stage on a measure which has already been agreed, in spite of the fact that formal agreement has not been reached on the Procedures Directive? The Hague Programme implies that the answer is negative, when it states that '[t]he European Council urges the Member States to implement fully the first phase without delay. In this regard the Council should adopt unanimously, in conformity with Article 67(5) TEC, the Asylum Procedures Directive as soon as possible' (point 1.3).

Regarding competences, there is a qualitative development in asylum policy, where the 'minimum standards' requirements of the Amsterdam and Nice Treaties have been replaced by calls for a 'uniform status' of asylum and subsidiary protection and common procedures.[75] The immigration Article contains an explicit legal base for measures defining the rights of third country nationals residing legally in Member States, including the conditions governing freedom of movement and of residence in other Member States.[76] It has been argued that this may solve the legal base problems that proposals on the right to paid employment have encountered.[77] Finally, and very importantly, Article III-169 states that asylum and immigration policies will be governed by the principles of solidarity and fair sharing of responsibility.

However, intergovernmental elements still remain, most notably in the area of legal migration. There is a reference to the integration of legally resident third country nationals, but due to Member States' sensitivities this will exclude any harmonisation.[78] There is also an explicit provision stating that the immigration Article will not affect the right of Member States to determine the number of third-country nationals, coming to their territory in order to seek work, who are admitted.[79] Lastly, no change regarding the position of the UK, Ireland and Denmark is proposed – the Protocols remain.[80]

CONCLUSION

Those who had high expectations for the development of meaningful common EU standards on immigration and asylum post-Amsterdam and Tampere must be disappointed. The development of common standards was hampered by unanimity in the Council, with Member States trying to export their domestic standards, leading at times to harmonisation on the basis of the lowest common denominator. In the light of heated domestic debates on immigration and asylum, which at times led to the lowering of domestic standards of law in Member States, the standards in EU instruments were lowered during negotiations. The growing securitisation of immigration and asylum, has led to a plethora of EU instruments of enforcement against illegal immigration, a number of instruments on asylum with watered-down standards and a minimal number of laws on legal migration and the rights of third country nationals; the Commission has pertinently noted

---

75　Article III-266. It is interesting, in this regard, that the Commission has recently floated the idea of a single asylum procedure. See the Commission Communication entitled 'A more efficient common European asylum system: the single procedure as the next step', COM (2004) 503 final, 15 July 2004.

76　Article III-267(2)(b).

77　See the chapter by Cholewinski in the companion volume.

78　Article III-267(4).

79　Article III-267(5).

80　The Foreign Office White Paper on the Treaty establishing a Constitution for Europe (Cm 6309) emphasises the maintenance of the UK border controls. It states explicitly that the Constitution 'preserves unchanged the UK's right to carry out checks at its borders' (para 71).

that the Union has so far failed to produce a common concept of admission for economic purposes.[81]

Will things change in the future? In the short term, with unanimity in a Union of 25 countries, and in view of the fundamental differences in perception of the asylum and immigration phenomena in Member States, it is rather unlikely. Moreover, new Member States may be reluctant to agree more laws before fully implementing what has been agreed thus far. In the field of asylum, it has been argued that enlargement may have an impact on the direction of legislation, as 'after enlargement any attempt to develop the *acquis* in a more liberal direction will need to overcome the new Member States' affinity with the first version of the *acquis*'.[82] However, in view of the fact that many of the enforcement measures adopted thus far were aimed at addressing the perceived shortcomings in the ability of new Member States to effectively guard the new EU border, enlargement may have the effect of new Member States pushing for more liberal measures. This is especially the case in the area of border controls with neighbouring countries in the East (the EU's 'new neighbours'), with which new Member States have historical, economic and social ties, which may be disrupted by imposing tight border controls at the EU external border.[83] New Member States may also be reluctant to support proposals for further integration in the operational sphere, such as the transformation of the European Border Agency to a European Corps of Border Guards guarding the EU's external border.[84]

A change in the legislative procedure, on one hand, and a move to majority voting on the other hand – envisaged across the board in the draft Constitutional Treaty – may lead to further harmonisation and a different direction in the content of EU legislation. At the moment the Nice arrangements are a step forward compared to Amsterdam, but are not quite there. The Protocol on Art 67 TEC, attached to the Nice Treaty, states that from May 2004 the Council will act by qualified majority on Commission proposals and after consulting the European Parliament in order to adopt the measures referred to in Art 66 TEC (which

---

81 Communication on the results of the Tampere programme and future guidelines, staff paper SEC (2004) 680 at p 17. In its first annual Report on migration and integration, the Commission stresses the failure of Member States to reach agreement on the draft Directive on the admission of third country nationals for employment purposes, and calls for a level playing-field in terms of admission policies for economic migrants across the EU, COM(2004) 508 final, 16 July 2004, pp 7 and 9.

82 Byrne, R, Noll, G and Vedsted-Hansen, J, 'Understanding refugee law in an enlarged European Union' (2004) 15 European Journal of International Law 355, p 371.

83 For the problems of the new EU external border see Mitsilegas, V, 'The implementation of the EU *acquis* on illegal immigration by the candidate countries of Central and Eastern Europe: challenges and contradictions' (2002) 28 Journal of Ethnic and Migration Studies 665.

84 This idea was proposed by the Commission some years ago, but was frozen in the negotiations toward the establishment of an Agency for the Management of the EU's external border (political agreement on which was reached in spring 2004). The Commission however has re-tabled the idea in its Tampere-II Communication. The Hague Programme once again watered down the Commission wording by speaking of a European System of Border Guards. On the issues arising from such proposals and the stance of new Member States see the Report by the House of Lords EU Committee *Proposals for a European Border Guard*, 29th Report, session 2002–03, HL Paper 133.

concerns operational co-operation between national administrations) – so on operational co-operation we have majority voting, but only consultation (and not co-decision) of the European Parliament. As said above, measures on asylum will be adopted by co-decision 'provided that the Council has previously adopted Community legislation defining the common rules and basic principles governing these issues'.[85] Law-making in other Title IV areas (including border controls and illegal immigration) can be adopted under the co-decision procedure if the Council agrees unanimously.[86] The only area that moved to co-decision in May 2004, explicitly under the Nice Treaty, involves rules on the issuing of visas and rules on a uniform visa.[87] As Pastore has noted, 'it will consequently be a confused patchwork of different decision-making methods that will govern the development of the entry control system of the enlarged EU'.[88]

This complex situation has been addressed by the Hague Programme, which calls on Member States to make use of the Treaty provision and move from unanimity in the Council and consultation of the European Parliament to qualified majority and co-decision in the remaining areas of immigration and asylum law (with the exception of legal migration) by 1 April 2005 (point 1.2). The Dutch EU Presidency has tabled a proposal to that effect,[89] and has prioritised its adoption by the end of the Presidency in December 2004. There were disagreements between Member States on whether issues such as guidelines on the integration of migrants in EU Member States (which in any case will not amount to harmonising measures) will be moved to the Art 251 procedure (some Member States want to keep unanimity in this area). Agreement was finally reached at the end of the Dutch Presidency. A Council Decision moved decision making on most of the areas of immigration and asylum law to qualified majority voting and to decision as of 1 January 2005. Measures on integration were formally excluded.[90]

---

85   Article 67(5) TEC.
86   Article 67(2) TEC. Declaration No 5 concerning Art 67 annexed to the Nice Treaty contains a political commitment to change over to co-decision immediately after 1 May 2004 for the measures provided for by Arts 62(3) and 63(3)(b) concerning the free movement of third country nationals, and illegal immigration and residence. The Commission, in its Tampere II Communication, notes that this must be taken into account in interpreting Art 67(2) TEC and that it would be legitimate to make use of this facility immediately after 1 May; COM (2004), 2 June 2004, p 5.
87   Article 67(4) TEC. Rules on common visa lists and a uniform format for visas were subject to majority voting already, post-Amsterdam, but with the European Parliament being only consulted – Art 67(3) TEC.
88   Pastore, F, 'Visas, borders, immigration: formation, structure, and current evolution of the EU entry control system', in Walker, N (ed), *Europe's Area of Freedom, Security and Justice*, 2004, Oxford and New York: OUP, p 137.
89   Document 14497/04, 12 November 2004. According to recital 4 of the document, the adoption of the asylum procedures Directive is a pre-requisite to the move to the second (majority voting) stage of the EU asylum policy.
90   Council Decision of 22 December 2004 providing for certain areas covered by Title IV of Part Three of the Treaty establishing the EC to be governed by the protective laid down in Art 251 of that Treaty – OJ L396, 31 December 2004, p 45. The Decision contains a recital aiming to regulate the move to the second stage of the Common European Asylum System (Recital 4) where the procedure in Art 251 TEC will apply. The wording is not entirely clear, but the UK Government has interpreted it as requiring a unanimous agreement to the procedures Directive to be necessary to allow MSC to move on to the second stage – EM of 18 November 2004, by Caroline Flint to the HL EU Committee.

It remains to be seen whether, and how, Member States' attitudes will change when negotiating EU proposals on immigration and asylum under co-decision. It is noteworthy that the UK, which has participated actively in the first stage of negotiations about the asylum proposals, now argues that there is no need for further legislation and common standards[91] (although the Constitutional Treaty envisages such progress). It will be interesting to see whether majority voting on immigration and asylum will result in an increase in opt-outs for the UK and Ireland and whether Member States, old and new, will make use of the provisions on enhanced co-operation to move ahead regarding certain policies.

The role of the European Parliament is central in this process. Judging from its current action in the fields of immigration and asylum, the Parliament's greater involvement may improve legislation both in terms of aiming for common standards and in terms of enhancing the rights of third country nationals. European Parliament involvement may also 'Europeanise' the debate on immigration and asylum. At the moment, these are largely viewed as purely national issues in Member States,[92] with very different kinds of debate taking place in different parts of the EU. The European Parliament may help to focus on the need for a common approach to these issues in a borderless Europe, most notably in the area of legal migration where little progress has been made thus far. The European Parliament may shift the focus of EU immigration and asylum policy from enforcement to protection – but it remains to be seen how Member States will react in this context. It may be possible for such moves to be countered by joint initiatives outside the EU framework, a good example being the summits of the G5 countries (the UK, France, Germany, Italy and Spain), which are already discussing counter-terrorism matters and which have recently discussed the issue of extra-territorial asylum processing and the creation of 'asylum camps' outside the EU territory.

In this context of competing interests and perceptions, a fundamental contribution to the development of common EU standards on immigration and asylum, respecting the rights and dignity of immigrants and asylum seekers, can be made by the Court of Justice in Luxembourg. The Court has already developed a protective approach to third country nationals, its case law creating principles that have many times constrained national enforcement action against them. If there is one advantage in the adoption of EU standards, even in their current, watered-down form, it is that it gives an opportunity to the Court to interpret the standards. The current ambiguities may be developed into common standards and the position of third country nationals examined in the light of the ECHR and (increasingly) the EU Charter of Fundamental Rights.

---

91 Explanatory Memorandum on the Tampere II Communication, para 16.
92 As Jorg Monar has noted, the 320-page 2001 Sussmuth Report evaluating the immigration situation in Germany first mentioned the EU dimension of immigration policy rather briefly on p 176. Monar, J, 'Justice and Home Affairs: Europeanization as a government-controlled process' (2003) 119 Proceedings of the British Academy 309, p 318.

CHAPTER 7

DETENTION OF ASYLUM SEEKERS AND REFUGEES AND INTERNATIONAL HUMAN RIGHTS LAW

Dan Wilsher

Detention of asylum seekers is a common and increasing practice amongst states.[1] This is a response to larger numbers of migrants fleeing alleged persecution. This use of detention has become closely entwined with the operation of the 1951 Convention on the Status of Refugees and concern that it is being exploited by large numbers of migrants. Detention is one response to this perception of abuse. States have sought thereby to regain a measure of control over their territorial sovereignty and prevent those not entitled to admission from entering. Another issue has been the deportation of non-nationals, including recognised refugees, perceived to be a threat to public order. Detention has been employed more frequently to remove such criminal non-nationals from society pending expulsion. Immigration detention is, however, ostensibly non-punitive although its consequences can be severe.

Immigration legislation relating to asylum seekers and refugees in general, permits such administrative detention to be indefinite. Asylum seekers and deported refugees are often subject to lengthy periods of detention, sometimes amounting to several years. Delays in both the processing of the decision to expel or refuse admission (which may be subject to prolonged appeals and reviews) are common. Even when a final decision has been made, there can also be grave difficulties in securing permission from another state to admit non-nationals after they have exhausted all remedies against return. Such lengthy, or even limitless, administrative detention raises serious human rights concerns. Within the common law tradition, habeas corpus was one of the central guarantees against infringement of the right to liberty by arbitrary detention.[2] The concern for protecting individual liberty against executive detention is reflected in the texts of the key international human rights conventions.

A claimed human right of asylum seekers and refugees to respect for their liberty, however, conflicts with the well-established right of states, conferred by both national and public international law, to control the admission and expulsion of non-nationals. Detention pending a decision on whether a non-national shall be

---

1   *Recommendations as Regards Harmonisation of Reception Standards for Asylum Seekers in the EU, Part A: Summary of State Practice*, July 2000, Geneva: UNHCR, p 31.

2   See Holdsworth, WS, *A History of English Law*, 1926, London: Methuen, Vol IX, pp 104–25. For the position in the US, see Duker, WF, *A Constitutional History of Habeas Corpus*, 1980, Westport: Greenwood Press. For a comparative examination of Commonwealth countries, see Clark, D and McCoy, G, *The Most Fundamental Right*, 2000, Oxford: Clarendon. See, for a modern review, Sharpe, RJ, *The Law of Habeas Corpus*, 2nd edn, 1989, Oxford: Clarendon.

admitted is arguably necessary in order for territorial sovereignty to be respected. Should a state be required to allow an asylum seeker to be at large on their territory until satisfied that they are indeed a refugee under the 1951 Convention? Likewise, where a state has made a decision to expel a refugee on public order grounds, should such a person be permitted to remain at liberty on the territory of that state pending their expulsion?

Non-discrimination norms certainly call into question the use of detention against non-nationals in situations where nationals would not be incarcerated. If the liberty of non-nationals is worthy of equal respect, much immigration detention is of dubious justification. Even if non-nationals do not have exactly the *same* liberty rights as nationals, it is important to set proper limits to their detention so that it is not arbitrary. This chapter considers the international legal jurisprudence on this question and attempts to formulate some principles that might be useful in striking the correct balance between state sovereignty and individual liberty.

It is important before considering the detailed case law, to distinguish between direct and indirect challenges to immigration detention. Many human rights claims are brought seeking to prevent deportation itself on the grounds that a detainee may be tortured if removed. The effect of a successful challenge to an immigration decision upon the legality of an underlying detention decision is limited. The European Court of Human Rights, for example, has held that where the deportation order itself is illegal because it violates national or Convention law, detention pending execution of that order is, however, not a breach of the right to liberty.[3] This is an example of the 'fourth instance' doctrine adopted by the Strasbourg court. This states that the merits of an underlying administrative decision or criminal conviction cannot be reviewed by the international court in order to impugn the compatibility of a detention order with the European Convention.[4] This view has been implicitly endorsed in relation to the International Covenant on Civil and Political Rights by the Human Rights Committee.[5] This chapter seeks to concentrate upon direct challenges to immigration detention. The reasons why states seek to deport persons should remain a separate question from the one under consideration, namely when is detention considered justifiable as a matter of international and domestic law.

Before moving on to the substantive analysis, it should be noted that this chapter proceeds on the basis that the rules governing detention of asylum seekers and refugees are essentially the same as those relating to migrants generally. The reason a migrant has entered or applied to enter another country does not, in general, affect the legality of their detention in international law terms. Thus, whilst a person fleeing persecution might be thought to deserve

---

3   See *Chahal v United Kingdom* (1997) 23 EHRR 413.
4   App 3245/67, *X v Austria*, 4 February 1969, (1969) 12 Yearbook 206, 236.
5   See *C v Australia* No 900/1999. Meeting on 28 October 2002. In this case, a detainee was refused asylum and held in detention for two years before this decision was reversed and he was awarded refugee status. His detention was in breach of Art 9, but not on the ground that the immigration decision had been wrong in domestic and international law.

greater respect for their liberty than an economic migrant, the case law does not on the whole support such a view. There is some indication from, for example, the United Nations High Commissioner for Refugees (UNHCR) that detention should be used sparingly in relation to asylum seekers.[6] This is however no more than guidance and has not featured significantly in the human rights case law. The reality is that many asylum claims are unfounded and that for a liberty interest to depend simply on the nature of the application would be wrong in principle. Weak asylum claimants would have more right to liberty than others and it seems hard to justify this. Perhaps a distinction of more importance is that between legal resident non-nationals and those who have never been granted status. There is some support for the view that the former have greater rights to liberty than the latter. This perhaps accords with the intuitive view that migrants' rights should increase if they become integrated into their new country.

CUSTOMARY INTERNATIONAL LAW AND DETENTION OF ASYLUM SEEKERS AND REFUGEES

Public international law is clear in laying down a firm rule that sovereign states have the right to control the admission to and expulsion from their territories of non-nationals.[7] This right is restricted in that limits are imposed both by customary international law and by treaties.[8] These include Arts 32 and 33 of the Convention on the Status of Refugees and Arts 3 and 8 of the European Convention on Human Rights (ECHR). Pursuant to customary international law, a state must have some form of administrative and/or judicial procedure for determining if a non-national should be either expelled or denied admission.[9] State practice in the form of legislation commonly confers executive power to detain until a non-national has been returned to another country.

These powers are entirely consistent with the general customary international law power to control admission and expulsion of asylum seekers and refugees.

---

6   UNHCR Executive Committee Conclusion No 44 (1986) Detention of Refugees and Asylum Seekers.

7   See Jennings, R and Watts, A, *Oppenheim's International Law*, 9th edn, 1992, London: Longman, pp 897–98 and 941; *Attorney-General for the Dominion of Canada v Cain* [1906] AC 542, p 546, where Lord Atkinson stated: 'One of the rights possessed by the supreme power in every State is the right to refuse to permit an alien to enter that State, to annex what conditions it pleases to the permission to enter it and to expel or deport from the State, at pleasure, even a friendly alien, especially if it considers his presence in the State opposed to its peace, order and good government, or to its social or material interests: Vattel, Law of Nations, book 1, S.231; book 2, s 125.' See also *Chahal v UK* (1996) 1 BHRC 405 at 422.

8   See Goodwin-Gill, G, 'The limits of the power of expulsion in public international law', (1974–75) 47 *British Yearbook of International Law*, pp 55–156; Goodwin-Gill, *International Law and the Movement of Persons between States*, 1978, Oxford: OUP.

9   *Op cit*, Goodwin-Gill, fn 8; and Jennings and Watts, fn 7, p 941: '... while a state has broad discretion in exercising its right to expel aliens, its discretion is not absolute. Thus, by customary international law it must not abuse its right by acting arbitrarily in taking its decisions to expel an alien, and it must act reasonably in the manner in which it effects an expulsion.'

Detention in such cases is a power ancillary to the primary power to control immigration. In terms of customary international law, as long as the underlying decision to refuse admission or expel a non-national meets the minimum international standard then detention, too, would appear to be lawful although there is little explicit consideration of the point in the case law. The law of state responsibility does, in theory at least, lay down standards for the treatment of non-nationals by other states.[10] These standards include treatment during expulsion, which should be effected 'with as much forbearance and indulgence as the circumstances and conditions of the case allow and demand, especially when expulsion is decreed against a domiciled alien.'[11] This standard is, however, only applicable to a limited class of ill-defined cases.[12] It is highly subjective and does not provide any clear limitations on when detention pursuant to immigration control should be lawful as a matter of international law.

INTERNATIONAL HUMAN RIGHTS LAW AND DETENTION OF ASYLUM SEEKERS AND REFUGEES

Customary international law does not therefore provide sufficiently clear limits to detention. International human rights law, as embodied in treaties, does, however, expressly or impliedly limit immigration detention. It is clear that most norms in international human rights law apply to all those within a state party's jurisdiction, regardless of nationality or immigration status.[13] Therefore, a state wishing to detain a non-national pursuant to immigration control should conform to international treaty standards in so doing. Whilst many treaty provisions exist, which regulate arbitrary detention, two treaties which have generated case law on the issue of immigration detainees specifically are the ECHR and the International Covenant on Civil and Political Rights (ICCPR). These will be considered in turn.

European Convention on Human Rights (ECHR)

The European Court of Human Rights ('the Strasbourg Court') (ECtHR) has the most extensive body of case law of any international human rights tribunal. Its decisions are widely referred to even beyond Europe. The approach of the ECtHR to immigration detention is therefore of some importance in making any assessment of the state of international law. The key provision is Art 5 which,

---

10 See, for a general discussion, Brownlie I, *Principles of Public International Law*, 1998, Oxford: OUP.

11 *Op cit*, Jennings and Watts, fn 7, p 945.

12 See the cases cited in *op cit*, Jennings and Watts, fn 7, p 945.

13 There are some obvious examples of norms which are specific in their application. For example, considering the International Covenant on Civil and Political Rights, Art 12 refers to 'Everyone lawfully within the territory of State shall ... have the right to liberty of movement and freedom to choose his residence.' In addition, Art 13 states that: 'An alien lawfully in the territory of a State Party ... may be expelled therefrom only in pursuance of a decision reached in accordance with law ...' Article 25 confers the right to vote upon citizens only.

unlike Art 9 (the equivalent in the ICCPR), explicitly authorises immigration detention. Article 5(1) states:

> Everyone has the right to liberty and security of person. No one shall be deprived of his liberty save in the following cases and in accordance with a procedure prescribed by law:
>
> ...
>
> (f) the lawful arrest or detention of a person to prevent his effecting an unauthorized entry into the country or of a person against whom action is being taken with a view to deportation or extradition.

It should immediately be noted that there is no prohibition upon 'arbitrary' detention under Art 5. This must be because the Article sets out an exhaustive list of permissible, and therefore presumably non-arbitrary, grounds for detention. Detention for any other reason would breach Art 5 *ipso facto* without any need to enquire into whether it was arbitrary or not.

(a) Is there a deprivation of liberty within the meaning of Art 5?

A fundamental question not considered by the Human Rights Committee in its jurisprudence, arose in *Amuur v France*[14] – is incarceration for immigration purposes a deprivation of liberty at all? In *Amuur* a group of asylum seekers flew by plane from Syria to France. They were held in the transit zone and in a secure hotel. After 20 days they were returned to Syria without their claims for asylum being determined. The Court decided two points relating to the deprivation of liberty question. The first issue related to the quality and duration of the incarceration. Was this merely a restriction on liberty and hence outside Art 5?[15] At first sight, it would seem obvious that being physically restrained for 20 days could not be other than a deprivation of liberty. The Court was, however, equivocal on this, stating:

> ... such holding should not be prolonged excessively, otherwise there would be a risk of it turning a mere restriction on liberty – inevitable with a view to organising the practical details of the aliens' repatriation or where he has requested asylum while his application for leave to enter the territory for that purpose is considered – into a deprivation of liberty.[16]

The Court also noted that the detainees had not been able to gain access to the refugee procedure, nor to seek judicial review of their detention. In light of the duration and conditions of detention, the Court concluded that there was a deprivation of liberty.

This reasoning is not entirely clear. The Court appears to be suggesting that the status of non-nationals seeking asylum means that they can be physically

---

14 (1996) 22 EHRR 533.

15 See *Guzzardi v Italy* (1980) 3 EHRR 333 and *Engel v Netherlands* (1976) 1 EHRR 647, in which the Court distinguished between a deprivation of liberty and a mere restriction on liberty which is now regulated by Art 2 Protocol No 4.

16 *Amuur* at para 43.

detained for a period without this constituting a deprivation of liberty. Beyond that period, a former mere restriction would become a deprivation. This suggests that non-nationals may be detained without either judicial review or clearly accessible lawful authority for an unspecified period, and this will be a mere restriction on liberty. That would render Art 5 much less effective in the protection it affords to non-nationals and is not justified by the text of the Art 5 itself. A more consistent approach would be to simply acknowledge that immigration detention is a deprivation of liberty, but that it is justified by Art 5(1)(f). It is also then possible to make more sense of the Court's reference to the duration of detention being significant. It is suggested that duration is important because detention is only justified whilst the application for entry is being considered. This process should not be unduly delayed, as otherwise the underlying grounds for detention will fall away.

The second point arose from the French Government's argument that there was no deprivation of liberty contrary to Art 5(1) because the detainees had been free to return to Syria at any time, thus making their detention consensual. This is sometimes referred to as the 'three-walls' situation. In rejecting this, the Court said that '[t]his possibility becomes theoretical if no other country offering protection comparable to the protection they expect to find in the country where they are seeking asylum is inclined or prepared to take them in'.[17] Syria was not a signatory to the Refugee Convention and therefore there was no legal guarantee that their asylum claims would be considered (much less recognised) there. The principle behind this argument is unclear. It might be that those fleeing persecution cannot be said to be acting freely in refusing to go back to a country that might return them to such persecution. They are acting under duress in 'choosing' to remain in detention and therefore their choice is not one which amounts to a valid consent to deprivation of liberty.

The problem with this view is that it would apply only to those fleeing serious harm. Thus, non-nationals not seeking asylum could never be said to be 'detained' unless no country would accept them back. In addition, even in asylum cases, only those genuinely having such fears could be truly said to be under duress. This would involve determining the asylum claim on the merits to assess whether a detainee was in truth under duress or rather validly consenting. In cases similar to *Amuur* an investigation into the law and practice of the third country would be required to see if its standards were equivalent to that of the state party detaining the victim. The duress model also rests entirely upon the actual knowledge of the detainee. Thus persons would be 'detained' or not, simply based upon their knowledge of the laws of, for example, Syria. There could be serious disputes as to whether a person was being detained at all for Art 5(1) purposes despite their being physically confined to a prison cell.

It is suggested that this introduces an undesirable lack of clarity into the scope of Art 5(1) protection. Surely it is better to apply a single standard to all non-nationals incarcerated for immigration purposes, based upon the objective

---

17　At para 48.

physical nature of their detention. This would then require a factual analysis based upon the Strasbourg Court's case law regarding the level of physical restraint constituting a deprivation of liberty.[18] This would accord with common law tort principles relating to false imprisonment.[19] Immigration detention in locked rooms, or even in locked facilities permitting some degree of movement inside a perimeter, should generally constitute a deprivation of liberty for Art 5(1) purposes.[20] In summary, *Amuur* is a confusing and unhelpful decision to the extent that it leaves the definition of a deprivation of liberty in immigration cases entirely unclear.

(b) What justification is required to detain under Art 5(1)(f)?

Amuur did not consider in any detail the separate issue of the scope of the justification under Art 5(1)(f) for such a deprivation in immigration cases. *Chahal* is the leading authority on this later point. This case concerned an Indian national who had been a lawful resident of the UK. A deportation order was made against him on national security grounds related to his alleged sponsorship and participation in political violence in the UK and India. He remained in detention for three and half years during the national proceedings because it was argued he posed a threat to national security if released. His applications for bail and judicial review of his detention were rejected by the national courts, which had only limited access to the intelligence material relied upon by the executive. He had been detained for six years by the date of the Strasbourg Court's judgment.

The Court held that the Article '... does not demand that the detention of a person against whom action is being taken with a view to deportation be reasonably considered necessary, for example to prevent his committing an offence or fleeing'.[21] The Court made clear that this is in contrast to the position of detainees on remand pending prosecution, which requires specific reasons, such as a risk of absconding, for continuing detention by virtue of judicial interpretation of Art 5(3).[22] It is also important to note that the Court has been prepared to 'read down' other provisions permitting detention under Art 5 so as to impose a proportionality test despite the lack of a clear textual basis for doing so. This has been necessary where the provisions on their face authorise detention without any clear public interest being served by it. Thus, the Court has ruled that mental patients detained under Art 5(1)(e) must present a threat to themselves or others if at large, despite the wording of that sub-Article, which imposes no such

---

18 See cases at fn 15.

19 *Meering v Grahame-White Aviation Co Ltd* (1919) 122 LT 44.

20 See *Secretary of State for the Home Department ex p Saadi and Others* [2002] UKHL 41, where detention in a military barracks, which allowed movement within it but not beyond it, was held to be caught by Art 5(1).

21 At para 112. This is in contrast to those detained on bail pending criminal charges under Art 5(1)(c) who must present such a risk of absconding or further offences.

22 See *Scott v Spain* (1997) 24 EHRR 391; *Caballero v United Kingdom*, App 32819/96, judgment of 8 February 2000; *Barfuss v Czech Republic* (2002) 34 EHRR 948.

limitation.[23] A similar approach has been taken to those detained for being under the influence of alcohol.[24] This approach is, in essence, based upon the same proportionality test that is explicitly articulated in Arts 8–11.

In the field of immigration control under Art 5(1)(f), the Court was not prepared to adopt a similar approach in *Chahal*. This would appear to exclude the principle of proportionality as a control on detention under Art 5(1)(f). The state need not show that detention is proportionate to meet the requirements of maintaining immigration control or public order, due to a risk of absconding or committing offences. It is possible that the national security justification for detention in the context of *Chahal* led the Court to be reluctant to interfere with the discretionary judgment of the UK Government. A Chamber of the Strasbourg Court has, however, more recently confirmed that the position is the same in cases not touching upon national security.[25] By contrast, the UK House of Lords has since held that, in its view, Art 5(1)(f) does contain a type of proportionality limitation.[26] Thus detention, which was mandatory in that case, required justification in terms of the need to speedily process asylum claims in one dedicated facility.

However, interestingly the *Chahal* Court did rule that the domestic courts' failure to review on the merits the national security justification for continued detention (as opposed to the grounds for deportation) was a breach of Art 5(4). This confers the right to judicially challenge detention. The reasoning of the Court is a little opaque, but it would appear to be based upon the fact that the UK authorities relied upon national security (and not simply the deportation proceedings) as the reason for detention. The Court's reading of Art 5(4) requires the domestic law basis for detention to be subject to review on the merits. This safeguard might in principle be evaded if, rather than claiming national security requires detention, the executive were simply to give no reason save for the fact that deportation proceedings are afoot. According to the ruling in *Chahal*, that would be enough to justify detention under Art 5(1). Article 5(4) would have no role to play apart from ensuring that executive *bona fides* and due diligence standards are met. The result is that, perversely, the executive might be driven to adopt less discretionary immigration detention policies because detention would not then be subject to judicial review under Art 5(4).

(c) The due diligence standard in justifying detention

In an otherwise largely permissive decision, the Court in *Chahal* did impose one important, if ambiguous, limit upon immigration detention. Following some of the thinking in *Amuur*, it held that:

---

23 See *Winterwerp v Netherland* (1979–80) 2 EHRR 387.
24 See *Wittold Litwa v Poland* (2001) 33 EHRR 1267.
25 App 51564/99, *Conka v Belgium*, 5 February 2002.
26 *Secretary of State for the Home Department ex p Saadi and Others* [2002] UKHL 41.

... any deprivation of liberty under Article 5(1)(f) will be justified only for as long as deportation proceedings are in progress. If such proceedings are not prosecuted with due diligence, the detention will cease to be permissible under Article 5(1)(f).[27]

This reading of the Article is not based upon explicit textual material, but, it is suggested, derives from the more general principle of effectiveness that is used by the Court in relation to all Articles of the Convention.[28] In the absence of a due diligence requirement, states could detain non-nationals indefinitely simply by formally making them subject to deportation proceedings. Such a reading would allow the executive to engage in arbitrary detention or disguised punitive measures. However, the Court did not make clear what the position would be where a state is unable to remove a detainee because no state will accept them. In principle, the detaining state might be said to be acting diligently so long as it continues to make serious diplomatic attempts to persuade potential recipient states to receive a detainee. Even where a state refuses repeatedly to accept a detainee, there is always the theoretical possibility that their position might shift in the light of new evidence or political change. The strength of the legal and factual case linking the detainee to the proposed recipient state might be relevant here. If there is only weak evidence of citizenship or former residence then it might be thought that the deportation proceedings are most likely bound to fail. The due diligence test enunciated by the Court does not, however, provide any clear guidance on such questions and is therefore unhelpful.

Even with this caveat, the Court's application of the due diligence test, as seen in *Chahal* and other cases, has been criticised.[29] Detention for six years in total, including periods of six and seven months waiting for initial and fresh decisions from the immigration authorities, is difficult to reconcile with the due diligence standard. The Court recognised this but noted the exceptional nature of this factually complex case, which also raised national security issues. By contrast, in another, extradition, case the Court ruled that delays of three and ten months violated Art 5(1).[30]

It is difficult to draw any firm conclusions from the case law on what periods of detention will fall on the wrong side of the line. The proper assessment of what amounts to due diligence is made more complex because delay may be a result of a combination of the detaining state's inefficiency and that of another state or even the detainee's obstructive behaviour. For example, in *Kolompar*[31] it was held that two separate delays of over two years and eight months in making decisions pending deportation did not amount to a violation of Art 5 because they were not attributable to the detaining state. Clearly, allocating responsibility for the delays in such cases is an imprecise process and this further undermines the precise content of the legal rights of the detainee.

---

27 At para 113.
28 See, for example, *Airey v Ireland* (1979) 2 EHRR 305.
29 See Ovey, C and White, RCA, *Jacobs and White: European Convention on Human Rights*, 3rd edn, 2002, Oxford: OUP, p 130.
30 *Quinn v France* (1995) 21 EHRR 529.
31 *Kolompar v Belgium* (1993) 16 EHRR 197.

Summary: the ECHR and unrestricted territorial sovereignty

The Strasbourg Court has an unduly restrictive position in relation to the detention of non-nationals. Article 5 of the ECHR only permits detention of non-nationals in order to prevent illegal entry or whilst deportation action is being taken. Although a prohibition on 'arbitrary' detention is absent from Art 5 the Strasbourg Court itself stated in *Chahal* that: 'any deprivation of liberty should be in keeping with the purpose of Article 5, namely to protect the individual from arbitrariness.'[32] The Court has imposed a proportionality test in relation to other grounds for detention, particularly Art 5(1)(e) in relation to mental patients and alcoholics. The failure by the Strasbourg Court to do so in relation to immigration detention is both inconsistent and unfortunate. The use of a proportionality test embodies the general approach of the Court, which requires there to be a fair balance struck between protection of the wider community and any interference with individual rights.[33] This test would provide a much higher level of protection for the liberty of non-nationals subject to immigration detention than the due diligence standard.

The approach of the Strasbourg Court reflects very clearly the influence of customary international law regarding the status of non-nationals. There is no right to be at large on the territory of a signatory state simply on the ground that a particular non-national does not pose a threat to a legitimate public interest. The Court suggests that detention pending the conferring or denial of immigration status is sufficiently justified by reason of the absence of such status. The *Chahal* principles would appear to apply equally to admission and expulsion cases, although the text of Art 5(1)(f) is drafted differently. Admission might appear to be more demanding of the state because detention in this circumstance must be 'to prevent' an illegal entry. This might imply a necessity test. By contrast, in deportation cases, the only obligation is for the state to show that 'action is being taken'. This distinction was rejected by the House of Lords in *Saadi*[34] and it is suggested that it would be counter-intuitive to allow greater protection for newly arrived migrants as compared with those already established. *Amuur* certainly gives no support for the need to show necessity in order to justify detention in admission cases.

---

32 *Chahal*, at para 118.
33 *Soering v United Kingdom* (1989) 11 EHRR 439, at para 89. There is however some divergence amongst academics on the question of whether proportionality has a role to play throughout the Convention or whether it is largely confined to Arts 8–11. See fn 29 (p 5) where only qualified rights are said to give rise to questions of proportionality. By contrast, see, Starmer, K, *European Human Rights Law*, 1999, London: Legal Action Group, p 169, who states that: '[t]he principle of proportionality is the defining characteristic of the Strasbourg approach to the protection of human rights.'
34 See fn 26 above.

International Covenant on Civil and Political Rights (ICCPR)

The ICCPR has been ratified by a large number of states and commands wide respect as a key source of human rights standards across the world.[35] It is also significant in that it established the Human Rights Committee, a quasi-judicial body, which can deliver non-binding opinions ('communications') in relation to individual complaints under the Covenant where a state has become party to the Optional Protocol to the ICCPR.

The basic provision of the ICCPR relevant for present purposes is Art 9(1) which states:

> Everyone has the right to liberty and security of person. No one shall be subjected to arbitrary arrest or detention. No one shall be deprived of his liberty except on such grounds and in accordance with such procedure as are established by law.

This is supplemented by Art 9(4), which entitles a detained person to bring proceedings in order that a court may decide on the legality of their detention.[36] It should be noted at the outset that Art 9 does not specify the circumstances in which detention is justified. This is in contrast to the approach taken in the equivalent Art 5 of the ECHR, which provides an exhaustive list of permissible grounds for detention. On one view, Art 9 is concerned purely with the formal legality of detention. It does not appear, on its face, to regulate the substantive grounds for detention. The only stipulation in Art 9 is that arrest not be 'arbitrary'. This term is commonly applied in legal contexts relating to detention and can be subjected to detailed linguistic analysis.[37] A better approach is to consider the manner in which 'arbitrariness' has been interpreted in practice. Recourse to the *travaux preparatoires*[38] of the ICCPR reveals that those drafting Art 9 had a broad view of the word. Thus, the majority of the delegates to the drafting committee were of the view that meaning went beyond mere unlawfulness to

---

35 148 States have ratified. See Brownlie, I and Goodwin-Gill, G (eds), *Basic Documents on Human Rights*, 4th edn, Oxford: OUP. See Joseph, S, Schultz, J and Castan, M (eds), *The International Covenant on Civil and Political Rights: Cases, Materials and Commentary*, 1995, Oxford: OUP; McGoldrick, D, *The Human Rights Committee: Its Role in the Development of the International Covenant on Civil and Political Rights*, 1991, Oxford: Clarendon.

36 Article 9(4) states: 'Anyone who is deprived of his liberty by arrest or detention shall be entitled to take proceedings before a court, in order that the court may decide without delay on the lawfulness of his detention and order his release if the detention is not lawful.'

37 See, for example, the definitions given in *New Shorter English Dictionary*, 1993, Oxford: Clarendon: '1. Dependent on will or pleasure; *Law* (now *Hist*) dependent on the decision of a legally recognised authority; discretionary... 2. Based on mere opinion or preference as opp to the real nature of things; capricious, unpredictable, inconsistent ... 3. Unrestrained in the exercise of will or authority; despotic, tyrannical ...' These are clearly rather different in character and range in their pejorative force.

38 See Art 32 of the Vienna Convention on the Law of Treaties, which allows recourse to the preparatory work of the treaty where general rule of interpretation in Art 31 'leaves the meaning ambiguous or obscure'.

encompass injustice, unpredictability, unreasonableness, capriciousness and unproportionality.[39]

This approach has been adopted by the Human Rights Committee in its Communications on Art 9. Thus, in *Van Alphen v Netherlands*[40] the Committee held that '"arbitrariness" is not to be equated with "against the law", but must be interpreted more broadly to include elements of inappropriateness, injustice and lack of predictability'. Therefore, although the arrest of the particular complainant was lawful in national law, it was 'unreasonable' (and therefore arbitrary) because there had to be a risk of flight, interference with evidence or of a crime being committed to justify detention on the facts. The Committee therefore clearly ruled that Art 9 imposes substantive limits upon detention.

This approach was adopted in the landmark immigration case of *A v Australia*,[41] which concerned the detention of a Cambodian asylum seeker who had entered Australia illegally. A was detained as part of a policy of mandatory detention of all undocumented persons arriving by boat. His asylum application was initially refused after one and half years and finally rejected on appeal after three years. He was later released after over four years in immigration detention. Drawing upon its decision in *Van Alphen*, the Committee noted that 'arbitrariness' should not be equated merely with unlawfulness, but must be interpreted more broadly to include inappropriateness and injustice. The Committee held that it was not arbitrary *per se* to detain persons requesting asylum. However, it stated that:

> ... remand in custody could be considered arbitrary if it is not necessary in all the circumstances of the case, for example to prevent flight or interference with evidence: the element of proportionality becomes relevant in this context.[42]

Turning to the particular situation of immigrants, the Committee said:

> ... detention should not continue beyond the period for which the State can provide appropriate justification. For example, the fact of illegal entry may indicate a need for investigation and there may be other factors particular to the individual, such as the likelihood of absconding and lack of cooperation, which may justify detention for a period. Without such factors detention may be considered arbitrary even if entry was illegal. In the instant case, the State party has not advanced any grounds particular to the author's case, which would justify his continued detention for a period of four years ...[43]

---

39 See Bossuyt, MJ, *Guide to the 'Travaux Preparatoires' of the International Covenant on Civil and Political Rights*, 1987, Amsterdam: Martinus Nijhoff Publishers, p 172. Interestingly, an earlier draft of Art 9 was modelled upon Art 5 of the European Convention and included a specified set of grounds for detention. This was abandoned when other drafting parties began to add further grounds of their own such that the text became unworkable with a list a comprising some 40 grounds! No consensus could be reached on a concise list and this led to the adoption of the term 'arbitrary' being substituted. See Bossuyt, p 164.

40 No 305/1988.

41 No 560/1993.

42 At para 9.2.

43 At para 9.4.

The Committee therefore concluded that there was a violation of Art 9(1). In addition, it found a violation of Art 9(4) because domestic legislation limited the power of national courts to review the detention of persons such as the complainant. From 1992, judicial review was limited to merely ascertaining that the detainee fell within the category of persons subject to mandatory detention. There was no power in the domestic courts to review the merits of continuing detention and thus to authorise release if found to be 'arbitrary' within the meaning of Art 9(1). The Committee therefore explicitly held that Art 9(4) required that domestic courts have power to restrain breaches of Art 9(1). This is important because the use of ouster clauses in conjunction with immigration detention legislation has been a feature of both Australian and American law in recent years.

More recently, the Committee also decided another similar complaint in *C v Australia*.[44] The complainant sought asylum after arrival at an Australian port whilst in possession of a valid visa. Mandatory detention was begun and lasted for two years before he was released by executive order on the basis of medical grounds after his mental health gradually declined and he developed psychosis. Judicial review was ousted by the primary legislation. In contrast to the decision in *A*, *C*'s asylum claim had been refused more quickly (after two months) and his review was rejected six weeks later. He was, however, later awarded refugee status after his release. He contended that his detention violated Art 9(1) and (4).

In this case, the Australian Government mounted a general defence of the mandatory detention regime on policy grounds. These grounds included: maintaining the integrity of the immigration system; ensuring that only those entitled to enter were permitted to do so; processing claims swiftly by ensuring ready access to migrants; facilitating removal of rejected applicants; general past experience of absconding; difficulties in tracing absconders, particularly given the lack of a system of identify cards. The Government also adduced specific evidence, relating to the detainee's dishonesty when questioned upon arrival, to support the argument that he had been an absconding risk.

The Committee rejected these arguments and found breaches of Art 9(1) and (4). Unfortunately it did not address the general arguments for mandatory detention that had been put forward by the Government. Thus, it is not possible to know exactly what it thought about these grounds, but the conclusion must be that it believed indefinite mandatory detention to be unacceptable. The reasoning offered first recalled the requirement in *A* that detention must not be longer than that for which the state can provide appropriate justification and then continued:

> In the present case, the author's detention as a non-citizen without an entry permit continued, in mandatory terms, until he was removed or granted a permit. Whilst the State party advances particular reasons to justify the individual detention ... the Committee observes that the State party has failed to demonstrate that those reasons justify the author's continued detention in the light of the passage of time and intervening circumstances. In particular, the State party has not demonstrated that, in the light of the author's particular circumstances, there were not less invasive means of achieving the same ends, that is to say, compliance with State

---

44   No 900/1999. Meeting on 28 October 2002.

party's immigration policies, by, for example, the imposition of reporting obligations, sureties or other conditions which would take account of the author's deteriorating condition. In these circumstances, whatever the reasons for the original detention, continuance of immigration detention for over two years without individual justification and without any chance of substantive judicial review was, in the Committee's view, arbitrary and constituted a violation of Article 9, paragraph 1.[45]

In finding a breach of Art 9(4), the Committee simply concluded, as it had in *A*, that because domestic legislation excluded substantive judicial review of the merits of detention of non-nationals in C's position, there was no effective remedy against a breach of Art 9(1).

The decision in C was followed in the later case of *Baban v Australia*,[46] where mandatory detention for two years was also declared to be in breach of Art 9(1). *Baban* was interesting in that the Iraqi complainant had actually escaped from detention and was in hiding at the time of the decision. The Committee found that, even where absconding had actually occurred, the length of the earlier detention had been excessive given the possibility of supervised release. The Committee also noted that removal of Iraqis had not been logistically possible during the detention period, rendering further detention unreasonable. The Committee also appear to have had regard to the harsh effects of detention upon the complainant's son (aged three) as a factor in the complaint's case. By contrast, in *Jalloh v Netherlands*,[47] detention of three and half months whilst making the administrative decision on an asylum claim was not unreasonable. This was on the basis that the complainant had previously absconded from supervised release and that he was released as soon as it became clear that there was no realistic prospect of removing him due to the impossibility of securing his acceptance by another state.

Summary: the Human Rights Committee and the proportionality approach

The decisions in *A* and *C* take a proportionality approach, which is rather reminiscent of that adopted by the ECtHR in other areas of its jurisprudence.[48] The Committee accepted the legitimacy of immigration control as an objective of policy. However, the detention practised in these cases was unnecessary and/or disproportionate. In addition, the Committee decided that, whilst illegal entrants could be arrested in order to conduct an initial investigation, detention beyond a short period would be arbitrary in the absence of specific risk factors. The fact of illegal entry *per se* was not enough to justify lengthy detention. In the case of *A*, it

---

45 At para 8.2.
46 Communication No 1014/2001 of 18/09/2003 (CCPR/C/78/D/1014/2001).
47 Communication No 794/1998 of 15/04/2002 (CCPR/C/74/D/794/1998).
48 See the voluminous case law emphasising this point summarised in Ovey, C and White, RCA, *Jacobs and White: European Convention on Human Rights*, 3rd edn, 2002, Oxford: OU P, pp 209–10. *Silver v United Kingdom* (1983) 5 EHRR 347, at para 97, is one example.

would appear that the lack of specific grounds for flight risk was decisive in the Committee's view. If there was no evidence of likely absconding, then immigration control could be maintained by less intrusive means. Detention was not necessary. In C, by contrast, the Committee appear to have concluded that the initial detention might have been justified given the risk of the detainee absconding. Extended detention was, however, disproportionate.

This represents a balanced view of the status of non-nationals' liberty rights: state sovereignty is recognised in that detention to investigate a claim for admission is generally permitted. Such detention may be prolonged if there is a specific risk of flight or offending, as in the *Jalloh* decision. The decisions in C and *Baban* confirm that the duration of detention may be disproportionate with regard to its effects on detainees and the risks they pose if released. Detention might be 'necessary' to prevent absconding, but it would be disproportionate to detain indefinitely merely because of such a risk. On the other hand, the balance might favour detention where a serious risk of violent criminality is present.

The Committee's case law appears to suggest that broadly similar principles apply to admission and expulsion cases. Thus, A and C both concerned initial detention pending applications for admission and then, following refusal, further periods of incarceration pending expulsion. One possible difference is that the Committee did allow a state a short initial period of detention in admission cases for investigation, irrespective of any specific justification for detention.[49] The Committee has not considered a deportation case, but it is arguable that where a state is taking away a pre-existing right of residence, it should not detain unless this is clearly justified on grounds of absconding or criminal behaviour.

NON-DISCRIMINATION NORMS AND DETENTION

Discrimination on the basis of nationality is of course inherent in immigration law and is perfectly compatible with international law. Only non-nationals can be detained in order to maintain immigration control, because only they are subject to it. The more difficult question arises when detention ancillary to deportation is employed to prevent criminal activity or protect national security. Clearly nationals also have a propensity to commit crime and yet preventive detention is generally not employed against them. This amounts to discrimination on the basis of nationality in relation to the relevant issue, namely criminal proclivity.

In *A and Others v Secretary of State for the Home Department*,[50] the House of Lords recently held that preventive detention of non-nationals who were subject to

---

49 This is the approach taken by the UN Economic and Social Council Working Group on Arbitrary Detention in their Deliberation No 5 (E/CN.4/2000/4, 28 December 1999), which stipulates that the maximum period of detention should be set by law and may not be excessive. See also UNHCR Executive Committee Conclusion No 44 (1986), which opines that detention should be avoided but may be justified, *inter alia*, in order to 'determine the elements on which the claim to refugee status ... is based' and should not be 'unduly prolonged'.

50 [2004] UKHL 56.

deportation but who could not be removed on legal grounds was discriminatory and disproportionate. The power of indefinite detention of suspected international terrorists pending their deportation was a breach of Arts 5 and 14 of the ECHR. The discrimination finding is of key importance. The background to the case stemmed from the effect of the *Chahal* judgment which meant that in normal times, a non-national must be deported with due diligence or released from detention. The UK Government argued that in a time of emergency it was lawful under the ECHR to derogate from Art 5 in respect of deportable non-nationals who posed a danger to national security. This was despite the accepted fact that UK nationals also posed similar threats to national security through association with the same terrorist groups as the detained non-nationals. The Government's case was that the difference in treatment between non-nationals and nationals was justified by the fact that the former were deportable and therefore had no right to be in the UK any longer. Furthermore it was argued that they had the option of ending their detention by returning to their own country. Nationals did not have this possibility. Finally, it was contended that international law allowed states to intern non-nationals during wartime and that emergencies should give a similar power. For these reasons the liberty interest of deportable non-nationals was therefore less than that of nationals. The Court of Appeal had accepted this argument.[51] Following a review of international treaties and custom relating to the status of non-nationals during wartime,[52] Lord Woolf said that deportable aliens who cannot in fact be deported 'have, unlike nationals, no more right to remain, only a right not to be removed, which means legally that they come into a different class from those who have the right of abode'.[53]

On appeal, however, the House of Lords decisively rejected these arguments and held that for the purposes of protecting national security, nationals and non-nationals were in a similar situation. Their liberty interest in being free from preventive detention was therefore the same. 'Suspected international terrorists who are UK nationals are in a situation analogous with the appellants because in the present context, they share the most relevant characteristics of the appellants.'[54] The threat posed by both groups was the same and therefore they should be treated the same. It was therefore discrimination on grounds of immigration status to detain only non-nationals who were suspected of terrorist activity. A difference in treatment directed at immigration control is clearly justified because nationals are not deportable and so cannot be detained to effect that aim. The House of Lords however concluded that the legislation was in reality a public security measure and not an immigration measure.[55] The

---

51 [2003] 1 All ER 816.
52 Articles 41 and 42 of the Geneva Convention Relative to the Protection of Civilian Persons in Time of War (1949); Arts 9, 32 and 33 of the Convention Relating to the Status of Refugees (1951); Art 4 of the International Covenant on Civil and Political Rights.
53 At para 47.
54 *Per* Lord Bingham at para 53.
55 'But it would be a serious error, in my opinion, to regard this case as about the right to control immigration. This is because the issue which the Derogation Order is designed to address was not at its heart an immigration issue at all. It was an issue about the aliens' right to liberty.' *Per* Lord Hope at para 103.

Government's attempt to use indefinite preventive detention pursuant to immigration control measures was discriminatory because non-nationals had an equal right to respect for their liberty, save for where they were the subject of efficiently prosecuted deportation proceedings.[56]

Flowing from the finding of discrimination, the House also ruled that the indefinite detention of non-nationals was disproportionate to the threat to the nation. This was because the Government had concluded that equally dangerous nationals could be dealt with by less draconian means such as surveillance. It was therefore clearly not necessary to detain non-nationals since similar measures should suffice against them. It was also arbitrary to allow suspected terrorist non-nationals to have their freedom outside the UK if they could find a place to go whilst detaining those who could not.[57]

This decision, although only one of a national court applying the ECHR, is of great importance because it is makes clear that the liberty interest of non-nationals is to be accorded the same level of respect as nationals under Arts 5 and 14. The Strasbourg Court's decision in *Gaygusuz v Austria*[58] makes clear that discrimination on grounds of nationality generally requires strong justification. The same applies to discrimination in relation to detention where deportation cannot be effected for any reason. Article 5(1)(f) allows a difference in treatment for non-nationals only for the purpose of deportation. The power of detention under Art 5 (1)(f) is very much confined and is effectively limited to situations where a non-nationals can be deported. Outside this situation, non-nationals cannot be detained other than in the other situations permitted by Art 5 in relation to all persons present in the jurisdiction. The existence of a state of emergency justifying a derogation from Art 5 does not affect the non-nationals' right of non-discrimination. They can only be treated differently in an emergency if they are truly differently situated. This would depend on showing that they present a degree of threat that nationals do not for some reason. This might be true if they are enemy aliens in wartime but even in this scenario a difference in treatment might not be justified. There might be nationals as or more sympathetic to the enemy than the enemy aliens themselves. Where a mass influx of migrants is causing public order problems, it might be arguable that a difference in treatment is justified here because nationals do not pose problems of the same nature.

---

56   'The Secretary of State was, of course entitled to discriminate between British nationals on the one hand and foreign nationals on the other for the purposes of immigration control, subject to the limitations established in the *Chahal* case. What he was not entitled to do was to treat the right to liberty under Article 5 of the Convention of foreign nationals who happen to be in this country for what ever reason as different in any respect from that enjoyed by British nationals.' *Per* Lord Hope at para 105.

57   '[T]he choice of an immigration measure to address a security problem had the inevitable result of failing adequately to address that problem (by allowing non-UK suspected terrorist to leave the country with impunity and leaving British suspected terrorists at large) while imposing the severe penalty of indefinite detention on persons who … may harbour no hostile intentions towards the United Kingdom.' *Per* Lord Bingham at para 44.

58   (1996) 23 EHRR 364.

What *A v Secretary of State for the Home Department* makes very clear is that a revocation of immigration status does not justify a revocation of the right to liberty of non-nationals. This should not however be taken to mean that preventive detention of non-nationals cannot be practised where detention of nationals posing a similar threat is not authorised by national law. When a non-national is subject to deportation action, they may be detained, as in *Chahal*, in order to protect national security or prevent crime. Indeed they may be detained simply to effect deportation. Thus preventive detention is still lawful but this must be ancillary to immigration control. It cannot be indefinite detention because deportation must be carried out with due diligence. Where it becomes indefinite then it ceases to be truly ancillary to immigration control but is rather a pure public security measure and therefore falls outside the Art 5(1)(f) justification.

In terms of Art 9 of the ICCPR, the Human Rights Committee has not specifically addressed this issue, but the following can be deduced. *A v Australia* allowed discrimination against non-nationals in relation to detention because it clearly permitted preventive detention pending admission. This might be put on the alternative basis that such non-nationals were not in the same situation as nationals. Thus, lack of immigration status justified holding in detention those likely to commit crimes. As with Art 5 of the ECHR, preventive detention is permissible under Art 9, but only ancillary to effective deportation proceedings. Where these proceedings are ineffective, then continued preventive detention will be discriminatory.

It is suggested that it does not matter that a state of emergency pertains. Whilst customary international law and treaties allow detention of non-nationals in wartime for example, such laws are entirely concerned with the plane of state responsibility to other states. They simply seek to regulate inter-state relations and control treatment of hostile aliens. Indeed, the modern law demands that internment not be based on nationality alone, but rather that necessity requires it. They, however, say nothing about discrimination between nationals and non-nationals within domestic law, which is the subject of regulation by Art 14 of the ECHR and Art 26 of the ICCPR. The core concern of non-discrimination clauses is to ensure that vulnerable minority groups are not singled out for special measures. As Jackson AJ famously put it in the US Supreme Court:

> ... nothing opens the door to arbitrary action so effectively as to allow those officials to pick and choose only a few to whom they will apply legislation and thus to escape the political retribution that might be visited upon them if larger numbers were affected. Courts can take no better measure to assure that laws will be just than to require that laws be equal in operation.[59]

It will be discriminatory and contrary to ECHR and ICCPR jurisprudence to practise preventive detention during an emergency without detaining nationals who pose a similar threat. There is no possible basis for such a distinction. Deportable status of non-nationals is a relevant distinction only to the extent that such persons can be removed in timely fashion.

---

59   *Railway Express Agency v New York* (1949) 336 US 106, pp 112–13.

DEROGATIONS AND IMMIGRATION DETENTION

Human rights treaties generally contain provision for derogation from their provisions in the face of national emergency.[60] Could large-scale immigration influxes be said to amount to public emergencies justifying derogation from the safeguards against arbitrary detention outlined above? In practice, states have not sought to argue this point in legal proceedings thus far.[61] Whilst there have been derogations entered, they have been in the face of armed threats to public order.[62] They must overcome the fairly stringent test laid down by the ECtHR, for example requiring there to be 'an exceptional situation of crisis or emergency which affects the whole population and constitutes a threat to the organized life of the community of which the State is composed'.[63] Set against this, the test does not require the threat to be of a criminal nature and the Court has left a wide margin of appreciation to states to decide whether such a situation exists.[64] Perhaps it is arguable that a massive migration of people across a border might threaten the life of a nation if it caused public order to break down; but it is submitted that migration that simply imposes financial burdens on the host state or leads to absconding in a number of cases would not be serious enough.[65] The essence of an emergency is a threat to life and limb from some source, natural or human. Amongst Western states, there have not been such large migrations of this character.

Even if such a large-scale migration might be such an emergency, the derogation provisions within the ECHR and ICCPR also require that the measures taken in response to the emergency must be no more than necessary to overcome the situation.[66] Mandatory detention under the ICCPR could only be employed if public order measures had failed to remove the emergency by restoring public security. Any such restriction of liberty would have to be accompanied by positive

---

60 The provision in ICCPR is Art 4, which speaks of 'public emergency which threatens the life of the nation and the existence of which is officially proclaimed, the States Parties ... may take measures derogating from their obligation under the present Covenant to the extent strictly required by the exigencies of the situation....' The ECHR Art 15 says 'In time of war or other public emergency threatening the life of the nation any High Contracting Party may take measures derogating from its obligations under this Convention to the extent strictly required by the exigencies of the situation...' Some rights are non-derogable, such as the prohibition on torture and right to life.

61 Australia did not seek to derogate from Art 9 ICCPR.

62 See, for example, *Ireland v United Kingdom* (1979–80) 2 EHRR 25.

63 *Lawless v Ireland* (1979–80) 1 EHRR 1, para 28.

64 *Ireland v United Kingdom* (1979–80) 2 EHRR 25, where the Court said at para 207: 'By reason of their direct and continuous contact with the pressing needs of the moment, the national authorities are in principle in a better position that the international judge to decide both on the presence of such an emergency and on the nature and scope of derogation necessary to avert it. In this matter, Article 15(1) leaves those authorities a wide margin of appreciation.'

65 See the discussion in Novak, M, *United Nations Covenant on Civil and Political Rights: CCPR Commentary*, 1993, Kehl: NP Engel, p 79. See, also, *Siracusa Principles on Limitation and Derogation provisions in the ICCPR.* E/CN.4/1985/4.

66 See *Aksoy v Turkey* (1996) 23 EHRR 553, in which the internment of terrorist suspects for fourteen days incommunicado was held to be beyond what was necessary to meet the emergency.

steps to speedily process immigration applications. As a result of *Chahal*, the ECHR appears to permit mandatory detention even in the absence of an emergency. Detention need only be pending removal and due diligence be exercised in effecting this. Even such limitations as are imposed by the Strasbourg Court can in principle be set aside in an emergency. The decision of the House of Lords on preventive detention in *A v Secretary of State for the Home Department*[67] discussed above concerned a situation of a derogation occasioned by a threat to national security emanating from terrorists. The House held that the derogation order was not lawfully made under Art 15 of the ECHR because it was not proportionate and was discriminatory. Nationals posed a similar risk as non-nationals. The decision is noteworthy for the particularly close scrutiny given by the court to the Government's justification for the measures taken pursuant to the derogation. Whilst a majority of the House[68] reluctantly accepted the Government's decision that there was an emergency, they did not accept that preventive detention of non-nationals was a lawful response. This decision did not however touch upon the situation of mass influxes of migrants under discussion here and the potential public disorder that that might occasion. In a situation like this, a difference in treatment between nationals and non-nationals could be justified on the basis that the 'danger' to public order emanated from incoming migrants and not nationals. This would still leave open the question of the proportionality of detention as a response to the emergency. The decision in *A v Secretary of State for the Home Department* appears to demonstrate that a state will face a heavy burden in justifying extended detention.

CONCLUSIONS ON THE AMBIT OF THE POWER OF IMMIGRATION DETENTION

We are now in a position to review the material set out above with a view to discerning different rationales for immigration detention.

Unrestricted detention in the absence of an immigration law right to enter or remain

This embodies the traditional customary international law power given to states to control access to their territory. For those who have no subsisting immigration law right to enter or remain, detention simply reflects the state's denial of this right or, at least, the failure to confer such a right. In this view, non-nationals have no right to liberty in the receiving state until they have been given a positive permission to enter or remain. This approach makes a clear distinction between lawful residents (including nationals) and others. Only the former have a right to personal liberty. Of the international human rights jurisprudence, *Chahal* is arguably consistent with this reasoning because the ECtHR made it clear that no

---

67 [2004] UKHL 56.
68 Only Lord Hoffmann was prepared to hold that there was no emergency.

justification need be offered for immigration detention beyond the fact that deportation or removal action is pending.

On this view, judicial review on the merits of detention is inappropriate and should be confined to the pure *vires* question of whether a non-national falls into a category of persons defined in national law. Such detention could also be supported on the substantive basis that there is nothing capricious about ensuring that only those non-nationals entitled to be at liberty are at liberty. This represents a basically unfettered view of the right of states to protect their territorial sovereignty as a matter of international law. It therefore fails to acknowledge the influence of human rights standards developed in the post-war era. It is suggested that the Human Rights Committee, in *A v Australia*, took the correct approach by acknowledging the influence of the principle of proportionality as a general control upon state interference with fundamental human rights.

Prevention of future migration by the detention

Deterrence of migration itself has not been an official justification for detention policies. Detention is thereby an aspect of criminal, not administrative, law. As such, according to orthodox theory it should be imposed by the judicial branch not the executive branch. Punitive immigration detention would conflict with the fair trial provisions of international human rights treaties. This issue has not been tackled by any international court, but the Australian High Court has done so in some detail in *Chu Kheng Lim and Other v Minister for Immigration, Local Government and Ethnic Affairs and Another*.[69] One factor pointing against immigration detention being punitive was said to be the 'voluntary' nature of immigration detention. There is an implicit endorsement of this in the *Amuur* decision, which seemed to conclude that only asylum seekers could be said to be involuntarily detained. Some domestic judges have instead considered voluntariness as part of the assessment of reasonableness of the period of detention in the *Hardial Singh* case.

There is also certainly some evidence that lesser protection afforded to admission cases over those facing deportation may be partly grounded in a recognition of the voluntariness of new migrants. Thus, a person newly seeking admission has chosen to migrate and seek entry. A lawful resident, who is being deported, is being deprived against their will of something they already have. Thus admission cases are accorded less protection by legislatures and courts. For example, Canadian law allows a period of detention to process migrants' applications regardless of proportionality issues. Similarly, the US courts allow indefinite detention in such cases. The UK House of Lords in *Saadi* allowed for a reasonable period of detention. At international level, the Human Rights Committee in *A v Australia* afforded an initial period of detention to process an application. These decisions are not based upon the conclusion that such persons are not 'detained' (due to their consent), but rather that their liberty interest is not

---

69   [1992] 176 CLR 1 FC 92/051.

as extensive as that of a lawful resident because they have chosen to seek entry into another country. The decisions also reflect the intuitive concept that those who have established themselves in another country are entitled to more protection than those who have not yet gained a foothold.

Protection of public safety or national security

Criminal or security threats posed by non-nationals are standard grounds for detention in national law. Detention of nationals on such preventive grounds is generally considered unacceptable. This discrimination has, however, been questioned by the majority of the US Supreme Court in *Zadvydas v Davis*.[70] The approach that appears to represent the consensus of opinion is rather more modest. This would follow from the proportionality test adopted by the Human Rights Committee in *C v Australia*, which appeared to accept that it was justifiable to employ preventive detention against non-nationals. Clearly it must be used in a manner not disproportionate to the threat posed by release. Thus trivial previous offending might not be sufficient to justify detention even though the legislature might lawfully deem deportation appropriate for such offences. The burden should be upon the detaining authorities to show a substantial risk of offending. It is suggested that, following the US District Court in *Fernandez-Roque v Smith*,[71] this should be a demanding standard higher than the normal civil balance of probabilities, but not beyond reasonable doubt. Finally, and most importantly, the House of Lords in *A v SSHD* confirmed that preventive detention cannot continue indefinitely. Where removal of a non-national proves impossible due to legal or practical obstacles, they must be released as a result of the *Chahal* decision.

Detention necessary to ensure removal of person without immigration status

This approach acknowledges that detention is essentially a means to secure removal and that it should only be used for that purpose. Where removal can be secured without detention, for example by ensuring a detainee surrenders to bail, incarceration is not necessary. There are a number of factors to consider here. At the international level, it is clear that the Human Rights Committee, in *A v Australia* and *C v Australia*, required that evidence of an absconding risk be adduced. The burden was clearly upon the detaining authority. The Committee decided that judicial review on the merits of any such finding must be available to satisfy Art 9(4). By contrast, the ECtHR, in *Chahal*, seemed to leave unclear the role of the judiciary. Clearly the ECtHR decided that it was not necessary to justify detention under Art 5(1)(f) by reference to an absconding risk. However, if a state

---

70   533 US 678 (2001).
71   See *Fernandez-Roque v Smith* 567 F Supp 1115 (1983).

argued that such a risk did exist as its justification, this finding should be subject to review under Art 5(4);[72] but, where detention is prolonged, both the underlying rationale for detention (removal or processing an application for admission) and the principle of proportionality suggest that supervised release is the appropriate course.

The doctrine of proportionality enunciated in *A v Australia* also embodies temporal limitations upon detention even where a risk of absconding is present. Thus the length of detention appeared to be important, even in cases where an absconding risk was present, as in *C* and *Baban*. The famous decision of the UK High Court in *R v Governor of Durham Prison ex p Hardial Singh*,[73] given by Woolf J,[74] articulated this idea in the context of common law rights. It is arguable that an absconding risk provides only limited justification for detention and that it does not support very lengthy periods of incarceration.

CONCLUSION

Immigration detention is lawful under international law, but there is an unfortunate lack of clarity in the extent of states' power in this regard. The case law is not well developed and there is a conflict between the ECHR and ICCPR tribunals. The later is much more generous in conferring rights upon detainees. Its decisions form the basis for a recognition of the universal liberty rights of all persons, regardless of citizenship or immigration status.[75] Whilst not wishing to exaggerate the case law, it does appear to represent a right to be free from physical restraint in any country in the world once the state has had a reasonable period to investigate an immigration application. Mass migration continues to raise questions as to the appropriate balance between states' rights and detainees' liberty. Asylum seekers will continue to present themselves within other countries in response to civil disorder and war. Whilst some will be 1951 Convention refugees and others will not, the decision to detain them is a separate question from *refoulement*. Asylum seekers have a liberty interest regardless of the ultimate outcome of their asylum applications. It is suggested that the Human Rights Committee has achieved a sensible balance between the two competing interests of state sovereignty and individual liberty. Although many find the idea that migrants should be allowed to gain their liberty without an immigration right to

---

72   The point is moot because the Court there was considering a risk to national security, not absconding, but the reasoning would appear to be identical.

73   [1984] WLR 704.

74   At 706: 'As the power is given in order to enable the machinery of deportation to be carried out, I regard the power of detention as being impliedly limited to a period which is reasonably necessary for that purpose. The period which is reasonable will depend upon the circumstances of the particular case.'

75   See Hill Maher, 'Who has a right to rights? Citizenship's exclusions in an age of migration', in Brysk, A (ed), *Globalization and Human Rights*, Berkeley: University of California Press, pp 28–29.

enter or remain abhorrent, the reality is that states have never achieved anything like total control over their borders. Many migrants are not removable due to practical or legal problems. Others can be re-detained at a later stage in their proceedings to secure their removal, if necessary. It is neither a sensible use of resources nor proportionate in relation to detainees' liberty to incarcerate for long periods pursuant to immigration control.

CHAPTER 8

JUDGING ASYLUM

Colin Harvey

Asylum, immigration and nationality law have all been used in the 'war against terrorism' in, for example, the UK, the US and Canada.[1] Anti-terrorism law and policy is having an impact on refugees and asylum seekers. There is, however, no necessary connection between national security and asylum and what tends to be neglected is that refugee law, as a legal regime, was designed precisely to regulate the 'exceptional situation' of forced migration. The existence of the humanitarian institution of asylum need not raise security concerns, and refugee law contains well-established mechanisms to address the issue. This chapter reflects my view that claims to novelty must be approached with caution. In recent years concern about asylum has reached the highest political levels and extended beyond national contexts. The UN Security Council, for example, made clear after 11 September 2001 that there should be no safe havens for terrorists and that refugee status should not be 'abused' by 'perpetrators, organizers or facilitators of terrorist acts'.[2] A particular focus for states remains on the possible use of the asylum system by those posing a risk to national security. However, these debates must be seen as part of a pattern of responses to migration that is not novel.[3] Refugee lawyers have noted for some time that a 'security discourse' is being constructed around the treatment of forced migration.

---

1   Note, for example, in Canada the provisions of the Immigration and Refugee Protection Act 2001. See Roach, K, *September 11: Consequences for Canada*, 2003, Montreal: McGill Queens Press; Adelman, H, 'Refugees and border security post-September 11' (2002) 20 Refuge 5. For developments in the US, see Martin, K, 'Preventive detention of immigrants and non-citizens in the United States since September 11th' (2002) 20 Refuge 23. See, generally, *Rasul v George W Bush* 542 US (2004), decided 28 June 2004. There has also been extensive discussion of this issue in the EU.

2   See UNSC 1373, 28 September 2001 and UNSC 1377, 12 November 2001. For comment, see UNHCR, *Addressing Security Concerns without Undermining Refugee Protection*, 2001; Gilbert, G, 'Protection after September 11th' (2003) 15 International Journal of Refugee Law 1; Bruin, R and Wouters, K, 'Terrorism and the non-derogability of non-refoulement' (2003) 15 International Journal of Refugee Law 5.

3   See Shah, P, 'Taking the "political" out of asylum: the legal containment of refugees' political activism' in Nicholson, F and Twomey, P (eds), *Refugee Rights and Realities: Evolving International Concepts and Regimes*, 1999, Cambridge: CUP, pp 119–35. He views this as part of a trend designed to contain the political activism of asylum seekers. The question he poses (at p 134) remains a pressing one: 'The question that arises is the extent to which the "political" dimension of asylum remains relevant and whether it can survive the manoeuvres of Western governments to suppress it.' See UNSC, *op cit*, fn 2, where it is made clear that political motivation should not be accepted as a ground for refusing the extradition of alleged terrorists. This reflects the steady erosion of the political offence exception in extradition law.

Human migration continues to play a prominent role in the development of states and the international community generally. The aim of the forcibly displaced is usually to seek the conditions that might make a fully human life possible. The reasons for flight are often complex and can include political, social or economic factors. The number of displaced persons is significant, and forced migration is accorded a central place in political discussions at all levels.

The focus of this chapter is on refugees and asylum seekers and the interaction with national security. As noted, asylum and terrorism are now often linked in political discussions. This has the potential to do lasting damage to the institution of asylum. The rule of law is under threat when national security concerns assume excessive prominence in the asylum debate. This is not a novel suggestion. When credible security threats exist (and there is often debate about whether threats are 'credible') there is a tendency to focus on the executive as best placed to address the matter. The argument is often made that the executive is in the best position to decide and has greater access to information upon which to reach balanced conclusions. The risk with this argument is that it can neglect the rigorous scrutiny of the interpretation of the legal standards that regulate exceptional situations. On this matter of legal interpretation, the judges are well placed to make decisions. My concern is primarily with how the senior judiciary addresses the arguments over the meaning of asylum law and policy. In order to understand the debates that have taken place over asylum and national security an examination must also be undertaken of the role of the judiciary in this area of public policy. Do different elements emerge when security concerns are raised? Are there, for example, any patterns in the approach adopted thus far?

The debate in the UK is similar to that in other common law jurisdictions. The suggestion made by some politicians is that the courts are interfering excessively in government asylum policy and have on occasions undermined the will of Parliament. In contrast, commentators and human rights advocates argue that deference to executive decision making is a continuing problem. The arguments are familiar ones and reflect long-established debates within constitutional democracies. These arguments, which continue in asylum law, are therefore not unique. It is, however, possible to test the merit of the arguments with reference to decided cases.

The senior judiciary is not undermining government asylum policy in the UK. Judges are aware of their institutional and constitutional roles, but are prepared to advance incrementally the interpretation of refugee law and on occasions question executive and administrative decision making. There is a danger, however, that when national security is raised, undue deference is accorded to the executive. The suggestion is not that deference is inappropriate (public law must retain some concept of due deference), but that there are risks if it becomes too extensive. On this, one must keep in mind that transnational judicial dialogue in human rights law will not necessarily result in more progressive interpretations of refugee law, or in robust judicial protection of human rights. Judges may just as easily discuss the merits of more deferential positions, particularly when there is a general climate of insecurity.

The debate in public law is polarised (and has been for some time) between those who are sceptical of the judicial role and those who believe the judges do not go far enough in defence of individual rights; but this is not an either/or choice. Some construction of the judicial role must form part of any analysis of public law that has not abandoned adjudication as a form of decision making. This suggests the need for an approach which recognises both the importance of parliamentary democracy (properly understood) and the robust parliamentary and judicial protection of the rights of vulnerable groups[4] (through the common law and statute law). This will not be found in excessive deference to the wishes of the executive, particularly when national security concerns are raised. It will also not be discovered in attempts to romanticise the judicial role. Attention should shift to legal argument and to those arguments that deserve recognition within a constitutional democracy that is committed to the rule of law. Less reliance should be placed on the institutional question of 'who should decide' and, instead, the arguments which surround the interpretation and application of legal norms should assume primacy. When national security concerns are prominent, it is essential that the existing normative framework is interpreted and applied appropriately. This process of intensive scrutiny need not be exclusively undertaken by the judiciary, and in the UK judges do not necessarily have the last word. Parliamentary committees, MPs, human rights and equality bodies, and NGOs all have responsibility in a functioning democracy to argue for the values that underpin legal order. However, criticism of judicial activism or deference suggests that some understanding of the judicial role is at work. The argument here is that this understanding needs to be positively argued for and not simply assumed. This approach places considerable emphasis on the values that underpin legal order and the arguments that best serve those values. These are values that are of particular relevance to non-nationals and which remain in place even when national security threats are raised.

DOES THE RULE OF LAW MATTER?

Even AV Dicey believed that arbitrary power was necessary in times of social disturbance or disorder.[5] He was of the view that 'order can hardly be maintained unless the executive can expel aliens'.[6] While framed within a conception of the rule of law where this was viewed as exceptional, it nevertheless highlights a common theme of assuming that certain actions *must* be permissible in times of serious disorder. The assumption that there are exceptional areas where legal order must not go, or if it does, that it must tread lightly needs to be challenged.

Before any attempt is made to consider asylum law, thought should be given to the rule of law and the judicial role. As I hope will become clear in the sections to follow, in advance of reflecting on national security and asylum a settled view

---

4   On this, see Singh, R, 'Equality: the neglected virtue' [2004] EHRLR 141.
5   Dicey, AV, *Introduction to the Study of the Law of the Constitution*, 8th edn, 1915, London: Macmillan, p 271: 'Under the complex conditions of modern life no government can in times of disorder, or of war, keep the peace at home, or perform its duties towards foreign powers, without occasional use of arbitrary authority.'
6   *Ibid.*

on these broader matters is necessary. Even if the starting point is scepticism about the judicial role, it is worth reflecting on what the judicial role *should be* or *might be* in this context.

It is usual to hear discussion of the rule of law in the context of citizenship. Does the rule of law, as a political ideal, depend upon national status, or is physical presence within the state sufficient? If asylum seekers have no effective say in the democratic process how can national law be legitimate for this group? The straightforward answer is the practical one: the asylum seeker is protected in law. Both common law and statute law recognise the asylum seeker; but in general discussions the link is still made between citizenship and legality. Citizenship is then constructed as the principal basis for entitlements and protection within a democratic state. In the UK there is currently a sharpened politics of citizenship. Despite much talk of a culture of respect for *human* rights, British citizenship and identity is accorded primacy in the treatment of individuals and groups. For those who lack this identity, separate, unequal and exceptional treatment is often regarded as acceptable, or is simply tolerated. The challenge in the democratic state is to make the commitment to respect for *human* rights meaningful. This argument is sometimes heard within democratic deliberation, but in practice it is often left to judges to articulate precisely what the normative ideals mean in individual cases.

There is no universal agreement on the meaning of the rule of law or the values that attach to it. The suspicion arises that it is rhetorical cover for the lack of a substantive argument, and disagreement continues over what it means to govern within a legal order. Does it, for example, mean that judges should defer consistently to the express wishes of the democratic branch of government? Are there areas of public policy where judges should not interfere? Are there values that stand above ordinary law? If not, are there values which inhere in the process of interpretation and application of the law? Debates on the meaning of the rule of law continue. To the human rights lawyer or activist some of these discussions will appear unnecessarily abstract. However, the outcome of debates on such jurisprudential issues do matter in the practical interpretation and application of substantive areas of legal regulation. Let us start by examining what views are held about the meaning of the rule of law.

First, there is what may be termed the 'formal tradition'. Writing from within this tradition, Joseph Raz notes the importance of the rule of law as a formal concept that means that legal rules must be general, prospective, open, clear and stable.[7] This description may appear uncontentious. In legal theory, the ongoing debate is on whether legal order is devoid of substantive moral or political content. The label 'formal tradition' is a simplification of the issues, but it captures a shared belief in the importance of separating legal validity from moral or political views. In this 'formal tradition' the rule of law may exist in a range of democratic contexts.

---

7   Raz, J, 'The rule of law and its virtues' (1977) 93 LQR 195.

Secondly, there are 'value-based' schools of thought on the rule of law. These approaches vary, but appear to influence those who attach more significance to the rule of law than the mere existence of formal legal rules and processes. In popular usage the concept is often deployed in place of a substantive argument about justice, suggesting that we invest it with political and moral ideals. When we talk about the principle of legality we appear to mean more than simply mechanically following enacted rules.

Dicey famously linked the concept to the supremacy of regular law as opposed to arbitrary power.[8] The basic idea is that extensive discretion is incompatible with the rule of law and, in this sense, it becomes a political ideal. This distrust of discretionary power is reflected in a number of accounts of the concept. It is a view that has particular relevance in the asylum context. A significant concern in asylum law is the discretion which the legal framework affords. Dicey's approach, often now described as constitutional law orthodoxy, remains of interest. This is the case, as asylum law demonstrates, even when it is accepted that discretion can be exercised in a number of ways. Arbitrary power in the asylum context has raised questions about the basic fairness of procedures. For Dicey, no one could be punished except by law, everyone must be equal before the law (in the sense that all classes of persons are subject to it) and law must be administered by the ordinary courts.[9] His key ideas are the applicability of the law to officials and citizens alike, and a preference for specific protections and real remedies rather than grand declarations of rights. The key themes identified by Dicey are evident in other conceptions of the rule of law that reflect a distrust of arbitrary power and a commitment to equality before the law. These core values underpin modern understandings of the rule of law, even if one accepts that law is, by nature, contested. These values have particular significance for marginalised groups. One fear of extensive discretionary power, for example, is precisely that vulnerable individuals and groups will suffer as a result. How this approach is classified in legal theory is of less interest than the values that it reflects and seeks to promote. What it suggests is that the rule of law has a substantive value and is not simply a formal or procedural concept.

Finally, some prefer to view the rule of law as political rhetoric and as, potentially, an obstacle to the achievement of social change. This is, of course, a crude simplification. However, it does capture a view that regards all talk of the rule of law or legality as a mask for power relations. This can either take the form of viewing law as political in indeterminate or determinate senses. In other words, law is contested in nature and simply reflects power relations within wider society and it should therefore be approached from a strategic and instrumental perspective. The commitment to legal order thus becomes a tactical one, and law, if useful at all, is constructed as a tool, in appropriate circumstances, to advance or impede wider political struggles. In this conception law becomes one arena of political contestation where interest groups operate to achieve political objectives.

---

8   *Op cit*, Dicey, fn 5.
9   *Op cit*, Dicey, fn 5.

Law is viewed here in instrumental terms; it has no independent normative value beyond the politics of particular factual circumstances. The strategic attitude towards the rule of law is often discussed in the human rights context. However, even if we accept the arguable and political nature of law this does not mean that we also must agree that the rule of law, or the principle of legality, is indeterminate.

The disagreement over the meaning of the rule of law reflects basic disputes in law and politics. Modern approaches that aim to hold onto a substantive understanding of the rule of law remain convincing. There are two main implications of adopting this position. First, it should promote a general legal and political culture where reasoned debate is possible in the formal and informal public spheres. This might be described as a procedural consequence of the principle of legality. The principle should keep channels of accountability, scrutiny and deliberation open. Secondly, the substantive moral aspect of the political ideal of legality rests on respect for the equal dignity and worth of the individual. Legality has fundamental procedural implications; but as a concept its basis is a political conception of the dignity of the individual. As David Dyzenhaus argues, the rule of law is therefore a political ideal, but one which should promote a culture of justification based on respect for the person.[10] The traditional categories in legal theory are not always helpful in this respect. The aim should be to highlight the arguable and dynamic nature of law and its basis in distinct values.[11] The focus should be on the substance of legal argument, as opposed to the sometimes oppressive institutional focus of the debate in the UK. Many of the values are reflected in the traditional approach. The idea of equality before the law and the distrust of arbitrary power are part of this. The attention shifts to the contribution the rule of law makes to the promotion of a general political culture of rational justification and the values that underpin it. The argument is that it means something, in substantive political terms, to be committed to legal order, as opposed to discretionary power administered on a case-by-case basis. The rule of law, in this understanding, is essential to the construction of a democratic culture in which people are treated equally, but the debate shifts towards legal reasoning as opposed to a rigid focus on the decision maker. If this approach is adopted, then when national security is raised there is no reason of principle why judges should not treat exceptional situations as being fully within the principle of legality. Legality is an important normative ideal for non-nationals.

The question is, however, how is this relevant to the debate on refugees and asylum seekers? Surely this focus on the arguable nature of law simply brings instability and uncertainty with it? These are genuine concerns and many

---

10 See Dyzenhaus, D, 'The permanence of the temporary', in Daniels, RJ, Macklem, P and Roach, K (eds), *The Security of Freedom: Essays on Canada's Anti-Terrorism Bill*, 2001, Toronto: University of Toronto Press, pp 21–37.

11 Dyzenhaus, D, 'Recrafting the rule of law', in Dyzenhaus, D (ed), *Recrafting the Rule of Law*, 1999, Oxford: Hart, pp 1–12; MacCormick, N, 'Rhetoric and the rule of law', in Dyzenhaus (ed) *ibid*, pp 163–77.

democracies do not have a proud record on protecting the rights of asylum seekers. However, legal orders generate mechanisms to resolve disagreement on the basis of existing norms and, often, foundational constitutional norms and values. Law is arguable, but it is not indeterminate in the sense this word is sometimes used. The turn to rational argumentation is convincing as a way to move the debate beyond the currently dominant preoccupation with 'who decides'. The obsession with the decision maker eventually weakens the protection of vulnerable groups in constitutional democracies and in some cases simply exacerbates the problem of Westminster executive dominance in the UK's democratic order.

I do not wish to underestimate the importance of the legitimacy of law-making processes, or the significance of judges who should be reflective of the societies they serve; but the judicial role must primarily revolve around the interpretation and application of norms and standards in particular cases, without undue anxiety about the political environment. The emphasis should be on continuing conversation over the terms of asylum law within the constraints of legal order. These are constraints that protect vulnerable individuals and groups. The political ideal of the rule of law is important not simply for citizens within the state, but for all persons who are subject to the jurisdiction of the state. In particular, this is because the rule of law promotes a democratic culture of equal concern and respect; and in the asylum context this becomes significant as it assists in the task of promoting a reasoned approach to this highly contested area of public policy. The justification of policy within law must *deserve* recognition within the terms of legal argumentation, and not solely on the basis of its pedigree. In the asylum context, it is not enough for judges to defer to executive decisions on the basis that Ministers are best placed to make them. Such deference simply shifts the responsibility to another institution, which will then be charged with making a substantive decision on what the law requires. Judges are obliged to address the substance of the legal arguments, even in cases where immigration, asylum and national security collide. In this respect, Dicey's emphasis on the ordinary courts and concerns about discretionary power retain their significance in asylum law and policy. This approach does have its limitations and these are well known. There is, for example, value in encouraging the development of expert bodies with knowledge of particular subject areas, such as immigration and asylum. These bodies can, in practice, arguably reach better decisions than the ordinary courts and ones which accord with the culture of justification mentioned here. This simply confirms the view that respect for the rule of law need not accord with established judicial hierarchies, but there are, at the same time, dangers in suggesting that certain groups require exceptional processes removed from normal legal processes.

As noted, the strength of the approach rests, in my view, on respect for the individual and the basic principles of fairness that this implies; but we need to move beyond the idea that this respect is owed solely or mainly to citizens. This is an area where judges may well be ahead of political and legal theorists. It is still too often the case that status is used unreflectively, thus neglecting the many people who are not nationals of the state they are in. In asylum law, where there are often extensive pressures placed on government and public administration to deliver quick results, the insistence on the importance of each individual is of particular significance. A commitment to legalism thus has an ethical dimension.[12] However the argument in favour of legalism as a positive conception does not mean support for a particular institutional belief in the courtroom as the only forum for its vindication.

SECURING ASYLUM

The legal framework

Asylum law in the UK has developed in the last decade as a specific area of public law.[13] There is now an extensive statutory framework and a substantial body of case law.[14] In addition, the Human Rights Act 1998 changes the human rights context.[15] There are other measures of relevance. For example, the Anti-terrorism Crime and Security Act 2001 deals specifically with immigration and asylum.[16] This legislation remains controversial and it has been subjected to extensive criticism. The 2001 Act increases the powers of the Home Secretary in relation to the deportation, removal and detention of 'suspected international terrorists'. Someone certified as a suspected international terrorist may be refused leave to remain, deported or removed from the UK. A person may also be detained even when it is unlikely that their removal will in fact be executed. An appeal is available to the Special Immigration Appeals Commission (SIAC) against certification. As a consequence of these measures the Government had to derogate from Art 5 of the European Convention on Human Rights (ECHR). Concerns were consistently raised about the 2001 Act and whether the indefinite detention of suspected international terrorist was a proportionate response.[17] In December 2004 a majority of the Law Lords ruled that the derogation was disproportionate and that the relevant provisions of the Anti-terrorism Crime and Security Act 2001

---

12 *Ibid*, MacCormick.

13 See, generally, Stevens, D, *UK Asylum Law and Policy: Historical and Contemporary Perspectives*, 2004, London: Sweet & Maxwell; Blake, N and Husain, R, *Asylum, Immigration and Human Rights*, 2003, Oxford: OUP; Shah, P, *Refugees, Race and the Legal Concept of Asylum in Britain*, 2000, London: Cavendish Publishing; Harvey, C, *Seeking Asylum in the UK: Problems and Prospects*, 2000, London: Butterworths.

14 The Asylum and Immigration (Treatment of Claimants, etc) Act 2004, Nationality, Immigration and Asylum Act 2002, Immigration and Asylum Act 1999, Asylum and Immigration Act 1996, and Asylum and Immigration Appeals Act 1993 constitute only the recent primary legislation in this field.

15 There is an extensive literature on the Human Rights Act 1998. See, generally, Bonner, B, Fenwick, H and Harris-Short, S, 'Judicial approaches to the Human Rights Act' (2003) 52 ICLQ 549; Gearty, C, 'Reconciling parliamentary democracy and human rights' (2002) 118 LQR 248; Leigh, L, 'Taking rights proportionately: judicial review, the Human Rights Act and Strasbourg' [2002] PL 265.

16 Part IV.

17 See, for example, Privy Counsellor Review Committee, *Anti-terrorism, Crime and Security Act 2001 Review: Report*, 18 December 2003, HC 100, pp 48–68; Joint Committee on Human Rights, *Anti-terrorism, Crime and Security Act 2001: Statutory Review and Continuance of Part 4* (2003–04) Sixth Report, HL Paper 38, HC 381.

were incompatible with ECHR rights. The Act deals directly with the interpretation of the key provisions in refugee law; these are Arts 1F (exclusion clauses) and 33(2) (permissible *refoulement*) of the Refugee Convention.[18] The 2001 Act grants the Home Secretary the power to certify that a person is not protected against *refoulement* because Art 1F or Art 33(2) applies and their removal would be conducive to the public good. In this context, the exclusion clauses are applied before inclusion is considered. The Act also makes clear that there is no balancing exercise involved in the assessment of these provisions. There is, of course, an ongoing debate within refugee law on this subject.

National security *may* become relevant to the asylum process at different stages. I stress '*may*' to emphasise that there is no necessary connection between the asylum system and national security. A link may emerge if asylum seekers, like other individuals, engage in specified actions in the asylum state or before entry. Some asylum seekers and refugees will have been politically active in their state of origin. This activism may have taken a number of forms. The issue of security may arise when the exclusion clauses are being considered during the status determination process. National security is not intended to be the primary concern at this stage, but there is evidence that it does enter into consideration. If a person is still awaiting determination of their claim, or is recognised as a refugee, their actions in the asylum state may trigger concern about a possible security risk. At this point their removal may be sought with reference to national security considerations. Removal in this context presents particular challenges where the individual faces a real risk of serious ill-treatment upon return to another unsafe state. While removal is an option, there is no necessary impediment to prosecution under existing anti-terrorism and/or criminal law. The legal framework currently in existence thus includes provision for dealing with asylum seekers and refugees who are suspected of being involved in terrorism.

The interpretation and application of refugee and asylum law

In order to advance the argument, I highlight two themes in asylum law: first, the contested meaning of refugee status and the treatment of asylum seekers awaiting a determination of their claim; and secondly, national security. A pattern emerges in the case law and it is one which does not support the argument that the judges are undermining asylum policy in the UK. What it does suggest is a senior judiciary intent on bringing clarity to the meaning of refugee law and mindful of its institutional role. This does not mean that agreement with executive decision making is always the result, but it does demonstrate a willingness to try to combine fairness to the individual with effective management of the asylum process. This tension, evident throughout public law, becomes particularly problematic in the area of asylum law where the management of the process, and the concerns of the executive, are on occasion accorded excessive weight. The

---

18 See Hathaway, JC and Harvey, C, 'Framing refugee protection in the New World disorder' (2001) 34 Cornell International Law Journal 257.

danger is that substantive legal arguments can lose out to managerial imperatives in the asylum process.

Refugee status determination is at the core of the asylum process. Who is a refugee in law? Although it is not strictly a part of domestic law, the definition used is contained in the 1951 Refugee Convention. An individual is a refugee if she has a well-founded fear of persecution for a 'Convention reason' and is unwilling or unable to seek the protection of their state of origin.[19] An individual also cannot be returned if this would be contrary to relevant provisions of the ECHR. The 1951 Convention definition is applied in domestic law in the UK, as is the ECHR, particularly since the entry into force of the Human Rights Act 1998. The House of Lords has attempted to establish a clear approach that will facilitate asylum decision making. It has also, on some occasions, been prepared to advance the interpretation of the definition to reflect the purpose of the law and modern legal developments in the protection of human rights.

In *R v Secretary of State for the Home Department ex p Sivakumaran*, for example, the issue was whether six Tamil asylum seekers were entitled to refugee status.[20] Their applications for asylum were refused by the Home Secretary. At first instance their applications for judicial review were rejected. However, on appeal to the Court of Appeal they were successful, and the Home Secretary appealed to the House of Lords. The Court of Appeal concluded that, from the perspective of someone of reasonable courage, the 'fear' (in 'well-founded fear') could be shown to be misconceived, but this fact alone did not necessarily transform its subjective nature. While the court accepted that fears which were simply paranoid could be discounted, those which were fully justified on the face of the situation could not be ignored, even if they were subsequently shown, by objective evidence, to have been misconceived. This approach was challenged in the House of Lords (the Court of Appeal did not find that the appellants were entitled to refugee status, this was a matter for the Home Secretary in the light of the new test). Lord Keith was critical of the reasoning. He shifted the attention back to the 'well-founded' nature of the fear. In other words, he stressed that the fear had to be objectively shown to be justified and not merely subjectively felt by the individual. Lord Keith stated:

> In my opinion the requirement that the applicant's fear of persecution should be well-founded means that there has to be demonstrated a reasonable degree of likelihood that he will be persecuted for a Convention reason if returned to his own country.[21]

Lord Templeman followed the same approach:

> My Lords, in order for a 'fear' of 'persecution' to be 'well-founded' there must exist a danger that if the claimant for refugee status is returned to his country of origin he will meet with persecution. The Convention does not enable the claimant to decide whether the danger of persecution exists.[22]

---

19   Article 1A(2).
20   [1988] 1 AC 958 (HL).
21   *Ibid*, p 994.
22   *Ibid*, p 996.

The approach of the Court of Appeal was rejected and the House of Lords opted for an interpretation which, in its view, would assist the process of asylum adjudication. By placing the emphasis on the 'well-founded' nature of the 'fear', the ruling guaranteed that, in practice, the objective element in the test would trump any subjective considerations. In the first important disagreement over the meaning of refugee status to reach the House of Lords, the focus thus shifted decisively to the conditions in the state of origin as the principal matter in the assessment of asylum claims. (It was not strictly the first refugee law case – see *Bugdaycay* discussed below.) The Law Lords opted for an interpretation that reflected the Government's preferred view of the refugee definition, and that focused on making the interpretation of refugee status manageable.

Disagreements are evident within states on the meaning of refugee law. These are resolved by domestic courts and tribunals. However, in the context of European integration, difficulties have arisen over divergent interpretations between member states of the EU. What happens if states disagree over the meaning of refugee law when a system is in place to transfer responsibility for the substantive assessment of claims? The issues were addressed in *R v Secretary of State for the Home Department ex p Adan*.[23] The case involved two appeals before the House of Lords from decisions in the Court of Appeal on applications for judicial review. Adan, a citizen of Somalia, had unsuccessfully sought asylum in Germany. After the refusal of her claim she travelled to the UK and claimed asylum. The Home Secretary determined, however, that the Dublin Convention 1990 (a treaty designed to facilitate the transfer of responsibility for asylum claims) was applicable and that Germany should take responsibility. The German authorities accepted responsibility and her claim for asylum in the UK was refused without consideration of the merits. Adan sought leave to move for judicial review of the certification of her case. The Divisional Court dismissed the application, but the Court of Appeal allowed Adan's appeal.

Aitseguer, a citizen of Algeria, had travelled through France on his way to the UK. He claimed to be at risk from an armed group in Algeria and that the Algerian Government was unable to protect him. The Home Secretary determined that Aitseguer should be returned to France in line with the Dublin Convention 1990. The French authorities agreed to take him back and his case was certified. Aitseguer successfully challenged the decision in judicial review proceedings on the basis that the Home Secretary had not taken the French position fully into account. This decision was subsequently upheld by the Court of Appeal.

In this instance the approach of the Law Lords had serious implications for government policy, and for hundreds of other similar cases. The problem involved the contested meaning of the refugee definition in different states and the impact this had on the operation of the Dublin Convention 1990. As Lord Steyn noted, a minority of states confined protection to those who could link persecution to the state. France and Germany followed this approach. The UK did not take this view. The consequent problems, stemming from conflicting

---

23 [2001] 2 AC 477 (HL).

interpretations of refugee law within the EU, were well illustrated in both of these cases. Adan feared persecution in Somalia as a result of being a member of a persecuted minority clan, while Aitseguer claimed to be the target of the Groupe Islamique Armé in Algeria. The feared persecution could not be attributed directly to the state. The Home Secretary accepted the argument that if they were returned to third countries both might be sent to their states of origin, due to the interpretation of the Convention applied in Germany and France. The Home Secretary did, however, suggest that there were alternative forms of protection in both states, which might offer protection to Adan and Aitseguer. An important question emerged: is there a true and 'international meaning' of the 1951 Convention, or do a range of possible interpretations exist, some of which the Home Secretary is entitled to regard as legitimate? Lord Steyn stated that the Refugee Convention did have a relevant autonomous and 'international meaning' and that this included persecution which emanated from non-state agents. Lord Slynn stated:

> The question is not whether the Secretary of State thinks that the alternative view is reasonable or permissible or legitimate or arguable but whether the Secretary of State is satisfied that the application of the other state's interpretation of the Convention would mean that the individual will still not be sent back otherwise than in accordance with the Convention. The Secretary of State must form his view as to what the Convention requires ... His is the relevant view and the relevant obligation is that of the United Kingdom.[24]

Lord Slynn rejected the argument that the Home Secretary could simply adopt a list of permissible interpretations of the Convention. The appeals by the Home Secretary were therefore dismissed. What the case demonstrated was a judicial insistence that the UK fulfil its obligations in refugee law by forming a view of the correct interpretation of the law. The question for the Home Secretary was not whether some other form of protection might be available in France or Germany, but what the 1951 Convention required. Would the individual in fact be sent back to their state of origin? The case reveals again the way that the legal system strives to promote internal certainty by encouraging determinate outcomes. In my view, by directing the Home Secretary to the correct interpretation of refugee law, the House of Lords effectively defended the notion that refugee law has a determinate content even in the face of disagreement in the EU. In particular, the Home Secretary was not permitted to evade responsibility by insisting that a range of reasonable interpretations existed outside of the UK. This case reflects a judicial insistence on the importance of according a determinate content to legal norms and the judges laid down important guidance on the approach that should be taken in the UK to refugee status in the context of European integration. The case is a useful example of how the law, through the process of adjudication, places a value on coherence and determinate outcomes in the context of ongoing disagreement.

---

24 *Ibid*, p 509.

It is difficult to view this as a case of the court stepping beyond the law to interfere with public administration. Even though the judgment had an impact on the application of the safe third country rule, the Law Lords were not prepared to defer to the argument of the Home Secretary. Their approach was based on the fundamental value of respect for the individual and the protection of the person in the determination of asylum cases. This judgment suggests where the limits to disagreement rest within refugee law and why those limits exist. The Law Lords accepted that disagreement over the meaning of the definition of refugee status existed, but then advanced an approach which openly acknowledged the potential unfairness and risk to the individual. If the Home Secretary was allowed simply to rely on reasonable disagreement within Europe, then risks would follow for the individual asylum seeker. The Home Secretary was thus obliged in law to reach a definite view of the true meaning of the definition of a refugee. The case neatly highlights an instance of how the legal system finds a determinate way out of disagreement and, in this case, in a way that reflects a concern for the rights of the individual. In my view, what underpins this is respect for the value of individual human dignity and a concern with the fairness of procedures.

Adan must now, however, be considered in the light of *R (Yogathas) v Secretary of State for the Home Department* and *R (Thangarasa) v Secretary of State for the Home Department*.[25] These cases involved the application of the safe third country rule to Germany. The House of Lords held that the Home Secretary had not acted unlawfully. A number of factors were significant. The Law Lords concluded that the German approach was not significantly different on persecution by non-state agents and on internal relocation. They concluded there was no real risk in either case that Art 3 of the ECHR would be violated. Lord Bingham stressed the importance of the 'anxious scrutiny test' (discussed below), but argued there were two further considerations. First, that courts should not infer that 'a friendly sovereign state which is party to the Geneva Convention will not perform the obligations it has solemnly undertaken'.[26] Only significant differences, in his view, should be allowed to prevent return in such cases. Secondly, he stated that the key issue was the prevention of return to places where the person will suffer persecution. The Law Lords relied on the reference to the German legal position as described in *TI v UK*.[27] They distinguished the position of Yogathas and Thangarasa from *ex p Adan* on the basis that in *Adan* they had not reflected fully on other forms of protection and German domestic law. The comments of Lord Hoffmann in *R v Secretary of State for the Home Department ex p Zeqiri*[28] are relevant here:

---

25 [2003] 1 AC 920 (HL).
26 *Ibid*, para 9.
27 [2000] INLR 211.
28 [2002] UKHL 3.

While therefore I entirely accept that Mr Zeqiri's wish to remain in the United Kingdom is an important matter to be taken into account, I do not think that it justified the courts in placing unnecessary obstacles in the way of the administration of the Dublin Convention.[29]

These cases suggest an awareness of the problems faced by the Home Office in the administration of asylum. They also are evidence of a judicial retreat from the position in *ex p Adan* and one influenced by the problems experienced in trying to make the system function effectively.

Two further cases reveal the tensions in the contests over the meaning of refugee law. In the first case, *Horvath v Secretary of State for the Home Department*,[30] the appellant was a member of the Roma community and a citizen of the Republic of Slovakia. He left Slovakia with his family and came to the UK to claim asylum. He argued that he feared persecution from skinhead groups that targeted Roma and that the Slovak police had failed to provide adequate protection. His application was refused and a special adjudicator dismissed his appeal on the basis that he was not a credible witness. The Immigration Appeal Tribunal (IAT), however, did find his evidence to be consistent and reviewed the finding on credibility. The IAT accepted that he had a well-founded fear of violence by skinheads, but that this did not constitute persecution because he had not demonstrated that he was unable or unwilling to seek the protection of the state. The Court of Appeal dismissed his appeal.

The issue for the House of Lords was the failure of the state to provide protection. What was the link to the persecution feared? Lord Hope stated that the purpose of the 1951 Convention was to offer surrogate protection when an individual no longer enjoyed the protection of their state of origin. He further stated that this purpose had implications for the interpretation of the word 'persecution'. Lord Hope suggested that the failure of state protection was central to the entire system of refugee law. He concluded that the word 'persecution':

… implies a failure by the state to make protection available against the ill-treatment or violence which the person suffers at the hands of his persecutors.[31]

The House of Lords dismissed the appeal. The case is a useful example of the UK Government's concerns about asylum policy entering fully into the assessment of the interpretation of refugee status. Rather than decide on the meaning of 'persecution', as a distinct concept, the Law Lords were more focused on the availability of protection in the state of origin. The case also reveals an unwillingness to accept that treatment in other European states might generate a valid refugee claim. In particular, the House of Lords relied heavily on an argument about the surrogate nature of refugee protection when it was assessing the meaning of the term 'persecution'. The assumption in this case, and one that is evident in other cases, is that sufficient protection is available in other European states.

---

29   *Ibid*, para 59.
30   [2000] 1 AC 489 (HL).
31   *Ibid*, p 497.

The case can be contrasted with *R v Immigration Appeal Tribunal ex p Shah; Islam and Others v Secretary of State for the Home Department*.[32] The appellants were two Pakistani women who had been forced from their home by their husbands and risked being falsely accused of adultery. They argued that they would be unprotected by the state if sent back and that they ran the risk of criminal proceedings for sexual immorality. They sought asylum in the UK on the basis that they had a well-founded fear of persecution as a result of membership in a particular social group, within the terms of the 1951 Convention. The issue before the House of Lords was the precise meaning to be given to 'membership in a particular social group'. A majority of the House of Lords concluded (Lord Millett dissenting) that the phrase could be applied to groups that might be regarded as coming within the Convention's anti-discriminatory objectives. This meant it applied to those groups that shared a common immutable characteristic, and were discriminated against in matters of fundamental human rights. In certain circumstances women could constitute such a group if they lived in societies like Pakistan. Unlike in *Horvath*, the majority in the House of Lords was prepared to be generous in the interpretation of refugee law, and in its assessment of the conditions in Pakistan.[33]

Although *Shah/Islam* might appear to extend the applicability of refugee law widely, the Law Lords were careful to stress the particular circumstances of the cases. The exercise of a more purposive interpretation within refugee law thus promotes, at best, incremental advances. The law is not static and is subject to development on the basis of the values that refugee law protects. The Law Lords were influenced by arguments about what a modern interpretation of refugee status should be in the light of ongoing developments in human rights law. In this construction the 1951 Convention is viewed as a 'living instrument'.

An individual is also protected from return if this would be contrary to the ECHR. It is well established that this obligation primarily relates to Art 3. However, the Law Lords have recently addressed, in the cases of *R v Secretary of State for the Home Department ex p Razgar*[34] and *R v Special Adjudicator ex p Ullah*,[35] the question of whether other Convention rights may prevent return. Both cases concerned a challenge to removal based on Articles other than Art 3 (*Razgar* involved Art 8 and *Ullah* involved Art 9). *Razgar* confirms the position that reliance may be placed on Art 8 to resist expulsion even where this is based only on the consequences for the mental health of the person if returned. The threshold is high, but if the facts of the case are strong enough then Art 8 may apply. *Ullah* again confirms that Art 9 may in principle be used but, as Lord Bingham noted, it is difficult to see how a claim that was sufficiently strong would not then be

---

32 [1999] 2 All ER 545 (HL).
33 Cf *Sepet and Another v Secretary of State for the Home Department* [2003] UKHL 15. Lord Bingham stated (at para 4) that the Convention should be viewed as a living instrument: 'While its meaning does not change over time its application will.' The case provides significant judicial guidance on how persecution should be interpreted.
34 [2004] UKHL 27.
35 [2004] UKHL 26.

successful under the Refugee Convention definition.[36] In other words, the person would have a well-founded fear of persecution for a Convention reason (religion).

The second main area of dispute in asylum policy is the treatment of asylum seekers while they are awaiting a decision and the decision-making process itself. Disagreement between some members of the judiciary and the executive is evident from the case law.[37] The tensions were demonstrated in *R v Secretary of State for the Home Department ex p Saadi*.[38] Saadi was one of four asylum seekers who appealed against the decision of the Court of Appeal that his detention at Oakington detention centre was lawful. At first instance it was held to be unlawful with reference to Art 5 of the ECHR.[39]

A fast-track procedure was introduced at the detention centre in 2000, whereby asylum seekers could be detained for seven days if it was felt that their claims could be determined quickly. Saadi and others challenged their detention. The first instance decision in their favour was subsequently reversed by the Court of Appeal. Their appeal to the House of Lords was also dismissed. The House of Lords concluded that their compulsory detention could not be said to have been arbitrary or disproportionate. In fact, the court argued, the process was highly structured and tightly managed. The Law Lords concluded that this structure would be disrupted if asylum seekers were able to live wherever they wished. The Law Lords stated that a balance had to be struck between the deprivation of liberty and the need for speedy decisions in order to prevent long delays. The House of Lords argued that conditions at Oakington were reasonable and that the periods of detention were not excessive. As a result, the balance was in favour of recognising that detention at Oakington was reasonable and proportionate. The judgment demonstrated a willingness to defer to the overall objectives of asylum policy, and judicial 'understanding' of the concerns of public administration. The Government's argument that detention was required in order to facilitate the speedy processing of selected asylum claims was found to be persuasive. In reaching this conclusion the Law Lords were evidently influenced by concerns about the overall management of the asylum process. The first instance judgment had, in particular, triggered an angry reaction from the Home Secretary. The judgment was, however, based on an interpretation of the meaning of the limitations to Art 5 of the ECHR, which suggested that the deprivation of liberty could be justified given the specific nature of the Oakington regime.

The Home Secretary was also not impressed with the first instance decision of Justice Collins in *R (Q and Others) v Secretary of State for the Home Department*.[40] The applicants challenged the lawfulness of a policy adopted under s 55 of the Nationality, Immigration and Asylum Act 2002. In order to meet Government

---

36	*Ibid*, para 21.
37	See *R v Secretary of State for the Home Department ex p Joint Council for the Welfare of Immigrants* [1997] 1 WLR 275 (CA).
38	[2002] UKHL 41.
39	Article 5 guarantees the right to liberty and the security of the person. It is not an absolute right and there are listed limitations.
40	[2003] EWHC 195 (Admin). See also the discussion by Keith Puttick in the present volume.

targets on the reduction of the number of asylum claims, the Home Secretary embarked on a policy of refusing welfare support to asylum seekers who did not make a claim 'as soon as reasonably practicable' upon entering the UK. The 2002 Act prohibits the provision of support to the destitute,[41] but allows the Home Secretary to offer support if it is necessary in order to prevent a breach of Convention rights.[42] The question the courts are faced with by the legislation is the level of destitution to which an individual has to fall before his or her suffering or humiliation reaches the minimum level of severity to amount to inhuman and degrading treatment under Art 3 of the ECHR. The precise meaning of s 55 was unclear, but more significantly the Act and its practical implementation were having a negative impact on asylum seekers in various parts of Britain. This problem was effectively left to the courts to resolve.

All the applicants were asylum seekers who were refused support because they had not made their claims as soon as reasonably practicable upon entering the UK. The applicants challenged the lawfulness of the decision and argued that their human rights were violated because the refusal to offer support meant they had no way of gaining access to food and shelter. Justice Collins held that the policy was unlawful. He found flaws in the decision-making process relating to a general failure to consider each case on its merits. He concluded that there was a real risk of a violation of Art 3 (prohibition on torture or inhuman or degrading treatment or punishment) and Art 8(1) (the right to privacy) of the ECHR on the basis that a person would be left destitute once benefits were refused. He also held that there had been a violation of Art 6 (right to a fair trial) with respect to the flawed procedures for challenging the initial refusal of support. In his judgment, Justice Collins referred to the fact that the Joint Committee on Human Rights at Westminster had noted possible problems under Art 3 and Art 8 during the legislative stage. The Home Secretary therefore had access to information suggesting human rights problems.

The Home Secretary appealed. The Court of Appeal, in rejecting the appeal, clarified the meaning of the relevant provisions of the 2002 Act with reference, in particular, to Art 3 of the ECHR. However, the more significant aspect of the judgment related to the assessment of the overall fairness of the procedures. The court held that the process was unfair for a range of reasons including: the flaws in the interview process; the fact that the purpose of the interview was not fully explained; the fact that the Home Secretary had not taken into account the state of mind of the individuals involved; and the use of standard form questionnaires. The Home Secretary opted not to appeal and reforms to the process were promised and introduced. Problems continued and in *R (Limbuela) v Secretary of State for the Home Department* the Court of Appeal held (Lord Justice Laws dissenting) that the Home Secretary had wrongly declined to provide support to asylum seekers under s 55(5) of the 2002 Act.[43] The Court of Appeal provided some further clarity on the meaning of the test to be applied. The Home Secretary

---

41 Section 55(1).
42 Section 55(5).
43 [2004] EWCA Civ 540.

has been given permission to appeal to the House of Lords. However, in response to the many problems that had arisen a decision was also taken to reform the s 55 process.

The importance of these cases rests in the careful scrutiny of the procedures applied and the emphasis, at first instance and in the Court of Appeal, on the importance of a proper assessment of each individual case.[44] This aspect of the application of the rule of law is sometimes neglected, but in a climate of hostility towards asylum seekers, the stress on the fairness of procedures, and the precise factors which need to be incorporated, is valuable. Judges may therefore fulfil an important role in ensuring procedural fairness and that equality before the law has meaning in practice for each individual. The stress on fairness is essential in the face of an asylum process that is under severe pressure from the executive to deliver quick results.

This rigorous assessment of asylum procedures by the judiciary has a history. An early example of concern about aspects of the asylum process is *Bugdaycay v Secretary of State for the Home Department*.[45] The appellants were granted temporary leave to stay in the UK and had remained beyond their designated leave. They were arrested and admitted that they had lied about their reasons for coming to the UK. They stated that they did not wish to return as they feared that they would be arrested for their political activities. Their applications for asylum were refused. As Lord Bridge acknowledged, this was the first time the House of Lords had to consider the 1951 Convention (although not the definition of refugee status).[46] In rejecting the argument of the appellants (that the immigration rules prohibited their removal), Lord Bridge noted that the matter was essentially a question of fact to be determined by an immigration officer or the Secretary of State and thus only open to challenge in the courts (at that time) on *Wednesbury* principles.[47] He stated:

> There is no ground for treating the question raised by a claim to refugee status as an exception to this rule.[48]

The first three appellants also sought to argue that the UK would be acting against recommendations advanced by the Executive Committee of the United Nations High Commissioner for Refugees (UNHCR) and that this was contrary to the obligation contained in Art 35 of the 1951 Convention.[49] Article 35 contains an undertaking by state parties to co-operate with UNHCR in the exercise of its functions. On this point Lord Bridge stated:

---

44 For an example of how the Law Lords have addressed the issue of dispersal and the provision of accommodation for destitute asylum seekers, see *Al-Ameri v Kensington and Chelsea LBC; Osmani v Harrow LBC* [2004] UKHL 4.

45 [1987] AC 514 (HL).

46 *Ibid*, p 521.

47 *Ibid*, p 523.

48 *Ibid*.

49 Article 35 deals with the obligation on states to co-operate with UNHCR.

I express no opinion on that question, since it is as it seems to me, neither necessary nor desirable that this House should attempt to interpret an instrument of this character which is of no binding force either in municipal or international law.[50]

Lord Bridge thereby rejected their argument. The case of the other appellant (Musisi) raised a distinct issue. He was a Ugandan national, and in this instance the Secretary of State argued that even if he was a refugee there was no obstacle to him being returned to Kenya. The issue to be addressed was whether there was any available ground by which the discretionary decision to remove Musisi to Kenya could be challenged in judicial review. On this Lord Bridge noted that:

> ... a detailed examination of the way in which the application made by the appellant for asylum was dealt with by the immigration authorities gives cause for grave concern.[51]

Lord Bridge was critical of the original asylum interview conducted by the immigration officer.[52] In particular, he was surprised to see such an important interview being undertaken by an immigration official with no knowledge of the country of origin.[53] The immigration officer rejected the appellant's arguments, but this view was not the one eventually relied on by the Home Office. The Home Office preferred to leave the question of refugee status 'open' in this case. The thrust of the argument was that a safe country (Kenya) existed to which the appellant could be returned. After stating the limitations on the role of the court in judicial review proceedings Lord Bridge noted:

> The most fundamental of all human rights is the individual's right to life and when an administrative decision under challenge is said to be one which may put the applicant's life at risk, the basis of the decision must surely call for the most anxious scrutiny.[54]

Applying this test to the case of Musisi, Lord Bridge concluded in the appellant's favour. The Secretary of State's decision to place faith in the Kenyan authorities was, according to Lord Bridge, misplaced.[55] Following a similar approach Lord Templeman stated:

> In my opinion where the result of a flawed decision may imperil life or liberty a special responsibility lies on the court in the examination of the decision-making process.[56]

The case is an example of the judicial use of rights discourse in administrative law long before the Human Rights Act 1998. It revealed a concern with the treatment of the individual in the asylum context and an acknowledgement of the serious human rights implications. As Nicholas Blake notes, the introduction of the

---

50 *Op cit*, fn 45, p 524.
51 *Op cit*, fn 45, pp 526–27.
52 *Op cit*, fn 45.
53 *Op cit*, fn 45.
54 *Op cit*, fn 45, p 531.
55 *Op cit*, fn 45, p 533.
56 *Op cit*, fn 45, p 537.

'anxious scrutiny' test in this case resulted in a sharp rise in judicial review applications and assisted in the eventual creation of a comprehensive appeals system.[57] The judgment recognised that where fundamental rights are at risk (in this instance the right to life), the courts, in judicial review proceedings, should examine the decision-making process very closely to ensure that there is no unfairness to the individual. The House of Lords in this case therefore introduced a more rigorous assessment of the asylum decision-making process, which had a practical impact on Government policy. A more recent example of this stress on the importance of procedural fairness and fundamental rights is *R (Anufrijeva) v Secretary of State for the Home Department*.[58] The issue was when an asylum case would be considered to have been determined for social security purposes. A note was placed on the internal departmental file that the asylum claim had been refused. From that date the Home Office treated the claim as having been refused. The claimant thus ceased to be an asylum seeker and was no longer entitled to income support. The House of Lords held (Lord Bingham dissenting) that constitutional principle required an adverse administrative decision to be communicated before it could have the character of a determination with legal effect. The majority held that general statutory words could not override fundamental rights and would be presumed by the court to be subject to those rights. Lord Steyn referred to the 'fundamental and constitutional principle of our legal system'.[59] He argued that the ECHR was not an exhaustive statement of fundamental rights:

> Lord Hoffmann's *dictum* applies to fundamental rights beyond the four corners of the Convention. It is engaged in the present case ... This view is reinforced by the constitutional principle requiring the rule of law to be observed. That principle too requires that a constitutional state must accord to individuals the right to know of a decision before their rights can be adversely affected. The antithesis of such a state was described by Kafka: a state where the rights of the individual are overridden by hole in the corner decisions or knocks on doors in the early hours. That is not our system ... Fairness is the guiding principle of our public law.[60]

Lord Bingham presented the dissenting view:

> I would not for my part question the principle of legality, let alone the importance of maintaining the rule of law. It is however a cardinal principle of the rule of law, not inconsistent with the principle of legality, that subject to exceptions not material in this case effect should be given to clear and unambiguous legislative provision.[61]

---

57 See Blake, N, 'Judicial review of expulsion decisions: reflections on the UK experience', in Dyzenhaus, D (ed), *The Unity of Public Law*, 2004, Oxford: Hart, pp 225–52.
58 [2004] 1 AC 604 (HL). Cf *R v Secretary of State for the Home Department ex p Salem* [1999] AC 450 (HL).
59 *Ibid*, para 26.
60 *Ibid*, paras 27–30. For Lord Hoffmann's *dictum*, see *R v Secretary of State for the Home Department ex p Simms* [2000] 2 AC 115, at 131.
61 *Op cit*, fn 58, para 20.

Making the principle of legality matter: National security, terrorism and the asylum process

I now turn specifically to the second area of relevance to this chapter – that is national security and the asylum process. Both the institution of asylum and the law of refugee status contain express provision for the exclusion of certain persons from protection.[62] The idea that certain persons, because of their actions, are undeserving of protection is not new to this area.

A willingness to defer to executive decision making is particularly marked. This is a trend which is not confined to asylum and immigration law. When a credible security threat exists there is a temptation to defer to the expertise and knowledge available to the executive; but as has often been stated, this is precisely when heightened judicial vigilance is required. Non-nationals are particularly vulnerable at such times and judges have a significant role in interpreting and applying the law in order to ensure that there are no exceptions to the presuppositions of legal order.

The first case of interest concerns the exclusion clauses in refugee law. There is ongoing debate about the scope of the exclusion clauses. The UNHCR has recently provided updated guidance on their interpretation and application.[63] It suggests:

> Their primary purpose is to deprive those guilty of heinous acts, and serious common crimes, of international refugee protection and to ensure that such persons do not abuse the institution of asylum in order to avoid being held legally accountable for their acts.[64]

The guidance does address the issue of terrorism. It provides:

> Despite the lack of an ... agreed definition of **terrorism**, acts commonly considered to be terrorist in nature are likely to fall within the exclusion clauses even though Art 1F is not to be equated with a simple anti-terrorism provision. Consideration of the exclusion clauses is, however, often unnecessary as suspected terrorists may not be eligible for refugee status in the first place, their fear being of legitimate prosecution as opposed to persecution for Convention reasons.[65] [Original emphasis]

The UNHCR stresses that each case requires individual consideration and the fact that someone may be on a list of terrorist suspects may trigger assessment under

---

62 Article 14(2) of the Universal Declaration of Human Rights 1948; Art 1F of the Convention relating to the Status of Refugees 1951. See, also, Arts 32 and 33 of the 1951 Convention.

63 UNHCR, *Guidelines on International Protection: Application of the Exclusion Clauses – Article 1F of the 1951 Convention relating to the Status of Refugees*, 4 September 2003, UN Doc HCR/GIP/03/05. See, also, Türk, V, 'Forced migration and security' (2003) 15 International Journal of Refugee Law 113; Gilbert, G 'Editorial' (2004) 16 International Journal of Refugee Law 1. See also the EU Council Qualification Directive of 29 April 2004, Articles 12 and 14, OJ (2004) L304/12.

64 *Ibid*, UNHCR, para 2.

65 *Ibid*, para 25.

the exclusion clauses, but should not in itself justify exclusion.[66] In addition, it suggests that the exclusion decision should in principle be dealt with within the regular status determination process.[67]

The Law Lords have addressed the issue of exclusion. In *T v Home Secretary*[68] the appellant was an Algerian citizen who claimed asylum in the UK. His claim was rejected by the Home Secretary and his appeal to a special adjudicator was unsuccessful. The appellant had been involved in a bomb attack on Algiers airport in which ten people were killed and then on a raid on an army barracks in which one person was killed. The special adjudicator concluded that this brought him within the exclusion clause in Art 1F(b)[69] because, as provided in that provision, 'there were serious reasons for considering' that he had committed serious non-political crimes. His appeals to the IAT and the Court of Appeal failed. The House of Lords also dismissed his appeal. However, the ruling contains extensive consideration of the meaning of 'serious non-political crime' within the context of refugee law. It demonstrated again the role of the House of Lords in resolving a disagreement over the meaning of refugee law with reference to the values the law was intended to promote. The House of Lords concluded that there were serious reasons for considering that the appellant had committed a serious non-political crime. The result was that the appellant could be legitimately excluded from refugee status. The debate in this case primarily involved the precision of the exclusion clauses rather than whether or not the appellant should have been excluded. The Law Lords displayed a desire to advance a clear definition that could be straightforwardly applied in the process of decision making and adjudication. Underpinning this, however, was a view of the purpose of refugee law and the values it is intended to uphold, in particular, that some individuals should be excluded from refugee status because of their criminal activity outside the state of refuge.

A related issue is what to do about those who are seeking asylum from persecution arising from anti-terrorism operations in other states. While a state may seek to arrest and prosecute terrorists, there is ample evidence of human rights being abused in the process. In *R (Sivakumar) v Secretary of State for the Home Department*, the claimant was a Tamil from Sri Lanka whose claim for asylum was rejected by the Home Secretary.[70] This was not a case where Art 1F was raised. On appeal, the adjudicator accepted the claimant had been detained and tortured, but held that this was due to the suspicion that he was involved in terrorism and not related to his political opinions. The IAT refused permission to appeal and the

---

66 *Ibid*, para 26.
67 *Ibid*, para 31.
68 [1996] AC 742 (HL). See also *Canada (Minister of Citizenship and Immigration) v Ward* [1993] 2 SCR 689; *Pushpanathan v Canada (Minister of Citizenship and Immigration)* [1998] 1 SCR 982; *Zrig v Minister of Citizenship and Immigration* (2003) FCA 178; *INS v Aguirre-Aguirre* (1999) 526 US 415.
69 Article 1F(b) provides: 'The provisions of this Convention shall not apply to a person with respect to whom there are serious reasons for considering that: (b) he has committed a serious non-political crime outside the country of refuge prior to his admission to that country as a refugee.'
70 [2003] UKHL 14.

claimant's application for judicial review was refused also. On appeal the Court of Appeal held that there was a strong inference that the claimant was persecuted for reasons of imputed political opinion or ethnicity, and the decision of the IAT was quashed. The Home Secretary appealed, arguing that persecution by agents of the state in the process of investigating suspected terrorist acts fell outside the protection of the 1951 Convention. The House of Lords upheld the decision of the Court of Appeal. Lord Steyn stated that not all terrorist acts fall outside the Convention:

> In other words not all means of investigating suspected terrorist acts fall outside the protection of the Convention.[71]

By suggesting that being investigated for involvement in terrorist acts took a person outside the protection of the Convention the adjudicator had got it wrong. Lord Steyn noted that there was a strong claim for refugee status in this case but, as four years had since elapsed, it was decided to remit the case back to the IAT. Lord Hutton stated that the proper conclusion was that the acts of torture were inflicted not solely to obtain information to tackle terrorism, 'but were inflicted, at any rate in part, by reason of the torturers' deep antagonism towards him because he was a Tamil ...'.[72]

The cases reveal that when national security, immigration and asylum collide, judges are likely to defer to the views of the executive. This trend remains the dominant one, though there is some evidence of a more robust attitude in recent case law. The general trend was confirmed in *Secretary of State for the Home Department v Rehman*.[73] The appellant, a Pakistani national, arrived in the UK in February 1993 after being given entry clearance to work as a minister of religion in Oldham. Both his parents were British citizens. His application for indefinite leave to remain was refused. The Home Secretary cited information that linked the appellant to an Islamic terrorist organisation and argued that his deportation from the UK would be conducive to the public good in the interests of national security. Rehman appealed to the Special Immigration Appeals Commission (SIAC). The SIAC was established under the Special Immigration Appeals Commission Act 1997.

It was created in response to the judgment of the European Court of Human Rights in *Chahal v UK* and the concerns raised in that case about the procedures for challenging deportation in the national security context.[74] *Chahal* is an important judgment because of the stress placed on the absolute nature of the Art 3 protection in removal cases and the rejection of the argument that a balancing exercise is necessary.

In his open statement to SIAC, the Home Secretary stated that the appellant had directly supported terrorism in the Indian subcontinent and, as a result, he was a threat to national security. The Commission held, contrary to the argument

---

71 *Ibid*, para 17.
72 *Ibid*, para 29. See also the judgment of Dyson LJ [2001] EWCA Civ 1196.
73 [2001] UKHL 47.
74 (1996) 23 EHRR 413.

of the Home Secretary, that the term 'national security' should be narrowly defined. The Commission stated:

> ... we adopt the position that a person may be said to offend against national security if he engages in, promotes, or encourages violent activity which is targeted at the United Kingdom, its system of government or its people. This includes activities directed against the overthrow or destabilisation of a foreign government if that foreign government is likely to take reprisals against the United Kingdom which affect the security of the United Kingdom or of its nationals. National security extends also to situations where United Kingdom citizens are targeted, wherever they may be.[75]

The Commission concluded that it had not been established in fact that the appellant was likely to be a threat to national security. The test adopted was that of a high civil balance of probabilities. The Home Secretary appealed successfully to the Court of Appeal.[76] The Court of Appeal considered that too narrow a view of national security had been adopted by the Commission. On appeal to the House of Lords, Lord Slynn acknowledged that the term 'in the interests of national security' could not be used to justify any reason the Home Secretary had for seeking the deportation of an individual.[77] However, he did not accept the narrow interpretation suggested by the appellant:

> I accept that there must be a real possibility of an adverse affect on the United Kingdom for what is done by the individual under inquiry but I do not accept that it has to be direct or immediate. Whether there is a real possibility is a matter which has to be weighed up by the Secretary of State and balanced against the possible injustice to that individual if a deportation order is made.[78]

Lord Slynn stressed the need for the Commission to give due weight to the assessment and conclusions of the Home Secretary in the light of his responsibilities.[79] Lord Steyn agreed with the reasoning of Lord Slynn and added that 'even democracies are entitled to protect themselves, *and* the executive is the best judge of the need for international co-operation to combat terrorism and counter-terrorist strategies'.[80] In rejecting the Commission's reliance on the civil standard of proof, Lord Steyn made reference to the events of 11 September 2001.[81] He concluded by acknowledging the well-established position that issues of national security do not fall beyond the competence of the courts. However, he stated that it was, 'self-evidently right that national courts must give great weight to the views of the executive on matters of national security'.[82] Lord Hoffmann

---

75   *Op cit*, fn 73, para 2.
76   [2000] 3 WLR 1240 (CA).
77   *Op cit*, fn 73, para 16.
78   *Op cit*, fn 73, para 16.
79   *Op cit*, fn 73, para 26.
80   *Op cit*, fn 73, para 28. Original emphasis.
81   'While I came to this conclusion by the end of the hearing of the appeal, the tragic events of 11 September 2001 in New York reinforce compellingly that no other approach is possible.' *Ibid*, para 29. For developments in Canada, see *Suresh v Canada (Minister of Citizenship and Immigration)* [2002] SCC 1, where the deferential approach in *Rehman* was mirrored.
82   *Op cit*, fn 73, para 31.

continued this theme, stating that the Commission had failed to acknowledge the inherent limitations of the judicial function that flowed from the doctrine of the separation of powers.[83] This brought with it the need 'in matters of judgment and evaluation of evidence, to show proper deference to the primary decision-maker'.[84] This restraint did not limit the appellate jurisdiction of the Commission and the need for it 'flows from a common-sense recognition of the nature of the issue and the differences in the decision-making processes and responsibilities of the Home Secretary and the Commission'.[85] In a postscript Lord Hoffmann stated:

> I wrote this speech some three months before the recent events in New York and Washington. They are a reminder that in matters of national security, the cost of failure can be high. This seems to me to underline the need for the judicial arm of government to respect the decisions of ministers of the Crown on the question of whether support for terrorist activities in a foreign country constitutes a threat to national security ... If the people are to accept the consequences of such decisions, they must be made by persons whom the people have elected and whom they can remove.[86]

The ruling endorsed a very broad interpretation of 'national security'. The notion that the executive must be deferred to because of its democratic legitimacy and expertise, particularly in times of crisis, raises several problems. Lord Hoffmann's comments suggest that the executive can step outside the normal application of the rule of law in times of public emergency by making its own decision about what the law is.

As Trevor Allan suggests, surely the focus should be on the quality of the reasons advanced.[87] The main question should be whether the legal reasoning is worthy of support or not in the individual case. To defer mainly because it is a decision of the executive, based on rather sweeping assessments of the national security threat, is problematic. This view is reinforced if one considers that in the national security context there is a heightened risk to the human rights and civil liberties of the individual, both with respect to suspects and those likely to be at risk from terrorism. It is on these occasions that the rule of law is tested, both in the sense of protecting individual rights and ensuring that an effective regulatory framework exists within which to offer security. By according conclusive weight to the views of the executive, the judges are not discharging their responsibilities on either of these matters. It is for the judges to take a view on the meaning of law, and not to defer excessively to the meaning preferred by the executive. If the courts do not do this they risk abandoning one of the values of the rule of law: the defence of the person against arbitrary power. Why the House of Lords was

---

83 *Op cit*, fn 73, para 49.

84 *Op cit*, fn 73.

85 *Op cit*, fn 73, para 58.

86 *Op cit*, fn 73, para 62. This statement can be usefully contrasted with his views in *R v BBC ex p Life Alliance* [2003] UKHL 23, at para 74 ff and *R v Secretary of State for the Home Department, ex p Simms and O'Brien* [2000] 2 AC 115.

87 See Allan, T, 'Common law reason and the limits of judicial deference', in Dyzenhaus, D (ed), *The Unity of Public Law*, 2004, Oxford: Hart, pp 289–306.

prepared to insist on its approach in *Shah/Islam* and *ex p Adan* and not in *Rehman* remains unclear, if one approaches this on the substantive legal arguments only.

Although dealing with a different issue, similar trends are evident in *A and Others v Secretary of State for the Home Department*.[88] The case concerned a challenge by a number of individuals detained under the provisions of the Anti-terrorism, Crime and Security Act 2001. That Act, and the Human Rights Act 1998 (Designated Derogation) Order 2001, were introduced after the terrorist attacks of 11 September 2001.[89] The Act granted the Home Secretary the power to issue a certificate if he reasonably believes that the individual's continuing presence in the UK is a risk to national security and suspects that the person is a terrorist. Suspected international terrorists may be detained. There is a right of appeal to the SIAC.[90] A challenge was brought against the provisions of the 2001 Act. The Government derogated from Art 5 of the Convention for the specific purpose of these provisions. The SIAC held that the measures were discriminatory in effect, and were contrary to Arts 5 and 14 of the European Convention, as they did not apply equally to British nationals.

On appeal against the SIAC decision, the Court of Appeal reached a different conclusion. Following a similar approach to that expressed in *Rehman* Lord Woolf stated:

> Decisions as to what is required in the interest of national security are self-evidently within the category of decisions in relation to which the court is required to show considerable deference to the Secretary of State because he is better qualified to make an assessment as to what action is called for.[91]

Lord Justice Brooke adopted a similar line of reasoning.[92]

The Court of Appeal held that British nationals were not in the same position as foreign nationals in this context. Lord Woolf noted that the non-nationals involved in this case no longer had a right to remain, only a right not to be removed.[93] This distinguished their plight from that of nationals. He also stressed that international law recognised the distinction between the treatment of nationals and non-nationals. The court accepted that Parliament was entitled to limit the measures to foreign nationals on the basis that Art 15 of the European Convention permitted measures that derogate only 'to the extent strictly required by the exigencies of the situation'. The tension between Art 14 and Art 15 had,

---

88   [2002] EWCA Civ 1502.

89   On the operation of the legislation, see Amnesty International, *Justice Perverted under the Anti-terrorism Crime and Security Act 2001*, 11 December 2003.

90   For criticism of SIAC from a former member, see Sir Brian Barder, 'The Special Immigration Appeals Commission' 26(6) London Review of Books, 18 March 2004.

91   *Op cit*, fn 88, para 39.

92   *Op cit*, fn 88, para 81(6): 'The events of 11th September are a reminder that in matters of national security the cost of failure can be high. Decisions by ministers on such questions, with serious potential ... require a legitimacy which can be conferred only by entrusting them to persons responsible to the community through the democratic process.'

93   *Op cit*, fn 88, para 47.

Lord Woolf argued, an important impact. The Secretary of State was obliged to derogate only to the extent necessary and widening the powers of indefinite detention would, Lord Woolf stated, conflict with this objective.

While acknowledging the importance of human rights protection, the Court of Appeal also accepted that it had to accord a degree of deference to the views of the executive in this area. Lord Woolf stated:

> The unfortunate fact is that the emergency which the government believes to exist justifies the taking of action which would not otherwise be acceptable. The ECHR recognises that there can be circumstances where action of this sort is fully justified. It is my conclusion here, as a matter of law, and that is what we are concerned with, that action is justified. The important point is that the courts are able to protect the rule of law.[94]

The case reveals again the measure of deference accorded to the executive when national security is raised. Lord Woolf's reference to the rule of law rests uneasily with other aspects of the case. What the statement reveals is, in this case, a concern to check that the Government's policy could be justified with reference to established legal norms; but there was not the sort of rigorous assessment that has emerged in other immigration and asylum cases. The view of the Court of Appeal did not persuade the majority in the House of Lords. As noted, in December 2004 a majority of Law Lords ruled that the derogation was unlawful and that the relevant provisions of the legislation were incompatible with Convention rights. It is also evident from the SIAC ruling and the House of Lords' judgment that scope for disagreement on the content of the law existed in the case. The weight given to the views of the executive (by both the SIAC and the Court of Appeal) on what was necessary in this context, and whether there was in fact an emergency which threatened the life of the nation, is revealing. Again, there is evidence that the views of the Home Secretary were being accorded excessive weight. This is an area where 'anxious scrutiny' of the reasons provided is most needed. In my view, this is not happening when national security is raised.

Suspected international terrorists have not fared much better on other aspects of their detention. In *R (A) v Secretary of State for the Home Department*, the BBC and the *Guardian* newspaper applied to interview those detained.[95] Conditions were attached to the interview process, such as the journalists not being permitted to tape- record interviews. The media agreed, but the detainees did not. Their judicial review of the decision to attach conditions was dismissed. Justice Kennedy concluded that they were justifiably suspected of being terrorists and the additional national security dimension provided ample justification for the conditions attached. The balance struck by the Home Secretary was not one against which the court would interfere. This deferential trend was halted to some extent in *Secretary of State for the Home Department v M*.[96] In this case the SIAC allowed an appeal against certification and the decision of the Home Secretary to make a deportation order against a Libyan national. M was a failed asylum seeker,

---

94   *Op cit*, fn 88, para 64.
95   [2004] HRLR 12 (Admin).
96   [2004] EWCA Civ 324.

he was not removed and it came to be accepted that he could not be returned. He was certified in November 2002 as a suspected international terrorist, his deportation was sought and he was subsequently detained. M's argument was that he feared persecution on return to Libya as a result of his opposition to the Ghadafi regime. The Home Secretary believed that he had links to Al Qaida. The judgment of the Lord Chief Justice, Lord Woolf, contained strong comment on the value of SIAC, which can perhaps be viewed in the light of the public criticism of this body.[97] Lord Woolf stressed the critical nature of the value judgment which SIAC had to make and noted that it was the body which was qualified to make this assessment. He stated:

> While the need for society to protect itself against acts of terrorism today is self evident, it remains of the greatest importance that, in a society which upholds the rule of law, if a person is detained, as 'M' was detained, that individual should have access to an independent tribunal or court which can adjudicate upon the question of whether the detention is lawful or not. If it is not lawful, then he has to be released.[98]

This was the first time the SIAC had allowed an appeal under the 2001 Act and thus also the first time that the Home Secretary had reason to challenge the decision under this legislation. Another case arising from the work of the SIAC was G v Secretary of State for the Home Department.[99] The case again involved an individual who had been certified as a suspected international terrorist. He applied to the SIAC for a grant of bail, claiming that his mental and physical health had deteriorated rapidly as a result of detention. The SIAC held that once certain conditions were met he should as a matter of principle be granted bail. The Home Secretary appealed against this decision. The Court of Appeal held (Pill LJ dissenting) that it had no jurisdiction to hear the appeal since bail was not a final determination of an appeal for the purposes of the legislation. It decided it would reconstitute itself as the Administrative Court and hear the application to apply for judicial review of the SIAC decision. The Government's response was to introduce an amendment to the Asylum Bill then going through Parliament.[100]

Although not specifically in the national security area, a case involving public order further supports the general argument. In R (Farrakhan) v Secretary of State for the Home Department,[101] the claimant was an African-American US citizen who was refused entry to the UK on public order grounds. The Home Secretary appealed against the decision of Justice Turner to allow the claimant's application for judicial review. Justice Turner held that the Home Secretary was required to provide objective justification for excluding the applicant and he had failed to provide this. The issue was whether Art 10 of the ECHR was engaged in a decision

---

97   Op cit, Barder, fn 90.
98   Op cit, fn 96, para 34(iii). See also Lord Woolf, 'The rule of law and a change in the constitution', Squire Centenary Lecture, 3 March 2004.
99   [2004] EWCA Civ 265.
100 Mr Browne, HC Deb 421 Col 778w, 17 May 2004. See s 32 of the Asylum and Immigration (Treatment of Claimants, etc) Act 2004.
101 [2002] 3 WLR 481 (CA).

to exclude an individual to prevent his expressing opinions in the UK. The Court of Appeal held that Art 10 was engaged, but concluded that the exclusion of the individual was for a legitimate aim under Art 10(2). Disagreeing with the judge at first instance, the Court of Appeal held that the Home Secretary had provided sufficient explanation for the decision. While the issue of public order involves a difficult assessment, it was not evident in this case that a 'significant threat to community relations' would be the result of the visit.

As noted in the cases above, beyond the national security context the views of the Home Secretary, and the administrative perspective, are accorded significant weight, but they are not generally regarded as a decisive argument. While one can understand a certain judicial unease in addressing national security matters, excessive deference to the views of the executive is inappropriate if there is a principled commitment to the consistent interpretation and application of the law. Evidence suggests that this is precisely the time when the values that underpin the rule of law need to be upheld. While the Home Secretary will have access to detailed factual information, and is the person who will face democratic accountability for the decision, the courts should not automatically defer to the Home Secretary's understanding of the substantive content of the law. On this matter the Home Secretary is in no better position than a judge. This view is reinforced when one considers that human rights standards are now a secure part of domestic law in the UK in the form of the Human Rights Act 1998. The judges have a responsibility to ensure that the law, properly understood, is applied to all on an equal basis. The risk is that exceptional treatment of particular groups and particular legal subject areas will lead to further erosion of existing guarantees.

Talking about asylum law

The cases examined address some key areas of disagreement over the meaning of asylum law. Questions were raised over the definition of 'refugee', the management of the asylum process, the effective implementation of international agreements, as well as the matter of national security. The House of Lords has now clarified central elements of the refugee definition in an attempt to resolve disputes within the process of adjudication. The Law Lords, in my view, have not adopted an approach that can be easily reduced to a single or unified theme. It is not possible, based on the current evidence, to be wholly dismissive or unequivocally supportive of the role of the senior judiciary. There is no simple pattern that emerges from the cases. However, it is inaccurate to describe the judicial approach as a concerted attempt to undermine Government asylum policy. When they might have been robust they have been deferential. While there have been incremental advances in doctrinal development, and in ensuring procedures are applied fairly to each individual, the senior judiciary consistently display a measure of deference toward the executive and a rather generous understanding of the managerial problems faced by successive governments. The risk in this approach is that the value that the rule of law attaches to the protection of the individual is steadily eroded and the responsibility for applying legal standards consistently is neglected. However, any balanced assessment must acknowledge the invaluable work of judges and lawyers in upholding the rights of asylum seekers. Significant constitutional debates are now occurring within this area of law and there is evidence of a principled stand being taken by several members of the judiciary. There is often intense political pressure not to impede the priorities of the executive.

On the issue of national security and public order, decisions reveal an established trend of deference toward the Government's view. This is evident in *Rehman* and *Farrakhan*. In these cases, the judges selected an approach designed to facilitate Government policy and relied on deferring to the executive on the basis of its democratic mandate and/or special position with regard to the facts. The reference made to the rule of law in *A and Others* by Lord Woolf reflects a rather 'thin' version of the concept. This general 'facilitative approach' goes beyond national security and is evident in the other cases examined above. The *M* case does not necessarily signal a major shift in approach, although the comments about the role of SIAC are significant when viewed in context.

The cases reveal a senior judiciary that places considerable weight on the overall management implications of judicial decision making and which is inclined to defer to the executive, particularly if national security is raised. From the analysis of these cases, and despite recent advances concern expressed by politicians about judicial activism appears to have little validity. In my view, this is a cause for concern. Even in areas where a clash with the Government is likely, the judges should insist on following the most persuasive legal argument in the context of the asylum case before it. Fairness to the individual and equality before the law (both inherent in a proper understanding of what it means to function within a legal order) should not be abandoned when judges are faced with difficult choices. These values are more (not less) important when national security concerns are raised or when a marginalised group is at risk. In this context, each individual (whatever the collective ambitions of Government policy) relies on institutions willing to remain consistently focused on the rule of law and the values that underpin it. The defence of legality is not the exclusive preserve of the judiciary. Those who are, for example, serious about creating a culture of respect for human rights know that the principles of legal order must be reflected throughout public administration and the parliamentary system.

CONCLUSION

In this chapter I placed the judicial role in asylum cases within a wider conception of legal order. In particular, I argued that 'dialogic' approaches, which shift attention away from institutions and sources of power towards argumentation and justification, are useful for both understanding and evaluating the existing case law. The traditional values associated with the rule of law are of particular significance for refugees and asylum seekers in all cases whether national security is at issue or not. The protection against arbitrary power and the basic principles of fairness, which are built into legal order, are important for marginalised groups in society. Judges, and others, have a duty to uphold the rule of law even when they risk serious public criticism and even when there is a general political climate of insecurity. The protection from arbitrary power that the concept should bring is undermined if judges refuse to engage with contested areas of public policy.

Under the substantive concept of legality advanced here, adherence to the rule of law is founded on a commitment to respect for the dignity of the individual. While its application is associated with the judiciary, this is not the only institution responsible for ensuring respect for the principle. In my view, the senior judiciary has demonstrated an understanding of the significance of the principle of legality in asylum law. However, when national security is raised there is a danger of deference undermining a thorough examination of the substantive legal issues. Asylum seekers, in particular, depend on judges and decision makers who are prepared to give meaning to the principle of legality.

CHAPTER 9

ASYLUM APPEALS: THE CHALLENGE OF ASYLUM TO THE BRITISH LEGAL SYSTEM

Robert Thomas*

This chapter addresses the challenge posed by asylum to the British legal system, by considering the system of asylum appeals, which exists to determine appeals against the Home Office's refusal of refugee status. The challenge, as I define it for the purpose of this chapter, is this: how is the asylum adjudication system to balance the competing demands placed upon it? Given the nature of the issues at stake, the system operates within a context of intense political scrutiny, which demands efficiency, speed and finality. At the same time, the system is under pressure to produce accurate and consistent decisions through fair procedures. Furthermore, the system must be operationalised in practice. The Government must seek to translate these competing goals into operational reality, a task that, in a world of restricted financial and organisational resources, inevitably imposes its own limitations. The principal objective of any workable adjudication system ought to be to attain some coherence amongst these goals. The purpose of this chapter is to seek to identify the values that underlie the adjudication system and suggest criteria by which it may be evaluated. Furthermore, the chapter will also attempt to consider some of the recent and proposed changes to the appellate system, in particular the move from the present two-tier appellate process (whereby appeals are determined initially by adjudicators and then on appeal by the Immigration Appeal Tribunal (IAT)) into a single tier of appeal (the new Asylum and Immigration Tribunal (AIT)).

The structure of this chapter is as follows: first, I identify the competing models of administrative justice that underlie contemporary debates about how asylum adjudication should be organised and suggest that such debates may only be understood against the broader political debate over asylum policy; secondly, I highlight the distinctiveness of asylum decision making; thirdly, I identify the principal values that the adjudication process seeks to promote, and examine how these values are promoted within the asylum adjudication system.

ASYLUM ADJUDICATION AND ADMINISTRATIVE JUSTICE

Broadly speaking, 'administrative justice' concerns the justice inherent in administrative and legal decision making. Mashaw offers a simple definition: administrative justice means 'those qualities of a decision-process that provide

---

*   I would like to acknowledge grateful financial assistance from the British Academy.

arguments for the acceptability of its decisions.'[1] The justice of an administrative-legal decision-making process is intimately connected with the extent to which the decisions produced are acceptable and legitimate. If the decisions produced command a high level of acceptance, then the justice inherent in the decision-making process achieves a more optimal level. However, different individuals and institutions may have different conceptions of what comprises an acceptable and legitimate decision-making process.

While much recent administrative justice scholarship has examined primary decision making, it is clear that the scope of the subject also includes the operation of appellate processes. Tribunals, it has been frequently observed, occupy a difficult position between the executive and judicial branches of government.[2] In the context of asylum appeals, this tension is perhaps more evident than in other areas. At one level it is played out in debates between government departments and the courts.

At a higher level of abstraction, this tension may be reflected in the competition between the two principal models of administrative justice that underlie asylum adjudication: a bureaucratic model and a legal model.[3] The goal of a bureaucratic model would be to maximise the common good through the statutory scheme by processing the aggregate number of applications. One important value of this model would be the efficiency of the administrative process through the application of rules. Another would be the effective and accurate implementation of public policy; individual cases are only relevant insofar as they contribute toward the achievement of the broader policy objectives. In the asylum context, this model is perhaps most clearly reflected in the Home Office's desire to process asylum claims expeditiously to ensure that genuine refugees are recognised, in the fast turnaround of manifestly unfounded cases and in the more effective enforcement of immigration control.

A competing model of administrative justice might be termed a legal or judicial model. While this model would also place value on the accurate and effective application of the relevant rules, the emphasis is on accuracy and propriety in each individual case rather than the aggregate. This model emphasises the importance of fair treatment to individuals and the independence of the decision maker. In the context of asylum adjudication, this model can be seen reflected in the appellate system with its emphasis on the individual consideration of each appeal, judicial independence, legal representation, fair procedures and review by the higher courts.

Both of these competing models of administrative justice can be detected within the asylum adjudication system. The tension between them can be seen in debates over how asylum adjudication should be structured and conducted.

---

1   Mashaw, JL, *Bureaucratic Justice: Managing Social Security Disability Claims*, 1983, New Haven: Yale UP, pp 24–25.

2   As Wraith, RE and Hutchesson, PG, *Administrative Tribunals*, 1973, London: Allen & Unwin, p 17 note: '[t]he British constitution tries to keep law and politics apart ... but administrative tribunals inhabit a twilight world where the two intermingle.'

3   See, *op cit*, Mashaw, fn 1, pp 25–34; Galligan, DJ, *Due Process and Fair Procedures: A Study of Administrative Procedures*, 1996, Oxford: OUP, pp 237–40.

Should the appellate process move from a two-tier to a single-tier structure? Should the Government have persisted with its proposal to oust the jurisdiction of the High Court to review judicially Tribunal and executive decisions in the asylum context? What amount of resources should be devoted by the state to ensure that asylum claimants are properly and effectively represented and advised? More generally, the broader normative question is this: what should be the role of law in the administration of asylum policy? The different answers to these questions may depend upon which underlying conception of administrative justice is preferred. In order to appreciate this basic tension, it is essential to situate the debate over asylum adjudication in its political context.

Asylum is a high profile area of public policy and governments place a high priority on seeking to ensure that policy is administered effectively.[4] This pressure arises from the very nature of asylum itself: applicants are by definition foreign nationals who may not otherwise qualify to remain in the UK; their continued presence poses a threat to effective immigration controls. Given the difficulties faced by the Home Office in securing the removal of unsuccessful asylum applicants, the legal process has been identified as an important cause of delay and therefore an impediment to the effective administration of removals. Extensive procedures for challenging the legality of decisions may prolong the whole decision-making procedure, delay the final resolution of claims, encourage further false or abusive applications and therefore undermine the maintenance of legitimate border controls. There are also broader concerns, such as the possible threat to community relations and social cohesion and the degree to which far-right political parties might exploit the situation. These political imperatives have clearly motivated the Government to restructure administrative and legal decision-making processes.

At the same time, there are compelling arguments as to why decisions refusing asylum should be subject to extensive legal controls. Such decisions intimately affect individuals' fundamental rights; as the costs of incorrect decisions to the individual concerned are extremely high, they should be subject to the 'most anxious scrutiny'.[5] If decisions to refuse asylum were not subject to legal controls, then this could result in the UK failing to adhere to these obligations and therefore weaken the international system of protection for refugees. Furthermore, refusals of asylum by the Home Office are administrative decisions and, in an area of government with a reputation for inefficient and low-quality decision making, it is essential that such decisions are subject to judicial procedures to ensure that they are both legally and factually sustainable by way of appeals on the merits of the decision, as determined by the immigration appellate authorities, with the opportunity for further legal challenges to the higher courts.

---

4   See generally Steiner, N, *Arguing About Asylum: The Complexity of Refugee Debates in Europe*, 2000, New York: St Martin's Press; Shah, P, *Refugees, Race and the Legal Concept of Asylum in Britain*, 2000, London: Cavendish Publishing; Schuster, L, *The Use and Abuse of Political Asylum in Britain and Germany*, 2003, London: Frank Cass; Gibney, MJ, *The Ethics and Politics of Asylum: Liberal Democracy and the Response to Refugees*, 2004, Cambridge: CUP.

5   *Bugdaycay v Secretary of State for the Home Department* [1987] AC 514, 531 (Lord Bridge of Harwich).

In short, the issue of how we organise asylum adjudication cannot be separated from the politics of asylum itself. As this is itself a highly contentious matter, it will be necessary, when designing an adjudication system, to strike trade-offs between different approaches to administrative justice. The issue of which particular model of administrative justice is preferred, and how the tensions are resolved, cannot be settled at the level of deeper theory, but depend on judgments that are ultimately political. It is, however, possible to identify the principal values that underlie such an adjudication system and examine the extent to which these values are promoted in the present system.

THE DISTINCTIVENESS OF ASYLUM ADJUDICATION

Before proceeding further, it is important to recognise the distinctiveness of asylum adjudication. There are several reasons why asylum adjudication is a distinctive form of adjudicative decision making, in addition to being deeply problematic. First, asylum decision making involves an assessment of future risk: is there a reasonable degree of likelihood that the claimant would, if returned to their country of origin, have a well-founded fear of persecution for a convention reason? This test requires an examination of the risk of persecution an applicant might face on return to their country of origin, and will typically involve both assessing whether or not the core elements of the applicant's story are sustainable and considering the conditions in the country of nationality.

Secondly, asylum adjudication is to be distinguished from most other forms of litigation, such as civil and criminal litigation; asylum decisions are more appropriately described as administrative decisions concerning, at one and the same time, the obligations of the state to provide international protection to foreign nationals and the (non-)enforcement of immigration controls. Asylum decisions are administrative not merely in the sense that initial decisions are taken by the executive, but also in the sense that the decision maker is not bound by the rules of civil litigation in establishing whether or not the claimant has a well-founded fear of persecution, but is bound to take into account all relevant considerations.[6] Furthermore, appeals determined by the appellate authorities are most appropriately described as 'essentially administrative enquiries, albeit they have all the trappings of a judicial adversarial process'.[7] A related point is that the distinctive elements of asylum adjudication – the lower standard of proof, the difficulties of proof and disproof of claims under both Conventions and the clear public interest – mean that the usual distinction drawn between adversarial and inquisitorial adjudication may not apply so clearly in this area. As the IAT has recently explained, '[t]he lower standard of proof, and obligations of fair dealing and co-operation where one party' – the asylum applicant – 'is possessed alone of

---

6   *Karanakaran v Secretary of State for the Home Department* [2000] 3 All ER 449, 479 (Sedley LJ).
7   *Benkaddouri v Secretary of State for the Home Department* [2002] UKIAT 04994, para 18.

almost all the relevant personal knowledge and the other' – the state – 'is better placed to deal with general country conditions, dictate together that this is a unique jurisdiction'.[8]

A third distinctive feature is that a claim for refugee status will usually be accompanied by a human rights claim under the ECHR. The burden of proof in human rights claims –where the question is, is there a real risk of a breach of human rights – is the same as that in asylum claims, and asylum and human rights claims will usually stand or fall together.[9] Both the Tribunal and the courts have recently stressed that the threshold to engage Arts 3 and 8 is extremely high: mere hardship will not suffice; there must be some particular reason why an individual's ECHR rights will be infringed.[10]

A fourth point to note is that while asylum decision making and adjudication concerns the application of rules drawn from both Conventions – whether those rules are contained in the Immigration Rules or the jurisprudence of both Conventions – discretion is endemic throughout asylum decision making. In other words, while the legal framework is composed of both legal rules and the Secretary of State's extra-statutory discretion, routine decision making in relation to asylum claims necessarily involves questions of judgment. This point can be illustrated by considering some of the elementary legal rules. Decision makers must, for example, examine whether there is a *reasonable degree* of likelihood that the claimant would face *persecution* or *ill-treatment* on their return to their country of origin; whether internal relocation to a different part of the same country would be *unduly harsh*; and whether the claimant has presented a *credible account* of their personal history; whether the removal of an appellant who has established a private and/or family life (under Art 8 of the ECHR) would be *disproportionate* in the circumstances. There is plenty of scope for judgment and intuition in asylum adjudication. As Laws LJ has noted, 'there are no sharp legal tests in this area'.[11] Furthermore, decision makers face difficult factual questions concerning the weighing-up of evidence as to conditions in countries producing asylum applicants. As the higher courts have recognised, in asylum cases the facts are

---

8   *Secretary of State for the Home Department v RK (Obligation to investigate) Democratic Republic of Congo* [2004] UKIAT 00129, para 46.

9   *Kacaj v Secretary of State for the Home Department* (Starred determination) [2002] Imm AR 213.

10 See *Secretary of State for the Home Department v Qosja* [2002] UKIAT 00756, para 8. See, also, *N v Secretary of State for the Home Department* [2004] INLR 10 (removal of AIDS victim will not contravene Art 3 in the absence of particularly compelling humanitarian circumstances); *Djali v Immigration Appeal Tribunal* [2003] EWCA Civ 1371 (removal of individual with severe Post-Traumatic Stress Disorder not contrary to Art 8). In *R v Special Adjudicator ex p Ullah; Do v Secretary of State for the Home Department* [2004] 3 WLR 23, the House of Lords held that an individual could only successfully rely on ECHR rights other than Art 3 when challenging removal if the violation of the right in the receiving state would be so exceptional and flagrant that it would completely nullify the right altogether.

11 *Op cit, N v Secretary of State for the Home Department*, fn 10, p 30 (Laws LJ).

often difficult to establish; the law is sometimes not clear; and even when the facts are established and the law is clear, there can nevertheless be room for legitimate differences of opinion as to whether an individual has made good their claim.[12]

A fifth point is that the asylum adjudication system is, by its very nature, volatile. Its caseload is dependent on trends in global migration, international conflict and instability and the integrity of immigration controls. The caseload of the system has in recent years been extremely high: in 2002, there were 83,540 initial decisions and 64,405 appeals and in 2003, these figures were 64,940 and 81,275 respectively.[13] However, while the Government may be able to reduce the intake of applications in the short term, it is difficult to predict with any degree of certainty what the future volume of applications (and the legislative response) may be. A related point is that, as the statistics indicate, the rate of challenge against negative decisions is exceptionally high. In contrast to social welfare adjudication systems, which typically experience a low take up of mechanisms to challenge decisions, asylum adjudication has been said to be characterised by a culture of pervasive challenge. The consequence of these trends is that the system has been subjected to intense pressures and has been in a state of almost perpetual reform.

THE UNDERLYING VALUES OF ASYLUM ADJUDICATION

How then are we to evaluate asylum adjudication? What are the principal values that underlie the operation of the system? One problem with this task is that different values may be advanced by different individuals and institutions. For instance, the Government has criticised the appeal process for being too slow and cumbersome to provide an efficient and timely decision making procedure, whereas sections of the legal establishment have expressed concern that the emphasis on the expeditious processing of appeals comes at the expense of fair procedures.[14] It is therefore necessary to be cautious when considering the criteria that define the overall quality of the adjudication system. With this caveat in mind, I would suggest that the following values underpin asylum adjudication: accuracy; timeliness and finality of decision making; fairness; and consistency.

Accuracy

Accuracy concerns the degree to which the substantive outcome of a decision corresponds with the true facts of an individual's circumstances, through the correct application of the relevant rules and is perhaps the most important value

---

12 *Saad, Diriye and Osorio v Secretary of State for the Home Department* [2002] Imm AR 471, 479 (Lord Phillips MR).

13 Home Office, *Asylum Statistics United Kingdom for 2002 and 2003*, London: HMSO.

14 See, eg, Council on Tribunals, *Annual Report 2002/2003* (2003–04 HC 1163), Ch 5.

15 Sainsbury, R, 'Administrative justice: Discretion and procedure in social security decision-making', in Hawkins, K (ed), *The Uses of Discretion*, 1992, Oxford: OUP, p 302.

of any adjudicatory system.[15] If a system fails to deliver accurate decisions, then it is failing to apply the law correctly and objectively. In the asylum context, accurate decision making raises very serious considerations. An incorrect decision to refuse an individual asylum may, at the worst, result in persecution, torture or even death; an incorrect decision to grant an individual asylum will undermine the policy objective of maintaining legitimate immigration control. In light of the legal-policy context of asylum adjudication, there is an important public interest in ensuring accurate decision making.

While accuracy is the substantive ideal, there are clearly inherent limitations on the degree to which any adjudicatory system can actually achieve this goal. The principal difficulty in the achievement of accurate decision making is that asylum adjudication, while superficially simple, conceals 'a mass of detailed, difficult and very problematic factual and legal issues'.[16] Determining the possible risk of future events occurring, based on necessarily limited and uncertain facts, is an onerous task, and is further complicated by the cultural, social and linguistic distances that separate decision makers and applicants. Furthermore, decision makers are under intense pressure to determine these difficult and complex cases within compressed time-limits, a managerial pressure exerted by government in light of the political imperatives of asylum policy. To some extent, the difficulty for applicants in establishing their claim to asylum is ameliorated by the adoption of the lower standard of proof – a reasonable degree of likelihood – which 'reflects the difficulties of proving the degree of future risk or the nature of the future risk which would be run, and the difficulties of proof and disproof of the allegations which, by their nature, underlie claims for protection under both Conventions'.[17]

However, the nature of asylum adjudication itself poses unique challenges to decision makers. The decision maker must make correct findings of fact with regard to both subjective facts – is the applicant presenting a truthful and credible account? – and objective facts – if so, would they face persecution on return to their country? Different decision makers may reach different conclusions as to whether an applicant is credible and though country conditions are described as 'objective facts', different conclusions may be reached as to whether the claimant would face persecution on return. Furthermore, there is the diversity of the clientele. The UK receives asylum applications from nationals of over 140 countries; decision makers must attempt to keep up to date on the situation in those countries. Such difficulties are compounded by the fact that many applicants do not possess any form of identification and some claimants may

---

16 Blake, CG, 'Judicial review, second tier tribunals and legality', in Partington, M (ed), *The Leggatt Review of Tribunals: Academic Seminar Papers*, 2001, Bristol: University of Bristol, Faculty of Law, p 68.

17 *Op cit, RK (Obligation to investigate)*, fn 8, para 46.

18 The Home Office has piloted language testing to detect such fraudulent claims, while the Tribunal, in *Khan v Secretary of State for the Home Department* (Starred determination) [2002] UKIAT 04412, has determined that an adjudicator who disbelieves that an appellant is from the country they claim to be from is entitled simply to say so.

fraudulently claim to be from a different country from that of their own nation.[18] Asylum adjudication, as the Court of Appeal has stressed, 'is immensely difficult and certainty in one's conclusions as to the facts is seldom to be found'.[19]

Examination of the desire for accurate decision making, however, leads to further complexities, in particular, the realisation that there is no objective standard for determining the quality and accuracy of decision making. This statement might seem somewhat strange; after all, the whole purpose of appeal processes is to provide a corrective to inaccurate initial decision making; furthermore, some 20% of appeals are allowed by adjudicators, a statistic frequently cited by non-governmental organisations in support of the proposition that Home Office decision making is of inferior quality.

There is, however, good reason to doubt whether the success rate of appeals before adjudicators and the Tribunal is an adequate measure of the quality of initial decision making. Asylum appeals, unlike entry clearance appeals, are not restricted to an examination of the correctness of the initial decision but are determined *de novo*. The fundamental purpose of the appeal is not to identify errors in the initial decision, but to determine whether there would be a risk of persecution on return, based on the facts in existence *at the date of the hearing*. As the Court of Appeal has explained, in asylum cases the appellate structure is to be regarded as an 'extension of the decision-making process' as opposed simply to a process whereby the initial decision may be reviewed.[20] Appeals may be determined months or even years after the date of the initial decision and the factual circumstances of the case may have changed substantially. Country conditions also change quickly and appellants can advance new evidence not before the initial decision maker. This inevitably means that new material, which was not before the initial decision maker, is frequently placed before the appellate authority. Legal representatives may also advance new arguments, which were not put forward at the initial decision making stage, before the appellate authority. It is therefore often difficult to determine whether reversal on appeal really is an indication of error in the initial decision or merely the result of having *de novo* hearings that frequently include evidence that was not before the initial decision maker.

The recognition that the rate of appeals allowed provides little systematic evidence as to the frequency of error at the initial level does not, of course, imply that initial decision making is of a high quality. Quite the contrary, concerns have been frequently raised that Home Office decision making is of indifferent quality, poorly reasoned, inadequately engages with the evidence of the applicant and frequently discloses factual inaccuracies about conditions in the applicant's country. The concerns expressed by the Tribunal that 'the lack of skilled and professional care in reaching the initial decision necessarily places extra burdens

---

19   *Oleed v Secretary of State for the Home Department* [2003] Imm AR 499, 506 (Schiemann LJ).
20   *Ravichandran v Secretary of State for the Home Department* [1996] Imm AR 97, 112 (Simon Brown LJ). See s 85(4) of the Nationality, Immigration and Asylum Act 2002.

on adjudicators' cannot easily be dismissed as the conventional displacement of blame to the level below.[21] The Home Affairs Committee has further concluded that the pressure to speed up the decision making process and increase throughput may have been responsible for some erosion in the quality of some initial decision making.[22]

That appeals do not provide much systematic evidence of the accuracy of initial decision making, together the repeated concerns as to quality, strongly support the introduction of additional safeguards to ensure accuracy. The Home Office has to some extent responded to such concerns by introducing both internal and external quality assurance of initial decision making, but more could be done. The National Audit Office has recently recommended that the Home Office invest more in initial and continuing training for its caseworkers, improve the quality of information about countries of origin, review more of its own decisions and improve the quality of feedback to caseworkers following appeal hearings.[23]

It is perhaps part of the culture of asylum adjudication that concerns as to quality are not confined to Home Office decision making, particularly in a high-pressure, high-volume jurisdiction. It is not therefore surprising that both the adjudicators and the Tribunal have been criticised for the variable quality of their decisions. For instance, in 2002 the Tribunal remitted back for a rehearing 44% of decisions of adjudicators.[24] Such a high rate may indicate that the Tribunal is concerned as to the quality of determinations and that adjudicators frequently make serious procedural, legal or factual errors. However, while adjudicators may make such errors, contributory factors may include the considerable pressure, to which they have been subjected in recent years, to determine increasing numbers of appeals within increasingly compressed time frames, a pressure which they are sometimes obliged to resist in the interests of justice to the parties. In line with the underlying culture of the asylum jurisdiction, however, the Tribunal itself has not escaped criticism by the Court of Appeal for the variable quality of its decision making.[25] At the same time, there is, underlying the statement of the Court of Appeal that not all (or even most) of its own decisions in this unusually fact-sensitive context should be seen as laying down propositions of law, an implicit recognition of the inherently problematic nature of asylum adjudication and the consequent concerns as to accuracy.[26]

---

21 *Horvath v Secretary of State for the Home Department (United Nations High Commissioner for Refugees intervening)* [1999] Imm AR 121, 129–30.
22 House of Commons Home Affairs Committee, *Second Report: Asylum Applications* (2003–04 HC 218), para 143.
23 National Audit Office, *Improving the Speed and Quality of Asylum Decisions* (2003–04 HC 535), Pt 4. It has also been argued that improved feedback in the entry clearance context may raise the quality of initial decision making, see Thomas, R, 'Immigration appeals for family visitors refused entry clearance' [2004] PL 612, pp 639–41; National Audit Office, *Visa Entry to the United Kingdom: The Entry Clearance Operation* (2003–04 HC 367), p 9.
24 Hansard HC Debs Vol 415 Col 592w, 11 December 2003.
25 See, eg, *Koller v Secretary of State for the Home Department* [2001] EWCA Civ 1267, para 26 (Brooke LJ).
26 *E v Secretary of State for the Home Department; R v Secretary of State for the Home Department* [2004] 2 WLR 1351, 1382 (Carnwath LJ).

Timeliness and finality

One of the persistent criticisms from the Government is that the appeal system can be used to delay finality of decision making because of the multiple layers of appeal. Asylum legislation has introduced a range of devices to ensure that decision making and appeals can be processed quickly. The 1999 Act introduced the 'one-stop' appeal whereby appellants have to put forward all their possible grounds of appeal when an appeal is raised, whereas previously appellants could lodge multiple appeals. The 1999 Act also re-enacted the certification of certain appeals considered manifestly unfounded, with the consequence that such appellants could not appeal to the IAT, though they could apply for judicial review. While the 2002 Act removed this cumbersome certification procedure, it also introduced further changes seeking to cut down on the delays within the appeal system. One cause of concern to the Government has been the tactical use of judicial review by claimants wishing to prolong the decision-making process. In order to reduce such delays, the Nationality Immigration and Asylum Act 2002 replaced judicial review of IAT decisions to refuse leave permission to appeal with a fast-track statutory review procedure.[27]

The latest piece of legislation introduces the most radical change to the appellate system: the move to single tier of appeal.[28] The Asylum and Immigration (Treatment of Claimants, etc) Act 2004 provides for the replacement of the existing two-tier structure, in which appeals are determined by an adjudicator with a right of appeal, with permission, on a point of law to the IAT, with a single tier of appeal. Appeals will be determined by the Asylum and Immigration Tribunal (AIT). The move to a single tier of appeal has been criticised on the basis that it is unlikely to improve the timeliness of the appellate process as the changes introduced by the 2002 Act have removed much of the delay. Furthermore, the proposal runs against the grain of the general model proposed by the Leggatt review of tribunals, which is to establish a coherent tribunal service based on the premise of two-tier appellate structures.[29] It is, at present, unclear exactly how the new appellate system will operate.

In this 2004 Act the Government had originally intended to remove the jurisdiction of the High Court by introducing a highly controversial ouster clause, but felt compelled to back down from this controversial measure following criticism from Parliamentary Select Committees and the higher judiciary.[30] The Government therefore tabled new provisions, which enable an applicant to request a review by a High Court judge on the papers only for an error of law in

---

27 See Thomas, R, 'The impact of judicial review on asylum' [2003] PL 479, pp 506–09.

28 Section 26 of the Asylum and Immigration (Treatment of Claimants, etc) Act 2004.

29 The Leggatt Report, *Tribunals for Users: One System, One Service* (2001); Department for Constitutional Affairs, *Transforming Public Services: Complaints, Redress and Tribunals*, Cm 6243 (2004).

30 House of Commons Constitutional Affairs Committee, *Second Report: Asylum and Immigration Appeals* (2003–04 HC 211), Ch 6; Lord Woolf, 'The rule of law and a change in the constitution' [2004] CLJ 317.

the AIT's determination. Given the volume of judicial review claims concerning asylum decisions in recent years, the issue of what supervision should be exercised by the High Court is not solely a matter of constitutional principle; clearly, the volume of cases also becomes relevant. Furthermore, while the courts have viewed the proposed ousting of judicial review as a threat to their supervisory jurisdiction, they have recently become increasingly vocal in their criticism of abusive and unmeritorious claims for judicial review.[31] The new provisions will therefore introduce a transitional filter mechanism for the modified statutory review procedure; review applications will initially be considered in the first instance by a senior immigration judge on behalf of the High Court; if the application is refused by the senior immigration judge, the applicant can opt to have the application looked at by a High Court judge. The purpose behind this new transitional filter mechanism is to meet concerns about the volume of cases reaching the High Court.

These legislative changes must also be situated against managerial pressures on the appellate system to process cases expeditiously. The Immigration Appellate Authority (IAA) has adopted a '1+1' hearing pattern whereby adjudicators will hear appeals one day and then are expected to write their determinations the next day so that their decisions can be promulgated quickly. Adjudicators are frequently expected to hear three asylum appeals on each hearing day. In light of the difficulty of the issues raised, the importance of correct decisions and fair procedures, the fact that evidence must usually be taken through an interpreter, adjudicators operate within a pressurised environment to determine cases within compressed time frames. The Department for Constitutional Affairs (DCA) and the Home Office have joint targets for the IAA to determine an agreed number of appeals. The DCA aims to ensure that 65% of appeals are completed – from receipt to determination – by the IAA within 12 weeks.[32] Although such managerial pressures are not confined to the asylum appellate process,[33] it is remarkable that adjudicators are pressurised to produce determinations so quickly in relation to matters of such importance to the individuals concerned.

It is a paradox though, that while the Home Office places such emphasis on the timeliness of decision making and appeals, its own management of cases has been a main cause of delays with respect to the time taken to reach a decision, then to forward appeal files to the appellate authority and in relation to the removal of unsuccessful claimants. Evidence of such delays can be seen in individual cases. For instance, in *Shala*, where the Home Office had delayed for four years its

---

31 See, eg, *R (Nine Nepalese Asylum Seekers) v Immigration Appeal Tribunal* [2003] EWCA Civ 1892. In *R (Pharis) v Secretary of State for the Home Department* [2004] EWCA Civ 654, para 17, Brooke LJ stated that: '[e]xperience has shown that the practice of pursuing a further appeal to this court in a judicial review matter in the immigration and asylum field has given rise to very serious abuse, with appellants pursuing wholly unmeritorious appeals simply to delay the time when they are to be deported.'

32 Department for Constitutional Affairs, *Annual Report 2003/4* (2004), p 43.

33 See, eg, Wikeley, N, 'Burying Bell: Managing the judicialisation of social security tribunals' (2000) 63 MLR 475.

decision as to whether the applicant was entitled to asylum, the court commented: 'the relevant procedures were designed to take a few months and yet have in practice, through no fault of the applicant, taken the Home Office several years.'[34] The Tribunal has also been critical of Home Office's delays. In one determination, a failed asylum applicant had repeatedly contacted the Home Office over a period of three years for a decision to remain under Art 8. As the Tribunal put it: '[t]he case was never let to go to sleep by the solicitors, and the IND [Immigration and Nationality Directorate] had every opportunity to give it its proper priority. That they did not do so is a public disgrace.'[35]

Other aspects of the system also enable the Home Office to delay the processing of appeals. For example, one of the features of immigration and asylum appeals is that an appellant must lodge the notice of appeal 'by serving it on the respondent'.[36] In other words, an individual in receipt of a refusal decision may only appeal if the appeal is first lodged with the Home Office who must then forward the appeal file to the appellate authority. As a result, '[t]he speed at which the appeal proceeds … is entirely in the hands of the Home Office … the inability to control its own cases is a mark of weakness on the part of the appeals system'.[37] Cases that have been refused months, or even sometimes years, ago may languish in the Immigration and Nationality Directorate's appeals processing department waiting to be forwarded to the appellate authority, which cannot act until it receives the appeal file from the Home Office. This procedure, which, in effect, enables the Home Office, which is party to all asylum appeals, to manage the speed at which appeals are heard, has raised concerns over the independence of the appellate process. In response to such concerns the Government has recently acknowledged that in principle it would seem sensible that the notice of appeal should be lodged directly with the Tribunal when the new system is brought into effect.[38]

Perhaps the most spectacular example of Home Office induced delay arose from the introduction of human rights appeals under the 1999 Act, which coincided with the implementation of the Human Rights Act 1998.[39] Contrary to expectations, secondary legislation stated that individuals could appeal on human rights grounds only in relation to immigration decisions taken after 2 October 2000.[40] As there was a considerable backlog of appeals being processed

---

34 *Shala v Secretary of State for the Home Department* [2003] INLR 349, 357 (Schiemann LJ). See also *Xhacka v Secretary of State for the Home Department* [2002] UKIAT 03352.

35 IAT Unreported (HR70696-02), para 8.

36 The Immigration and Asylum Appeals (Procedure) Rules 2003 SI 2003/652, r 6(2).

37 Blake, CG, 'Immigration appeals – the need for reform', in Dummett, A (ed), *Towards a Just Immigration Policy*, 1986, London: Cobden Trust, p 179.

38 Department for Constitutional Affairs, *Government Response to the Constitutional Affairs Select Committee's Report on Asylum and Immigration Appeals*, Cm 6236 (2004), p 9.

39 Section 65(1) of the Immigration and Asylum Act 1999.

40 Schedule 2, para 1(7) of the Immigration and Asylum Act 1999 (Commencement No 6 Transitional and Consequential Provisions) Order 2000 SI 2000/2444.

through the system, the coming into force date meant that claimants refused asylum before that date could not lodge a human rights appeal. However, in *Pardeepan*, the Home Office assured the Tribunal that individuals whose asylum claims and appeals had been refused could raise human rights objections to their removals and that the Home Office would 'generate' a separate human rights appeal, giving rise to the phenomenon of second appeals.[41] The consequence of this concession did not become apparent for three years; in light of the cost of supporting such individuals and processing their claims and appeals, the Home Office announced a 'one-off exercise' under which 12,000 families, who applied for asylum before October 2000, would be allowed to remain and work in the UK, a substantial number of whom, it may be assumed, would not otherwise have qualified to remain.[42]

The adjudication of claims is, however, only part of the problem; the other is implementation, which in this context implies removal of unsuccessful claimants from the country which, as the Home Office is acutely aware, poses huge logistical problems. Given the comparatively low number of removals, the whole decision making process may simply become an academic exercise.[43] As the Tribunal has put it: 'the Secretary of State does not, in the majority of cases, attempt promptly to enforce decisions of the immigration appellate authorities. Broadly speaking, an adverse decision ... has no immediate effect on the claimant's continued presence in the United Kingdom.'[44]

The problem of removals is undoubtedly complex and compounded by numerous practical difficulties.[45] In view of the issues at stake, it is not surprising that claimants – whether viewed as economic migrants or genuine refugees wrongly refused – have sought to utilise all procedures of the legal system to challenge decisions throughout the process. The culture of pervasive challenge is, however, only one barrier to removal. Protracted delay by the Home Office before removal, owing to a lack of co-ordination in the system, may also delay removal. Furthermore, an extended period of time between refusal and removal, claimants may form family ties and relationships, which may provide a basis for challenging

---

41 See *Pardeepan v Secretary of State for the Home Department* (Starred determination) [2002] Imm AR 249; *Devaseelan v Secretary of State for the Home Department* (Starred determination) [2003] Imm AR 1, 9–10.

42 Home Office press notice, 'Clearing the decks for tough new asylum measures – Home Secretary' 295/2003, 24 October 2003.

43 In *Number 19 v Secretary of State for the Home Department* (01TH00093), para 44, the Tribunal stated that: '[n]ormally, the appellate authority is bound to assume that the respondent will enforce removal and that the appeals are not academic exercises ... Our knowledge that the Home Office does not remove because of lack of resources or difficulties in locating individuals cannot be used to displace the assumption that removal will take place.'

44 *Op cit*, Devaseelan, fn 41, p 10.

45 See, generally, House of Commons Home Affairs Committee, *Fourth Report: Asylum Removals* (2002–03 HC 654).

removal under Art 8 of the ECHR.[46] Other barriers to removal include a lack of appropriate travel documentation for some claimants and a reluctance of some countries of origin to accept the return of their nationals. Furthermore, some claimants will not be returnable because of the conditions in their country of origin. Finally, individuals may abscond; they may either deliberately go to ground or lose contact with the authorities.

However, the difficulties do not pertain solely to the removal of unsuccessful applicants, but also to the absence of a procedure for removing refugee status from those individuals recognised as refugees who, owing to a change of conditions in the country of origin, no longer fear persecution. While the Immigration Rules state that refugees will be granted limited leave to enter, the normal practice of the Home Office is to grant such people indefinite leave to remain.[47] The Home Office does not therefore seek to implement the cessation clause of the Refugee Convention to remove refugee status from those individuals who, in light of changes in country of origin conditions, may safely be returned.[48] The concept of surrogate protection under the Convention is, after all, envisaged as a temporary protection during a period of risk, not necessarily a permanent immigration status. While it would appear sensible to give limited leave to those individuals where the situation in their country is fluid, as for example is the case in relation to Sri Lanka or Turkey, this practice is not adopted by the Home Office.[49]

Fairness

Fairness is an important legitimising value of public law; if fair procedures are adopted, then individuals are treated in accordance with the value of dignity. Fair procedures are also likely to promote accurate decision making. In the asylum context, fairness must, however, be balanced against other considerations, such as efficiency, cost and the need for expedition in the determination of appeals. In the context of asylum adjudication, procedures are created by Parliament and the executive, through primary legislation and the appeal procedure rules. One of the principal functions of the IAT has been to ensure that hearings before adjudicators are fairly conducted; a finding of unfairness by the Tribunal will typically result in

---

46 For instance, in *Ul-Haq v Secretary of State for the Home Department* [2002] UKIAT 04685, the Tribunal concluded that an applicant with a 'shocking immigration history' who had deployed 'deliberate delaying tactics' nevertheless succeeded in his Art 8 appeal because of 'negligent delay by the Home Office'.

47 Immigration Rules (1994 HC 395), para 330.

48 Refugee Convention 1951, Art 1C(5).

49 See *Jeyachandran v Secretary of State for the Home Department* [2002] UKIAT 01869, para 9; *Secretary of State for the Home Department v IA HC KD RO HG (Risk – Guidelines – Separatist) Turkey* CG [2003] UKIAT 00034, para 47. Section 76(3) of the Nationality, Immigration and Asylum Act 2002 confers a power on the Home Secretary to revoke indefinite leave to remain, granted pursuant to refugee status being recognised, if the individual either voluntarily avails themselves of protection of their country of nationality, voluntarily re-acquires a lost nationality, acquires a new nationality or establishes themselves in a country in respect of which they were a refugee.

the appeal being remitted back to a different adjudicator. Furthermore, the higher courts have also ensured fair procedures, though they have been reluctant to displace the ability of the executive to define the principal ground rules. This reluctance has perhaps been motivated by a recognition of the nature of the politically sensitive issues of asylum adjudication. As Parliament has frequently reformed the appeal process, it is not for the courts to intervene. This reluctance is also reflected in the exclusion of asylum and immigration decisions from the scope of Art 6 of the ECHR, which provides for the right to a fair trial by an independent and impartial tribunal. In addition, decisions concerning the entry of foreign nationals are regarded as exclusively administrative.[50]

The tension between speed and fairness is perhaps best illustrated by the introduction of non-suspensive appeals.[51] Under this appeal mechanism, asylum claimants from designated countries, which are in general considered to be safe, may have their claim certified as clearly unfounded by the Home Office with the consequence that they may only appeal from outside the UK. The justifications behind this appeal mechanism included that it would help reduce the intake of applicants from those countries considered to be generally safe, but at the same time retain an element of individual consideration and also reduce the burden on the state in terms of supporting asylum applicants during the processing of their claims and appeals. So far, comparatively few applicants have been processed through the non-suspensive appeal system; there have been approximately 250 non-suspensive appeals, of which two have been allowed.[52]

But how are we to evaluate non-suspensive appeals? From a legal perspective, the consequence of such appeals is bizarre: appellants may only appeal after the implementation of the decision the validity of which the appeal is intended to test. Non-suspensive appeals may subject appellants with genuine cases to the very persecution that they are seeking refuge from. The appeal process will provide scant consolation to a genuine applicant whose claim was incorrectly certified as clearly unfounded. Furthermore, the quality of such an appeal is unlikely to match that of an in-country appeal: the appellant will not be available to present oral evidence that, given the importance of credibility, may be crucial to the outcome of the appeal.

On the other hand, non-suspensive appeals may be effective in preventing future applicants from designated states from entering the UK in order to claim asylum, thereby reducing costs (for example, of processing applications and supporting and removing applicants) and promoting the Government's policy of maintaining immigration controls. After all, requiring some applicants to appeal from abroad prevents further pressure being put onto an overburdened system by people who, once they are in the system, may never realistically be removed

---

50 *Maaouia v France* (2001) 33 EHRR 42; *MNM v Secretary of State for the Home Department* (Starred determination) [2000] INLR 576; *AM v Secretary of State for the Home Department* (*'Upgrade' Appeals: Art 6?) Afghanistan* (Starred determination) [2004] UKIAT 00186.
51 Section 94 of the Nationality, Immigration and Asylum Act 2002 and s 27 of the Asylum and Immigration (Treatment of Claimants, etc) Act 2004.
52 *Op cit*, Department for Constitutional Affairs, fn 38, p 5.

irrespective of the outcome of their appeal. Furthermore, with regard to many of the designated states, the Tribunal has found there to be, in general, little risk of ill-treatment or persecution.[53] Non-suspensive appeals may then be effective in deterring people from even entering the country in order to claim asylum and also, because they can only appeal from abroad, from challenging a refusal decision. Finally, applicants subject to this procedure may still challenge, by way of judicial review, the decision to certify their claim as clearly unfounded.[54]

While the clear policy objective of reducing the intake of asylum applicants may raise concerns as to the fairness of non-suspensive appeals, other factors may also limit the fairness of appeal hearings. For instance, the large volume of appeals that have been heard in recent years has outstripped the ability of the Home Office to be represented before each appeal. In the year up to August 2003, Home Office presenting officers only attended 72% of appeals.[55] Given the central role of adjudicators in making findings of fact, the frequent inability of the Home Office to be represented before them has been placed strain on the adjudication process. As the Tribunal has explained:

> ... in what is essentially an accusatorial system, the adjudicator is all too frequently placed in a near impossible situation on the one hand in avoiding descending into the arena and on the other hand wishing to have the evidence properly tested in order for findings of fact to be made.[56]

The adjudicator cannot be expected to conduct the Home Office's case as this would risk the appearance of bias. At the same time, the adjudicator will be understandably reluctant to allow what they regard as an improbable or exaggerated account by the appellant to be accepted at face value, potentially leading to a wrong decision because it has not been tested or all relevant material has not been produced.

The Tribunal has produced guidance – the *Surendran* guidelines – that stipulate that in the absence of a presenting officer the adjudicator may only ask questions for the purpose of clarification; but this has prompted debate as to whether an adversarial procedure is the most appropriate procedure for asylum

---

53 For example, *op cit*, in *Jeyachandran*, fn 49, para 8, on the return on Tamils to Sri Lanka, the Tribunal stated that: 'having regard to present trends it is only exceptional cases that will not be able to return in safety.'

54 See, eg, *ZL and VL v Secretary of State for the Home Department* [2003] Imm AR 330; *R (Oppilamani) v Secretary of State for the Home Department* [2004] EWHC Admin 348; *Atkinson v Secretary of State for the Home Department* [2004] EWCA Civ 846.

55 Hansard HC Deb Vol 416 Col 981w, 19 January 2004.

56 *Op cit, Secretary of State for the Home Department v IA HC KD RO HG (Risk – Guidelines – Separatist) Turkey CG* [2003] UKIAT 00034, fn 49, para 46. In, *op cit, RK (Obligation to investigate)*, fn 8, para 1, the Tribunal noted that: '[o]nce again the Adjudicator's task was made more difficult than it should have been because the Secretary of State was not represented before her.' In *M v Secretary of State for the Home Department (Chad)* [2004] UKIAT 00044, para 4, the Tribunal noted that difficulties in the adjudicator's determination 'stemmed from the difficult situation in which the adjudicator was placed, once again, by the now notorious inefficiency of the Home Office, in failing to field a presenting officer before her, in insignificant and far-flung Birmingham'.

appeals.[57] In light of the distinctive function of asylum adjudication, the public interest in correct outcomes and the possible effects of reduction in legally funded representation, there has clearly been a move away from the traditional adversarial model toward a more inquisitorial or 'enabling' approach, a development that has to some extent already been taken on board by the Tribunal.[58]

The presence of the Home Office in appeals does not of itself necessarily guarantee an adequate and proper hearing; poor quality administration is part of the culture of the appellate process, and indeed immigration processes more generally. For example, in *Tatar*, a Tribunal chaired by Collins J, after detailing routine Home Office handling of appeals before the Tribunal as 'files are not provided, documents are not available, they do not put in evidence that they ought to put in, they fail totally to produce any skeleton arguments, the list goes on and on and the Tribunal is simply getting fed up with it', concluded that the Home Office does 'not seem capable of dealing with the appeals in the manner in which they ought to be dealt with. The result is that the Tribunal is left in an impossible position'.[59] In *Razi*, the Tribunal noted that, if it took the charitable view that the Home Office's lamentable conduct of the appeal, which involved repeated failures to comply with directions issued by three successive adjudicators, was no more than institutional incompetence, 'it is hard to imagine any other department of state in this country where such incompetence would be tolerated'. However, as the Tribunal continued, the Home Office's failings were so severe that it 'begins to go beyond mere institutional incompetence, into the realm of an institutional culture of disregard for adjudicators, who are the primary judicial authority … for making sure that immigration powers are efficiently, as well as fairly, exercised'.[60]

It should, however, be noted that there is evidence of good practice by the Home Office and that such incompetence is not the exclusive preserve of the Home Office. The quality of representation for appellants is also at a variable standard. While there are plenty of anecdotes, the following statement from the Tribunal in 2002 is instructive:

> There is an increasing tendency to suggest that unfavourable decisions by Adjudicators are brought about by error or incompetence on the part of representatives. New representatives blame old representatives, sometimes representatives blame themselves for prolonging the litigation by their inadequacy (without, of course, offering the public any compensation for the wrong that from which they have profited by fees).[61]

---

57 *Surendran v Secretary of State for the Home Department* (21679) (HX/70901/98).

58 *Yildizhan v Secretary of State for the Home Department* [2002] UKIAT 08315; *K v Secretary of State for the Home Department (Côte d'Ivoire)* [2004] UKIAT 00061; *WN v Secretary of State for the Home Department (Surendran – Credibility – New Evidence) Democratic Republic of Congo* [2004] UKIAT 00213.

59 *Secretary of State for the Home Department v Tatar* (00TH01914), paras 3–4.

60 *Secretary of State for the Home Department v Razi* (01TH01836), paras 16–17.

61 *Op cit*, Devaseelan, fn 41, p 14.

In light of such concerns about poor quality representation, in 1999 Parliament established the Office of Immigration Service Commissioner, the powers of which have been enhanced by the 2004 Act. At the same time, however, the Government has sought to reduce the overall amount of resources expended on immigration and asylum cases by reducing publicly funded advice and representation, which was done by removing funding, in all but exceptional cases, for attendance of representatives at interviews and introducing financial thresholds for the preparation of appeals.[62] In short, while action has been taken to weed out poor quality providers, simultaneous funding restrictions run the risk of pushing out quality providers from the sector.

Consistency

A further concern is that the adjudication process has not been able to deliver consistency. Consistency in decision making – such as treatment of like cases – is inevitably difficult to achieve in a system that currently comprises of some 600 adjudicators and a Tribunal composed of 26 full time vice presidents, 50 part time legally qualified chairpersons and 60 lay members. One source of inconsistency has been in relation to important questions of law; as a statutory tribunal the IAT is not, strictly speaking, able to establish legal precedents that bind lower tier decision makers, such as adjudicators. However, in order to ensure consistency in relation to points of law, the Tribunal, under the lead of Sir Andrew Collins, introduced the system of starred determinations, under which those Tribunal decisions that settle important points of law must be followed unless they are inconsistent with authority binding on the appellate bodies. As the Tribunal has explained, starred determinations are 'heard by a tribunal consisting of the President and two legally-qualified members ... [and] ... and must be followed by all tribunals and will be regarded as binding upon all adjudicators'.[63] The special status and precedential value accorded to starred determinations are further indications of the judicialisation of asylum adjudication. The 2004 Act provides for the new AIT to sit as a panel of 'three or more legally qualified members' for the purpose of determining those cases that raise important questions of law.[64]

While the Tribunal has introduced the starring system, it has also limited the proliferation of other determinations by ceasing the practice of publishing all its determinations and by introducing a system of 'reported' and 'unreported' decisions, the former being cases considered to have wider importance than the

---

62 Hansard HC Debs Vol 415 Cols 34–37WS, November 27, 2003; The Community Legal Service (Scope) Regulations 2004 SI 2004/1055. See, also, House of Commons Constitutional Affairs Committee, *Fourth Report: Immigration and Asylum: The Government's Proposed Changes to Publicly Funded Immigration and Asylum Work* (2002–03 HC 1171).

63 *Ali Haddad v Secretary of State for the Home Department* (Starred determination) (00/HX/00926), para 2.

64 Section 26 of the Asylum and Immigration (Treatment of Claimants, etc) Act 2004, inserting new s 103E into the Nationality, Immigration and Asylum Act 2002.

mere resolution of the dispute in hand.[65] One reason for this has been the sheer volume of Tribunal determinations, which has been at the level of 6,000 a year, and which has given rise to concerns of 'selective citation' of determinations. In restricting the number of reported decisions, the Tribunal has sought to ensure consistency and to provide guidance to adjudicators, though reported decisions are not binding.

The introduction of country guideline (CG) determinations has been a positive action to ensure consistency with regard to the treatment of categories of asylum applicants from certain countries when assessing whether an individual's subjective fear of persecution is objectively well-founded, that is, whether the claimant has in fact established a reasonable likelihood of persecution if returned. Whether or not this test has been satisfied will usually depend upon an examination of the objective evidence about the situation in the country concerned by an examination of Home Office Country Information Policy Unit (CIPU) reports, as well as those reports published by non-governmental organisations, such as the UNHCR and Amnesty International, and the US State Department and reports submitted by individuals with expertise in country conditions. In light of the volume of material regularly submitted at appeals and the nature of the exercise being undertaken, both the adjudicators and the Tribunal have, in the past, reached different conclusions, which has lead to a degree of inconsistency of approach in relation to the conditions in certain countries. As the Tribunal has recognised:

> It is perfectly possible for differing views reasonably to be held about the same country conditions but it would be wholly undesirable whether at Adjudicator or Tribunal level for there to be a divergence of practice in relation to essentially similar cases.[66]

For example, in *Shirazi,* an appeal by an Iranian apostate, in light of conflicting Tribunal determinations about conditions in Iran for Christian converts from Islam, the Court of Appeal noted that: '[i]t has to be a matter of concern that the same political and legal situation, attested by much the same in-country data from case to case, is being evaluated differently by different tribunals.'[67]

The Tribunal has therefore instituted the practice of issuing country guideline determinations to provide authoritative factual guidance on conditions in countries and to provide guidance to adjudicators and other Tribunal panels. Such determinations are intended to be definitive unless there is a change of circumstances that materially affects those asylum applicants concerned. This development has been approved and actively encouraged by the higher courts, which have recognised that it would be beneficial to the general administration of asylum appeals for the Tribunal to set out its views on the situation in a particular country in order to guide future decisions that engage questions concerning the

---

65 Practice Direction No 10 of 2003 [2003] INLR 358.

66 *Secretary of State for the Home Department v BD (Application of SK and DK) Croatia CG* (Starred determination) [2004] UKIAT 00032, para 56.

67 *Shirazi v Secretary of State for the Home Department* [2004] INLR 92, 101 (Sedley LJ).

same state. As the Court of Appeal has explained, '[c]onsistency in the treatment of asylum seekers is important in so far as objective considerations, not directly affected by the circumstances of the individual asylum seeker are involved'.[68] More recently, Laws LJ has recognised that the establishment of factual precedents through country guideline determinations may be 'exotic', but it is also 'benign and practical' in the context of asylum adjudication, as:

> [there] is no public interest, nor any legitimate individual interest, in multiple examinations of the state of the backdrop … [of general country conditions] … at any particular time. Such revisits give rise to the risk, perhaps the likelihood, of inconsistent results; and the likelihood, perhaps the certainty, of repeated and, therefore, wasted expenditure of judicial and financial resources upon the same issues and the same evidence.[69]

Country guideline determinations therefore enable the Tribunal to investigate the likelihood of persecution of specific groups of people, which may not be dealt with in sufficient detail in the general background information reports. Subsequent appeals from the same country can be listed and heard together in order to follow an authoritative CG determination in order to promote both efficiency and consistency in decision making. The Tribunal has recently adopted the practice of listing so-called 'follower' cases so that they are be dealt with together in light of the relevant CG determinations. Furthermore, CG determinations provide guidance to adjudicators; if an adjudicator failed to take into account a relevant CG determination, then this could be classified as an error of law.

While CG determinations seek to promote a consistency of approach, there are some inherent limits. As conditions in countries can change, there will always be a need for the Tribunal to revisit the factual situation in certain countries producing asylum applicants, and to reassess matters in light of new evidence. Furthermore, consistency must at times be combined with sufficient leeway for individual cases; after all, the general conditions in a particular country might not be such as to support a refugee claim for all nationals, but certain individuals or groups may nevertheless be at risk on return. For example, the Tribunal has, in relation to Sri Lankan Tamil appeals, determined that 'it is only the exceptional cases that will not be able to return in safety' and that, in relation to appeals by Serbs from Croatia, no ethnic Serbs should be able to establish an asylum claim unless 'special circumstances can be shown in an individual case'.[70] Country guideline determinations are intended to provide guidance about the approach to be taken in relation to general country conditions, but do not override the need to pay close attention to the specific circumstances of the individual asylum claim.

---

68 *Manzeke v Secretary of State for the Home Department* [1997] Imm AR 524, 529 (Lord Woolf MR).

69 *S and Others v Secretary of State for the Home Department* [2002] INLR 416, 435–436 (Laws LJ).

70 *Op cit, Jeyachandran*, fn 49, para 8; *Secretary of State for the Home Department v SK* (Starred determination) [2002] UKIAT 05613, para 46.

CONCLUSION

The objective of this chapter has been to address the challenge posed by asylum to our legal system and to do so by examining the operation of the asylum appeal system and proposed reforms. Asylum adjudication has developed into a discrete sub-system of administrative law decision making. However, the nature of this administrative law system has proved to be extremely volatile in light of the political pressures that bear down upon it. In seeking to understand the system of asylum adjudication, this chapter has drawn upon administrative justice scholarship in order to identify the two principal models of decision making in this context. Recent reform of the asylum adjudication system is best understood as embodying an inherent tension between the bureaucratic and legal models of administrative justice. In addition, this chapter has sought to identify the principal values that this system seeks to foster – accuracy, timeliness and finality, fairness and consistency – and to recognise the inherent conflicts among them.

Administrative justice scholarship can therefore enhance our understanding of asylum adjudication, but it cannot tell us how the tensions should be resolved. The reason for this is clear: administrative justice does not itself embody any fundamental values that dictate how adjudication systems should be organised. There is no fundamental theory of justice that awaits discovery and hence no definitive conception of administrative justice; both of these ultimately rely on broader political understandings and beliefs.[71] In short, administrative justice is an essentially contested concept; different actors will hold different conceptions of what comprises justice within administrative and appellate decision making, dependant upon their political presuppositions. Given the highly contentious nature of asylum policy there are, therefore, no easy answers to the challenge posed by asylum adjudication as to how the system should seek to achieve an appropriate balance between the competing values.

This chapter has, however, sought to identify the principal values that underlie asylum adjudication in an attempt to appreciate the difficult task of managing the competition between them. While the weight to be attached to them is ultimately a matter of political judgment, this chapter has indicated that more action could be taken to improve the overall quality of the adjudication process. There is clearly more scope for more training for initial decision-makers, as well as feedback from appeals and the enhancement of quality assurance systems, in order to raise the level of primary decision making. With the establishment of the single tier of appeal, it will be essential for initial decisions to be more carefully prepared and for the Home Office to be represented at all appeals. In this context it is, therefore, unfortunate that while the Government has sought to raise the quality of representation through the Office of the Immigration Services Commissioner, it has restricted publicly funded legal advice and representation. Higher quality and more robust appeal decisions are likely to be produced by a combination of a more extensive training programme for adjudicators and a reduction in the pressure to determine appeals quickly.

---

71 *Op cit*, Sainsbury, fn 15, p 327.

In short, there is a strong normative case for strengthening the legal model of asylum adjudication in order to enhance decision making quality and to impose some order on the primary decision making process. The values underpinning this model – fairness, independence and accurate decision making in each individual claim – are necessary to ensure that the adjudication system does not become downgraded into mass processing without due regard to the individual circumstances of each claim. The strong political pressure to increase throughput should be resisted. It is essential that individual claimants are treated fairly in order to ensure that claims are correctly determined and to protect individual dignity. It is therefore unfortunate that the current adjudication system is susceptible to pressures which lean toward mass processing. It might, however, be questioned whether UK-based asylum adjudication has any long-term future. In light of current political pressures surrounding asylum, policy makers have been increasingly looking toward either dismantling the present system or replacing it with out-of-country procedures. Current policy debates concern options which range from withdrawal from, or redrafting of, the Refugee Convention to the establishment of either offshore processing camps or processing centres located in regions that produce refugees. As such options will clearly signal a more drastic reduction of legal values in the determination of asylum claims than that outlined in this chapter, the consequence will inevitably be a concomitant reduction of protection for genuine claimants.

CHAPTER 10

COMMUNICATIVE BARRIERS IN THE ASYLUM ACCOUNT

Roxana Rycroft

This chapter scrutinises some of the key factors that govern the narration of the asylum account from within the perspective of immigration interpreting. Through the asylum account, by which I mean a plurality of successive interpreted narrations of the asylum seeker's story, the asylum seeker can demonstrate an objective fear of persecution in their own country and therefore entitlement to refugee status under the Refugee Convention 1951, as amended by the 1967 Protocol. The account is therefore a crucial piece of evidence in the legal proceedings that govern the allocation of refugee status. I will take the asylum account as the framework for a situational analysis of immigration practices and the role of the immigration interpreter in the asylum procedure.

Very little is known about the application of legal procedures for the determination of refugee status, as this is a domain where immigration officials and civil servants have wide discretionary powers. Nonetheless, the issue of asylum is highly politicised and as such it receives much media attention, mainly confined to reporting changes in legislation, hair-raising statistics of numbers of asylum seekers and the costs of running the asylum procedure. Judging by what makes its way into the press, one could be forgiven for believing that the asylum determination process is a black box that swallows vast numbers of illegal entrants and spits out equally vast numbers of bogus asylum seekers. This chapter sets out to provide empirical knowledge about the 'black box', which is actually a highly intricate enmeshing of screenings, procedures and deadlines, adding up to a bureaucracy employing thousands of people.

It is assumed that everything taking place during asylum-process encounters is verbalised, then interpreted so that everyone present knows exactly what is happening, and finally written down so that the decision makers are presented with a neutral and accurate record of the proceedings. This chapter, written from the perspective of immigration interpreting, sets out to dispel this myth. The sociological interaction in the context of the asylum account may actually comprise linguistic, as well as extralinguistic, behaviours, that is: dialogue, interventions, silent behaviour (for example, glances, gestures, blank looks and other body language), fragmented speech that defies interpretation, and crying. Most extralinguistic behaviour holds important clues for the emotional state of the asylum seeker, which constitutes evidence for decision-making purposes. However, such evidence tends to be ignored instead of being treated sensitively. The notes of the asylum account constitute a linguistic reduction of the asylum encounter.

Immigration interpreters are privy to the gap between the real structure of the encounter and that part of it that is recorded on file, and can see how reducing the bilingual asylum encounter to its spoken dimension translates into loss of meaning. This results in incorrect decision making, putting asylum seekers' lives at stake. The handwritten mode of recording the asylum account forbids any independent method of checking its accuracy because the written record is all that is left of the encounter. The gap cannot be reconstituted *post facto*, therefore it can only be analysed at the time of its fleeting occurrence. This chapter contributes to the situational analysis of asylum encounters because it is contemporaneous with the gap, and thus in an almost singular position to document it. The existence of gaps shows this form of recording the asylum account to fall well short of legal standards for treating evidence, meaning that the law is not conducive to proper fact-finding despite its internal myths.

Unusual for being written from within the state apparatus, this chapter offers a uniquely close perspective to the sociological interactions amongst asylum seekers, immigration personnel and interpreters in asylum face-to-face encounters. It goes beyond the mere application of immigration law. The common sense understanding that immigration law applies to asylum cases after they are fully made out is badly misplaced. By looking at law in its informal settings, as social practice in action, we will observe the procedures by which, in the first instance, immigration procedure interferes with the very asylum account to which, in the second instance, it will apply itself. The problematic relationship between immigration law and the asylum account shows the former to be a biased allocator of refugee status, and as such it brings out the inherent contradictions in a seemingly benign asylum determination procedure. This analysis thus contributes to the work of human rights activists concerned with the implementation of the law behind the formal guarantees of legality in the field of asylum.

One category of personnel on which the work of the immigration system crucially rests consists of interpreters. I have worked as a freelance immigration interpreter for the Romanian language for over eleven years, being mostly engaged in procedures relating to the registration of the claim, the substantive interview, and the appeal against refusal. One reason for choosing the standpoint of interpreting for carrying out this analysis is that I can contribute my first-hand experience to it; but more strikingly, this standpoint is not bound to a particular asylum moment. It uniquely straddles three main stages of the asylum process, therefore affording interpreters unique insights into the articulation of the different stages of the asylum procedure.

Through the interpreting perspective, I will show the rendered asylum account to be actually a product mediated by three objective factors. I analyse *the legal conditions and the physical setting* that regulate the transmission of the asylum account and thematise the *presence of the interpreter and the interpreting process* in the narration of the account. The analysis of the interpreting process entails an evaluation of the Janus-faced role of interpreting, as both facilitator and obstacle, in the communication process between the immigration authorities and asylum seekers. I then introduce the concept of *silent actors*. By these I mean the un-verbalised assumptions that structure the line of questioning by the decision makers, in the sense that the questions are informed by a grid of legal and cultural understandings serving to categorise the answers. This will allow the pinpointing of, and commenting upon, the gap between the narrated experiences of asylum seekers, and the legal concepts that claim to capture the 'truth' of the 'genuine' refugee experience.

Thus the provision of interpreters, while indispensable to the decision-making process, is not sufficient by itself to overcome the culturally grounded silences and the inevitable gaps in comprehension born out of them and that make their way arbitrarily into the decision-making process. In summary, this chapter mounts a socio-legal critique, from within the context of interpreting, of the procedures by which the asylum account is elicited from asylum seekers. It also has policy relevance in that it signals the need to rethink the standards expected of immigration interpreters, as the legal criteria defining their conduct are not relevant to the reality of interpreting and compound the procedural obstacles facing the asylum seekers.

LITERATURE REVIEW

A common focus of studies of interpreters is the disparity between the legal expectations of the interpreters' role and the reality of interpreting. Such legal expectations are coded in the 'conduit' approach, demanding that interpreters only act as mechanical devices for transmitting utterances. The failings of the 'conduit' approach are numerous. Morris shows that in court it is incompatible with the defendant's perception of interpreters as linguistic, cultural and legal saviours; it ignores the necessity for linguistic negotiations that aim for the best interpretation; it is also inappropriate for understanding interpreters' repertoire of individual strategies to deal with their role predicaments.[1] Barsky points out that it undervalues immigration interpreters, who are in the ideal position to help articulate the asylum account.[2] He argues for the extended role of immigration interpreters who should be trained as intercultural agents charged with assisting and supporting claimants, thus avoiding cultural and factual misunderstandings. In her study of American court interpreters, Berk-Seligson provides a useful analytical framework for the distinct participatory role of interpreters in judicial proceedings, a participatory role that is wished away by the legal profession and obscured by the 'conduit' approach.[3] Interpreters are shown to change the rendition of image and character of speakers by altering the pragmatics of speech, while their actual role may vary between usurping the power of the attorney to coercing the witness. Additional interpreter-related factors affecting the proceedings reside in extralinguistic features like voice, which adds or eliminates nuances from testimony, and personality, which intervened in the Nuremberg

---

1   Morris, R, 'The gum syndrome: predicaments in court interpreting' (1999) 6(1) Forensic Linguistics 6.
2   Barsky, RF, 'The interpreter as intercultural agent in Convention refugee hearings' 2(1) The Translator 45.
3   Berk-Seligson, S, *The Bilingual Courtroom: Court Interpreters in the Judicial Process*, 1990, Chicago: Chicago UP.

proceedings when interpreters who refused to interpret derogatory language had to be replaced.[4]

All these arguments point to the inadequacy of the conduit role of the interpreter as a model for understanding the realities of interpreting. However, the focus on the penal procedure does not fully illustrate the problematic role of immigration interpreters in asylum proceedings. Interpreters must also contend with the discursive conflict between refugee procedure and asylum account. Identified by Blommaert through the use of discourse analysis, this conflict is played out in the bureaucratic 'text trajectory' that objectifies and deducts meaning from the narrative.[5] Useful for understanding the ideological source of the discursive format imposed on asylum accounts, and the essential incompatibility between the two, this chapter brings to the fore the issue of cultural gaps in comprehension, so salient to the work of the immigration interpreter. The concept of 'text trajectory' renders well the dynamic of procedural interference with the text, of which interpreting is a necessary part.

THE CONDITIONS FOR THE ASYLUM ACCOUNT

The asylum account is a crucial piece of evidence in the determination of refugee status. It can only be rendered within the framework of asylum procedure in the sense that it is governed by a set of legal conditions and that it takes place in a certain physical setting. Blommaert's 'text trajectory', comprising instances when the applicant narrates their story interspaced with translations, interpretations, note-taking and codification into questions, fits the asylum procedure quite well. At all these stages immigration personnel actively negotiate the asylum information: eliciting details considered relevant, omitting 'irrelevant' details, and editing, as well as making mistakes. Throughout this process the applicant's account is re-centred from personal experience to objective categories that fit the procedure. Although the applicant has limited input into this multi-authored bureaucratic circulation of text, ultimately they are held as being its sole author. The corollary of this is that there can be no asylum account outside the designated procedure. Therefore the decision-making process does not apply retroactively to a fully made out account, but is actively involved in selecting and processing accounts before applying itself to them.

To make an asylum claim, applicants must present themselves to immigration officers at the port of arrival in the UK, or to the Home Office. Generally speaking, there are three main stages in the decision-making process. The initial screening of the asylum seeker ascertains the applicant's identity, travel route and eligibility for support, and is carried out at the port of application. The applicant is then issued with forms to be filled in, including an asylum questionnaire calling for

---

4   Gaiba, F, *The Origins of Simultaneous Interpretation: The Nuremberg Trial*, 1998, Toronto: Ottawa UP.

5   Blommaert, J, 'Investigating narrative inequality: African asylum seekers' stories in Belgium' 12(4) Discourse & Society 413.

their personal data and the reasons for claiming asylum. Secondly, the applicant is called for a substantive asylum interview. Thirdly, there is an appeal in cases where the Secretary of State refuses the claim. Many applicants are represented by solicitors, which means that applicants get to explain their reasons for asylum outside the stages outlined above. Although I limit my analysis to the procedure as described above, as this is where my personal knowledge comes from, there are a number of other procedures not discussed here: detention of applicants, where decisions and removals are swift and access to legal representation limited; refusal for non-compliance without the benefit of a substantive interview if the questionnaire is not submitted on time; appeal determination 'on papers', that is, without the appellant's evidence or submissions by the Home Office and without appellant's legal representative, and 'out-of-country' appeals for nationals of countries on the 'white list'. These procedures involve severe limitations being imposed on the narration of the asylum account.

The initial screening interview

The people allowed in the Asylum Screening Unit (ASU) are the applicants and their dependents on the asylum claim and, if they are represented, their solicitors (who may have their own interpreters) and social workers and/or guardians in the case of minors. The solicitors, etc, can enter the building only at the same time as their clients. The Home Office also makes interpreters available for the screening procedure.

If a prospective applicant is not allowed into the building no asylum account can be made out. Access to the ASU is therefore the gateway into the asylum procedure. Once inside, the wait can extend to many hours. Metal benches, two vending machines and the toilets are the only available facilities. The place can get very noisy when there are small children around. The seats in front of the desk are about one metre away from it, so applicants have to bend forward into an uncomfortable position to get close to the glass pane separating the desks from the waiting room. The dialogue is facilitated by a microphone,[6] but is nevertheless possible only when people raise their voices. It is standard practice for exchanges to be carried out with raised voices only when communicating across the screen, not behind it. This spacing arrangement that bounds the hearing range to the area behind the screen permits the desk officers to include or exclude applicants from the verbal exchange at will, thus providing a strategic means for constraining their participation in the claim registration, as well as placing them on a lower footing. Here we find an ideal illustration of Carlen's analysis of the use of social space in magistrates' courts:

> The spacing and placing of people on public occasions is strategic to their ability to effectively participate in them ... spatial arrangements ... will, in addition to determining the mode and range of verbal interaction, emphasise the relative status of those present.[7]

---

6   The audio system is falling apart: broken microphones are common, despite the building having recently undergone extensive refurbishment.

7   Carlen, P, *Magistrates' Justice*, 1976, London: Martin Robertson, p 21.

The screening starts with the interpreter reading out a convoluted explanation of procedure, which ends with a threat of criminal proceedings if the applicant is later found to have given false information. Then the desk officer reads out questions from a form and takes down the answers. Part of the form only accepts answers that fit into boxes. Most of the answers do not.

The officers are completely in charge of the dialogue. They dictate the pace, decide what part of an answer constitutes the answer and subsequently take it down, turn the microphone off to consult or chat with a colleague or the interpreter and then turn it back on to resume the dialogue, or walk off to get papers or make phone calls. No explanations are given to the applicant about any of these moves. Most important is the issue of 'negotiating' the answers given in response to less than straightforward questions. The recorded answer is sometimes exactly what the applicant said, at other times a concise or partial version of it, arrived at either by further consultation with the applicant, or the interpreter, or both, or no consultation at all. If the applicant launches themselves into long explanations, the officers busy themselves with other form filling and ask the interpreter at the end: 'What was that all about?' Alternatively, the officers will stop the applicant from giving explanations.

This approach wrong-foots the applicant on two counts: as a matter of procedure they are told they are potential liars; then, as a matter of the officer's behaviour, they may be marginalised from their own account by having their answers curtailed and being excluded from the desk interaction altogether when the microphone is turned off. Not all officers I observed are unfair towards applicants, at least not all of the time. However, some may, and do, treat applicants unfairly with impunity, sometimes being downright coercive. One Sunday[8] I witnessed a heated exchange between a supervisor and an elderly, black lady. The supervisor was shouting: 'You told my officer that you are Congolese, now sign here that you are Congolese!' I could not hear the reply, but the supervisor carried on: 'It's 3 o'clock on Sunday, my officers have had a long week and they must go home, now sign that you are Congolese!' The lady signed.

The performance of the interpreters is not monitored either. The interpretation is not always delivered consecutively, meaning that the interpreter will wait for the end of the answer and then relay it to the officer. Because the environment is noisy and the officer has their attention on filling in as many forms as possible, the interpreter is often put in the situation of having to clarify the answer before interpreting it. This is often the case when it comes to asking the applicant if they believe their circumstances to be covered by the definition of a refugee. That moment usually signals the start of long explanations, when the screening form only provides one small box for the reply, so the interpreter is left to negotiate an answer that actually fits in the box.

In yet another type of frequent intervention, the interpreter has to elucidate geographic and cultural matters to officers who cannot believe what they are being told. One of my colleagues told of an occasion when the officer reluctantly

---

8   Case code: Congo/ASU (12 January 2003).

agreed to enter Romania as a country of nationality, as she was convinced that it was a former province of Yugoslavia;[9] and I personally had to explain to an officer that Eastern Europe was not a continent.[10] It will be clear that the interpreter's interventions are permitted, in some cases even expected, and many times taken on board.

The record of the screening interview is the 'foundation' of the asylum file, in the sense that everything an applicant says at a later stage is crosschecked against it, and any discrepancies or mistakes will undermine their credibility. It is therefore crucial that the record is an accurate account of the answers given. From what we have seen above, there is no monitoring to ensure that this is the case. A copy of the record is handed to applicant, so that they know what is held on file about them. However, this safeguard against inaccuracies is inadequate because if there are any mistakes the Home Office refuses to correct them without evidence, which seems illogical given that the information was recorded on the say-so of the applicant in the first place.

We have seen so far that the ASU is the scene of deployment of various techniques of control over the manner and the contents of the initial asylum encounter. These techniques are actualised in the spatial arrangement of the fixtures, the officers' monopoly over the flow of conversation, and the lack of monitoring of the performance of officers and interpreters. The registration procedure is the beginning of the 'text trajectory'. The notes on file take on the status of 'evidence' that will precede the applicant in all their encounters with the officials, and will constitute the reference for all other stages in the procedure. The boxed format for recording the applicant's circumstances on the screening form starts off the objectification process by which the applicant's story will be stripped of its 'irrelevant' elements and inserted into the asylum procedure.

The substantive asylum interview

The following people may be present in the interview room: the applicant, their solicitor, their interpreter, the Home Office interviewing officer, one Home Office observer, and the Home Office interpreter. The applicant's solicitor and interpreter are present as observers only, and may make comments at the end of the interview. The interview room is all grey – that is walls, carpet, table and sometimes the chairs too. The applicant, the officer and the Home Office interpreter sit at the table in a triangle, while the applicant's solicitor and interpreter sit behind the applicant.

The applicant is first asked to confirm their details and if they understand the interpreter. They are then told that there is no need to repeat what is already written in the Statement of Evidence Form (SEF), as that information is on file and will be considered. The applicant is also asked to break their answers into smaller

9   Pers comm.
10   Case code: E Europe/ASU (5 December 2002).

parts so that they can be interpreted and written down, which takes time. The interview may then proceed.

Time is not neutral, it belongs to the immigration procedure. It is a valued institutional resource.[11] Apart from the strict booking procedure that must be complied with, the interview is therefore governed by other time pressures that show up in the briskly efficient manner of conducting it. The interview starts as soon as people sit down – there is no 'Make yourself comfortable' or any other courteous remarks. Many times I have had to tell applicants to take off their jackets, put their bags on the floor or papers on the table, rather than holding them on their laps. The officers never protested about this, but did not initiate courteous behaviour either, as if a concern with the applicant's comfort would amount to an invitation to talk too freely.

All officers have a list of questions drawn up on the basis of the questionnaire, but, apart from that, the format of the interview varies. Some officers conduct a very structured interview, by going through the questions, ticking them off one by one, and moving to the next one without engaging with the answers. This method sometimes confuses the applicant and as a consequence the answers tend to get briefer. Other officers run a loosely structured interview, letting people speak freely, as well as going through their list. In stark distinction to the initial screening interview, the general rule is that every single word is noted on paper, explanations about the procedure are comprehensive and forthcoming, and the officers do not mind being asked questions.

All lists of questions insist on quantitative data: names, dates, frequencies and numbers, in the form of: How many times were you detained or harassed? Date and lengths of detention(s)? Who was the leader of your party? When was it founded and by whom? If the applicant cannot remember a date, or approximate a frequency, they are prodded into producing a firm answer by which they commit themselves to a version that then becomes the official one. To me, this indicates a serious cultural misunderstanding because the insistence on precision about dates, times and other quantitative data is specific to the Western scientific rational discourse, and is not necessarily appropriate as a tool in the understanding of the experiences of asylum seekers.

Any inconsistencies, omissions or untimely revealing of new material will affect the credibility of the claim, as the applicant is unfairly expected to tell their story exactly in the same way every time, instead of allowances being made for human factors like memory, emotional state, trust in those present and circumstances of story being told. Asylum Aid documents credibility as being the most frequent reason for refusing asylum claims,[12] while Rousseau et al found that, in the Canadian asylum procedure, many refusals based on lack of credibility were the result of mishandling the evidence and constituted breaches of procedure: many contradictions and inconsistencies were either explained at a

---

11 *Op cit*, Carlen, fn 7, p 27.
12 Asylum Aid, *Still No Reason At All: Home Office Decisions on Asylum Claims*, 1999, London: Asylum Aid.

later stage but the explanation was rejected because of its timing, or could have been explained had the questions been asked.[13] This finding ties in with my observation that most applicants are not asked to clarify any inconsistencies.

Other constant questions on the officers' lists relate to: attempts to relocate in the face of persecution; attempts to make complaints; employment and means of subsistence; and the timing of departure vis à vis the risk to life and body. These questions aim at establishing whether the applicant reacted to their situation as a 'rational' asylum seeker, exhausting all domestic routes of redress before escaping political persecution, or if they were driven to flee by other reasons. In reply to such specific questions, many asylum seekers tend to expand their explanations of what they did or did not do, as a means of ascribing meaning to their actions. They rightly feel that actions divorced of their wider social and political meaning can be misconstrued. Blommaert refers to these richly contextualised accounts as 'home narratives', and identifies them as a tool for centring the account onto personal experience.[14] However, most of the interviewers I have observed discourage these home narratives either because they are seen as irrelevant, or because they disturb the 'appropriate' chronology of the account; here we can see another instance of the institutional appropriation of time. The insistence on short, specific answers strips the asylum story of its context and produces an objectified, easily categorised account.

Apart from time and procedure constraints, the narration of the account is also subject to interpreting-related stress factors. The applicant has to answer in small chunks, broken apart by sometimes quite long pauses while waiting for their words to be first interpreted and then written down, thus proceeding at a speed much slower than a normal conversation flow might allow. The interpretation and recording of the account thus act as objective constraints on the speech flow. Another mediating factor comes into play if the answer is delivered fast, or in long chunks. The applicant will be interrupted, which proves to be a strain for many applicants who, once interrupted, cannot remember where they stopped.[15]

In the substantive interview there is less room for interpreter intervention by comparison with the screening stage. It is acceptable to ask the speaker to repeat, to ask for permission to clarify an answer or question, and it is acceptable to step in if there are any misunderstandings. Other than that the interpreter must not intervene, even if they suspect that the meaning of the question or answer has escaped the other party.

At the end of the interview the applicant is asked to sign the notes, without having them read back, to accept them as an accurate account of what was said in the interview. This record of the interview constitutes evidence, even if the

---

13 Rousseau, C, Crepeau, F, Foxen, P and Houle F, 'The complexity of determining refugeehood: a multidisciplinary analysis of the decision-making process of the Canadian Immigration and Refugee Board' (2002) 15(1) Journal of Refugee Studies 43.
14 *Op cit*, Blommaert, fn 5.
15 Interview with Rada (11 February 2003).

applicant challenges it at a later stage. This step in the process shows up the presumption that the interpretation and the recording of the account cannot be faulted. The solicitor's interpreter can challenge the interpretation if needs be, but there rarely is an interpreter since the Legal Services Commission has reduced its spending and, in any event, the interpreter would not know what the officer actually took down. The position is the same for the solicitor. The applicant and solicitor get a copy of the interview notes, and if they spot any mistakes they can write to the Home Office, but they are in no position to challenge the interview notes before accepting them as a true record.

Problems may arise if the interviewing officer unwittingly takes down something other than what is being said by the interpreter, who is the only one in the room close enough to the see what is being recorded, and thus able to spot inaccuracies. From what I observed, if the interviewing officers genuinely misunderstand the interpreter they will not mind amending the notes if the interpreter calls their attention to the mistake. Spotting inaccuracies thus depends on the interpreter's ability to read the interviewing officer's writing at the same time as interpreting, which is not easy, as well as their goodwill in monitoring the record, as this is not stipulated as a professional requirement.

The substantive interview is the one stage in the process where, according to the law, the applicant is assumed to have had every opportunity to explain their case to the decision makers. However, in reality, the rendering of the account is subject to interpreting-related stress factors, as well as major procedural interference. The latter consists of discouraging the applicant from explaining their experiences in their own way, and failure to engage with the account positively, that is, to ask for clarification of inconsistencies or to elicit information that would assist a positive decision. While on the face of it, the Home Office is there to protect those in need of asylum, in practice it employs covert adversarial tactics to set them up to fail.

The court hearing

The Immigration Appellate Authority (IAA) runs 19 hearing centres throughout the UK – most of them are dedicated immigration appeal centres, but some immigration hearings are held on the premises of Magistrates' and Crown Courts. In the hearing room the interpreter and the appellant share one desk, the Home Office and the legal representative flank them facing each other, and the special adjudicator's raised desk completes the square.

At the start of the day all parties in the appeal cases converge in the hearing room. Everybody rises to greet the adjudicator, who starts with the 'housekeeping': finds out who are present, who is ready to proceed, what files the Home Office does and does not have, and then starts the hearings. Throughout this, all parties sit down or stand wherever they can, and it may well be that interpreters will sit next to the person they will interpret for. However, they are strictly forbidden from talking to the appellants outside the hearing, unless permission is granted by the adjudicator. So, interpreters may either ignore the appellant altogether, try a half-concealed greeting and, if the appellant takes that as an encouragement, be prepared to explain they cannot talk, or just openly exchange greetings with the appellant and hope for the best. Whichever way, due to the proximity with the appellant and the natural human need for communication that many appellants display before the hearing, the interpreters must ignore either the court dictum or the feelings of the appellant. In the latter case it is difficult to see how this professional behaviour can engender the appellant's trust. I once had to interpret for a man I had met on previous occasions in the company of his wife and son. I stuck to the rules and gave them the briefest nod of greeting, which earned me a very sad look from the wife. She followed me into the ladies' room after the hearing with the same sad look, and asked: 'Madam, are you allowed to talk to me in here?'[16] It turned out she only wanted to say a proper 'Hello'.

Unlike at the Home Office premises, at court interpreters and appellants share the corridors and the facilities. Therefore, if approached by appellants, the interpreters are expected to discharge the delicate task of explaining that they are not allowed to talk to them outside the proceedings. When doing so I have come across reactions ranging from incomprehension to disbelief and even anger. It must be particularly confusing for those appellants who have been in other interpreted encounters where this rule does not apply, such as hospitals, social services or magistrates' courts. I personally explain that I would be sacked if seen talking to them – however, it must be an unsatisfactory explanation since one burly Roma male admonished me with: 'Oh, forget it, other interpreters treat us well.'[17]

At the beginning of the hearing the adjudicator explains their role to the appellant, tells them there is no need to repeat what has been already recorded on file, asks if they understand the interpreter, and may also ask the appellant to explain how they travelled to the court for the hearing – this latter question is meant as a mini-test to ensure that the interpreter and appellant understand each other. The appellant's representative will ask questions first. Then the appellant will be tendered to the Home Office Presenting Officer (HOPO) for cross-examination. The hearing can last anything from half an hour to over three hours. The questions tend to be quite narrow and, yet again, if the appellant gives long answers they are stopped and reminded that they are to answer briefly. If there are discrepancies (for example, concerning dates, frequencies or names of local or national political leaders) the appellant will be asked to explain them. At the end of the questioning the appellant is to listen to the interpretation of the submissions, which mark the end of the hearing. Most special adjudicators reserve their decision.

The interpreter's job is to interpret consequently during the dialogue, and simultaneously (whispered) during the submissions. There are specific challenges and skills involved in court interpreting, as compared to the previous stages of the asylum process. Most importantly, the interpreter will interpret what is said by

16   Case code: Maria/IAA (30 August 2002).
17   Case code: Ion/IAA (22 May 2003).

four different parties and must maintain consistency with the tone and demeanour of each one. For example, the interpretation of the cross-examination must be rapid, sharp and delivered in a raised voice if that is the way the HOPO is talking. If the adjudicator is laid back, that must be put across through the interpretation, and so on. In this respect the interpreter is a bit like an actor playing several roles. The more the interpreter can maintain linguistic and demeanour consistency with all the parties, the less they will intrude upon the dynamics of the encounter.

Demeanour consistency poses problems to the interpreter simply because it is difficult to maintain. I also feel that it looks silly, as if the interpreter were mocking the speaker. Linguistic consistency is often impossible to keep, as the appellant may be of uneducated background and the court and representatives simply do not adjust their register to the situation. They mostly address each other over the appellant's head and leave it to the interpreter to make communication possible by talking up to the court and down to the appellant. The submissions are especially crammed with legal terminology which marginalises the appellant as, in order to keep up with the flow, the interpreter can either unpack the meaning of concepts and get left behind with the interpretation, or give a verbatim interpretation that will not mean anything to the appellant. Article 3 is a good example. The three parties say 'Art 3' (three seconds), the interpreter must somehow explain what Art 3 rights are about and how they fall outside the political claim (one to two minutes).

The dynamics of the interpreter's presence in court differ once again from the previous stages. First of all, the entire set-up discourages interpreters from intervening directly. There is an assumption that they are there as mouthpieces, and nothing else. There have been cases when the interpreter pointed out to the adjudicator that something was wrong with the appellant, just to be asked why they were interfering.[18] On the other hand, the physical proximity between the appellant and interpreter, and the fact that no one is paying attention to them during submissions, never mind understanding what is being said by way of interpretation, can give rise to a certain degree of complicity manifested in chatting or explanations about the hearing being proffered by the interpreter.

At this stage it is important to emphasise the marginalisation of the asylum seeker's narrative throughout the determination procedure. At the ASU the asylum seeker is told not to explain their case, the substantive interview uses the cover of the non-adversarial system to deploy selective tactics for limiting the Home Office responsibility towards them, and the hearing rules instruct the asylum seeker specifically when to talk and what to talk about.

The degree of permissibility of interpreter's intervention in the dialogue rises and falls in inverse proportion with the distance between them and the applicant: the degree of permissibility peaks in the ASU, where the interpreter and applicant are separated by a glass pane and can only communicate with the help of a

---

18 Interview with Amy (15 April 2003).

microphone, and is at its minimum in the courtroom, where the two sit next to each other. Thus, the assistance that the interpreter could give the applicant is permanently held in check by the interplay of two institutional arrangements: physical proximity to applicant and degree of permissible intervention.

THE PRESENCE OF THE IMMIGRATION INTERPRETER

The National Register of Public Service Interpreters (NRPSI) code of conduct lays down clear procedural standards for interpreters. They must 'interpret truly and faithfully what is being said, without anything being added, omitted or changed',[19] and their intervention in the exchange is limited to asking for clarification, pointing out a possible misunderstanding or a missed cultural inference, or asking for accommodation of the interpreting process. On the ethical side, interpreters are expected to observe confidentiality, act impartially and professionally, and not discriminate against parties. However, at the top of the list of aptitudes considered necessary for becoming an interpreter the International Association of Conference Interpreters (AIIC)[20] lists intuition and the ability to analyse and construe facts. The above exposition illustrates the contradictory demands harnessing the interpreting process: the interpreter must not add, omit or change anything, but it is important that they can construe facts and use their intuition! This is a contradiction in terms. In reality, faithful interpretation very often inhabits the threshold between accuracy and transformation, and the difficulty of incorporating this standard of performance into a realistic code of interpreting conduct is one index of the predicaments of the interpreter.

Just as the interpreting profession places contradictory demands on the interpreter, so do the parties in the interpreted encounter. Thus, Morris describes the interpreter as being caught between the 'conduit' approach, expected from them by the legal profession, where they perform as a linguistic device, and the 'saviour' status assigned to them by the linguistically disadvantaged party.[21]

In my experience too, many asylum seekers regard the interpreter as an authority figure. Knowledge of the language and familiarity with the procedure bestow on interpreters a hallowed aura of superiority keenly perceived by the asylum seeker. Despite being told at the beginning of the interview that the interpreter must interpret all that is said, throughout my interpreting career many asylum seekers have pleaded with me to speak for them because they did not know how to. Others have launched themselves in convoluted explanations and asked me to summarise the point for the interviewer, because they thought I knew what it was like in their home country and could explain it better. These examples show that some asylum seekers perceive the interpreter as an ally able to negotiate the divide between the cultures. They do not want the interpreter to be an

19   NRPSI Code of Conduct, available at www.iol.org.uk/nrpsi.
20   'Advice to Students Wishing to Become Conference Interpreters', available at www.aiic.net.
21   Op cit, Morris, fn 1.

impartial figure, but expect help to redress the imbalance of power in their position.

In these circumstances even the mildest reiteration of the interpreter's duty to interpret everything comes across as a rebuke, which will directly affect the rendition of the account. If the interpreter puts the applicant at ease, the interpreter is in breach of professional conduct and may raise the suspicions of the interviewing officer. Whatever the interpreter does will arbitrarily affect the rendition of the account, and the interpreter therefore always has a participatory role in the dynamics of the interpreted encounter. This role has not been envisaged by the rules of professional conduct, or by the institution that employs the interpreter, because their concern lies with interpretation *per se*.

Consider the following example from my experience. On this occasion, the interviewing officer was a burly, very abrupt man. I had worked with him in the past, and remembered well his aggressive behaviour. I found myself addressing young Ileana,[22] the interviewee, in a much tougher manner than usual, partly because I had to reproduce the interviewing officer's manner of address, and partly because I found it extremely difficult to be in his presence. To which Ileana said, chin trembling: 'Why are you talking like this, what is this here, is it the police?', and started crying inconsolably, face angry-red and big tears falling into her lap. The interviewing officer immediately ended the interview and (in my opinion) took the proper course of action. However, there is no way of knowing just how much psychological damage was inflicted on Ileana in that aborted interview. In a situation where I behaved by the book, that is, mirrored the officer's manner, I actually contributed to the breakdown of communication! Apart from graphically illustrating how authoritarian attitudes in the interview room drastically affect the fact-finding procedure, this case exemplifies one of the pitfalls of the 'conduit' approach.

One technique of direct interference with the account is to insist on concise answers. Certain interviewers run a very structured interview and interrupt the applicant whenever they feel the answer is straying. This continuous interruption and rebuking makes the applicant quite upset and unsure of how they are supposed to answer. As for me, I have difficulty in concentrating because, having memorised the answer, I am stopped from relaying all of it and I am directed to rebuke the applicant into being concise. So the applicant does not know how much of their answer was recorded and their evidence does not add up, quite apart from the fact that this impacts negatively on their ability to present their story. Why do the officers do this? It seems that they already have an idea of what constitutes an answer, so they will try to extract exactly that in the first place. Long answers mean more handwriting, which is tiring. When applicants persist in giving long explanations the officers get irritated: they sigh, exclaim, raise their voices, and show other signs of nervousness. By doing this they show their superiority, as this kind of behaviour would not be tolerated from anyone else in the room.

---

22   Case code: Ileana/Substantive Interview (8 March 2001).

Besides, time is precious, and it belongs neither to the applicant nor to the interpreter. It belongs to the institution that booked the interview and provides the resources for it to be carried out, as well as to the interviewer personally. This was starkly illustrated to me in Mihnea's[23] interview when the officer, a young woman, put a lot of pressure on him to answer to the point. Mihnea kept breaking down, but was doing his best to answer, and although his replies were rather convoluted he did address the questions in the midst of background information. This information clearly disclosed instances of persecution and ill-treatment, but as it did not relate to the question or emerge in a tidy manner, the officer was not pleased about it. For example, when she asked him whether there was an arrest warrant out for him, he said that the police gave him nothing, and went on to describe the appalling conditions of his detention and the torture inflicted on him. That was his way of telling the officer exactly what he had received at the hands of the police; but his long answers exasperated the officer, who rushed the interview to its end. I stayed behind after Mihnea and his solicitor left the room, and asked her, 'Did I annoy you? I noticed you were showing signs of frustration, did I do anything wrong?' To which she replied, 'No, you were OK, but I have to fetch my child at 4 o'clock, so now I'm using my time.'

Two issues come out of this example. First, the officer did not explore Mihnea's account of torture, and even cut the interview short. However, the interview is the only opportunity for applicants to put their case before the primary decision makers, and any evidence they might have that is not recorded in the interview will not be taken into consideration. Secondly, a vast amount of interaction did not get recorded in the notes. There was much extralinguistic behaviour, on behalf of both Mihnea and the officer. She was showing signs of frustration with the amount of writing she had to do, and he cried, spoke incoherently, put his medicine on the table for her to see (about 10 various packets) – she did not even glance at it – and rotated his head about 10 degrees to demonstrate the loud cracks in his neck. None of this made its way into the interview notes in the same way, as her prompts designed to circumscribe his answers did not. It is very disturbing that so much interaction is missed out from the asylum record, as it holds important clues about the mental state of the applicant at the time of the interview, as well as about the kind of pressure from the officer that may have steered the account. This means that the asylum record does not capture the reality of the encounter, and that missing information cannot be used at a later stage to challenge the primary decision maker's fact finding. I was troubled and uncomfortable throughout the interview because I knew something that he did not, that is, that by her behaviour the officer was depriving him of the opportunity to make his case fully. I nicknamed 'piggy in the middle' the particular predicament when the interpreter is acutely aware of injustice done to the applicant in the asylum encounter.

---

23   Case code: Mihnea/Substantive Interview (7 July 2003).

One further example of the interpreter as 'piggy in the middle' comes from one colleague[24] who returned from an interview quite upset that the interviewing officer, who in this case was an immigration officer as well, did not make an accurate record of the interview. My colleague told the officer that he was taking down things she had not said, but he carried on regardless. The applicant had no idea what was being written in his interview record, while she, who could see the notes, was in no position to do anything about it. Her experience can be taken as a litmus test for the clash between the interpreter's professional duties to interpret accurately and not to intervene, and the moral duty to challenge any injustices they may be privy to.

These examples illustrate the predicament of the interpreter who is caught in the crossfire between the logic of the institution that allows unfair treatment of applicants and the interpreter's personal ethical concerns about being cast in the role of the bystander in the face of injustice. The interpreter's hands are tied by the professional standards of conduct that forbid intervention apart from a strict list of circumstances, thus allowing their employer to use them as a institutional resource, rather than a facilitator of meaningful communication. What strategies interpreters deploy in order to resolve situations of predicament is a matter of further research that goes beyond this chapter. However, the fact that situations of predicament exist is an index of the insufficiency of the professional code of behaviour to respond to the reality of interpreting. It is also an index of the arbitrariness introduced in the rendition of the asylum account, as these strategies are not prescribed, known or evaluated.

We have seen that the code of practice prescribes that interpreters must interpret accurately everything that is being said. It is crucial for the rendition of the account that they are linguistically competent for the job. However, their performance is not monitored unless there is a solicitor's interpreter present, or the applicant understands some English and can spot mistakes. Otherwise, the applicant is left to the mercy of the interpreter's competence and professional conduct. By persisting with a job that exceeds their linguistic abilities, interpreters alter the asylum account fundamentally.

The following examples present us with unacceptable linguistic and professional interpreter misconduct. In one case, the interpreter mistook 'wealth' for 'health', and interpreted 'Did you leave for reasons of wealth?' as, 'Are you in good health?', to which the applicant answered 'Yes'. In the present political climate, where asylum seekers are branded economic migrants, this mistake would have cost the applicant a speedy refusal, had it not been for the intervention of the legal representative who could also speak the applicant's language.[25] The second example concerns a case where the grounds of appeal against the refusal of asylum include the incompetence of the interpreter who, aside from providing faulty interpretation, was clipping her nails during the

---

24   Pers comm.
25   Rada's interview, 11 February 2003.

substantive interview.[26] These examples put into question the interpreter's personal standards of conduct, as well as the organisational logic of the institution that tolerates substandard performance. They further illustrate the presence of the interpreter in the asylum account.

Other extralinguistic factors affecting the applicant's ability to narrate their account can be the differences in sex, age and/or ethnic group between themselves and the other parties to the encounter, as these factors may be strongly connected with social identities and issues of cultural prohibition or prejudice. Ethnic differences can be the *locus* of deep social or personal prejudice, and therefore a major impediment in the rendition and/or the interpretation of the asylum account. On one occasion, a Roma applicant behaved very aggressively towards me even before the interview started, accusing me of laughing about him because of his ethnicity;[27] and a Kurdish interpreter once told me there are serious interpretation-related issues between Turkish and Kurdish people. Some Turkish interpreters have trouble interpreting simple phrases like 'I am from Kurdistan' because for them Kurdistan does not exist.[28]

The latter example illustrates what Gaiba has already shown: interpretation is not a value-free activity.[29] Interpreters' powers of empathy are engaged during the interpreting process as they too have socially situated identities. This means that, maybe unconsciously, some interpreters tend to interpret in a manner that maintains consistency with their own cultural background and personal beliefs, which may enhance or diminish the applicant's image. This constitutes an alteration of the pragmatics of the speech acts, in the sense described by Berk-Seligson.[30] The resulting arbitrary element introduced in the account will affect the applicant's chances in the face of the law.

Age and appearance can also affect the amount of trust between applicants and interpreters, and therefore reflect on the rendition of the account. One young interpreter colleague told of a court hearing when the appellant, a middle-aged lady, treated her with high contempt throughout the encounter;[31] and from an asylum seeker I heard that he refused the services of one Home Office interpreter because he looked too much like a Securitate (former Romanian secret police) agent and that made the asylum seeker feel uncomfortable.[32]

---

26 Pers comm.
27 Case code: Roma/Substantive Interview (17 April 2003).
28 Pers comm.
29 *Op cit*, Gaiba, fn 4, pp 107–08.
30 *Op cit*, Berk-Seligson, fn 3.
31 Amy's interview, 15 April 2003.
32 Pers comm.

I have considered, from several points of view, the inadequacy of the 'conduit' role of interpreter to respond to the realities of interpreting in the context of asylum encounters. The interpreter who sticks to the 'conduit' role gives distressing messages to those most vulnerable asylum seekers who need assistance to make out their claim. In this respect the immigration interpreter's dilemma is, as Morris predicted, the same as that of any other interpreter in the legal field.[33] However, in asylum encounters the availability or otherwise of interpreter assistance may have serious consequences in terms of putting people's lives at risk. Procedural biases against asylum seekers are the source of another type of interpreter dilemma. This discussion lends support to Barsky's argument that interpreters could do a lot to help applicants articulate their claims, were their hands not largely tied by the 'conduit' role, which basically relegates them to the role of institutional resources.[34] Finally, interpreters' visibility in the asylum proceedings goes much further than their professional and institutional presence, insofar as they manifest their human condition in physical, social and mental traits that necessarily affect the process of communication. Thus the combined effect of the legal conditions of interpreting and the failings of the asylum procedure is materialised in the interpreters' dilemmas (which they tackle by means of individual strategies), as well as in the oversight of the interpreters' impact on rendering the asylum account.

THE 'SILENT ACTORS'

We have seen that the dialogical interaction in the asylum account does not always constitute meaningful communication, as the latter can be hindered by a plethora of linguistic, cultural, psychological and procedural obstacles. However, there is an additional factor that alters the pragmatics of communication in the asylum account: textual silences. Huckin has defined them as *'omissions of some piece of information that is pertinent to the topic at hand'*, and has divided them into five broad categories.[35] Of these, we are interested with *manipulative* silences that deliberately conceal information from the interlocutor. Here, I use the concept of textual silence to make visible certain presuppositions that steer the asylum account.

The decision-making process relies on a grid of legal concepts that enable the calculation of eligibility to refugee status. To paraphrase Foucault,[36] concepts constitute the refugee experience as an object of knowledge by cutting out from the ensemble of social phenomena those that enable a non-reductive analysis of the phenomena specific to persecution. Thus, forming legal concepts and

33 *Op cit*, Morris, fn 1.
34 *Op cit*, Barsky, fn 2.
35 Huckin, T, 'Textual silences and the discourse of homelessness' 13(3) Discourse & Society 347.
36 Foucault, M, 'Introduction', in Canghuilem, G (ed), *On the Normal and the Pathological*, 1978, Dordrecht and Boston: D Reidel Publishing, p xvii.

applying them to social reality is an activity inherent in refugee law and, more generally, dispensation of justice.

The function of the questions asked in the substantive interview is to elicit information that assists a decision. However, in asking particular questions and not others the interviewing officer has, at the back of their mind, the legal concepts that govern the allocation of refugee status, relating to economic circumstances, level of political activity, exhausting domestic remedies, etc. As a matter of procedure the applicant is not made aware of the material aspects informing the decision, presumably in order to discourage dishonesty; but by the same token, the applicant simply has no idea of the legal significance attributed to their answers and, therefore, they cannot properly represent themselves. Just like Carlen's 'dummy' player,[37] the defendant in a magistrates' court who absorbs the gains and losses of the information game in which court professionals play his hand over and above his head, our asylum seeker does not know what case they are answering. As the legal concepts referred to steer the line of questioning, they can be described as 'silent actors' in that they have an invisible textual presence in the asylum account.

During instances of manipulative silences, the very canons of interpreting obstruct the flow of meaningful communication between officers and applicants, since the interpreter is once again 'piggy in the middle' in a linguistic exchange where the officer means more than what he says, and the applicant digs their own hole by answering literally to questions whose larger contextual meaning they are ignorant about. The questions are narrow and elicit partial answers, and the applicant rarely elaborates their replies, especially if they have been dissuaded from giving long answers. For example, in order to assess one's economic circumstances, the officer usually asks: 'Were you in employment?' For many Romanians employment means working for a company, with the attendant social rights to pension and so forth. So many answer, 'No'. It is only in response to further prodding on the subject that they may add information about working on their farm or being self-employed otherwise, but not many officers ask additional questions. Another example: 'Was it always the same two policemen who beat you?' If the applicant says 'Yes', it will be inferred that the act of ill-treatment came from two individuals acting in their private capacity; but if the applicant says 'Yes, they were the only policemen manning the local station', such inference cannot be made. Yet another example concerns the concept of relocation. Under refugee law a person qualifies as a genuine refugee if they have exhausted all domestic protection options. Thus the ubiquitous question is: 'Have you tried to move to a different part of Romania?' Many applicants say, 'No, because the police are hand in hand.' The fact that they did not attempt to relocate will count against them, although, had the applicants known where the question was aiming, they may have explained that in Romania the police keep centralised records, and that in order to move away one has to request a residence visa from the police. Therefore, someone fleeing the police can hardly be expected to approach them for a visa.

---

37 *Op cit*, Carlen, fn 7, p 42.

Legal concepts are intrinsic to the interests of justice, but justice is not served as long as the applicants are put in procedural triple bind: they are not aware of the material points informing the decision; the questions asked of them are narrow and selective; and they are prompted to answer succinctly. Asylum Aid also argues that the asylum interview is hopelessly inadequate for establishing the facts of a case. Although the UNHCR handbook asserts that 'while the burden of proof in principle rests with the applicant, the duty to ascertain and evaluate all the relevant facts is shared between the applicant and the examiner',[38] in practice, a common complaint of applicants is that they did not divulge relevant information because they were not asked about it.[39] Little do they know that the Home Office does not consider that it is the role of the interviewing officer to elicit relevant information that would assist the decision.

This chapter has identified yet another type of constraint on the asylum account: 'silent actors' or legal concepts played out as manipulative silences. Their effect is to prevent evidence from being recorded in the asylum file, thus compromising the fair calculation of entitlement to refugee status. I coined this term to draw attention to the active role of textual silences in the gathering of evidence. I believe that the immigration interpreter, who is aware of the legal concepts that structure the questions and the legal arguments that shift through the asylum narrative, cannot but notice how they actually shape it from the outset. The 'conduit' role demands that the interpreters make abstraction of that knowledge, thus inevitably siding with the officer.

CONCLUSION

Having followed the rendition of the asylum account through the refugee determination procedure, we have seen it being mediated by several constraints. There are procedural constraints that tightly regulate the account every step of the way. Once the asylum seeker is admitted into the ASU, their asylum story will be put on the bureaucratic conveyor belt of the 'text trajectory'. Institutional conventions will produce it at the appropriate place and time, the boxed format of screening forms together with imposed chronological sequences as well as suppression of 'home narratives' will re-centre and streamline it to objectification, and legal concepts will shift through what is left probing for 'genuine' refugee experiences. When viewed like this the asylum procedure appears in its full dehumanising absurdity.

The substantive interview, purportedly the fair opportunity given to asylum seekers to make their case, is there for the eyes of the law and the public because in reality the 'fair' opportunity is the scene of deployment of covert adversarial tactics, best described from a verbal interaction point of view as negative

---

38 United Nations High Commissioner for Refugees, *Handbook on Procedures and Criteria for Determining Refugee Status*, 1992, Geneva, para 196.
39 *Op cit*, Asylum Aid, fn 12, p 65.

engagement with the account designed to set asylum seekers up for failure. The method of keeping interview records by hand is legally suspect from two points of view: it is tiring, therefore prone to genuine mistakes, and it allows the interviewer inordinate freedom to tamper with the record as it cannot be subsequently checked for accuracy; and anyway, the Home Office enlists the help of the obliging appellant, who never refuses to sign the interview record to vow for its accuracy, although it is not read back to them and they have no idea what was taken down. Their signature gives the interview record the status of evidence, and if they later try to contest anything in the record they will find that they have diminished grounds for legal challenges. The constraints discussed above can be understood as procedural 'squeeze factors' that act unofficially in tandem with admissibility procedures to limit state responsibility for asylum seekers.

The asylum account will also be mediated by interpreter and interpreting-related factors. The process of interpreting has to be accommodated, but it thereby imposes an artificial manner of speaking, which exacts psychological costs from asylum seekers; and the immigration interpreter, far from being the invisible mouthpiece dreamt up by the legal profession, will exert an arbitrary influence on both asylum seeker and account, depending on the interpreter's competence and professionalism, as well as physical and social traits.

The 'conduit' role, imposed by the legal profession on the interpreter, has been castigated by numerous commentators for its failure to represent the realities of interpreting, and for landing interpreters in various predicaments. In addition to those predicaments, the immigration interpreter faces other specific role-dilemmas. They find themselves to be the only person who can monitor the accuracy of the substantive interview record, and spotting mistakes may put them in a difficult position as the interpreters' code of conduct is silent on this matter. This predicament challenges the role-definition of the interpreter as, whatever they decide to do, they will side with either the appellant or the Home Office. Depending on their personal attitude and knowledge about the procedure, a benevolent interpreter may find themselves pushed to covertly intervene in the rendering of the account in order to compensate for procedural biases against asylum seekers, or for specific unfair treatment. By sticking to their 'conduit' role, the interpreter gives distressing messages to vulnerable asylum seekers who look to them for help. Therefore, their role in proceedings cannot be neutral by definition. Furthermore, the interpreter may well be informed about political, social or historical issues that would help bridge the gaps in comprehension between the parties in the encounter, as well as matters of asylum procedures that would help articulate the account, but the interpreter is gagged by the 'conduit' role. Thus the legal criteria defining the provision of interpreting end up compounding the procedural obstacles facing asylum seekers.

The specific dilemmas of immigration interpreters arise from the combined effect of the 'conduit' role and the inadequacies of the asylum procedure. They are continuously pushed out of the 'conduit' role by the asylum procedure, and pulled back by the 'conduit' role, which relegates them to the status of institutional resources. In light of this chapter, it can be stated that the standards of conduct expected of immigration interpreters are hopelessly inadequate to the job they have to perform, and need a speedy overhaul that would benefit by taking into account the points raised here.

There is urgent need also for asylum legislation that takes into consideration the arbitrary effect of all these communicative limitations on the asylum account. Until such legislation is in place the asylum procedure will continue to fail in its fact-finding mission, despite its internal and public myths. As a first practical step, tape-recording at least the substantive interview, as a safeguard to ensure accuracy, would increase asylum seekers' chances of due process.

CHAPTER 11

'DON'T BOTHER KNOCKING': AUSTRALIA'S RESPONSE TO ASYLUM SEEKERS

Ernst Willheim

On 26 January 1788, a small fleet of foreign boats arrived on the south-east coast of Australia, at a place now known as Sydney. They carried several hundred foreign nationals. They arrived without the permission or authority of the local people. Those on board were of a different race, a different colour, a different religion, a different culture. They brought with them many of the problems associated with boat people today. They brought the threat of terrorism – subsequent massacres of the local indigenous population are well documented. They brought disease – exotic diseases that soon decimated the local indigenous population. They established a form of military dictatorship. Their society was founded on a form of slavery. Arrival of these first boat people is variously remembered in Australia, by some as 'Australia Day', by others as 'Invasion Day'.

Australia today is a nation built on migration. For some time after the 'first fleet', the UK was the primary source. After the Second World War, Australia took large numbers of refugees and other immigrants from continental Europe. Over the last 30 years, refugees and immigrants have come also from Asia, Africa and Latin America. Since the Second World War, the number of people who have come to Australia to settle exceeds six million,[1] more than 620,000 of them as refugees or displaced persons.[2] A quarter of Australia's population was born overseas.[3] Many are now leading members of the Australian community.[4]

Australia is one of only about 10 countries that agree to accept an annual quota of refugees from UNHCR for resettlement. Australia's migration program has a humanitarian component of 13,000 places annually, including a refugee intake of 6,000.[5] The Migration Act 1958 establishes special classes of visas, known as protection visas, for people to whom Australia has protection obligations under the Refugee Convention 1951.[6] Yet Australia has established what are arguably the most formidable barriers to asylum seekers anywhere in the Western world.

---

1   Department of Immigration and Multicultural and Indigenous Affairs (DIMIA) Fact Sheet 2, *Key Facts in Immigration*.
2   DIMIA Fact Sheet 60, *Australia's Refugee and Humanitarian Program*.
3   DIMIA Fact Sheet 2, *Key Facts in Immigration*.
4   Five of Australia's eight billionaires were people whose families came to Australia as refugees: Peter Mares, *Borderline: Australia's Response to Refugees and Asylum Seekers in the Wake of the Tampa*, 2002, Sydney: UNSW Press (hereinafter cited as *Borderline*), p 2, citing *Business Review Weekly's* annual 'Rich 200' list.
5   These figures have recently been increased: Media release VPS 056/2004, 23 March 2004, Minister for Immigration and Multicultural and Indigenous Affairs.
6   Section 36.

Leaving aside the first fleet settlers, all those to whom I have referred arrived as part of an orderly program. Australia is an island nation. Not having any land borders, it did not have to contend with streams of uninvited people crossing its land boundaries. More recently, however, that comparative isolation and Australia's consequential complacency were broken. Asylum seekers, in small fishing boats, began to arrive in remote places on Australia's north-west coast. In the late 1970s and early 1980s, following the end of the Vietnam War, several thousand people from Vietnam arrived by boat, seeking asylum. These people were fleeing from a regime with which Australia had been at war. They were accepted with little debate. The next wave, fleeing from Cambodia following the troubles in that country, attracted less sympathy. They were followed in turn by Sino-Vietnamese, many of whom were forcibly returned to China.

A new wave, fleeing from the regime of Saddam Hussein in Iraq and from the Taliban in Afghanistan, started in 1998. It is this group that has generated the strongest reaction and the greatest controversy. 'Boat people' have taken centre stage as a political issue. The arrival of the *MV Tampa* in August 2001, together with the events in New York on 11 September 2001, created a new political climate. In a pre-election environment, politicians built on fear of Muslim refugees. National sovereignty and border protection overshadowed international obligations and human rights concerns. Radical new legislative and administrative measures have been put in place to deter boat people. Those who do arrive are treated harshly.

This chapter deals, first, with the arrival of the *MV Tampa* and substantive changes in Australian law relating to asylum seekers arriving by boat ('boat people'), including the enactment of retrospective laws to validate the Government's actions in relation to the *Tampa*; the conferral of wide new powers to intercept refugee boats; the excision of parts of Australia from Australia's 'migration zone' in order to prevent boat people from accessing Australia's legal system; off-shore processing of asylum seekers (the so-called 'Pacific Solution'); mandatory detention of boat people, including women and children; the introduction of new limited classes of temporary protection visas for boat people, with no right of permanent residence and no right of family reunion; and attempts to exclude judicial review of refugee decisions, leading to a landmark constitutional decision.

The second part of the chapter deals with the 'children overboard' affair and the wider impact of migration issues on the Australian legal and political system, leading to what may be seen as distortions or corruptions of Australian public affairs, including false claims by Ministers who alleged that asylum seekers had thrown their children overboard; disturbing developments in public administration; inappropriate intervention by Ministerial staff in public administration highlighting an accountability vacuum; serious memory lapses on the part of very senior officials; official involvement in disruption activities in a foreign country; a new role for the Navy, including deterring asylum seekers on the high seas from entering Australia and towing vessels out of Australia's contiguous zone into international waters; intemperate Ministerial criticism of the judiciary; significant new jurisprudence concerning the scope of judicial review;

abuse of executive power; changes in Australia's attitude to international human rights obligations, in particular, changes in Australia's relationship with the UN's human rights treaty monitoring bodies; changes in the political environment, in particular, the politicisation of refugee issues; and the development in the governing coalition parties of an increasingly harsh attitude to asylum seekers.

Since 1989, the number of boat people landing on Australia's shores has totaled about 13,500.[7] To put this in perspective, Australia is a country of about 20 million people. Has Australia been 'absolutely deluged' by the arrival these thousands of people, 13,500, spread over 15 years? Do boat people pose a substantial risk to Australia's security or to the stability of the nation? Readers will form their own conclusions as to the magnitude of the problem; the extent, if any, to which these people represent a threat to Australia; and the proportionality of the Australian responses.

MV TAMPA

The arrival of the MV Tampa at Christmas Island in August 2001 triggered dramatic changes to Australia's attitudes to asylum seekers. I have traced the course of the Tampa episode elsewhere.[8] In summary, the MV Tampa, a Norwegian container ship with a crew of 27, in response to a call from Australian Search and Rescue, picked up 433 Afghan asylum seekers and five Indonesian crew aboard a distressed twenty-metre, wooden, Indonesian fishing boat, the Palapa, and headed for Christmas Island, an Australian Indian Ocean territory. Australian authorities directed the Tampa to stay out of Australian waters and to change course for Indonesia. Seriously overloaded, with many passengers in need of medical attention, the Tampa issued distress calls and, contrary to the directions of the Australian authorities, entered Australian waters. Australia was unwilling to accept the rescued passengers. The ensuing impasse between Australian and Norwegian authorities attracted worldwide attention. The impasse was broken only when the asylum seekers were transferred to an Australian troopship, HMAS Manoora, to be transferred to Papua New Guinea, Nauru and New Zealand for processing, under arrangements hastily negotiated with those countries. These were not, of course, destinations chosen by the asylum seekers. Indeed, the asylum seekers were told only that they were to be transported to 'another place'. They were not told their destination.[9] Incredibly, this was to avoid reaction and resistance.[10] The Australian Government subsequently secured the passage of a package of new legislation that was to dramatically change Australia's

---

7   DIMIA Fact Sheet 74, *Unauthorised Arrivals by Air and Sea*. Fact Sheet 74a provides detailed statistics.

8   For a more detailed analysis of Australia's response to the *Tampa*, see Willheim, E, '*MV Tampa: the Australian response*' (2003) 15 International Journal of Refugee Law 159–91.

9   *Senate Select Committee for an Inquiry into a Certain Maritime Incident* (hereinafter 'CMI Report'), p 162, *Transcript of Evidence*, pp 866–67.

10   *Op cit*, CMI Report, fn 9, cites, at p 163, a File Note of 10 October 2001 attached to a witness statement.

arrangements for the processing of asylum seekers who arrived by boat, without authority.

The *Tampa* episode raised a series of international law issues which I have dealt with more fully elsewhere.[11] In particular, the impasse between Australia and Norway over responsibility for the rescued passengers exposed a serious deficiency in international maritime law. Although the *Tampa's* duty to render assistance to the distressed Indonesian vessel was clear, international maritime law was silent on responsibilities in relation to rescued passengers. Laws relating to rescue of life at sea had been developed in a different era, when the assumption was that those rescued would be only too anxious to return home. Maritime law had not responded to the new situations that now arose, where those rescued were fleeing from their original homes.

The impasse also exposed deficiencies in refugee law. Australia's primary obligation under the Refugee Convention was that it must not to send the asylum seekers back to a place of risk (the non-*refoulement* obligation). Was any of the Australian action, closure of the port of Christmas Island, refusal of access to Australia, removal of the rescued passengers to third countries, contrary to the non-*refoulement* obligation?[12] Views differ. Clearly, Australia's obligations under the Convention were enlivened. Australia did not return the asylum seekers to a place of risk. On the other hand, many will see Australia's action in forcibly removing asylum seekers to a third country for processing as contrary to the spirit of the Convention.

The *Tampa* episode also became the catalyst for a whole new system of processing asylum seekers who arrive by boat, without authority. At the time the *Tampa* arrived, Australian legislation required that asylum seekers arriving by boat be brought to the Australian mainland, placed in what was called immigration detention and processed in accordance with refugee determination procedures established under the Migration Act 1958. These processes included a right to have a rejection of refugee status reviewed by the Refugee Review Tribunal and some limited access to judicial review. The system was no more, but no less, than what one would expect in a civilised country with a common law legal system and a well-developed system of administrative law.

The arrival of the *Tampa* heralded the adoption of an entirely new policy. In the words of the Prime Minister, 'we will not allow these people to land in Australia'.[13] The Government's new objective was to prevent asylum seekers from landing and to prevent them from accessing Australia's statutory refugee determination procedures. Instead, they were to be processed 'off-shore'.

---

11   *Op cit*, Willheim, fn 8.
12   These issues are canvassed in more depth in *op cit*, Willheim, fn 8.
13   Doorstep interview, Melbourne, 31 October 2001.

Retrospective validation and prevention of judicial proceedings

The validity of the action the Government had taken in relation to the *Tampa* was open to serious doubt.[14] It was also clear that the existing legislation, providing for unauthorised arrivals to be brought to the mainland and placed in detention for processing under the Migration Act 1958, did not give effect to the Government's new objectives. Legislation was therefore enacted that purports to validate the government's action in relation to the *Tampa*. It also purports to prevent the initiation or continuation of any civil or criminal proceedings that would challenge that action.[15] These extraordinary provisions raise both policy and legal issues. Retrospective validation has been criticised by the Senate Standing Committee for the Scrutiny of Bills.[16] Legislation that purports to prevent a court from determining current proceedings is of doubtful constitutional validity.

There can be little doubt that the Australian Parliament has power to enact laws having a retrospective operation.[17] Parliament may also amend the law so as to alter the rights and liabilities of parties to a dispute that is already the subject of judicial proceedings.[18] Such a change in the law does not of itself constitute an unlawful interference in the exercise of judicial power. It may constitute such an interference where, for example, it exhibits an excessive degree of particularity, for example, in relation to the persons and time period to which it applies[19] or where Parliament purports 'to direct the courts as to the manner and outcome of the exercise of their jurisdiction'.[20] In most cases, the critical distinction will be between permissible alteration of substantive rights and impermissible interference with the judicial process itself.[21] Is the retrospective validation provision a law which retrospectively alters substantive rights and liabilities or is it a law which operates as an impermissible direction to courts, to treat as lawful that which was unlawful? The distinction is not always an easy one. In the present

---

14 The Federal Court challenge to the validity of the Government's actions is considered in the second part of this chapter.

15 *Border Protection (Validation and Enforcement) Act 2001.*

16 Alert Digest No 13 of 2001; First Report of 2002.

17 *Polyukhovic v The Commonwealth* (1991) 172 CLR 501.

18 *The Queen v Humby ex p Rooney* (1973) 129 CLR 231, 250; *Australian Building Construction Employees' and Builders Labourers' Federation v The Commonwealth* (1986) 161 CLR 88; *HA Bachrach Pty Ltd v Queensland* (1988) 195 CLR 547; see, generally, Gerangelos, P, 'The separation of powers and legislative interference with judicial functions in pending cases' (2002) 30 FLR 1. This chapter has benefited from Peter Gerangelos's helpful comments.

19 *Nicholas v The Queen* (1998) 193 CLR 173, 261 (note that Kirby J was in dissent) and 277; *Liyanage v The Queen* [1967] 1 AC 259; see, also, *Leeth v Commonwealth* (1992) 174 CLR 455, 469–70.

20 *Chu Khenh Lim v Minister for Immigration, Local Government and Ethnic Affairs* (1992) 176 CLR 1.

21 *Australian Building Construction Employees' and Builders Labourers' Federation v The Commonwealth* (1986) 161 CLR 88, p 96; *Lim v Minister for Immigration, Local Government and Ethnic Affairs* (1992) 176 CLR 1, 36–37, 50, 68.

case, the validating legislation has a high degree of particularity. Curiously, the legislation does not adopt the conventional drafting approach to retrospective validation. It does not, for example, use the formula, 'by force of this section'. In the New South Wales Court of Appeal, the expression 'for all purposes' has been seen as an indicator of a legislative directive that would breach the separation principle.[22]

Another possible source of invalidity is that the intended effect is to shield action by officers of the Commonwealth from judicial review. Arguably, the constitutional right to judicial review, guaranteed by s 75(v) of the Australian Constitution, cannot be circumvented by a law declaring to be lawful action of Commonwealth officers that would otherwise be unlawful.[23] Section 7 of the Act prevents the institution or continuation of proceedings against the Commonwealth, a Commonwealth officer or any other person who acted on behalf of the Commonwealth in relation to the *Tampa*. At the time this legislation was enacted, a Federal Court challenge to the validity of the executive action was already under way:

> To purport to divest jurisdiction from a federal court that has commenced to exercise judicial power vested in it by the Constitution in respect of jurisdiction vested in it by the Parliament, may be said to be an interference with judicial power not permitted by the Constitution.[24]

In so far as s 7 purports to prevent the continuation of proceedings that had already been commenced, s 7 appears to be an impermissible interference with the exercise of judicial power.

New powers to intercept refugee boats

In 1999, legislation was enacted to confer extensive powers to intercept, board, chase and search foreign ships and to bring ships suspected of being in contravention of migration laws to an Australian port.[25] Unauthorised arrivals may also be prevented from landing.[26] The circumstances in which the powers may be exercised vary according to whether a ship is in the Australian territorial sea, the contiguous zone or on the high seas.[27]

---

22 *Building Construction Employees and Builders' Labourers Federation of New South Wales v Minister for Industrial Relations* [1986] 7 NSWLR 372, 376, 379, 395.

23 *R v Hickman ex p Fox and Clinton* (1945) 70 CLR 598, 615–16; *Deputy Commissioner of Taxation v Richard Walter Pty Ltd* (1995) 183 CLR 168, and see the discussion below regarding exclusion of judicial review.

24 *Autistic Association of New South Wales v Dodson* (1999) 93 FCR 213, para [30]; *Minister for Immigration, Local Government and Ethnic Affairs* (1992) 176 CLR 1, 37; *Liyanage v R* [1967] 1 AC 259; *Building Construction Employees and Builders' Labourers Federation of New South Wales v Minister for Industrial Relations* [1986] 7 NSWLR 372, 378, 394, 409.

25 Sections 245B, 245C, 245F, 245G of the Migration Act 1958.

26 Section 249 of the Migration Act 1958.

27 For example, in relation to foreign ships on the high seas the relevant circumstances include a 'mother ship' reasonably suspected of being used in support of a contravention of the Act, ships covered by agreements with foreign countries and ships without nationality – s 245B of the Migration Act 1958.

The problem that came to light during the *Tampa* affair was that the legislation provided for those arriving without authority to be brought to the mainland, placed in immigration detention and processed under the Migration Act 1958 scheme. What the Government now wanted was the power to prevent people from accessing Australia's statutory refugee determination procedures. Schedules to the 2001 legislation introduced new provisions into the Customs Act 1901[28] and the Migration Act 1958[29] authorising detention and search of people found on detained ships and movement of those people to or from Australia (including to 'a place outside Australia').[30] Such detention, search and movement are protected from judicial scrutiny (subject to the retention of the High Court's constitutional jurisdiction under s 75(v)).[31] Exercise of these coercive powers is not confined to the territorial sea. Nor are the new powers required to be exercised subject to law of the sea principles.

The Senate Scrutiny of Bills Committee has criticised the width of these powers. Removal of the opportunity of judicial challenge (otherwise than in the original jurisdiction of the High Court) to such wide powers raises serious questions as to the abrogation of the rule of law and compliance with international legal obligations relating to access to courts.[32] Movement of persons, without their consent, to a foreign country may raise international law questions concerning the exercise of personal jurisdiction, especially where those persons have been detained on the high seas.[33]

Excisions from the 'migration zone': the 'Pacific Solution'

The Migration Amendment (Excision from Migration Zone) Act 2001, and a related Consequential Provisions Act, effectively restructured the administrative arrangements for processing asylum applications made by people who arrive by boat without authority. Instead of being brought into the 'migration zone', and processed under the Migration Act 1958 framework, including access to the Refugee Review Tribunal merits review process, the new provisions authorise Australian authorities to move these people to Pacific Island countries for processing. That processing is undertaken outside Australia and outside the framework of Australia's Migration Act 1958.

The first step in the Government's strategy was the excision of parts of Australia, including Christmas Island, Ashmore and Cartier Islands and the

---

28 Schedule 1.
29 Schedule 2.
30 Section 185(3A) (new) of the Customs Act 1902.
31 Section 185(3B) (new) of the Customs Act 1901; ss 245F(8A) and 245FA of the Migration Act 1958.
32 Article 16.1 of the Refugee Convention provides that: 'A refugee shall have free access to the courts of law on the territory of all Contracting States.'
33 A state may exercise controls necessary to prevent infringements of its immigration laws in its territorial sea and its contiguous zone (Arts 21 and 33 of the United Nations Convention on the Law of the Sea).

Cocos (Keeling) Islands and off-shore resource installations, from what is known as Australia's migration zone. These parts of Australia are now called 'excised off-shore places'. They include the islands where refugee boats have traditionally landed. People landing at an excised off-shore place are no longer able to activate Australia's statutory refugee application and determination procedures.[34] The stated intention is 'to discourage unauthorized arrivals, people smuggling and to promote the integrity of Australia's entry and visa processes'.[35] The excisions may have the appearance of purported geographic reservations to the Convention. Arrival of a refugee applicant at a place in Australia will still enliven Australia's obligations under the Convention, irrespective of whether that place be within the 'migration zone' for the purposes of Australian domestic law.[36]

The second step was statutory provision for people arriving at an excised off-shore place to be taken to a declared country. The Minister may declare a country if they are satisfied the country can provide assessment procedures that meets certain standards. The country does not have to be a party to the Refugee Convention. People who arrive without authority at an excised off-shore place may be taken to a declared country, using such force as is necessary.[37] Neither the Migration Act 1958 administrative review procedures nor judicial review under Australian law is available.[38] The Explanatory Memorandum states that this provision 'is intended to ensure that court proceedings are not used by an "offshore entry person" to frustrate the resolution of their immigration status or movement to a "declared country" or to obtain desirable migration outcomes'.[39]

Arrangements were made with Nauru and Papua New Guinea for the transfer of asylum seekers to detention centres in these countries for processing under the new powers. Processing centres have been established in Nauru and Manus Island. The very substantial costs of these centres are borne entirely by Australia. Substantial additional development aid has been provided as part of the overall arrangements,[40] bringing a range of financial benefits to the countries concerned.[41] Other countries were also approached.[42] In Fiji, the Australian Government's offer

---

34 Section 46A of the Migration Act 1958 prevents the making of a visa application.
35 Explanatory Memorandum, p 2. The Memorandum states: 'The amendments ... are being made in response to the increasing threats to Australia's sovereignty to determine who will enter and remain in Australia. These threats have resulted from the growth of organized gangs of people smugglers who bypass normal entry procedures.'
36 Under Art 28 of the Vienna Convention on the Law of Treaties, Australia is bound in respect of its entire territory.
37 Section 198A (new) of the Migration Act 1958.
38 Ibid, s 494AA.
39 Explanatory Memorandum, p 7. Exclusion of judicial review has been criticised by the Senate Committee for the Scrutiny of Bills (First Report of 2002, p 46).
40 Op cit, CMI report, fn 9, at p 296 gives details of additional aid to Nauru. Peter Mares, Borderline, 2002, Sydney: UNSW Press outlines some of the consequential distortions to the aid program. Apparently no additional aid was specifically provided to Papua New Guinea, but at p 130 Peter Mares, outlines assistance measures that appear to be linked to refugee arrangements.
41 Op cit, CMI Report, fn 9, p 312. Financial details of extra development aid to Nauru appear at p 329.
42 Op cit, CMI Report, fn 9, refers, at pp 293–95, to Kiribati, Fiji, Palau, Tuvalu, Tonga, France (in relation to French Polynesia).

of money in return for hosting a detention centre was described as 'a shameful display of cheque book diplomacy'.[43] More generally, the scheme has projected a negative image of Australia in the region.[44] Some argue that detention of asylum seekers in Nauru and Papua New Guinea is in breach of constitutional provisions in those countries, which prohibiting detention without trial.[45]

Processing of those removed to Nauru and Manus Island is undertaken by Australian and UNHCR officials. That processing is undertaken in a legal vacuum. Australian law has no application. Internal review by a more senior official is available, but the avenues of review and appeal available to unsuccessful onshore applicants under the Migration Act 1958 are not. There is no access to the Refugee Review Tribunal or to judicial review. Indeed, exclusion from those procedures was at the very heart of the scheme.[46] Nauru and Papua New Guinea do not have laws for refugee processing. Those refused asylum have no recourse under Australian, Nauru or Papua New Guinea laws. Independent legal advice and assistance are unavailable. Transparency and accountability are lacking. Those found to be refugees may continue to be detained for prolonged periods until a place is found for them: resettlement is not automatic.[47] This is the so-called Pacific Solution.[48]

Changes to the protection Australia offers to boat people: new limited classes of visas

While Australian law continues to recognise that Australia owes protection obligations under the Refugee Convention to refugees,[49] the nature of the protection Australia offers has progressively been diminished. Major changes have been made to visa arrangements, including new categories of visas for boat people. These new categories confer very limited rights. Until October 1999, all those recognised as refugees were eligible for permanent residence, including the right to apply for Australian citizenship after two years, and access to

---

43 Op cit, CMI Report, fn 9, p 294.

44 Op cit, CMI Report, fn 9, p 312.

45 Frank Brennan, Tampering with Asylum, 2003, St Lucia, Queensland, Queensland UP, pp 108, 110–11. Australian lawyers seeking to mount a constitutional challenge were prevented from boarding their aircraft for Nauru (conversation with Julian Burnside QC, the leader of the legal team).

46 Op cit, CMI Report, fn 9, p 316.

47 The UNHCR has expressed concern that:

> ... refugees who have been recognised and therefore have had their status regularised remain detained until a durable solution is found. This detention is without time limits or periodic review. The ongoing detention of persons recognised as refugees is a restriction of freedom of movement in breach of Article 26 ... Furthermore, such detention is not consistent with Article 31(2) ... (Response of the Office of the United Nations High Commissioner for Refugees to the Senate, Legal and Constitutional Committee request for comments on the Migration Legislation (Further Border Protection) Bill 2002, para 27).

48 The Labor Opposition's National Platform and Constitution includes, in Chapter Seven, a commitment to 'end the so called "Pacific Solution"'.

49 Section 36 of the Migration Act 1958.

comprehensive settlement and support arrangements. Families were able to join those granted permanent residence. After October 1999, those who arrived without authority (in practice, boat people) and were accepted as refugees were eligible only for three-year temporary protection visas (TPVs). They were reassessed after three years and only then were they eligible for permanent residence and family reunion. One unintended consequence was an increase in the proportion of women and children among those arriving by boat.

In 2001, after the *Tampa* incident, visa arrangements were further restricted. Now boat people who, since leaving their home country, have resided for at least seven days in a country where they could have sought and obtained effective protection,[50] are never eligible for a permanent protection visa. The initial three-year TPV can be renewed if there is a continuing need of protection,[51] but these people will never be eligible for permanent residence or for Australian citizenship. Their families will never be able to join them. If they leave Australia, for example, to visit family members unable to join them in Australia, they are unable to return (this restriction is in direct breach of the travel entitlements conferred by the Refugee Convention).[52] Unauthorised arrivals who did not reside for at least seven days in a country where they could have sought and obtained effective protection have access to a permanent protection visa after thirty months.

TPV holders are able to work. They are eligible for a limited range of social security and health care benefits. They are not, however, able to access the settlement services provided to refugees who enter lawfully[53] and they are not able to access mainstream social security benefits. Inability to access mainstream social security benefits appears to be contrary to the requirements of Art 24 of the Refugee Convention. A special restrictive regime for those who arrive without authority may be contrary to Art 31.

Most refugees who reach Australia by boat without authority have come via Malaysia and Indonesia and will have spent considerably more than seven days in one or both of these countries. The effect of the new provisions is to prevent these people from establishing a new life for themselves and their families in Australia. What were the reasons for these restrictions? The Minister's explanation was characteristically blunt: to deter further movement from, or the bypassing of, other safe countries.[54] The perception is that asylum seekers should take refuge in one of the countries through which they have passed on their way to Australia. Only those who are actually accepted as refugees are eligible for

---

50 Schedule 2 to the Migration Amendment (Excision from Migration Zone) Consequential Provisions Act 2001 amends the Migration Regulations. Schedule 2 is amended by insertion of new visa classes 200.212, 202.212 and 204.212 and a new sub-class 447 Secondary Movement Offshore Entry (Temporary).

51 Government moves to return people to Afghanistan after the fall of the Taliban gave rise to much controversy.

52 Article 28, Schedule, para 13.

53 Eg, English language classes.

54 Second Reading speech, House of Representatives Hansard, 18 September 2001, 30872.

TPVs, yet there was not a word of compassion in the Minister's second reading speech.[55]

Underlying these changes is a renewed emphasis on national sovereignty, including the right to control entry, together with a perception that many asylum seekers are brought to Australia by people smugglers from places where they are not at risk, but are attempting to choose Australia as a more desirable place to settle. Australia is not alone in restricting the opportunities for resettlement in respect of those who have passed through countries where they were not at risk. Short-term protection may not breach Convention obligations. Those determined to be refugees are not returned to a place of risk. Nevertheless, the importance given to time spent in third countries gives little weight to the practical circumstances in those countries, including the level of protection offered.

Mandatory detention

Undoubtedly the most controversial aspect of Australia's refugee processing arrangements is the requirement that asylum seekers who arrive without a visa are held in detention until their claims are determined and either a visa is issued or they are deported.[56] Boat people are removed to Nauru and Manus Island and detained there.

Detention is often prolonged, in many cases for years.[57] Identification, and resolution of possible security concerns, can be difficult, particularly where travel and identity documents have been destroyed. Those detained include women and children. Most Australian detention centres[58] are located in remote areas. Conditions in detention centres are in many respects similar to prisons, for example, constant roll calls, identification by number, and perimeter razor wire. In addition to physical hardship, many of those detained suffer severe psychological damage. Hunger strikes, sewn lips, self-harm and attempted suicides are graphic manifestation of desperation and despair.

---

55 Curiously, the right of centre government has not made any assessment of the economic efficiency of its policies. Arguably, given appropriate resettlement assistance, refugees could be expected to make significant contributions to the Australian economy. Current policies including mandatory detention and the uncertainty of short-term visas are, however, likely to create long-term problems, including long-term burdens on the Australian economy. The Labor Opposition's National Platform and Constitution includes in Chapter Seven a commitment to permanent protection after two years.

56 Sections 189 and 196 of the Migration Act 1958.

57 The number of people admitted to detention centres peaked at 8,205 in 1999–2000. By 4 February 2004, the number in detention had declined to 977, reflecting the decline in boat arrivals. DIMIA Fact sheet 70, *Border Control*; Fact Sheet 82, *Immigration Detention*.

58 Villawood, Maribyrnong, Perth, mainly accommodate over-stayers, people in breach of their visa conditions, or people refused entry at Australia's international airports; Port Hedland, Christmas Island and Baxter are primarily used for unauthorised boat arrivals.

The Refugee Convention does not specifically exclude detention of asylum seekers. It does prohibit the imposition of penalties on account of illegal entry.[59] Restrictions on movements may be applied only where they are necessary.[60] Article 9 of the International Covenant on Civil and Political Rights (ICCPR) prohibits 'arbitrary detention'. Article 10 requires that all persons deprived of their liberty be treated with humanity and with respect for their dignity. The Human Rights Committee has interpreted Art 9 as requiring that detention must be reasonable and necessary.[61] In a decision concerning a complaint from Australia, the Committee accepted that:

> [t]he fact of illegal entry may indicate a need for investigation and there may be other factors particular to the individual, such as the likelihood of absconding and lack of cooperation, which may justify detention for a period. Without such factors detention may be considered arbitrary, even if entry was illegal.[62]

The Committee urged Australia 'to reconsider its policy of mandatory detention of "unlawful non-citizens"'.[63] In another decision, the Committee held that detention of children (and their mother) for two years and eight months, without any right of review, was not justified. Australia had not demonstrated that other less intrusive measures could not have achieved the same end of compliance with Australia's immigration policies.[64] It followed that the mandatory detention was contrary to Art 9.[65]

Some of those in detention are children.[66] Article 24 of the ICCPR makes special provision relating to the protection of children. Article 37(b) of the Convention on the Rights of the Child (CROC) provides that: 'No child shall be deprived of his or her liberty unlawfully or arbitrarily.' Detention of a child is to be used only as a measure of last resort and only for the shortest appropriate period of time. Guideline 5 of the UNHCR's 'Guidelines on Detention of Asylum Seekers' provides that children: '... must not be held under prison-like conditions.

---

59   Article 31(1), but only in relation to refugees who come 'directly' from a territory where they are threatened. The term 'coming directly' has not been defined; in particular, how the term is to apply to refugees who have transited countries where they have not been able to obtain durable asylum. The Executive Committee in Conclusion No 22 (XXXII) endorsed the principle that asylum seekers should not be penalised on the ground that their presence in the country is considered unlawful.

60   Article 31(2).

61   *Alphen v Netherlands*, Communication No 305/1988.

62   *A v Australia*, Communication No 560/1993.

63   *Ibid*.

64   Communication No 1069/2002 at [9.3].

65   Communication No 1069/2002 at [9.3] in relation to Art 9.1 and [9.4] in relation to Art 9.4.

66   In February 2004, Australia was holding at least 172 children in immigration detention. See statistics compiled by A Just Australia at www.ajustaustralia.com/informationandresources_factsandstatistics.php. See, also, DIMIA Fact Sheet 83, *Residential Housing Projects*, regarding new arrangements for women and children. As at 1 October 2003, 62 children had been in detention for more than two years. The longest a child has been held in detention is five years, five months and 20 days: Human Rights and Equal Opportunity Commission, *National Inquiry into Children in Immigration Detention Report – A Last Resort?*, tabled in Parliament 13 May 2004.

All efforts must be made to have them released from detention and placed in other accommodation.'[67]

The Executive Committee has provided guidance on the circumstances that may make it necessary to detain refugees.[68] Detention should normally be avoided, but may be resorted to in order to verify identity, to determine the elements of the claim, to deal with cases where documents have been destroyed or fraudulent documents are used and to protect national security. Detention should not, however, be automatic or unduly prolonged.[69] Similarly, the UNHCR *Guidelines on Detention of Asylum Seekers* states that detention is inherently undesirable, especially for single women and children.[70] Asylum seekers should be detained only as a last resort on exceptional grounds after full consideration of all possible alternatives.[71] Detention to deter future asylum seekers is contrary to the norms of international law.[72] The Executive Committee has emphasised the need to assess a compelling need to detain, which is based on the personal history of each asylum seeker.[73] The Commission on Human Rights' Working Group on Arbitrary Detention, in a Report on Australia,[74] expressed concern about the automatic and indiscriminate character of arbitrary detention, its indefinite duration, the absence of judicial control, the psychological impact of detention on asylum seekers, the denial of family unity, children in detention, the lack of information given to detainees, the lack of a proper complaints mechanism and the implications of the management of the detention centres by a private company.[75] Australia's Human Rights and Equal Opportunity Commission has expressed similar views.[76]

The Australian requirement of mandatory detention of all unauthorised arrivals, often for long periods, is clearly arbitrary. It is not consistent with the

---

67 In May 2004, the Australian Human Rights and Equal Opportunity Commission reported on the effects of detention on children. Its findings, in a comprehensive 700 page report (HREOC, *National Inquiry into Children in Immigration Detention Report – A Last Resort*, May 2004) are chilling. Eg, at 9.4.5, the Report reads: 'The Inquiry finds that many children in detention have suffered a range of mental health problems including anxiety, bed wetting, nightmares, emotional numbing, hopelessness, disassociation, and suicidal ideation.' The paragraph goes on to refer to development delay, depression, a high level of self-harm, attempted hangings, lip sewing and hunger strikes.

68 Executive Committee Conclusion No 44, *Detention of Refugees and Asylum Seekers*, (1986) ExComm Conclusion 44, UN Doc A/AC.96/688, para 128; the General Assembly welcomed the Executive Committee's conclusion (Resolution 41/24, 4 December 1986, para 7).

69 *Notes on International Protection*, 15 August 1988 UN Doc A/AC.96/713, para 19.

70 Introduction, para 1.

71 Guideline 3.

72 *Ibid.*

73 *Detention of Asylum-Seekers and Refugees: The Framework, the Problem and Recommended Practice*, 4 June 1999, EC/49/SC/CRP.13.

74 E/CN.4/2003/8/Add.2.

75 *Ibid*, Executive Summary, p 2.

76 *Those Who've Come Across the Seas: Detention of Unauthorised Arrivals* (May 1998), Recommendation 3.1. In its very recent report, *National Inquiry into Children in Immigration Detention Report – A Last Resort?* (tabled 13 May 2004), the Commission expressed particular concern about the adverse effect of detention on children.

ICCPR, CROC, ExComm Conclusion 44 or the UNHCR's guidelines. Those international standards are not enforceable domestically. In the absence of a Bill of Rights, prolonged mandatory immigration detention cannot be challenged in an Australian domestic court.[77] Refugee issues of this kind highlight Australia's isolation from the burgeoning human rights jurisprudence in Europe and in other common law countries. There is an urgent need for consideration of practical alternatives to prolonged mandatory detention, including possible release into the community until claims are determined, subject to exceptions where identity is in serious doubt or where there is a risk to national security, better arrangements for children, periodic review of detention and an outer limit beyond which a person cannot be held without specific reason.[78]

Detention for purposes other than processing, for example, for the purposes of deterrence, may also be contrary to Australia's constitution.[79] The High Court has rejected a contention that the conditions in detention rendered the detention unlawful.[80] Kirby J, the sole dissentient, considered that the constitutional power that supported 'immigration detention' would not support prolonged confinement in conditions so inhuman and intolerable as to amount to 'punishment'.[81]

Legal issues have also arisen where the Government has continued to detain people found not to be refugees and the Government is unable to find a country that would take them. The Federal Court has held that once a failed asylum seeker has formally requested removal, continued detention requires 'a real likelihood or prospect of the removal of the person from Australia in the reasonably foreseeable future:[82]

> [C]onformably with Australia's obligations under Art 9(1) of the ICCPR, it would be necessary to read it as subject, at the very least, to an implied limitation that the period of mandatory detention does not extend to a time when there is no real likelihood or prospect in the reasonably foreseeable future of a detained person being removed and thus released from detention.[83]

---

77 *Secretary of State for the Home Department ex p Saadi* [2002] UKHL 41.
78 The Labor Opposition's National Platform and Constitution includes, in Chapter Seven, maintenance of mandatory detention, but in open hostel-style supervised accommodation, and removal of children from detention centres and a commitment to determine 90% of claims within 90 days.
79 It is clear that deterrence was one of the original purposes – see the Minister's second reading speech, *Hansard, House of Representatives,* 5 May 1992, 2372, and the submission of the Department of Immigration and Ethnic Affairs to the Joint Standing Committee on Migration's Inquiry into Detention Practices. The Australian High Court has upheld detention that is reasonably capable of being seen as necessary for processing, but punitive detention would contravene the judicial power provisions of the Australian Constitution (*Chu Kheng Lim v Minister for Immigration, Local Government and Ethnic Affairs* (1992) 176 CLR 1, 33).
80 *Behrooz v Secretary of the Department of Immigration and Multicultural and Indigenous Affairs* [2004] HCA 36 (6 August 2004).
81 *Ibid*, at [116]–[117].
82 *Minister for Immigration and Multicultural and Indigenous Affairs v Al Masri* [2003] FCAFC 70 (15 April 2003), para 136.
83 *Ibid*, para 155.

In a later, highly controversial, decision, the High Court decided by a narrow four to three majority that in these circumstances the Migration Act 1958 authorised indefinite detention.[84] McHugh J held that the legislation was unambiguous[85] and that the Constitution could not be read subject to provisions of international law accepted since the Constitution was enacted.[86] Hayne J rejected the contention that indefinite detention was punitive.[87] Kirby J, in a vigorous dissenting judgment, declined to construe the legislation as authorising 'unlimited executive detention', preferring an interpretation of the legislation that 'is consistent with the principles of the international law of human rights'.[88]

Exclusion of judicial review

Successive Australian governments have made several attempts to limit the availability of judicial review in respect of refugee determination decisions. Such attempts have run into constitutional difficulties. These developments need to be seen against the background that Australia has a well-developed system of merits review of administrative decisions by administrative tribunals[89] and of judicial review by the Federal Court of Australia.[90] Although Australia does not have a Bill of Rights, s 75(v) of the Constitution confers on the High Court original jurisdiction 'in all matters … in which a writ of mandamus or prohibition or an injunction is sought against an officer of the Commonwealth'. It follows that High Court review of migration decisions cannot entirely be excluded. Migration decisions can, however, be excluded from the jurisdiction of other courts established by statute, including the Federal Court.

Successive governments have long been cautious about both merits review and judicial review of migration decisions. Reasons for opposition to judicial review have included concern that judges have been too liberal, concern about 'opening the floodgates', concern about large numbers of unmeritorious appeals and concern that applications for judicial review are self-serving (applicants are not removed until the judicial process is completed).

Australia's general merits review body, the Administrative Appeals Tribunal (AAT), has never had a general refugee jurisdiction.[91] The Immigration Department resisted the establishment of independent external merits review of refugee decisions long after merits review of administrative decisions became

---

84   *Al-Kateb v Godwin* [2004] HCA 37 (6 August 2004).
85   *Ibid*, at [35].
86   *Ibid*, at [62].
87   *Ibid*, at [268].
88   *Ibid*, at [193].
89   Principally, the Administrative Appeals Tribunal, a general administrative tribunal, supplemented by a small number of specialist tribunals.
90   Under the Administrative Decisions (Judicial Review) Act 1977.
91   Note, however, that s 443 of the Migration Act 1958 makes provision for the Principal Member of the RRT to refer to the AAT a decision that involves an important principle or issue of general application. The power has rarely been exercised.

generally available.[92] The Refugee Review Tribunal (RRT), which provides independent merits review of departmental decisions relating to refugee status, began operating as recently as 1993.

The RRT differs significantly from Australia's mainstream Administrative Appeals Tribunal. It operates as a single member tribunal. No qualifications are required for appointment. All appointments are for short terms, not exceeding five years.[93] The former Minister once gave public warning that members might not be re-appointed.[94] One writer claims that re-appointments draw on appraisals by the Principal Member, which cover not only productivity, but also the member's set aside rate, which is compared with the Tribunal average, so it is possible to see whether a member's decisions are 'generous'.[95] Concerns about the re-appointment process cast doubt on the integrity, impartiality and independence of the RRT.[96]

RRT proceedings are inquisitorial in nature and are initially conducted 'on the papers'. Applicants have the opportunity to be heard in person before their appeals may be rejected,[97] but there is no right to legal representation.[98] Hearings must be conducted in private.[99] Public and judicial disquiet has been expressed over the RRT's handling of key credibility issues.[100] The Opposition has recently indicated its lack of confidence in the RRT and its intention to replace the RRT with a new three member tribunal.[101]

The RRT has a substantial caseload. In 2003–04, it received 3,344 applications and finalised 5,810.[102] The primary decision was set aside in 13% of the cases finalised.[103] The percentage set aside in respect of applicants from Afghanistan

---

92 Willheim, E, 'Recollections of an Attorney-General's Department lawyer' (2001) 8 AJ AdminL 154.

93 Section 461 of the Migration Act 1958. The Principal Member is to be appointed as a full-time member (s 459). Somewhat curiously, the current Principal Member concurrently holds another full-time appointment, as Principal Member of the Migration Review Tribunal.

94 Canberra Times, 27 December 1996.

95 Op cit, Mares, fn 4, p 156. The Principal Member of the RRT, in correspondence with the writer, has confirmed that affirm and set aside rates are available to those who process appointments, but goes on to say the suggestion that they are the basis for re-appointment is not true.

96 Senate Legal and Constitutional Committee, Refugee and Humanitarian Determination Processes, June 2000, 5.127; see also 5.133–5.138; see, also, op cit, Mares, fn 4.

97 Section 425 of the Migration Act 1958.

98 Ibid, s 427.

99 Ibid, s 429.

100 Senate Legal and Constitutional Committee, Refugee and Humanitarian Determination Processes, June 2000, 5.61, but see also 5.70 and the accompanying footnote 57 for a contrary view.

101 Hansard, House of Representatives, 31 March 2004, 26490. The Labor Opposition's National Platform and Constitution includes in Chapter Seven a commitment to a new Refugee Determination Tribunal with appeals to Federal Magistrates.

102 Refugee Review Tribunal Annual Report, 2003–04, p 3. One consequence of the statutory exclusion of 'boat people' from the Migration Act processes is a decline in those eligible to seek RRT review.

103 Ibid, pp 3 and 18.

was much higher, 90%.[104] There were 2,824 applications made for judicial review and 163 cases were remitted to the Tribunal for reconsideration.[105]

Some see the RRT as confrontational and as unsympathetic to refugees.[106] Tribunal decisions have from time to time given rise to trenchant criticism by the Federal Court. In one case, after describing Tribunal hearings as 'virtually unique in Australian legal procedures and in the common law system generally', the Court went on to say that '[t]hese methods contravene every basic safeguard established by our inherited system of law for 400 years'.[107] In another case, the Court described the Tribunal's reasoning as resembling 'a house of cards'.[108]

Having regard to the legislative requirement that detention be mandatory, review of the lawfulness of detention under Australian domestic law is limited to narrow, formal questions and rarely arises in practice.[109] No provision is made for a person validly detained under domestic law to seek judicial determination of whether the detention is consistent with Australia's international obligations.[110]

Judicial review of the lawfulness of refugee determination decisions has proved controversial. Two major attempts have been made to limit judicial review. The first was in the Migration Reform Act 1992 and was largely unsuccessful. The *Tampa* episode changed the political environment and the Government was able to gain support for new restrictive legislation.[111] The Migration Act 1992 now includes a new concept: 'privative clause decisions'. These decisions are 'final and conclusive', and are not subject to challenge and, in particular, are not subject to prohibition, mandamus, injunction, declaration or certiorari.[112] The definition of 'privative clause decisions' includes visa decisions of the Minister and of the RRT on review.[113] The explanatory memorandum explained that the privative clause 'affects the extent of judicial review by both the Federal Court and the High

---

104 *Ibid*, p 3.

105 *Ibid*, p 3. Apart from statistical and management information, the RRT's Annual Reports were initially uninformative and provided little background on the Tribunal's work, but have improved significantly under the current Principal Member.

106 *Op cit*, Mares, fn 4, pp 152–57.

107 *Selliah v Minister for Immigration and Multicultural Affairs* [1999] FCA 615 (12 May 1999), paras 3, 4.

108 *Sivaganeshan Kathiresan v Minister for Immigration and Multicultural Affairs* [1998] 159 FCA (4 March 1998).

109 But note *Chu Kheng Lim v The Minister for Immigration, Local Government and Ethnic Affairs* (1993) 176 CLR 1, above.

110 Article 9.4 of the ICCPR, Art 37(d) of CROC and Art 16 of the Refugee Convention may require such a right of review.

111 The principal changes are in the Migration Legislation Amendment (Judicial Review) Act 2001.

112 Section 474 (new) of the Migration Act 1958.

113 *Ibid*, ss 65 and 415.

Court'.[114] The intention is 'to provide decision-makers with wider lawful operation for their decisions'.[115]

This new attempt to exclude judicial review ran into constitutional difficulties. The original jurisdiction conferred on the High Court by s 75(v) of the Constitution cannot be removed by Parliament. The extent to which Parliament can, by a privative clause, validly restrict judicial review is an area of difficulty. A privative clause presents a conceptual problem: there is an apparent inconsistency between legislation conferring a defined power and a provision that seeks to prevent a court from adjudicating on an application for judicial review made on the ground that the power has been exceeded.[116] A decision by the Minister to grant or refuse to grant a visa[117] is clearly the exercise of a defined statutory power. So is the decision of the RRT to affirm, vary or set aside the decision of the Minister.[118]

In one of the most significant constitutional cases determined by the High Court in recent years,[119] the High Court rejected a challenge to the validity of the privative clause, but also rejected the Government's contention that the new privative clause excluded judicial review of refugee decisions.[120] The Court reached this result by reading down the operation of the privative clause. It also established clear limits to such clauses. The Court held that, as a matter of construction, the clause did not purport to oust the entrenched jurisdiction conferred by s 75(v). The expression 'decision ... made ... under this Act' did not include a purported decision by the RRT that involved a failure to exercise its jurisdiction or which was in excess of jurisdiction.[121] It followed that the privative clause did not protect a purported decision where the RRT failed to accord procedural fairness, since breach of procedural fairness constituted jurisdictional error.[122] Had the privative clause purported to protect RRT decisions against review for jurisdictional error, it would have been invalid.[123] Parliament cannot confer on a non-judicial body power conclusively to determine its own jurisdiction. These outcomes follow in part because the distinction between jurisdictional and non-jurisdictional error, apparently abolished in England in *Anisminic v Foreign Compensation Commission*,[124] remains in Australia.[125]

---

114 Revised explanatory memorandum to the Migration Legislation Amendment (Judicial Review) Bill 2001.

115 *Ibid*.

116 *R v Coldham ex p Australian Workers' Union* (1983) 153 CLR 415, 418; *Deputy Commissioner of Taxation v Richard Walter Pty Ltd* (1995) 183 CLR 168, 193–94; *Darling Casino Ltd v New South Wales Casino Control Authority* (1997) 191 CLR 602, 631.

117 Section 65 of the Migration Act 1958.

118 *Ibid*, s 415.

119 Kerr, D and Williams, G, 'Review of executive action and the rule of law under the Australian Constitution' (2003) 14 PubLR 219.

120 *Plaintiff S157/2002 v Commonwealth* (2003) 211 CLR 476.

121 *Ibid*, 506, 508, also 494.

122 *Ibid*, 508, 494.

123 *Ibid*, 506, 508.

124 [1969] 2 AC 147.

125 *Craig v South Australia* (1995) 184 CLR 163, 179.

The decision is a significant rebuff to the Government. It is to be welcomed as a significant victory for the rule of law in the sense of judicial supervision of administrative decisions to ensure that the executive adheres to minimum standards of legality. In the words of a former Chief Justice, the decision is 'a dramatic example of the tensions that can exist between the Executive Government and the judiciary and of the ultimate constitutional protection of the rule of law as defined by the High Court'.[126]

Attempts to exclude judicial review have been justified on the grounds of the extensive merits review rights, the high volume of litigation,[127] the high cost,[128] the self-serving nature of judicial review applications, in particular, the substantial number who used the legal processes to extend their stay in Australia[129] (deportation is deferred until the court proceedings are concluded) and the low success rate.[130]

There is substance in many of these claims. The number of appeals is high. The number that lead to a different outcome for the applicant is extremely low. Undoubtedly, many unsuccessful applicants for asylum pursue every available avenue of appeal solely for the purpose of delaying deportation. Nevertheless, as a former Chief Justice has recently said:

It is perhaps in this field that the independence and competence of the courts as the bastions of the rule of law becomes most significant.[131]

Moreover, resort to litigation to achieve a collateral objective is not unique to immigration cases. Large corporations regularly pursue legal proceedings in order to, for example, damage a competitor. Asylum decisions are absolutely fundamental to each of the individuals concerned. The systems for review of executive decisions whether persons are refugees should be no less than the systems provided for review of executive decisions generally. The availability of judicial review is fundamental to accountability.

A separate issue is whether exclusion of judicial review is consistent with obligations under the ICCPR and Art 16 of the Refugee Convention. The RRT exercises executive rather than judicial power.[132] *Prima facie*, RRT review does not satisfy Convention requirements. On the other hand, these international instruments have application to a wide range of countries with widely differing legal systems. The obligations they impose need to be understood having regard

---

126 Sir Gerard Brennan, 'The rule of law and the separation of powers in Australia', lecture at Australian Studies Centre, University of Indonesia, 2 July 2002, p 20.

127 1640 applications in 2000–01.

128 $A15 million in 2000–01.

129 One-third to one-half of applicants withdraw prior to hearing.

130 The information in the preceding four footnotes is drawn from the Minister's second reading speech, House of Representatives Hansard, 26 September 2001, 31560.

131 *Op cit*, Brennan, fn 126.

132 *SZ v Minister for Immigration and Multicultural Affairs* (2001) FCR 342, para 41, *NAAX v Minister for Immigration and Multicultural Affairs* [2002] FCA 263, paras 39–42.

to individual domestic constitutional arrangements.[133] On one view, the availability of merits review in the RRT may satisfy the substance of the ICCPR and Refugee Convention obligations. The composition of the RRT, the limited nature of RRT procedures and the modest status of the RRT in the Australian legal system all indicate to the contrary.

DISTORTION AND CORRUPTION OF AUSTRALIAN PUBLIC AFFAIRS

The coalition government has successfully turned refugee issues to its political advantage. The arrival of the *Tampa*, shortly before an election, was followed by a scare campaign culminating in full page paid advertisements showing a huge photograph of the Prime Minister and the slogan 'We will decide who comes to Australia'. Boat people were said to create 'increasing threats to Australia's sovereign right to determine who will enter and remain in Australia'.[134] Late in the election campaign, the Prime Minister raised concern about possible inclusion of terrorists among asylum seekers trying to enter Australia by boat from Indonesia, a claim that turned out to be contrary to the advice of the relevant intelligence agency.[135]

Equally disturbing are the consequential distortions and corruption of Australian public affairs, Ministers misleading the public, some quite extraordinary and disturbing developments in public administration, inappropriate behaviour by Ministerial staff, official involvement in disruption activities in a foreign country, extraordinary political criticism of the courts, abuse of executive power and lack of respect for the rule of law. Again, it is convenient to begin with a particular event and its aftermath.

The children overboard affair

In the UK, the Hutton Inquiry was a watershed in public administration, providing unprecedented insights into the inner workings of government. The Australian equivalent was earlier and its implications arguably more far reaching.

On 7 October 2001, the Minister for Immigration, Philip Ruddock, announced to the media that 'a number of children had been thrown overboard' from a suspected 'illegal entry vessel' ('SIEV') (referred to as the SIEV 4) just intercepted by the Australian Defence Force. The 'children overboard' story was repeated in subsequent days and weeks by senior Government Ministers, including the

---

133 According to Conclusion No 8 (XXVIII) of the Executive Committee, which advises UNHCR, the review authority may be administrative or judicial, according to the Contracting State's prevailing system.

134 This language is used repeatedly both in formal documents, such as Explanatory Memorandums to Bills and in statements by Ministers.

135 Marr, D and Wilkinson, M, *Dark Victory*, 2003, Crow's Nest, NSW: Allen & Unwin, pp 280–81.

Minister for Defence, Peter Reith, and the Prime Minister, John Howard. On 10 October, photographs were released purporting to be evidence of children having been thrown overboard on 7 October.

The children overboard story was untrue. After the elections, it turned out that the photographs, purporting to be of children thrown overboard on 7 October 2001, were in fact taken the following day, 8 October, when the vessel was sinking. On 11 October, the Chief of the Defence Force briefed the Minister that the photographs were of the wrong event.[136] On 7 November, the Acting Chief of the Defence Force briefed the Minister that 'there was nothing to suggest women and children had been thrown into the water'.[137] The public record was not corrected.

The significance of the children overboard claim was that it was made at the beginning of, and sustained throughout, an election campaign, during which 'border protection' and national security were key issues. That asylum seekers trying to enter Australia by boat were the kinds of people who would throw their children overboard was used by the Government to demonise them and as part of the argument for the need for a 'tough' stand against external threats and in favour of 'putting Australia's interests first'.[138]

After the election, when the children overboard claim was shown to be false, a Senate Committee was appointed to investigate why the claim was made and why it was not corrected. The Committee investigated the roles of government agencies and Ministerial staff. Its report was a devastating indictment of the Government, of Ministerial advisers and of the administration of the People Smuggling Taskforce (PST). It found that the former Minister for Defence 'stands condemned for his deliberate misleading of the public, his persistent failure to correct the record, and his refusal to cooperate with the Senate inquiry'.[139]

Central to the administration of asylum seekers arriving by boat was an interdepartmental group of officials, chaired by the Deputy Secretary of the Department of Prime Minister and Cabinet, and known as the PST. This was an extraordinary creation. Amongst other things, once each boat load of asylum seekers was intercepted, every decision in terms of what to do with the vessel was directed from Canberra, in practice from the PST.[140] In effect, a civilian authority was inserted into the chain of command in relation to an operational matter.[141] Between 27 August 2001 and 9 November 2001, the PST met at least 53 times.[142] One can only speculate as to the reasons for this extraordinary level of activity.

---

136 *Op cit*, CMI Report, p 83, *Transcript of Evidence*, p 742.
137 *Transcript of Evidence*, Estimates, Senate Foreign Affairs, Defence and Trade Committee, 20 February 2002, p 76, CMI Report 117.
138 *Op cit*, CMI Report, fn 9, p xxi.
139 *Op cit*, p 190.
140 Evidence of Rear Admiral Geoff Smith to the CMI, fn 9, 4 April 2002, p 447, cited in, *op cit*, Marr and Wilkinson, fn 135, p 133.
141 *Ibid*, p 133.
142 *Op cit*, CMI Report, fn 9, p 7.

Did the PST's activities extend beyond the normal bureaucratic functions of co-ordination between agencies to political support for the Government in the period leading up to a general election?

The Senate Committee was highly critical of the PST's *modus operandi*, finding 'weaknesses in its basic administrative operations, including record keeping, risk management and reporting back'.[143] The lack of adequate minutes rendered its activities inaccessible to subsequent scrutiny.[144] The PST did not operate with 'a clear governance framework which clearly defines accountability and reporting arrangements'.[145] The Committee also made important recommendations on significant aspects of public administration, including guidelines for record keeping, accountability, and the responsibilities of agency heads where a Minister fails to correct factual misinformation of public importance and the development of a code of conduct for Ministerial advisers and frameworks, mechanisms and procedures for the accountability to Parliament of Ministerial advisers.[146]

Amongst other things, the Senate Committee found a sequence of 'unusual' features surrounding the SIEV 4, including insistence by the Secretary of the Department of Prime Minister and Cabinet that everyone rescued was to go on board HMAS *Adelaide* and not to Christmas Island. In reply, he Chief of the Defence Force had said safety of life at sea was to be the paramount consideration.[147] He described his exchange with the Secretary as 'heated'.[148] The Senate Committee was also highly critical of the perceived failure of the three most senior civil and military Defence officials in relation to correction of the record.[149]

The Senate Committee was also highly critical of the role of Ministerial staff, who had clearly played a key role in relation to the failure to correct the public record in the children overboard affair. The inquiry revealed 'behaviour by advisers in their interactions with departments which is inappropriate at best, and grossly improper at worst'.[150] The Committee found that there now exists a group of people on the public payroll – Ministerial advisers – who seem willing and able, on their own initiative, to intervene in public administration and to take decisions affecting the performance of agencies, without there being a corresponding requirement that they publicly account for those interventions, decisions and actions.[151]

---

143 *Ibid*, pp xxxii, 167, 170.
144 *Ibid*, pp xxxii, 170.
145 *Ibid*, p 171.
146 *Ibid*, p xxxix.
147 *Ibid*, pp xxv, 56–57, 289.
148 *Ibid*, p 289.
149 *Ibid*, p xxviii.
150 *Ibid*, p 186.
151 *Ibid*, p 174.

It highlighted a serious accountability vacuum at the level of Ministerial offices, including the evolution of the role of advisers to a point where they enjoy a level of autonomous executive authority.[152] Concern was expressed about a Cabinet decision that Ministerial advisers were not to appear before the Committee, and the Committee recommended that Ministerial advisers be subject to parliamentary scrutiny in a similar manner to public servants.[153]

The Senate Committee was also critical of Government directions that centralised all defence media communications through the Minister's office, circumventing the usual Defence media machinery. Personalising or humanising images of asylum seekers were to be avoided. One objective was to ensure that the Minister retained absolute control over the facts that could or could not become public. The second was to ensure that no imagery that could conceivably garner sympathy or cause misgivings about the aggressive new border protection regime would find its way into the public domain.[154]

The Committee reported:

> Even before the 'children overboard' story broke, then, the facts show there was a determination on the part of the Minister and his office to manipulate information and imagery in support of the government's electoral objectives. Such preparedness to manipulate the factual record would be abhorrent and inimical to good governance at any time. That it occurred during the caretaker period of an election campaign, in which issues relating to 'border protection' were extremely significant, is inexcusable.[155]

A notable feature of the Committee's inquiry was the inability of some very senior officials to recall relevant matters. The Deputy Secretary of the Department of Prime Minister and Cabinet and chair of the PST could not recall whether she was informed that Defence had no documentary evidence of children being thrown overboard.[156] The Australian Police Commissioner, who visited Indonesia following cancellation by the Indonesian Government, in September 2001 (shortly after the *Tampa* episode), of a protocol between the Australian Federal Police and the Indonesian Police, could not recall whether he asked Indonesian officials why the protocol was cancelled.[157] What appeared to be significant memory lapses on the part of very senior officials may have damaged public confidence in the integrity and independence of public officials.

Disruption activities in a foreign country and the SIEV X incident

It emerged in the course of evidence to the inquiry that officials from a range of government agencies, including the Australian Federal Police, the Australian

---

152 *Ibid*, pp xxix, xxxiii, 173.
153 *Ibid*, p 187.
154 *Ibid*, pp 24–25.
155 *Ibid*, p 24.
156 CMI Transcript, 16 April 2002, p 955.
157 CMI Transcript, 11 July 2002, p 1971.

Secret Intelligence Service, the Department of Foreign Affairs and Trade and the Department of Immigration and Multicultural Affairs (as it was then known) were engaged in a range of what were euphemistically described as 'disruption activities', being activities in Indonesia designed to prevent people smuggling.[158] According to Ministers, the Government's policy of 'physically disrupting the work of people smugglers' was one of the main reasons for the decline in the number of asylum seeker boats coming to Australia.[159] The full extent of these disruption activities is unclear. They range from information campaigns to more direct activities, such as physical disruption, including preventing vessels from departing Indonesia.[160] The police evidence regarding active disruption was described as 'contradictory and misleading'.[161] According to a leading public affairs television program, a Mr Enniss, a police informant, had also confessed to paying Indonesians to scuttle people smuggling vessels.[162] The Committee expressed concern about the disruption activities and recommended an independent inquiry.[163]

One particularly tragic incident highlighted these concerns. A heavily overloaded Indonesian fishing vessel (referred to as the SIEV X), carrying several hundred asylum seekers, sank on 19 October 2001, a day after it set sail for Australia. Three hundred and fifty-three people, including 142 women and 146 children, drowned.

The exact location where the boat sank remains in doubt, but it appears it sank in or near Indonesian waters.[164] Survivors claimed that, during the night of 19 October 2001, two large vessels approached those in the water, shone lights on them but did nothing to rescue them.[165] Survivors have indicated that SIEV X, before it departed, was very low in the water and horribly overcrowded. Many passengers were forced onto the vessel at gunpoint. About 30 Indonesian police were present and beat passengers and forced them at gunpoint onto the boat. The police appeared to be actively involved in the people smuggling operation.[166]

Australian authorities have claimed they acted properly in relation to the SIEV X.[167] Questions have, however, been raised concerning Australian

---

158 Op cit, CMI Report, fn 9, pp 8–12; Senator John Faulkner's Additional Comments, pp 456–57.
159 Op cit, CMI Report, fn 9, Senator John Faulkner's Additional Comments, p 453.
160 Op cit, CMI Report, fn 9, Senator John Faulkner's Additional Comments, p 454.
161 Op cit, CMI Report, fn 9, Senator John Faulkner's Additional Comments, p 457.
162 Op cit, CMI Report, fn 9, Senator John Faulkner's Additional Comments, pp 455, 457.
163 Op cit, CMI Report, fn 9, p 12. One member expressed his concern that these disruption activities are occurring in Indonesia at the request of the Australian Government and no legal advice has been sought nor are any mechanisms in place to ensure nothing illegal or untoward is occurring in Indonesia (CMI Report, p 11, Senator John Faulkner's Additional Comments, p 459).
164 Op cit, CMI Report, fn 9, p 196.
165 Op cit, CMI Report, fn 9.
166 PM Program, ABC radio, Ginny Stein report, 24 October 2001; Op cit, CMI Report, fn 9, Senator John Faulkner's Additional comments, pp 466–47.
167 Op cit, CMI Report, fn 9, p 198.

government agencies' knowledge of the vessel's departure, its unseaworthy state, and whether Australian authorities could have acted to avert the disaster or rescued more survivors.[168] The Senate Committee found it 'extraordinary that a major human disaster could occur in the vicinity of a theatre of intensive Australian operation and remain undetected until three days after the event'.[169] Whether Australian authorities in any way connived in sabotage of this vessel remains mere speculation. Many consider, however, that Australian authorities were slow to set in train search and rescue operations.[170]

Before the *Tampa* episode, the role of the Navy had been to detect and intercept unauthorised boats inside Australian waters and escort them to Australian ports for processing. The new role, codenamed Operation Relex, was much more aggressive. Initially the Navy was to deter boats suspected of carrying asylum seekers from entering Australian waters.[171] Ultimately the new orders extended to boarding vessels before they reached Australia and returning them to Indonesia.[172]

The new Navy role led also to new behaviour on the part of the asylum seekers – frustration of their aim of reaching Australia led to instances of threatened and actual self-harm, violence and sabotage – to counter the Navy's strategies.[173] There is evidence that the new role for the Navy had an adverse effect on the psychological health of Navy crew[174] and that it gave rise to concern within the Navy.[175] Rescuing people from sinking boats was one thing. Boarding refugee boats and towing them back to Indonesia was quite another.

Ministerial criticism of the judiciary

Ministers reacted angrily to Federal Court decisions that the privative clause did not exclude all judicial review and to decisions overturning the RRT. The former Immigration Minister claimed that about half a dozen 'creative' Federal Court judges were 'out there on a frolic of their own'.[176] When one judge expressed concern, in a graduation ceremony speech, at the Government's efforts to circumvent the power of the Court, the Immigration Minister responded:

> I do remember a time when judges who wanted to be able to involve themselves in the political process saw it as being more appropriate to resign from the bench and stand for parliament.[177]

---

168 *Op cit,* CMI Report, fn 9, p 196.
169 *Op cit,* CMI Report, fn 9, p 288.
170 *Op cit,* Marr and Wilkinson, fn 135, p 288.
171 *Op cit,* Marr and Wilkinson, fn 135, pp 66, 120.
172 *Op cit,* Marr and Wilkinson, fn 135, p 217.
173 *Op cit,* CMI Report, fn 9, pp xx–xxi, 29–30.
174 *Op cit,* Marr and Wilkinson, fn 135, p 278.
175 *Op cit,* Marr and Wilkinson, fn 135, p 229.
176 *Op cit,* Mares, fn 4, p 158, *The Australian,* 7 December 1998.
177 *Op cit,* Mares, fn 4, p 163.

Only a few days before the hearing of a major appeal, the Immigration Minister on a major television program said:

> What we are finding is that, notwithstanding that legislation, the courts are finding a variety of ways and means of dealing themselves back into the review game.
>
> ...
>
> The High Court of Parliament is saying decisions of the Tribunal should be final and conclusive and if we need to give the court some further advice we may need your support again.[178]

A few days later, at the outset of the hearing of the appeal, the Chief Justice of the Federal Court addressed the Minister's counsel, the Solicitor-General:

> The most recent statement however raises a new issue since it would appear that it could only refer to the issues before the Court on these appeals – appeals to which your client is a party ... The statement was made only a matter of days before the date fixed weeks ago for the hearing of the appeals.
>
> You would of course know, Mr Solicitor, that the court is not amenable to external pressures from Ministers or from anyone else whomsoever, but we are concerned that members of the public might see the Minister's statement as an attempt to bring pressure on the Court in relation to these appeals to which he is a party.[179]

In judgments in immigration litigation the Court has been critical of Government action and of evidence by officials.[180]

Enlargement of Executive power?

I return to the *Tampa* episode. The Government's actions, removing the asylum seekers to Nauru and Papua New Guinea instead of processing them under the Migration Act 1958, were challenged in the Federal Court. The applicants were successful at first instance, but the orders made by the trial judge were set aside on appeal. The key issue was whether the executive power of the Commonwealth authorised the expulsion of the asylum seekers and their detention for this purpose. It was submitted that the Migration Act 1958 covered the field in relation

---

178 30 May 2002, Channel 9 *Today* Program, cited Brennan, fn 45, p 149.

179 Text of statement made by Black CJ of the Federal Court of Australia, *NAAV of 2001 v MIMIA* (N265 of 2002), *NABE of 2001 v MIMIA* (N 282 of 2002), *Ratumaiwai v MIMIA* (N399 of 2002), *Turcan v MIMIA* (V22255 of 2002), *MIMIA v Wang* (S84 of 2002), 3 June 2002, cited *op cit* by Brennan, fn 45, p 150.

180 For example: 'It is plain ... from the evidence of Mr Eyers that the policy of the government was to operate as clandestinely as possible and to provide no access to the plaintiff or her officers ... Not only were the plaintiff and her officers deliberately given the run around ... Behaviour of this kind usually implies that there is something to hide ... Even to this Court the information provided by Mr Eyers who was effectively the spokesman for the first and third defendants was quite minimal ... Mr Eyers ... said that he did not know whether any of the persons concerned had asked for legal assistance or not and did not know whether any of them had asked for asylum. Even allowing for the urgency under which this affidavit was sworn I found it incredible that the 1st and 3rd defendants' principal witness could not answer these questions.' *Cox v Minister for Immigration Multicultural & Indigenous Affairs and Others* [2003] NTSC 111 (20 November 2003), [10], [24].

to unlawful entry in a way that manifested an intention to displace any executive power in relation to the same subject matter.

The Court was divided, the majority holding that the Commonwealth was acting within the scope of its executive power. French J, who wrote the main judgment, held that the executive power of the Commonwealth, absent statutory extinguishment or abridgement, would extend to a power to prevent the entry of non-citizens and to do such things as are necessary to effect such exclusion:

> The power to determine who may come into Australia is so central to its sovereignty that it is not to be supposed that the Government of the nation would lack, under the power conferred upon it directly by the Constitution, the ability to prevent people not part of the Australian community from entering.[181]

A clear and unambiguous intention was necessary to displace the power.[182] The Act was facultative. It did not evidence an intention to take power away. The test was 'whether the Act operates in a way that is necessarily inconsistent with the subsistence of the executive power described'.

Black CJ, in a powerful dissent, held that it was at least doubtful that the asserted prerogative right to exclude aliens continued to exist at common law.[183] The test, whether a prerogative power has been displaced by statute, 'is whether the legislation has the same area of operation as the prerogative'.[184] Black CJ examined the provisions of the Migration Act 1958 in depth, noting its detailed provisions, 'which provide a comprehensive regime for the control; of Australia's borders ... The regime could have applied to the rescued people ... had the government "not taken a view" that it did not wish to apply the Act'.[185] '(O)nce a particular statutory regime is in place, there can be no parallel executive right in the area expressly covered ... It would be a strange intention to impute to the Parliament that a parallel system of unregulated executive discretion should be available.'[186] The conclusion to be drawn was that the Parliament intended that in the field of exclusion, entry and expulsion of aliens, the Act should operate to the exclusion of any executive power derived otherwise than from powers conferred by the Parliament.[187]

The judgments expose differences of considerable constitutional significance. French J's observation, that the power to determine who may come into Australia is central to its sovereignty, is unremarkable; but what are the consequences? Power to make the necessary determinations is exercisable by Australia as a sovereign state. The manner in which that power is to be exercised is a matter to be determined in accordance with Australia's domestic constitutional structure.

---

181 *Ruddock v Vardalis* [2001] FCA 1329, para 193.
182 *Ibid*, paras 184, 201.
183 *Ibid*, para 29.
184 *Ibid*, para 34; see also para 33 where the language used is 'where a statute, expressly or by necessary implication, purports to regulate wholly the area of a particular prerogative power or right'.
185 *Ibid*, para 60.
186 *Ibid*, para 61.
187 *Ibid*, para 64.

Issues of external sovereignty are legally distinct from issues as to the internal distribution of powers as between the executive and the legislative branches of government. It does not follow from the existence of the power as an attribute of Australian sovereignty that the power, in particular coercive power, is exercisable by the executive branch of government without legislative authorisation. Hitherto it had been accepted that no person (including non-citizens) could be detained in custody except pursuant to statutory authority.[188] Construction of the executive power to include significant coercive powers is both novel and troubling.

An equally important issue is whether relevant executive powers, assuming they were available, continue to be exercisable when the Parliament has legislated. The difference between the majority's formulation of the test as to abrogation of executive power by legislation and the formulation by Black CJ is significant. The 'same area of operation' test, or perhaps a 'covering the field' approach, along the lines adopted by Black CJ, seems preferable to the 'necessarily inconsistent' test adopted by French J. Whatever be the test, it is remarkable that, in the face of the extraordinarily detailed and complex statutory regime in the Migration Act 1958, the majority found that the executive power was not abrogated. Parliament has legislated to grant, or to confer, detailed powers and detailed responsibilities on the executive. Even if some of those powers were originally within the powers of the executive, pursuant to s 61 of the Constitution, Parliament has now regulated how those powers are to be exercised, for example, by imposing duties as well as conferring powers. Can it really be the case that Parliament envisaged that the executive would retain an unfettered discretionary power to, for example, detain aliens and to transfer them without their consent to foreign countries notwithstanding that the Parliament has enacted a comprehensive legislative regime establishing in detail how aliens attempting to enter Australia without authority were to be processed? In this respect the Full Court's decision represents a high point in the retention, under s 61 of the Constitution, of independent unregulated executive powers, exercisable without parliamentary authority, notwithstanding the enactment of a detailed regulatory scheme. Some of French J's analysis, in particular, his reliance on his assessment of the centrality of the relevant power to Australian sovereignty, is highly subjective. If followed, this approach may leave scope for unregulated coercive executive power, including serious inroads into individual liberty, contrary to safeguards established by Parliament. Arguably, reliance on the similar centrality of national security could authorise coercive powers to combat perceived threats of terrorism, notwithstanding statutory safeguards. In a country without a Bill of Rights, the courts are the traditional bulwark against abuse of executive power. The approach favoured by the majority is a matter for serious concern. Black CJ's view is to be preferred.

---

188 *Chu Kheng Lim v Minister for Immigration* (1992) 176 CLR 1, 13, 19, 67; *Re Bolton ex p Beane* (1987) 162 CLR 514, 528; *Koon Wing Lau v Calwell* (1949) 80 CLR 533, 555.

Abuse of executive power: the *Minasa Bone*

On 5 November 2003, an Indonesian fishing vessel carrying 14 Turkish Kurds landed at Christmas Island. Later that day, regulations were made excising Melville Island and other off-shore islands from Australia's migration zone.[189] The regulations took effect from the commencement of that day. The immediate purpose and effect was to prevent the asylum seekers from making asylum applications under the Migration Act 1958 and from having such applications determined under the Migration Act procedures. The fishing vessel was towed out to sea and eventually returned to Indonesia.

Asylum had in fact been sought, a fact initially denied by Ministers but eventually conceded. On 9 November 2003 the Minister for Foreign Affairs and the Minister for Immigration and Multicultural and Indigenous Affairs issued a joint media release (VPS 006/2003) in which they stated: 'The passengers on the *Minasa Bone* did not claim asylum in Australia.' On 13 November 2003, following media reports that the passengers *did* make asylum claims, the Minister for Immigration and Multicultural and Indigenous Affairs released without comment a departmental letter to her, which made it clear that asylum claims *had* been made. Curiously, the release of 9 November 2003 is included in the media releases on the Minister's website while the 13 November release, correcting the error in the earlier release, is not included.

The Prime Minister contended that whether asylum had been sought was irrelevant because Melville Island had been excised from Australia's migration zone.[190] The Prime Minister did not address Australia's obligations under the Refugee Convention.

In Australia, regulations are made by the Governor General. They may be disallowed by either House of the Parliament, but have effect until disallowed.[191] Similar excision regulations had been made in June 2002,[192] but had been disallowed by the Senate.[193] There was no reason to assume that the attitude of the Senate had changed. Indeed, the new regulations were subsequently disallowed on 24 November 2003. Arguably, the remaking of regulations in circumstances where disallowance is almost certain constitutes an abuse of executive power.[194]

---

189 *Migration Amendment Regulations 2003* (No 8). The regulations were disallowed by the Senate on 24 November 2003.

190 Transcript of interview with Fran Kelly, AM Program, ABC Radio, 14 November 2003.

191 The essential provisions relating to the making of regulations are found in s 48 of the Acts Interpretation Act 1901.

192 Migration Amendment Regulations 2002 (No 4).

193 Australia, Senate, *Debates* (19 June 2002) Vol 214, p 2178.

194 The issues are examined in more depth in Willheim, E, 'Government by regulation: deficiencies in parliamentary scrutiny?' (2004) 15 Pub LR 5.

CONCLUDING OBSERVATIONS

Why were the *Tampa* refugees sent to Nauru and Manus Island? Why were the Turkish Kurds on board the *Minasa Bone* towed out to sea? Why have parts of Australia been excised from the Australian migration zone? Why was the 'Pacific Solution' devised? Why has the Government sought to exclude judicial review?

There was no deficiency in Australian law. These measures were taken to prevent asylum seekers from invoking Australian law. Such measures reflect a fundamental lack of respect for the rule of law.[195] These and other measures considered in this chapter, such as mandatory and indefinite detention, reflect a fundamental lack of respect for international law. Recent obsession with national sovereignty and border protection has made a nation that was once pre-eminent in its respect for human rights one that now fails to meet basic human rights standards, standards in whose adoption Australia once played an active part.

Deficiencies in public administration identified by the Senate Committee show a fundamental lack of respect for core public sector values. Asylum seekers are kept behind razor wire for prolonged periods in the most appalling conditions. People accepted as refugees are denied the right to establish a new life for themselves and their families. No other subject area has given rise to similar departure from fundamental standards that lie at the heart of a free and democratic society. Australia's standing as a nation that respects human rights has been diminished.

How is it that this has happened? Border protection and the right to control entry of foreigners are legitimate interests. Those interests must be balanced against international human rights obligations and human rights standards. The Australian Government has failed to provide moral leadership. Rather, refugee issues have been the vehicle on which a desperate government has generated a climate of fear and uncertainty. Asylum seekers have become the victims of a crude attempt at domestic political advantage.

POSTSCRIPT

On 13 July 2004, the Minister for Immigration and Multicultural and Indigenous Affairs, Senator Amanda Vanstone, announced that 9,500 temporary protection visa holders would have the opportunity to apply for mainstream migration visas to enable them to remain in Australia permanently. The Minister also announced a new return-pending visa, which would allow people not in need of further protection 18 months in which to make arrangements to return to their home country or elsewhere. This would allow more time to make arrangements to

---

195 Sir Gerard Brennan, *Australia and the Rule of Law,* address to International Law Association, 4 December 2003.

depart.[196] Reaction from refugee support groups was mixed, doubts being expressed whether many holders of temporary protection visas would be able to satisfy Australia's strict criteria for mainstream migration visas. The fundamentally flawed temporary protection visa system remains in place and those recognised as refugees still have no right to permanent residence.

196 Media release VPS 99/2004.